CULLODEN

Recent Books by Trevor Royle

Crimea: The Great Crimean War, 1854–1856

Civil War: The Wars of the Three Kingdoms 1638–1660

The Flowers of the Forest: Scotland and the First World War

Montgomery: Lessons in Leadership from the Soldiers' General

The Wars of the Roses: England's First Civil War

Time of Tyrants: Scotland and the Second World War

Britain's Lost Regiments: The Illustrious Bands
of Brothers Time has Forgotten

Bearskins, Bayonets and Body Armour: Welsh Guards 1915–2015

CULLODEN

Scotland's Last Battle and the
Forging of the British Empire

TREVOR ROYLE

PEGASUS BOOKS
NEW YORK LONDON

CULLODEN

Pegasus Books Ltd
148 West 37th Street, 13th Floor
New York, NY 10018

First Pegasus Books hardcover edition November 2016

ISBN: 978-1-68177-236-3

10 9 8 7 8 6 5 4 3 2 1

Printed in the United States of America
Distributed by W. W. Norton & Company, Inc.

Contents

Preface and Acknowledgements

For many years the Battle of Culloden has been acknowledged as the last of the battles that have disfigured the frequently troubled relationship between England and Scotland. It was fought by two armies, one led by the Duke of Cumberland on the Hanoverian side (the government or royal army) and the other by Prince Charles Edward Stuart or Bonnie Prince Charlie (the Jacobite or Highland army). Contrary to popular belief, not all of the 9000 soldiers in Cumberland's army were English and not all of the 5000 in the Jacobite army were Scots or even Highlanders, but that did not stop the myth-making. In time Culloden was personified as a fight between the English and the Scots, or even as a battle involving romantic kilted Highlanders on one side and dastardly red-coated English and Lowland Scots on the other. Neither is true, but both viewpoints came to be accepted, largely as a result of a deep-seated need to mythologise the former and demonise the latter. As a result 'Culloden' became useful shorthand to delineate Scotland's history in terms of battles fought long ago, such as Bannockburn, a justly famous victory for the Scottish King Robert Bruce over the army of King Edward II in 1314; or Flodden, a disastrous setback two hundred years later when James IV, an otherwise sensible king, led his country's army to a quite unnecessary defeat at the hands of the English Earl of Surrey on 9 September 1513.

To be fair, modern historians have worked hard and successfully to correct those impressions; most recent accounts of the Battle of Culloden place it firmly within the context of a doomed French-supported rebellion raised in the name of the Catholic Stuarts and aimed at unseating the reigning Hanoverian royal family. It has also come to be regarded – rightly so – as one of the battles in the contemporaneous War of the Austrian Succession (1740–8), which took its name from the failure of the ruler of the Hapsburg monarchy to father a male heir and involved most of the European powers.

This violent struggle was fought initially in continental Europe, pitting Britain and her allies against the combined forces of France and Spain – both Catholic countries – and the threat of French invasion was rightly feared. It was not simply a religious war, in which Protestant fought Catholic – Britain's principal ally, Hapsburg Austria, was of the latter persuasion – but as the fighting spread into the Caribbean and North America it gave British foreign policy a religious dimension by stimulating anti-Catholic sentiments.

Prince Charles Edward Stuart was a Catholic and had been supported by King Louis XV of France, albeit somewhat half-heartedly. The inference was clear: at a time when Britain was engaged in a conflict aimed at suppressing what seemed to be Catholic tyranny, the Jacobites were viewed as part of an international conspiracy in which the Stuart cause was inextricably linked to the global interests of France and her allies.[1] It was perhaps not surprising that, not long after Bonnie Prince Charlie had arrived in Moidart with his followers during the summer of 1745, the government in London began enforcing long-dormant laws aimed at preventing Catholics from bearing arms, owning horses or gathering in large numbers for worship or other purposes. As one contemporary verse had it, the Catholic Antichrist had 'join'd with a Hellish Band of Jacobite Thieves'.[2]

At the time, and in the years following the uprising, the British government was quite sanguine about the fact that within Britain support for the Jacobites had been confined to Scotland and was prevalent mainly amongst the Highland population. That was known and understood, but there had also been widespread fears about the country's capacity to contain the Catholic threat. Cumberland's victory at Culloden eased those concerns by eliminating the Jacobite menace, putting paid to Catholic interference in domestic and foreign policy and thwarting, for the time being, the enemy's territorial ambitions. With those threats crushed or at least confined to the Scottish Highlands, which would shortly undergo a process of rapid and violent pacification, the government was able to turn its mind to determining the future of British power and to the prospect of expanding its influence in the wider world. Many of those involved in that imperial process were young officers of the British Army who had learned their trade while serving under Cumberland; as history was to show, they had learned their lesson well.

There was certainly no lack of opportunity for them to hone their military skills. No sooner had the Culloden campaign ended than many were back in action, fighting against the French and their allies in Flanders until the war ended in 1748. It was only a short respite. Within eight years Britain was to be at France's throat again, fighting the Seven Years War (1756–63), which forms most of the background for the present book. Not only was this one of the most successful wars ever fought by Britain, but it put paid to French hopes of building a world empire in North America, India and the Caribbean. At the same time a rival British empire was cemented in those same territories and in Britain the Hanoverian dynasty was secured once and for all.

There was to be further fighting between Britain and France in 1778, but that came about as a result of a revolt by the North American colonists who received French support. The final confrontation in 1793–1815 was prompted by the French Revolution and led to the collapse of the French Empire created by Napoleon Bonaparte. Although the latter two conflicts are not strictly part of the present story, they have been alluded to within the narrative as the lives and careers of many of the participants span all the wars fought against France in the second half of the eighteenth century. It is a well-attested fact that between the Act of Union, which brought Britain into being in 1707, and the final defeat of Napoleon in 1815, which ended French dreams of imperial domination, the two countries were rarely at peace; and that experience had an impact on the development of the British Army.

Most of the senior officers in the Duke of Cumberland's army came from English or Irish backgrounds or were Lowland Scots – in other words they were British – and after Culloden many of them went on to enjoy solid and in some cases spectacular careers in the British Army as a result of the patronage of their commanding general. They were Cumberland's men and they quickly became an identifiable military grouping within the British Army when they served in the European, North American and Indian theatres of military operations. In the parlance of a later age and usage they belonged to 'Cumberland's Ring'.

In so doing they showed that they had learned the lessons of the Jacobite campaign and remembered them in later operations. Perhaps the most pertinent, because it was the most potent, was the value of sustained and disciplined musketry. At Cumberland's insistence the lines of government infantrymen had been instructed in new drills to counter the ferocious charge of claymore-wielding clansmen when they clashed at Culloden, but it was the unrelenting volleys of rapid and accurate musket fire from the infantrymen which won the day. Backed by artillery the tactics soon became a battle winner, as was made evident during the later Battles of Minden and the Plains of Abraham, two of the most successful set-piece battles (from a British point of view) of the Seven Years War. Equally, in the counter-insurgency phase which followed Culloden, battalion commanders used tactics which would be employed later against native American allies of the French in the fighting in North America – displacing the population and destroying their property as part of a group punishment for supporting the opposition. Although they are to be deplored and achieved nothing other than alienation and a long-lasting bitterness, such tactics were not untypical of the period. However, more astute commanders came round to the belief that in warfare of that kind the population had to be won over. During the post-Culloden period there was considerable discussion about the value of using the army as a force for good in restoring order and obliterating the root causes of rebellion. But the main characteristic that unites the officers in the Cumberland Ring is that, like all good soldiers, they learned from their experiences in the Jacobite campaign, profited from them and put them to good use in the Seven Years War, especially in the fighting in North America and India which gained Britain its first empire. Telling that story is the main purpose of this book.

Its creation is very much the culmination of a lifelong interest in the history of the British Army and the British Empire. It would therefore be invidious of me not to thank the publishers and editors who have encouraged me over the years by commissioning books which

I hope have illuminated that abiding concern. Each one played a key role and across the years I offer them my thanks: Susan Watt (particularly for *The Last Days of the Raj*), Alan Samson (particularly for *Glubb Pasha* and *Crimea*), Hugh Andrew (particularly for *The Flowers of the Forest: Scotland and the First World War*) and Bill Campbell (particularly for *Death Before Dishonour* and the concise histories of Scotland's infantry regiments). For much support and encouragement I also wish to salute the following: Gloria Ferris, my erstwhile agent, John Bright-Holmes, a prince among editors, and Andrew Roberts, one of our great historians.

Histories of the Jacobite uprisings and the Battle of Culloden are legion and the subject has generated a huge amount of interest and debate in recent years. Amongst those authors who have illuminated my research I would like to acknowledge and thank the following: Christopher Duffy, Bruce Lenman, Frank McLynn, Murray Pittock, John Prebble, Stuart Reid and W.A. Speck.

For their customary courteous help and advice in identifying archive material from the period, thanks are due to the staffs of the British Library in London, the National Archives at Kew, the National Library of Scotland and the National Archives of Scotland in Edinburgh. While writing this book I had the good fortune to hold an Honorary Fellowship in the School of History, Classics and Archaeology at the University of Edinburgh which allowed me the privilege of making full use of the holdings of the admirable university library.

Over the years I have been privileged to enjoy a close relationship with the British Army and I would like to take this opportunity to thank the officers and men of The Royal Regiment of Scotland and their predecessor regiments. It is impossible to name each and every individual but they will know who they are and the extent of my gratitude.

Although he would not have known it at the time, the original impetus for this book came from my good friend and fellow military historian Iain Gale while he was editing the magazine of the National Trust for Scotland and encouraged me to write a piece arguing that consideration should be given to the idea of raising a monument at Culloden to commemorate the red-coated government soldiers killed in the battle. When I suggested this book to my publisher, the ever supportive and ever positive Tim Whiting at Little Brown, he happily fell in with the idea and provided equal help and encouragement as it came to fruition. During the editing process I received much valuable assistance and good advice from his colleagues Claudia Connal and Iain Hunt, who have my thanks. As ever, any remaining infelicities remain my responsibility alone.

Trevor Royle
Edinburgh/Angus
Winter 2015

CULLODEN

Prologue

Drummossie Moor,
dawn, Wednesday 16 April 1746

Dreich is a good Scots word. It means 'dreary, bleak', and it
describes perfectly the weather conditions on Drummossie Moor,
a desolate open plain some six miles to the east of Inverness, as a
bitterly cold, wet night gave way to a grudging dawn in the uncertain Scottish spring of 1746. A dreich day, but not untypical for
the time of year. Leaden skies and low scudding clouds brought
freezing cold rain in from the north-east, mist covered the high
ground along the ridge of Beinn Buidhe Mhòr and Carn nan
Tri-tighearnan to the south-east; while to the north, in the waters
of the Moray Firth, sea and sky were almost inseparable in their
uniform grey drabness.

As for the moor itself, it was unremarkable, a flat undulating
plain bounded to the east by the valley of the River Nairn, with
the foothills of the Monadhliath mountains rising beyond to the
south. On a summer's day, with the sun shining, Drummossie
Moor has its charms, but on a wet spring morning, chilled by a

rain-soaked wind, it is a desolate and unprepossessing place. As a contemporary description put it, 'the external appearance of the country is not very inviting, and must seem rather wild and romantic to a stranger.'[1] One thing was certain, as anyone living locally would have remarked: it was not a day to be out and about unless there was urgent business in hand.

But even at that early hour, and despite the discouraging conditions, the moor had been peopled. On its western limits lay a stretch of flat and often boggy open ground across which groups of obviously weary men were making their way in no particular order to form two lines facing north-east. The ground they were occupying crossed the spine of Drummossie Moor, being bounded to the north by the parkland of Culloden House, a gracious Jacobean pile owned by Duncan Forbes, Lord Chief Justice of Scotland, a man of Presbyterian principles who was widely admired for his good sense and sagacity. To the south of the ragged lines lay another walled enclosure known as Culwhiniac, one of the few parts of the moor which hinted at human habitation, having been built to offer shelter to the sheep which used the grazings on the moor in spring and summer.

The men who occupied that space were few in number, no more than five thousand, and most of them were hungry, dispirited and desperately tired, having been involved in a gruelling and pointless cross-country march which had taken them east towards the small neighbouring town of Nairn before turning back in the grey light of dawn. About half of them, perhaps even fewer, were mountain people from the Highland areas of Scotland, bound together by ties of blood and name which bred a fierce loyalty and provided the bedrock of one of the last feudal societies in eighteenth-century Europe.[2] To outsiders such men seemed little better than barbarians who spoke a strange lilting language and wore clothes made of animal skins and coarse patterned wool, but at home in their mountain fastnesses they were lords of all they surveyed, existing in closely knit communities ruled by a dynastic chieftain, the man to whom they owed utmost loyalty and devotion. This did not make them savages, as contemporary propaganda described them in order to belittle them as people and denigrate their soldierly abilities. On the contrary, most were skilled in field craft and proficient in handling weapons – sword or musket – and, serving in clan regiments, they had officers with some experience of the military life or of wars in Europe. Touchy, proud, strangely atavistic to the modern eye and immersed in a savage code of honour, these men were on the moor for only one reason – to support the claims of the House of Stuart to the throne of the Kingdom of Great Britain (as England and Scotland had become following the Act of Union of 1707).

Their hopes were centred on one man, Prince Charles Edward Louis John Casimir Sylvester Severino Maria Stuart, the eldest son of James Francis Edward Stuart, himself the eldest son of King James II of England and VII of Scotland, the last Catholic king to hold the British throne before he fled into exile in 1688. Commonly known as 'Bonnie Prince Charlie' or 'The Young Pretender', the prince had landed in Scotland in August 1745 with the intention of raising a rebellion which would return the crown to his father, who would then rule as King James III and VIII. Just under a year later that impulse had brought him on to the moor at the head of the Highland or Jacobite army whose soldiers were taking up their positions in the cold lifeless light of early morning.

Amongst them were men of Atholl and Stewarts of Appin on the right of the first line, with other clan regiments including Clan Chattan in the centre and Clan Donald on the left. This greatly angered the latter three regiments – Clanranald's, Keppoch's and

Glengarry's – which by tradition had occupied the right of the line ever since the privilege had been granted to them during the reign of King Robert the Bruce. Behind them were others who were neither Highland nor Catholic, but who were present out of allegiance to prominent supporters of the Stuart cause, such as the Duke of Perth, Lord Lewis Gordon and Lord David Ogilvy, wealthy Episcopalian landowners from Aberdeenshire, Angus and Perthshire; also in the ranks were Irish and French mercenaries in red uniforms and John Roy Stewart's Edinburgh Regiment, formed of adventurers and dreamers from the Lowlands, deserters from the royal army or those who had allowed themselves to be pressed into service through drink or bribes in pursuit of a romantic cause.

They all had their reasons for being there to support Prince Charles, but another element also united them: all were equal in the face of the grim conditions. Later one of their leaders, old Simon Fraser, Lord Lovat, would say: 'None but a mad fool would have fought that day.'[3]

Riding a grey gelding and dressed in a tartan jacket with a white cockaded bonnet on his head, Prince Charles cut a brave but incongruous figure as he rode through the sleet on to the moor. A few clansmen greeted him with huzzas, bonnets were raised in polite salute, but there were also grumbles from men who were exhausted and hungry and would soon be facing the shock of battle. To encourage them the prince cried out that 'the day will be ours!', but this was mere braggadocio. Already it was clear to the more experienced Jacobite officers that, with its bogs and exposed terrain, the moor was no place to take on the disciplined modern forces which would soon be confronting them.

Shortly before eleven o'clock the Highlanders got a first glimpse of their opponents as the leading columns of red-coated infantrymen marched on to the moor from the direction of Nairn, where they had camped the previous night. They too had been awake since first light, called to order by beat of drum at four o'clock in the morning to begin the task of assembling in columns to march the twelve miles which would take them towards their enemy. Parading by battalion – the standard infantry formation, each battalion numbering roughly four hundred and eighty soldiers – they moved into three columns with the colour parties leading the way, bravely carrying the standards which gave the regiments their identity – the Union flag of the King's Colour and the different facings of the Regimental Colours, blue, yellow, green or buff, carried by fresh-faced young ensigns who had scarcely entered their teens.

Behind the colour parties marched the first companies of men, taller and better built, with a swagger to their step and wearing mitre hats; these were the grenadiers, who once had been armed with spherical grenades but by the time of Culloden formed the right flank companies. Behind them came the rank and file: infantrymen wearing red coats, waist length at the front with short skirts to the rear, the high collar and cuffs yellow or blue and trimmed with white lace. Each man wore a black tricorn cap and carried a muzzle-loading flintlock musket topped with a socket bayonet – a weapon in time to be memorialised as the Brown Bess, which in the hands of an experienced soldier could fire off four rounds per minute. There were also three formations of mounted cavalry – Cobham's Dragoons, Lord Mark Kerr's Dragoons and Kingston's Horse – and an artillery detachment equipped with three-pounder guns possessing a range of five hundred yards. But the main cutting edge was provided by the infantry.

In addition to the presence of three companies of Highlanders who acted as skirmishers (often referred to as the Argyll Militia), three of the infantry battalions (Royals, Campbell's North British Fusiliers and Sempill's) were Scottish in make-up, one (Blakeney's) was Irish and the rest were English, although the muster rolls of all fifteen regiments show large numbers of Irishmen in the ranks. They were battle-hardened, too. Half of them had recently returned from Europe, where in June 1743 they had fought at Dettingen, which had seen the defeat of a French army by a joint British-Austrian-Hanoverian force. Others still had fought in May 1745 at the inconclusive Battle of Fontenoy, where their commander had been Prince William Augustus, the Duke of Cumberland, a younger son of the Hanoverian King George II. Born in 1721 and ennobled five years later, he had been something of a favourite with his parents, who denied him nothing. A precocious child, he was educated by private tutors and seems to have spent some time at Westminster School in London before joining the armed forces, first the Royal Navy and then the army after being commissioned in the Coldstream Guards in 1740. He was also the commander of the royal army on Drummossie Moor, a heavily built young man who believed in firm discipline and gave his orders in a style that was not 'softened by gentle persuasive arguments by which gentlemen, particularly those of a British constitution, must be governed'.[4]

By midday the two forces had arrived on the moor and the royal army was finalising its positions within six hundred yards of the Jacobite line, which now straggled out in two ranks around a thousand yards in length. There was still no let-up in the wretched weather; clouds scudded overhead, and the rain and sleet beat down remorselessly from the north-east as the drums continued to rattle from within the royal army and the Jacobite pipers replied in defiance.

1

THE HEAVIEST CURSE THAT
CAN BEFALL AN UNHAPPY PEOPLE[1]

On 9 August 1745 Major Hugh Wentworth, the garrison commander at Fort Augustus in Inverness-shire, received a letter he had long anticipated. Written by Captain Edward Wilson, who was deployed with around seventy infantrymen of Guise's Regiment in the Bernera barracks at Glenelg on the Sound of Sleat, directly opposite the island of Skye, it brought baleful news. A French man-of-war had been sighted off Skye, and it had landed a party of men and ammunition further down the coast at Borrodale in nearby Arisaig.

Two days later another letter reached Wentworth telling him that Wilson had spoken to a local informant, 'who had supped with the young Sheiffeleare the night before last at Knoidart'; a third letter from Wilson insisted that if the strangers were to 'attempt this barrack, we cannot hold out long, but shall give them all the powder and ball we have'. But by then Wentworth knew all that he needed to know.[2] The 'sheiffeleare', or chevalier, was none other than Prince Charles Edward Stuart, otherwise known as Bonnie Prince Charlie, the man who had returned to Britain through Scotland as regent to his father James in order to reclaim for him the thrones of Great Britain.

An experienced army officer from Yorkshire, Wentworth knew only too well what was afoot. Within the area of his operational command at Fort Augustus on the south-west corner of Loch Ness a potentially serious uprising was about to erupt, the latest in a chain of Catholic-inspired insurgencies which had bedevilled Scotland throughout the century.

The move was not unexpected. Support for the Stuart cause had remained strong in early eighteenth-century Scotland, maintained primarily but not uniquely in socially conservative Episcopalian and Catholic families who deplored the Union of the Parliaments of 1707 and the rule of the Whigs. (In general the Whig faction in British politics supported the Protestant succession and abhorred the possibility of a return to power by the Catholic Stuarts.) There was also a widespread belief in Scotland that whereas the Stuarts had abdicated the crown in England in 1689, they had only forfeited the Scottish crown and were entitled to reclaim it; in so doing they still had dynastic legitimacy north of the border. At the same time the performance of the Scottish economy was poor, especially once successive crippling tax regimes had been imposed following the union. All this led to disaffection with the government in London and helped to keep Jacobitism alive, not merely as a sentimental longing for times past but as a realistic alternative to the union and the House of Hanover, Britain's royal family since 1714. What gave substance to that disaffection was the presence in the Highlands of armed clansmen fiercely loyal to their clan chiefs who provided the basis of a credible and capable Jacobite army.

There was though a balancing factor. While considerable backing existed for the return of a Scottish parliament, many Presbyterian Scots in the Lowlands could not countenance the restoration of a Catholic monarch – especially if it involved French support, as indeed seemed to be the case in 1745. Britain had been at war with France since the previous year contesting the War of the Austrian Succession, fighting mainly in Flanders, and during that time the French government had given serious thought to using the Stuarts to foment and lead a Jacobite rebellion in Britain. At the end of 1743 King Louis XV had given his blessing to a plan which would have seen a French force of 10,000 soldiers assemble at Dunkirk, where they would cross the Channel and land at Maldon near Colchester prior to a march on London. The enterprise depended on the French navy winning command of the Channel from the Royal Navy, but a massive storm in February 1744 ripped apart the rival fleets off Dungeness, ensuring that no French invasion could take place that year.

Even so, the revelation of the French invasion plan concentrated minds in London, where the government under the leadership of Henry Pelham, who had been in office since December 1743, was well aware of the possibility that Scotland might provide fertile ground for a fresh Jacobite challenge backed by France. There had been several attempts at restoring the Stuarts earlier in the century, the most serious having been mounted in 1715, but by the 1740s support for the cause had narrowed itself down to Scotland, where the main centres of Jacobite influence were in the north-east and the Highland areas beyond the Great Glen. Of course there were still Jacobite sympathisers in England, but the harsh reality was that most of the great pro-Jacobite families had effectively embraced the Whig regime which had been in power since the succession of King George I in 1714 and was to reign supreme until the reign of King George III. Of particularly vital concern to them was the important patronage which this so-called 'Whig Supremacy' was able to offer. If any revolt were to be raised in the 1740s, the odds were that it would come from Scotland.

With that in mind, the government ordered their commander-in-chief in Scotland, Lieutenant-General Sir John Cope, to make preparations for the defence of the Highlands, as that remote land mass would be the most likely focus for the raising of a revolt in support of the Stuart cause. Cope was an experienced veteran who had fought at the Battle of Dettingen, and he acted quickly by making immediate use of the defences put in place by Field Marshal George Wade in the wake of the earlier Jacobite rebellion in 1715. As part of his pacification policy for the north of Scotland, Wade was responsible for the construction of defensive points at Fort George, Fort Augustus and Fort William, the aim being to control the important line of communication through Loch Ness and Loch Lochy, the route of the later Caledonian Canal.

Reacting to the government's orders, Cope ordered three companies of Guise's Regiment[3] to march to Fort William, the southernmost strongpoint, while an additional three companies moved to Fort Augustus and two others deployed to Fort George outside Inverness. At the same time single companies were sent to smaller garrisons at Bernera and at Ruthven near Kingussie. There was also a small presence at Castle Duart on the island of Mull.[4] Each company should have been about seventy strong, but detachments had had to be withdrawn to furnish working parties on the roads, so the garrisons in place were inadequate to mount a serious defence to a determined attacking force. The challenge was not long in coming.

The French warship sighted by Captain Wilson was the *Doutelle* (or *Du Teillay*), a trim little frigate lightly armed and made for speed. It was owned by a French privateer of Irish extraction called Antoine Walsh, a former French naval officer whose father Philip had transported James Stuart to France from Ireland following the disastrous Jacobite campaign of 1689. On board were Prince Charles and his party, which included seven boon companions who were later to become immortalised in Jacobite folklore as the 'Seven Men of Moidart'. As befitted those who had espoused the Jacobite cause in exile, they were 'a most extraordinary band of followers': the ailing and gout-ridden William Murray, Marquess of Tullibardine (also styled Duke of Atholl by his followers); Aeneas Macdonald, the expedition's banker, who was in the party to win over his brother Donald of Kinlochmoidart; Colonel Francis Strickland, the only Englishman and a member of an old Westmorland Jacobite family; and four Irishmen – Sir Thomas Sheridan, the prince's old tutor, George Kelly, a Protestant clergyman, Sir John Macdonald, a dipsomaniacal former cavalry officer, and Colonel John William O'Sullivan, a presumptuous Franco-Irish army officer. According to the memoirs of the Chevalier James Johnstone, an Edinburgh-born Jacobite sympathiser and later an aide to Prince Charles who kept a record of the enterprise, all had varying degrees of military experience but none were in the first flush of youth; they constituted in his opinion a 'ridiculous retinue'.[5] What bound them together was the prince's plan to sail to Scotland to raise a rebellion amongst Jacobite supporters and then to put his father back on the throne.

It is important not to underestimate the incredible willpower and enthusiasm which the young prince brought to the enterprise; he seemed to understand the absolute importance of getting to Scotland without further ado and of refusing to let any obstacles get in his way. He also realised that if the operation were successful it would force France's hand to support the cause by sending forces to invade England.

The frigate had sailed from the Loire at the end of June and had been joined at sea by the French man-of-war *L'Elisabeth*, armed with sixty-four guns. *L'Elisabeth* was carrying weapons and ammunition – broadswords, muskets and twenty field guns – as well as money and a token collection of around seven hundred volunteer soldiers drawn from the Irish Brigade, one of several mercenary formations which served in the French army; many of its members were veterans of the recent fighting in Flanders. The small squadron was bound for the north-west coast of Scotland and initially the two ships made good time, but on 9 July, while a hundred miles west of the Lizard, they were intercepted by HMS *Lion*, fifty-eight guns, under the command of Captain Percy Brett RN. A fierce close-quarter battle began between the two capital ships, while the smaller *Doutelle* stood off and awaited the outcome: the French and British vessels were evenly matched in terms of firepower and that parity prevented either from getting the upper hand. After five hours of heavy pounding, *L'Elisabeth* and the *Lion* were badly damaged and had taken substantial casualties amongst their crews, leaving Brett with little option but to break off as night fell and to limp back towards Plymouth. When it became clear that *L'Elisabeth* was unable to continue, Walsh had no option but to head north towards Scotland, even though that meant leaving behind the bigger ship's valuable cargo of weapons and soldiers.

Having taken leave of the stricken *L'Elisabeth*, Walsh made sail on a northerly course to reach Barra, the southernmost of the Western Isles, and on 23 July the *Doutelle* made its first landfall on the small island of Eriskay. There the prince was welcomed by Alexander Macdonald of Boisdale, half-brother to the Macdonalds of Clanranald and a powerful local Catholic magnate.

The information received by Macdonald was not encouraging; in response, aghast at the lack of money, arms and manpower necessary for an uprising, he advised the prince that he would not receive the backing of two influential West Highland supporters, Macdonald of Sleat and Macleod of Macleod, both of whom had earlier pledged their willingness to 'come out' in the Jacobite cause provided that Charles received military backing in Paris. At that, recalled O'Sullivan later, 'everybody was strock as with a thunderbolt'.[6] It could have signalled the end of the enterprise, but Charles was determined to continue, and next day the *Doutelle* set sail again to cross the southern waters of the Minch, its destination the remote and scarcely penetrable fastness of the mountainous coastline of Arisaig, Morar and Moidart.

It was at that stage that Captain Wilson sighted the French ship from his strongpoint in Glenelg and his dispatch started alarm bells ringing at distant Fort Augustus. There was now no doubt that Prince Charles had arrived in Scotland and would soon be stirring up the long-feared Jacobite uprising amongst the pro-Catholic clans of the western Highlands and islands. Having ascertained the facts, Wentworth sent a warning letter to Cope:

The people in general in this neighbourhood seem mightily rejoiced to find the Chevalier is so near them, and within these two days all the gentlemen of any figure in this part of the world are all gone off. One Glengarry said yesterday, before he left home, to the blacksmith that was shoeing his horses that these Barracks should be in his possession before Saturday night. I have taken all possible care ...[7]

Wentworth was right to take precautions, for Charles's arrival on the Scottish mainland had indeed excited considerable local interest and excitement. Having made a second landfall on the Scottish mainland in Arisaig, on the northern shore of Loch nan Uamh, Charles and his party took up residence inside the farmhouse of Borrodale belonging to the Clanranalds. There he received a number of delegations of local dignitaries who came to pay their respects and to weigh up their response to the prince's plea for assistance. From this point onwards, despite the defections of Macdonald and Macleod on Skye, the uprising started to gather the kind of momentum which was capable of growing into a realisable insurgency. Using his undoubted personal charm, Charles began to work on the local clan leaders both at Borrodale and then at Kinlochmoidart six miles to the south; his first converts were the Clanranalds, who were followed by their Macdonald kinsmen of Glencoe and Keppoch. At the same time the first support from outside the Highland bounds came from the unexpected arrival of John Gordon of Glenbucket, a venerable landowner from the north-east, the first of his class to declare for the prince's cause. The biggest prize though was Donald Cameron of Lochiel, hereditary leader of Clan Cameron.

Lochiel's decision to support the uprising cemented its viability and made worthwhile the prince's efforts in Moidart during the course of the late summer. As the other clans wavered and only the Macdonalds seemed likely to support the Jacobite cause, Lochiel's commitment was a turning-point, and many legends grew up around the way in which it happened. According to the playwright John Home, who got the story from the traveller Thomas Pennant, Lochiel was almost tricked into supporting Charles by nobly declaring, 'I'll share the fate of my prince; and so shall every man over whom nature or fortune hath given me power.'[8]

The truth is less romantic, but it gives some idea of the network of tribal loyalties that underpinned the Jacobite cause and intensified government concerns about a Stuart challenge to the throne. Lochiel came from an old-established Episcopalian Jacobite family which had supported risings in 1708 and 1715, and in their aftermath he had taken on the task of acting as agent for the Stuarts in the West Highlands. Somewhat rashly, given his family's relative poverty, Lochiel had promised to provide 20,000 soldiers to support the French invasion of 1744 and its failure had been a bitter disappointment to him. Thereafter he was of the opinion that no rising could succeed without massive French assistance, and initially he was in some despair when he heard that the prince and his party had arrived without the expected French military support.

To begin with, in his discussions with Charles, Lochiel was inclined to play for time in the hope that the absence of local backing would persuade the prince to return to France. It was not to be, and a combination of blandishments and an appeal to his honour seems to have weakened Lochiel's resolve. A deciding factor was Charles's promise to find the funds to compensate Lochiel's estate should the expedition end in disaster, and three weeks of negotiation ended with the Cameron leader throwing in his lot with the Jacobites and, more importantly, encouraging neighbouring clans to provide 2500 soldiers.[9] If any further argument were needed it was produced by Charles on 6 August, when he ordered Walsh to return to France in the *Doutelle* and then summoned the clans to join him at a rallying point at the head of nearby Glenfinnan on 19 August. In taking that course of action – figuratively burning his boats – there was no way back.

One other factor would act as a spur: the good omen of any early military success. And this was not long in coming. On 13 August Wentworth wrote again to Cope, warning him that the local people supported the Jacobites in general, and that he would be hard pushed to contain any Jacobite pre-emptive strike as he could not 'find one man that knows how to point a gun or ever saw a shot fired out of a mortar, there being only two gunners and they not much accustomed to it'.[10] By then too the first news of Charles's landing had arrived in London, where the initial reaction was one of muted indifference. The only member of the Cabinet alert to the threat was the Duke of Newcastle, Pelham's brother and foreign secretary, who wrote to the Duke of Cumberland, commander-in-chief of the government forces in Flanders, warning him that he might have to send back some of his infantry regiments. A warning was also sent to the Earl of Stair, who commanded the army in England, but the elderly field marshal believed that the 6000 soldiers at his disposal were ample to meet the challenge. At the same time Cope was proceeding with his intention of strengthening the lines of communication in the Highlands and had ordered two companies of the Royals to make their way without delay from Fort William to Fort Augustus to reinforce the garrison.[11] It was a distance of no more than thirty miles but the order was fraught with difficulty: the barely trained infantrymen were unused to the mountainous terrain, having served only at the depot in Perth prior to embarking for service in Flanders.

On approaching Wade's High Bridge (close to present-day Spean Bridge) on 16 August, the Royals, under the command of Captain Scott, were ambushed by a group of Highlanders loyal to Donald Macdonnell of Keppoch. Unnerved by the sudden and unexpected firing, Scott's men retreated back down the track, and after a brief skirmish they were forced to surrender to Keppoch. Scott and three other officers, together with eighty NCOs and infantrymen, were taken prisoner and marched off to Achnacarry, where Charles showed leniency by offering parole on condition that they did not serve against him again. The same treatment was meted out to Captain John Swettenham, a military engineer sent by Wentworth to gather intelligence who had also fallen into Jacobite hands.

Both incidents were good for the morale of Keppoch's men and they undoubtedly influenced Lochiel in his decision to support the uprising. From a military point of view the skirmish and Swettenham's capture would also influence the following course of events.

The key to the tactical situation lay in the government forts, which were suddenly open to attack. Wentworth recognised the danger and told his cousin Thomas Watson-Wentworth, Lord Malton and Lord Lieutenant of the West Riding, that 'the Pretender with 3,000 highlanders is six miles off'.[12] Cope also saw what was happening and realised that if the forts fell it would hamper his own plans to march into the Highlands to destroy the rebellion before it gathered momentum. On 19 August he rejoined the government forces in Stirling, before heading north to Dalwhinnie by way of Crieff and Dalnacardoch with a small force of 1500 infantrymen representing Murray's, Lascelles' and Lee's regiments, most of them under strength and all untested.[13] From there he proposed marching towards Fort Augustus, a route that would take him over the wilds of the Corrieyairack Pass, the only passable crossing place in the western Monadhliath mountain range – Wade had recognised its importance when he built his twenty-eight miles of zig-zag military road in 1731. Corrieyairack was the strategic equivalent of Afghanistan's Khyber Pass: the commander who held this position was in possession of the only viable route for a rapid descent from the West Highlands into the Lowlands.

Before leaving Edinburgh, Cope had discussed his tactics with

a number of leading grandees, including Lord President Duncan
Forbes of Culloden, and throughout his march he was in constant
correspondence with the Marquess of Tweeddale, the ineffectual
Secretary of State for Scotland, who was inclined to minimise
the threat posed by the Jacobites. With so many political masters
having to be placated, Cope was in a parlous position, but once he
had committed his force to move into the Highlands his military
thinking was sound enough. Recognising that in such terrain artillery and cavalry would not be helpful, he decided to leave behind
his field guns and two regiments of Irish dragoons and to move as
quickly as possible with his infantry. According to the testimony
of one of his officers, Lieutenant-Colonel Charles Whitefoord,
Cope 'kept the Highlanders always advanced, extended to the left
and right, with trusted officers who were to make signals, in case
of the enemy lurking in the hills'.[14] On 26 August Cope reached
the small village of Dalwhinnie, which justified its Gaelic name
Dail Chuinnidh ('meeting place'), for it was here that he had to
decide whether or not to continue towards the Corrieyairack Pass
or to veer north-east towards Inverness. It was here, too, that he
received the intelligence that a superior force of Jacobites had
already beaten him to the pass.

What is more, the information was confirmed by Captain John
Swettenham, who although on parole passed on the intelligence
to Cope as his superior officer. Earlier Swettenham had witnessed
one of the high points of the uprising (and an iconic moment in
Jacobite historiography) when he was present at the gathering of
Prince Charles's supporters at the head of Glenfinnan. Having
given instructions to muster at the meeting point of the glens
of the Shlatach, the Finnan and the Callop, Charles and his retinue arrived shortly after midday. To begin with he only had a
small bodyguard of some four hundred Macdonalds, a handful

of Macgregors and Glenbucket's Gordons, but as the afternoon dragged on and tensions no doubt grew, the sound of bagpipes was heard from the east, heralding the arrival of eight hundred Camerons. Lochiel had been true to his word and in so doing produced a wonderfully dramatic scene which Charles was able to milk to the full. The Jacobite standard was unfurled, James Stuart was proclaimed king and the blessing was provided by Hugh Macdonald, Bishop of the Highlands. Several onlookers remarked that Prince Charles had never looked happier than he did at that moment. He had 1200 men under his command and the rebellion was now a reality.

As happens so often in an enterprise of this kind, success breeds further success, and in the days that followed the raising of the standard other clans flocked to join the Jacobite army – Macdonalds of Glengarry, Grants of Moriston, Macdonalds of Glencoe and Stewarts of Appin. By the beginning of September the Jacobite army was joined by two commanders who were appointed lieutenant-general and who would play leading roles in the campaign which lay ahead – James Drummond, Duke of Perth, and Lord George Murray, younger brother of the Marquess of Tullibardine and an experienced soldier who had served the Jacobite cause in the previous uprisings of 1715 and 1719.

By then, too, it seemed inevitable that the first engagement would be fought on the heights of the Corrieyairack Pass. Charles was keen to make contact with an enemy whom he sensed might be in disarray, but this turned out to be the battle that never was. Cope managed to keep his head and assessed the situation correctly. Following a council of war, he and his senior officers decided against any attempt to take the pass; instead, they agreed to head north-eastwards up the Spey valley and over the Slochd Mor Pass to Inverness. On their departure they left behind a small party of twelve men from Guise's Regiment commanded by Sergeant Terence Molloy to garrison the nearby barracks at Ruthven, another of Wade's counter-measures to deter Jacobite activity in the Highlands.

On 29 August Cope reached the safety of Inverness, thus bringing to an end the first phase of operations in the West Highlands. For the Jacobite army this proved to be something of an anti-climax, as they had entertained hopes of engaging and beating the government army on the heights of Corrieyairack. With no other enemy in sight, they made an ineffectual attempt to capture the barracks at Ruthven, but this was easily beaten off by Molloy who refused to submit, saying that he was 'too old a soldier to surrender a garrison of such strength without bloody noses'. Although the Jacobite forces managed to set alight a number of buildings they suffered five casualties, while Molloy only lost one soldier who, as he informed Cope, was 'shot through the head by foolishly holding his head too high over the parapet, contrary to orders'.[15] As a result of that stout defence, the barracks at Ruthven remained secure under Molloy's command and would do so until the following year. But for the time being Prince Charles's army had a bigger prize: they now knew that the road to the Lowlands was open and that their march south would be unopposed.

Paradoxically, given the attempts to pacify the Highlands through construction of a decent transport infrastructure, the Jacobite army was greatly assisted by the creation of Wade's military road from Dalwhinnie through Dalnacardoch down to Dunkeld. Setting out on 29 August they reached Blair Castle two days later, after covering an average of seventeen miles a day. By 3 September they had crossed the Highland line and were in Dunkeld, having negotiated the Pass of Killiecrankie, a potential choke-point where an earlier Jacobite uprising led by John

Graham of Claverhouse, Viscount Dundee, had come to grief in 1689. The road to the Lowlands through Perth was now open, and the Jacobite army took full advantage of the easier marching conditions; they even found the time to spend a full week resting in Perth, where James Stuart was declared king at the cross. Rumours abounded about the presence of government troops, but the dragoons left behind by Cope kept out of sight, and when the Jacobite army passed by Stirling, garrison commander Brigadier-General William Blakeney kept his troops within the bounds of the castle and used his small six-pounder cannons to fire four rounds on the Jacobite line of march. Although they did not do any damage he reported to Pelham that his main intention had been to prevent Stirling falling into Jacobite hands:

> After having repaired the fortifications of the Castle, I have Barracaded [sic] all the Avenues to this Town, and obliged the Inhabitants to stop up all their back doors and Passages, by which I shall prevent the Town's being Insulted, and if the Men that I have placed to defend it happen to be pressed, I have secured a safe retreat for them into the Castle.[16]

Although little is known about Blakeney's early military career other than that he saw service with the 1st Foot Guards (later Grenadier Guards), his professional behaviour during his governorship of Stirling Castle would earn him rapid promotion to major-general (1746) and then lieutenant-general (1747) before becoming commander of the garrison on the island of Minorca. Very much a soldier's soldier, he had served previously in the West Indies and was present at the siege of Cartagena in 1741 and the abortive attack on Porto Bello a year later. He was typical of many army officers of the period: Irish-born, tough and no-nonsense, much better at military practice than theory but popular with his fellow officers. Like most of them, too, he was not particularly clever but was full of common sense and was forthright in his dealings with the men under his command.

As Charles continued his march south, the government in London thought that his army would swing west towards Glasgow in order to take the western route into England through Annandale and on to Carlisle and Preston, but at that juncture Charles was intent only on capturing Edinburgh. That much became obvious when he crossed the River Forth and followed its southern side towards the Scottish capital through present-day West Lothian. This took him towards the town of Linlithgow, where it would have been possible for one of the government cavalry regiments, the 13th Dragoons, to lay an ambush, but their commanding officer Colonel James Gardiner, a veteran of the Battle of Ramillies (1706), preferred caution to chance and retreated towards Edinburgh to link up with the 14th Dragoons. That was the last opportunity for government forces to engage the Jacobite army, by then 1800 strong, which had marched within range of Edinburgh by 16 September.

By then Cope had also left the Highlands and by using the government's superior logistics had brought his forces to within sight of the Scottish capital. It had been a tortuous journey. Having reached Inverness, Cope discovered two unpalatable facts. First, there had been no noticeable support for the government from Highland clans thought to be pro-Whig and anti-Jacobite; second, it was clear that Prince Charles's army had broken out into the Lowlands to threaten Edinburgh and that the only way to retrieve the situation was to transport his army south by sea. Cope immediately resolved to march his army to the east coast port of Aberdeen, where they would be met by transport ships sent up from Leith, the port of Edinburgh. This bold move was accepted by his senior officers as 'the only means to get there [Edinburgh] before them [the Jacobites]'.[17] It took a week to complete the march across the north-east through Banff, Turiff and Oldmeldrum, but on 15 September the fleet was on its way, and the following evening after a squally voyage it had reached the port of Dunbar in the Firth of Forth, some twenty miles east of Edinburgh. Cope's soldiers started disembarking on 17 September, at much the same time that an advance party of the Jacobite army led by Lochiel entered Edinburgh through the Netherbow Port, having tricked the guards into allowing them access while a coach was leaving the city.

Edinburgh was certainly a prize worth taking and the Jacobite entry into the city was another high point in Prince Charles's campaign. Not yet the sprawling mass it would become in later years, the city was a compact area bounded by the impregnable castle at its western end and the palace of Holyroodhouse to the east. Along the main thoroughfares of the Lawnmarket, the Grassmarket and the Canongate lofty tenements had been built, some of them eight storeys high, and according to the English traveller Edward Burt each storey accommodated 'a particular Family and perhaps a separate Proprietor'. It was a crowded, noisome place where it was the custom to discharge household and human waste into the streets each night at ten o'clock, forcing the inhabitants, according to Burt, 'to light Pieces of Paper, and throw them upon the Table to smoke the Room, and, as I thought, to mix one bad smell with another'.[18]

None of this impinged on Prince Charles and his army: he was lodged in Holyroodhouse and his army made camp in the adjoining parklands, where their behaviour was reported to be 'more regular than expected'. The arrival of the Jacobite army produced a schizophrenic response from the people of Scotland's capital. It had been anticipated for several days but the Lord Provost, Archibald Stewart of Mitcharn, and his fellow magistrates were unsure how to deal with the situation and were at first minded to refuse the Jacobites entry. According to John Home, who was present throughout, when Charles sent a summons demanding the city's surrender 'the cry against resistance became louder than ever; and it was proposed to send a deputation to the person from who this letter came, to desire that hostilities should not be commenced till the citizens had deliberated, and resolved what answer should be made to the letter.'[19] Clearly Provost Stewart was playing for time until Cope's forces were in a position to engage the Jacobite army.

The Lord Provost was in fact in an impossible situation. The castle was under the command of Lieutenant-General Sir Joshua Guest, an ancient cavalry officer who was described by Sir John Clerk of Penicuik (an astute observer of events) as having been 'in his time an Active, diligent Souldier [sic] but, being a man above 86 years of age, he cou'd scarcely stir out of his room'; his deputy Lieutenant-General Sir George Gordon was little better, being roughly of the same age and confined to a Bath chair.[20] The castle was well-nigh impregnable and defended by regular forces, but in the event of a pitched battle the crowded city would have been difficult to defend and large numbers of civilians would undoubtedly have been killed. Stewart could have called on over three thousand armed men to defend the city but the majority were half-trained (at best) volunteers or members of the Town Guard, a kind of police force composed mainly of 'old Highlanders, of uncouth aspect and speech, dressed in a dingy red uniform and cocked hats, who often exchanged the musket for an antique native weapon called the Lochaber axe'.[21] In short, these were hardly effective forces, and while Stewart was suspected of being a closet Jacobite he had little option but to negotiate with Charles's men once they were inside the city. Contemporary evidence suggests that, while there had been some displays of public support for the prince, backing for the government remained strong, if unspoken, and some leading citizens followed the example of the poet Allan Ramsay, author of pro-Jacobite and anti-Union verses, who diplomatically absented himself from the city pleading a sudden illness.

If anything, though, the initiative had passed to Prince Charles, ensconced in Scotland's capital. As for Cope, he had to make the running if he was to fulfil his obligations as the commander of the government forces in Scotland. On paper, from a military point of view he had little to fear. After landing at Dunbar he had met up again with his two regiments of dragoons, which provided him with reconnaissance, mobility and, potentially, a cutting edge in the field. While dragoons were more like heavy mounted infantry than cavalry and lacked the élan of light horse regiments, they were feared by infantrymen, and along with artillery they were especially disliked by Highland soldiers. Cope also had around twelve hundred infantrymen in Murray's, Lee's and Lascelles' regiments, plus two companies from Guise's, and these were supported by four mortars and six artillery pieces manned by marines. However, numbers and names counted for little. It was the steadfastness and experience of the infantrymen that decided everything and in this respect Cope's force was deficient. Most of his soldiers were little more than raw recruits who had been given basic infantry training in preparation for fighting in Europe and were unprepared for the kind of close-quarter engagement favoured by the Highlanders. As for the dragoons, they were suitably bellicose, but Gardiner's 13th Dragoons had already made fools of themselves outside Edinburgh when they panicked after encountering a handful of Highlanders and fled towards the coast in full view of the people of the city. This ludicrous incident became known as the Coltbridge canter, from the small village near Corstorphine where the flight began.

By that stage of the campaign Gardiner was a nervous wreck – as a young man he had undergone a profound religious conversion after falling from his horse – but Cope had some good regimental officers under his command. Amongst the more professional and capable were Lieutenant-Colonel Peregrine Lascelles from Whitby in Yorkshire, later to be a general, and Lieutenant-Colonel Sir Peter Halkett of Pitfirrane of Lee's Regiment, a Fife landowner's son and member of parliament for Dunfermline. As the government army marched westwards from Dunbar the men were in a bullish mood, and the officers later remarked that 'all expressed the strongest desire for action'.[22]

The first obstacle facing Cope's men was the crossing of the River North Esk at Musselburgh, just to the east of Edinburgh, and it was here that the location of the battle was decided. Cope halted his men close to the town of Tranent on open ground towards the sea between Seton and the coastal village of Preston-pans. At the same time, on learning of Cope's approach, Charles had ordered his army to leave Edinburgh and had also moved them towards Musselburgh, where they crossed the North Esk in the early morning of 20 September. Skirting to the south and led by Lord George Murray, the Jacobite army made its way through the village of Wallyford towards Tranent and it was on the ridge of Falside Hill that they got their first sight of the government forces. At first it was judged to be an unpromising location; one Jacobite officer complained that he 'saw no possibility of attacking it, without exposing ourselves to be cut to pieces in the most disgraceful manner'.[23] Not only did Cope enjoy the protection of the walls of Preston and Bankton Parks to the west (the latter location being Gardiner's family home), but to the south lay the marshy expanse of Tranent Meadows, a formidable physical obstacle for infantrymen.[24]

Taking advantage of the terrain, Cope drew up his force facing south towards the meadows, with the walled gardens on his right flank. It was the correct decision, but it was also to be his undoing. During the course of the evening the Jacobites held a war council at which Lord George Murray proposed a flanking move to the east of the marsh obstacle, and during the discussion a local farmer's son called Robert Anderson volunteered the information that he knew a shortcut which was passable and would take the Highlanders along a narrow track known as the Riggonhead Defile. This would get the Jacobites into a new position to the east before first light. The plan was adopted and the Highland army set out along the path, keeping total silence and marching three abreast.

Although Cope had posted pickets and lit fires, the move went undetected until it was too late. Commendably, Cope reacted quickly and ordered his force to wheel left to face the new threat, eventually forming a line with the infantry facing west–east, flanked by two squadrons of dragoons on either side and with the others in reserve.

It was the classic defensive formation of the age, but it had been made too late. Shortly before six o'clock in the morning the Highlanders charged out of the mist, and with the government artillery only able to fire off one round they were quickly in amongst the bewildered and increasingly panic-stricken government soldiers. As Cope's line staggered under the volleys of musket fire, the men had no time to regroup before the Highlanders drew their broadswords and charged into the broken ranks, hacking and stabbing. Lochiel's Camerons piled into the government left flank, followed by Clan Donald, and the combination of speed and aggression proved too much for infantrymen unused to this kind of combat. As Pelham later commented in a critique of Cope's performance, it had not helped matters that all of Cope's men had been ordered to leave their swords at Stirling at the beginning of the campaign and that the gunners were inadequate: 'the Engineers sometimes put powder into the Cannon & forgott the Ball, at others put the Ball in first & the Powder Afterwards.'[25]

At this point in the battle the dragoons could have intervened decisively, but they were the first to break and turn from the weight of the Jacobite charge, leaving the infantrymen in front exposed. As the dragoons started to wheel away from the lines, Gardiner found himself cut off with a small party of his men whom he tried to rally, but he was quickly wounded – mortally as it transpired – and carried from the field. Other officers also behaved bravely but ineffectually. Halkett attempted a stand outside the parkland walls to the west but was soon overwhelmed and forced to surrender. In other parts of the field the retreat was in full flight as terrified government soldiers attempted to make their way back to Edinburgh. Others fled east towards Berwick-on-Tweed, while some managed to escape south towards the Lammermuir Hills and on to the border at Coldstream. According to the evidence of Alexander Carlyle, whose father lived near Prestonpans and who later became a distinguished minister of the Church of Scotland, the whole business was over within a quarter of an hour, with Prince Charles left as master of the field before the sun had fully risen.[26]

As for Cope, he escaped once it became clear that all was lost, heading south towards Lauder and then Coldstream before following the River Tweed towards Berwick-on-Tweed. Under the circumstances he could not have done otherwise; his army had been trounced and humiliated and his baggage train at Preston-pans had fallen into enemy hands, thereby providing the Jacobites with much-needed ammunition and money. From a military point of view it could not have been worse. In the bleak arithmetic of war, the government army losses were computed at 300 killed, 400 to 500 wounded and 1400 to 1500 captured.[27] Around thirty Highlanders had been killed and several more badly wounded. In the words of the Chevalier de Johnstone, who was present, 'the field of battle presented a spectacle of horror, being covered with hands, legs and arms, and mutilated bodies, for they killed all with the sword.'[28]

At a stroke it seemed that Prince Charles was master of Scotland. His immediate opponents with their feared artillery and cavalry had been routed, Edinburgh was in his hands and apart from the Highland forts and the castles at Stirling and Dumbarton, the government had no remaining military presence in Scotland. After spending the night at nearby Pinkie House, Prince Charles returned to Edinburgh on 22 September to consider his next move. An immediate invasion of England immediately suggested itself, but there were massive logistical difficulties and the Jacobite army was still pitifully small. There were also tensions in the council of war, with Lord George Murray emerging as the leader of a rival faction. At the same time the position of Edinburgh Castle became a problem. The garrison was now under the command of General Preston, another octogenarian, who quickly gave notice that he would not surrender but neither would he resist by firing his big guns into the city and causing unnecessary damage and civilian casualties. Meanwhile no word came from France about the hoped-for military support, and recruitment into the Jacobite army proved to be extremely tardy. Otherwise Charles passed the time pleasantly enough, holding court at Holyroodhouse, where he spent much of his time issuing proclamations denouncing 'the pretended union of the two countries' and generally acted in his capacity as his father's regent.

The government, too, had to decide what to do next. It could no longer hide behind the pretext that Prince Charles's arrival in Scotland was a minor irritation and now had to face up to the fact that it had a major insurrection on its hands. Already, on 4 September, the Duke of Newcastle had written a concerned letter to the Duke of Cumberland in Flanders, expressing surprise that the Jacobites had made so much progress:

> I did not imagine that, in so short a time, the Pretender's son, with an army of 3,000 men, would have got between the King's troops and England, and be within a few days' march of Edinburgh, where, some think, we shall soon hear that he is; and that he may attempt to call a parliament there.[29]

When news arrived of the defeat at Prestonpans, it confirmed all of Newcastle's worst fears about the 'reality and danger' of the Jacobite challenge. Cumberland had already been ordered to detach ten infantry battalions from his army in Flanders and return them to Britain, a process which would take time after negotiation with his Dutch and Austrian allies, but now the government had to take immediate steps to strengthen the defence of the homeland. The first reinforcements, 6000 Dutch and Swiss mercenaries from Flanders, reached Cope in Berwick-on-Tweed immediately after his defeat, while the first British battalions arrived in the Thames estuary on 19 September. The rest sailed directly to Newcastle with Cumberland in the middle of October. Two further battalions – the 2nd Royals and Battereau's – were withdrawn from garrison duty in Ireland, having been reinforced by men from other regiments. By then the defence of the north of England had been placed in the hands of Wade, who was in his seventies; at the end of October his army numbered just under 11,000 men and had assembled at Newcastle, with a detachment at Berwick-on-Tweed composed of the remnants of Cope's force and one Dutch battalion. A second force of similar size guarded the English Midlands from its base at Lichfield with a small detachment at Chester. It was commanded by Lieutenant-General Sir John Ligonier, a remarkable French-born Huguenot who had been permitted to purchase a commission in the British Army in 1703, and it included three regiments of foot guards and fourteen other regiments of foot.

All this was accomplished with commendable speed, but it also has to be said that it was done against a background of fear and panic in the northern English towns, caused by the inexplicable defeat at Prestonpans and the anticipated arrival of the Highland hordes. Partly this was a race memory; the towns on the English side of the border remembered only too well the long history of cross-border raiding and the arrival of Scottish war parties bringing death and destruction in times of tension. Partly, too, the fear was exacerbated by anti-Catholicism; there was real dread in northern England that the Jacobite victory presaged a wider and bloodier invasion backed by the French, and there were reports of the burning of effigies of the pope and Prince Charles.[30] All down the east coast, from Berwick-on-Tweed as far as King's Lynn in Norfolk, local defences were strengthened and volunteer forces were raised to meet the expected onslaught. Similar steps were taken in towns on the western marches as worried townspeople tried to gauge which route the Jacobites would take, many people remembering that it was down the west coast that the Jacobites had marched during the previous invasion scare in 1715. What followed was a sorry mixture of dithering and poor judgement by the government military commanders, to which was added general incredulity that an invasion from Scotland was actually about to take place.

By then, Wade's best days were long behind him. A veteran of the War of the Spanish Succession at the beginning of the century, he had consolidated his reputation through his pacification of the Highlands in the aftermath of the 1715 Jacobite rebellion and had been promoted field marshal in 1743. However, his performance as commander-in-chief in Flanders had been weak and he was allowed to retire to England in March 1745, having failed to cope with the intricacies of coalition warfare and having been outmanoeuvred by the French. There was no shame in his recall as his opponent was Marshal Maurice de Saxe (1696–1750), one of the great commanders of the age, whose *Reveries upon the Art of War* (1757) is considered to be one of the most intelligent expositions on tactics and the military life.

Despite the setback, Wade retained the confidence of King George II and emerged as the leading military personality in the government's plans to contain the Jacobite threat. Ordered to take command of the army assembled at Newcastle, he took possession of a sizeable and experienced force which included twelve battalions of infantry, five regiments of horse and five Dutch or Swiss infantry regiments. His second-in-command was Lieutenant-General William Ann Keppel, 2nd Earl of Albemarle, and his cavalry was under the command of Lieutenant-General Henry Hawley; both were veterans of Fontenoy. Other officers worthy of remark were two experienced brigadier-generals, James Cholmondeley and John Mordaunt, both of whom had distinguished themselves in the fighting in Flanders and would continue to enhance their reputations in the British Army.

It took time for the government forces to assemble following their withdrawal from Flanders – Albemarle's reinforcements did not reach Newcastle until 26 October – and it was also true that Wade was hampered by lack of reliable intelligence about Jacobite intentions north of the border. Moreover, he had to retain sufficient forces to guard Newcastle and the strategically vital coalfields of the north-east, London's main source of fuel, while it was necessary to guard the main border crossing at Berwick-on-Tweed in case the Jacobites attempted to invade England by the eastern route. Even so, he was remarkably dilatory in his approach. Albemarle counselled an immediate move north to engage the Jacobites before their revolt gained momentum and they were able to build on their victory at Prestonpans. Somewhat reluctantly, Wade agreed to the plan, and in the first week of November the government army headed north towards Morpeth.

They did not get very far. On 3 November Wade received intelligence that elements of the Jacobite army had left Edinburgh for Dalkeith and from there were heading south towards Peebles. This suggested that they were on their way over the hills towards Moffat and into Annandale, the western route into England where their first obstacle would be Carlisle. To meet this new challenge Wade decided to retire back to Newcastle, where his army could use the route through the Tyne Gap to march westwards and locate the Jacobite army as it marched south down the western route. Bowing to Albemarle's insistent demands for an invasion of Scotland, he ordered the elderly Lieutenant-General Roger Handasyde in Berwick-on-Tweed to march immediately on Edinburgh, reasoning correctly that Prince Charles had abandoned the Scottish capital and that it could be quickly retaken. Following some unnecessary dithering by Handasyde, who was not convinced by Wade's arguments, government forces eventually reached Edinburgh on 14 November, allowing the city to come under government control with the aid of the garrison inside the castle.

Meanwhile, the unexpectedly easy victory at Prestonpans had raised Jacobite morale and had led to an increase in recruitment (not to mention the arrival in Montrose of a shipload of funds and weapons from France). The Jacobite command was nevertheless divided about what to do next. Prince Charles was all for moving swiftly into England, both to maintain the momentum created by success and to encourage the English Jacobites to rise in his support. His plan was to march immediately into the north-east and to engage Wade's army before it was on a war footing. He also realised that London was the seat of power and that its capture was essential if his campaign was to succeed; that could not happen while he remained in Scotland.

But a number of the clan chiefs had already supported Lord George Murray's counter-proposal to do just that. They believed that the Jacobite position in Scotland had to be consolidated by removing the last vestiges of government power, notably the castles and forts, and by mounting a recruitment campaign to increase the size of the Jacobite army. This would also give France the time and opportunity to send money, arms and soldiers to support the next stage of the military campaign. Both arguments prompted intense discussion and on 30 October the matter was settled by a single vote, thanks to a last-minute proposal by Murray to invade England via the western route through Carlisle. His reasoning was that it would avoid an immediate confrontation with Wade, as well as providing an easier route which would take them through Lancashire, with its potential for supplying Jacobite support.

By then, too, the size of Prince Charles's army had grown to respectable proportions, but contrary to popular belief not all of them were Highlanders. Although more clansmen had flocked to the cause, notably men of Atholl and Cluny's Macphersons, large numbers came from the north-east and from Angus and Kincardine, where Jacobite support was particularly strong thanks to the influence of the Episcopalian church.[31] Lord Ogilvy's Forfarshire Regiment numbered 300 men, drawn mainly from the estate of his father the Earl of Airlie at Cortachy, and was generally considered to be one of the most efficient and disciplined of the prince's forces. For the first time artillery appeared, in the shape of six field guns sent from France to join those captured at Prestonpans; these were placed in the Duke of Perth's regiment under the command of Colonel James Grante, a French artillery officer.

When the invasion began the Jacobite army numbered some six thousand men; it was established on regional lines with the Lowland formations, mainly horse and artillery, moving south towards the western route while the Highlanders feinted south-eastwards over the Lammermuir Hills towards Lauder and then Kelso. There they switched to a south-westerly direction down the valley of the River Teviot towards Hawick and Langholm, a route that would take them through Canonbie and then on to Carlisle, which was reached on 9 November.

By then Prince Charles's intentions were unmistakable and Wade had to respond. After leaving Edinburgh, the Jacobites had made remarkable progress and had also given notice that they were an invasion force, and not the 'ragged hungry rabble of Yahoos of Scotch Highlanders' imagined by the Whig press.[32] Once again, though, Wade's response was tardy and ill-considered; nor were the prevailing circumstances to his advantage. Morale was low due to the inhospitable conditions in the camp at Newcastle, and the weather was bad, with snow lying along the route which would take the force westwards through the Tyne valley. With winter already upon the countryside, an early start was necessary, but this was not achieved; the army eventually set out only on 16 November, a full week after the Jacobites had reached Carlisle. Hindered by the darkness and the wintry weather, the marching infantry regiments were in trouble by the time they had reached Hexham. Worse news followed, when it became clear that Carlisle had fallen and that the leading elements of the Jacobite army had already reached Penrith. Wade now had no chance of catching his opponents on the other side of the Pennines and he succumbed to the inevitable by ordering his army to march back over the frozen wintry roads through the Tyne Gap. In a dispatch to Newcastle he blamed the harsh weather, the bad roads and sickness amongst his men, but even though he did not admit it the truth was that Wade was commanding an army which had already been beaten without a shot being fired: 'I am sorry to tell Your Grace that, in all the service I have seen since my first coming into the army, I never saw more distress than what the officers and soldiers suffer at this time.'[33]

But not everyone was disheartened. Serving in Wade's army as a brigade-major in Barrell's Regiment was James Wolfe, an up-and-coming young officer with recent experience of fighting in Flanders, where he had caught Cumberland's eye.[34] Writing to his mother on 14 November he predicted that 'these rebels won't stand the King's troops'.[35] Partly this was the confidence of a young officer anxious to reassure his mother at home in Yorkshire, but it was also the observation of a professional soldier who had already been at war and whose horse had been shot from under him at Dettingen two years earlier.

Wolfe came from a military family and his father Edward, a

major-general, was also in Wade's army, in his case taking a party of reinforcements north to join Handasyde's force at Berwick-on-Tweed. Despite suffering from a severe dose of gout which required him to ride in a carriage, Edward Wolfe too was in a confident frame of mind. His view as expressed to his wife was quite simple: it was only a matter of time before the 'Pretender's Rabble' was crushed, allowing him and his son to be at home in time for Christmas.[36]

2

LIKE THE SAVAGE RACE THEY
ROAM FOR PREY

Wade's dithering in the north-east of England gave an immense advantage to Prince Charles and his army. Carlisle fell without a fight on 18 November and with no opposition ahead of them the Jacobite army began the long march south, setting their course towards Penrith and Kendal. Led by Lord Elcho's life guards they made good progress, and by the end of November the bulk of the force had reached Preston and the vital crossing of the River Ribble. This was not just a physical barrier but in Scottish minds a mental challenge: Scottish armies had faced defeat here before, in 1648 during King Charles I's civil war and in 1715 during an earlier Jacobite rebellion.

Given the state of the roads at that period, getting so far south in such a short time had been a remarkable achievement. Most roads were little more than rough tracks, and while some were paved to allow the passage of carriages and carts, their state of repair was uneven and horse-drawn vehicles could only move at a slow pace. Even so, the Jacobite infantry was able to make progress at a rate which had proved impossible for the soldiers in the government army – a tribute to the hardihood of the men involved and their willingness to crack on at first light. What is more, while on the march and during overnight stops the Jacobite army behaved with quiet dignity and succeeded in allaying the fears of the locals that they were a gang of undisciplined savages.

While this confounded most existing preconceptions about the Highlanders, it did not encourage many local people to join the Jacobite cause; recruitment proved to be a disappointment – especially for the prince, who was relying on large numbers of English Jacobites rising in his name in order to encourage the French to lend further support to his invasion. Hopes were high amongst Prince Charles's Irish advisors that the mood would change once the Jacobite army entered Lancashire, where Catholic influence was strong, but those expectations were dashed. There was some piecemeal recruiting in the north of the county, but it was not until the army reached Manchester at the end of the month that numbers started arriving in any quantity.

On St Andrew's Day, 30 November, potential recruits from the city were encouraged to join a new formation to be known as the Manchester Regiment, and around three hundred eventually answered the call at the mustering point in the grounds of the town's Collegiate Church. The regiment was commanded by Colonel Francis Townley, who had served previously in the French army; although Whig propaganda claimed that its volunteers were 'mostly people of the lowest rank and vilest principles'[1], three of the new regiment's officers were sons of Dr Thomas Deacon, a leading non-juring clergyman and bishop (one who had refused to swear allegiance to King William and Queen Mary in the aftermath of the Glorious Revolution of 1688), all of whom refused pay and contributed personally to the costs of running the regiment.[2] Much of the credit for its formation must be given to an intrepid former government soldier called Sergeant John Dickson from Perth, who had been taken prisoner at Prestonpans. Having thrown in his lot with the Jacobites, he had ridden ahead of the main army to beat up for recruits, accompanied by a drummer boy and a comely woman with a fine singing voice known to history as 'Long Preston Peggy'.[3]

But despite the trickle of recruits a pattern was beginning to emerge. There was little overt hostility surrounding the arrival of the Jacobite army, but while people turned out in numbers to satisfy their curiosity or to catch a glimpse of Prince Charles as the Highlanders passed through the towns of Lancashire, very few took the step of donning the white cockade worn by most of the Jacobite soldiers. At the same time, there was evidence that many young men were joining the militia forces whose call-out had been authorised by parliament on 14 November. For years the militia had embodied the ancient English principle of the citizen's duty to protect the realm in time of danger; although it had once been a reasonably effective instrument, by the middle of the eighteenth century it was a debased military force capable only of minor policing duties, being described by one historian of the British Army as 'useless'.[4]

Even at the time, opinions varied about the effectiveness of the militia forces. Major-General Humphrey Bland, newly returned from service in Flanders, thought the Lancashire militia was 'a very fine body of men, well-armed and tolerably well disciplined', who would greatly assist the regular army; others, notably Lord Derby, the Lord Lieutenant of Lancashire, considered them to be raw and undisciplined and no match for the Jacobite army.[5]

Bland possessed a shrewd military mind, being another of those Irish-born career soldiers who provided the backbone of the army during the reigns of George I and George II. Sensible, efficient and blunt to the point of rudeness, he had vast experience of campaigning in Flanders, having served in Marlborough's army earlier in the century and more recently as a brigade commander at Fontenoy. He was also highly respected as a theoretician and his work *A Treatise of Military Discipline* (1727) had emerged as a standard drill book, as well as being an intelligent and practical guide to officers' duties in quarters and in the field. It also brought Bland to the notice of the Duke of Cumberland, who respected him for his professional approach and listened to him over matters such as discipline and tactics.

However, for all his military experience, Bland was overly optimistic about the effectiveness of the militia. He was probably trying to bolster spirits amongst government ministers in London, where the invasion was now being treated with growing alarm, but he had been out of the country too long to have had much experience of the militia's effectiveness as a fighting force. In fact, it ended up being something of a broken reed as far as engaging the Jacobite army was concerned. Some units such as the Liverpool 'Blues' – so nicknamed on account of the colour of their uniform coats – did good service by carrying out an order to destroy the bridges over the River Mersey at Warrington to hinder the Jacobite advance, but overall the militia's lack of training, equipment and organisational coherence meant that they could do little other than supply a reassuring presence to the local population.

As the Jacobite army marched further south, Ligonier was ordered to move his forces from their defensive stop line centred on Lichfield in Staffordshire and to deploy them northwards to the River Mersey. This he put in hand, but then promptly fell ill and had to be replaced as commander of the government forces. Newcastle's choice fell on Cumberland, who had already expressed his annoyance at the removal of the infantry battalions from his continental army, having told Newcastle that he hoped that Britain was not about to be 'conquered by 3,000 rabble'. However, the king's second son was not the kind of soldier to shirk his duty and he answered the call immediately: 'it would be the last mortification to me when so much is at stake at home, and brought to the decision of arms, to be out of the way of doing my duty'.[6]

The news of Prince Charles's invasion had arrived when Cumberland was attempting to come to terms with the military situation in Flanders following Fontenoy. The bulk of the Austrian Netherlands was now in French hands, as were the ports of Ostend and Nieuport, and important towns such as Tournai and Ghent were quickly captured by Saxe's triumphant army. It had been a time of considerable danger to the coalition forces, yet at the very moment that they should have been regrouping to meet the French challenge, Cumberland had received the order from London to remove ten battalions of infantry from his field army and to send them back to Britain. Now, with Ligonier incapacitated, Cumberland had to take over command himself, and being senior in rank to Wade had to determine how the government forces should be used. On 27 November Cumberland arrived at Lichfield and set about deciding what should be done next.

One advantage was immediately apparent: the soldiers, mostly Flanders veterans, were inordinately pleased to see him and welcomed his arrival with acclaim, certain that matters would now take a turn for the better. Prince William Augustus, Duke of Cumberland, was still a young man aged twenty-four but he was already a battle-hardened soldier, having been wounded in the foot during the Battle of Dettingen where he had impressed those who had witnessed his composure under fire. At the beginning of 1745 King George II had appointed him captain-general of the forces in Flanders, a rank last used by Marlborough forty years earlier and only revived the previous year, when it was held by the Earl of Stair for his command in Europe. It would be easy to write off Cumberland as a king's son who owed his preferment to his father, but the so-called 'martial boy' had his good points, being a quick learner who made up for his inexperience by displaying courage in the field. At the Battle of Fontenoy, which he lost – albeit narrowly – to Marshal Saxe, he had been let down by poor intelligence and the indifferent performance of his Dutch cavalry forces, but had still managed to rally his advancing troops under withering French fire and learned the important lesson that it was no disgrace to retire when all was lost. In short, Cumberland did not just enjoy royal support but he was young and had recent experience of operational service – and as a king's son it was perhaps appropriate that he was about to engage an army commanded by his distant cousin Charles, who happened to be only four months older.

The position facing Cumberland on his return to England was not overly complicated, but he was let down by uncertain intelligence about the precise movements of the Jacobite army and the response to them. To the north, on the eastern side of the Pennines, was Wade's army; just under seven thousand strong, it had left Newcastle two days before Cumberland's arrival and was making its way south towards Durham to join the old Roman road of Dere Street. This should have given it the opportunity of striking west should the opportunity arise, but the conditions were taking their toll; by the time Wade's force reached Wetherby on 4 December, 670 soldiers were found to be incapable of continuing and were forced to fall out.[7] By then it was clear that the

Jacobite army would reach the Midlands ahead of Wade and that a pincer defence using Cumberland's army as the southern block would be impractical. Besides, Wade was feeling his age and had informed Newcastle that he would be unable to accept an offer to take over command of the government's forces in Scotland. With Ligonier out of the equation, that left Cumberland as the only realistic government commander in the field.

Fortunately Cumberland enjoyed the services of a shrewd staff officer in Charles Lennox, 2nd Duke of Richmond and Duke of Aubigny in the French nobility, who served in the rank of lieutenant-general and was close to the royal family, being both a privy councillor and Lord High Constable of England. Like others close to Cumberland, he had seen action at Dettingen, and the nexus of the king and his son gave him considerable influence. Although he persevered in clinging to a wrong-headed belief that the Jacobite army would eventually make for the mountain fastness of north Wales, where a leading landowner, Sir Watkins William Wynn, was known to be a keen Jacobite supporter, Richmond proved to be an astute reader of the situation unfolding to the north of Cumberland's position on the Lichfield defensive line. In his view, expressed to Newcastle in a letter of 30 November, the options facing the Jacobites amounted to engaging Cumberland's army, continuing the march south through Derbyshire, entering north Wales by way of Chester or retreating back into Scotland to regroup. The last idea was not fantastic: Prince Charles had left behind a sizeable force under the command of Viscount Strathallan, who had been succeeded by Lord John Drummond, brother of the Duke of Perth, on 26 November, and it had been reinforced by recruits from the north-east and by the arrival through the port of Montrose of additional forces from France, including a regular regiment of Royal Ecossais.[8]

Until Cumberland was ready to take charge, Richmond was effectively in command of the troops that had arrived in the Lichfield area, and on 25 November he advised the government that unless these were augmented and made ready 'this Kingdom may be undone in a fortnight'.[9] He was not being alarmist, merely sensible, as he was obliged to defend a line which stretched over thirty miles north as far as Newcastle-under-Lyme. Under his immediate command he had a small force of 2325 soldiers but amongst them were two cavalry regiments, Montagu's and Kingston's, as well as two experienced infantry battalions from Flanders, Sempill's and Johnston's. Three regiments of foot guards were expected to arrive from London within a few days, but it was already clear to Richmond that it would be impossible to retain a defensive position along the line of the Mersey as his battalions were over-stretched and scattered in billets over a wide area. Lack of intelligence remained a problem: put simply, Richmond and Cumberland could only guess what would be the Jacobites' next move, but they had the good sense to understand that they had to keep an army between their enemy and the road to London.

Matters became clearer for both sides at the beginning of December, when, following another acrimonious council of war, the Jacobite army left Manchester and headed south for Derbyshire by way of Macclesfield. At the same time Cumberland moved his headquarters to Stafford so that he could cover the route to London or to north Wales, depending on his enemy's intentions.

These moves were decisive. Two days into the march south, at Macclesfield, a Jacobite column of about 1200 led by Lord George Murray diverted west towards the town of Congleton, leaving the bulk of the army to continue south; they thereby gave the impression that they were heading towards Nantwich and then on into north Wales using the old pack-horse routes over the high ground linking Chester to inland Wales. Instead, having reached Congleton on 2 December, Murray swung his army back towards Macclesfield through the village of Ashbourne, where he demanded billets for his men.

This feint had the desired effect of persuading Cumberland that a battle was in the offing, and he prepared his army accordingly. Early in the morning of 3 December he gathered his forces and drew them up in battle order outside the old market town of Stone to the north of Stafford, on open ground already reconnoitred by Ligonier. Having waited overnight for the arrival of the enemy, Cumberland realised his mistake and reacted quickly by ordering his army to move swiftly south towards Northampton on 4 December. He also warned Newcastle that it was entirely possible that the Jacobite army would reach London before him and that the city's defences should be put on high alert.[10]

There was more: not only had Cumberland allowed himself to be duped by a simple ruse but he had permitted the Jacobite army to get a day's march between his forces and the road south. All that lay between Prince Charles and the 149 miles between Macclesfield and London was the distance itself and the hastily drawn-up forces which were being assembled on Finchley Common, twelve miles to the north-west of the capital, for the final defence of the city. Marching at the same rate that had taken them south, there was no reason why the Jacobite army should not reach London by the middle of December. But even before they set out from Macclesfield it was becoming doubtful just how far they would go. Throughout the journey south the faction around Lord George Murray had made it clear that progress depended on two factors – the support of the English Jacobites and firm pledges from France that military support would be forthcoming in the shape of an invasion of England. Unless these materialised, and unless solid proof could be shown to the council, it would be madness to continue. Prince Charles, though, had remained deaf to all appeals and had come to believe that he was marching in step with destiny, that one more push and a display of confidence would see him arrive in triumph in London. The next stopping place was the town of Derby, and it was there that a decision had to be made.

Matters came to a head on 5 December when the prince and his council sat down in the first floor drawing room of Exeter House, a handsome seventeenth-century brick-built mansion in Full Street, to discuss the next move. It soon became apparent that only Prince Charles was minded to continue the advance; indeed it became clear that he had no other thought than to capitalise on his army's unopposed progress south and descend immediately on London. Murray spoke first and in mild-mannered tones expressed the opposite point of view, namely that retreat back into Scotland was now the only option. Not only did the Jacobites face the overwhelming force of three government field armies – Wade's, Cumberland's and the force assembling at Finchley – but the promised support from France and the English Jacobites had failed to appear and would probably never materialise. In vain did Prince Charles try to counter by ignoring the argument and concentrating on the proposed line of march. As the debate continued it soon emerged that Murray was supported by the main Jacobite magnates, including Lord Elcho and Lord Ogilvy, and that the decision to retreat was a fait accompli, mainly because there was no counter-argument forceful enough to refute it. In an attempt to stave off the decision a further meeting was held in the evening, but not even the news of Drummond's arrival in Scotland could change minds about possible French intervention. If anything, the initiative seemed to provide further proof that any French efforts would be concentrated not in England but north of the border.

As the meeting drew to a close the decision to retreat was inevitable. The conditions for continuing had been laid down from the outset at Edinburgh, then at Carlisle, Preston and Manchester, and as they had not been met, the Scottish Jacobite commanders felt that without English or French support for their cause they had no option but to retreat back to their own country. It was difficult to refute Murray's comment that 'if there was any party in England for him, it was very odd that they had never so much as either sent him money or intelligence or the least advice what to do'; perhaps the *coup de grâce* was provided by Lochiel, the last of the clan leaders to add his agreement to Murray's proposal.[11]

The decision at Derby has given history one of its great 'what if?' moments. Although most historians agree with the argument that revisiting the decision is 'to indulge in an interesting but unprofitable speculation',[12] it is only human to weigh up the conflicting evidence and attempt to reach a conclusion concerning the rival arguments. First, it has to be said that there was much to recommend in the prince's argument to push on to London. With momentum behind them and the road to the capital open, everything seemed to point to a continuation of the march south, especially as the Jacobite arrival in Derby had been greeted in London with apprehension bordering on panic, leading Horace Walpole to christen 6 December 'Black Friday'. The Londoners were right to be apprehensive. If the Jacobite army had continued its rapid march south it would have arrived ahead of Cumberland's pursuing force, and if the Highland shock troops had shown the same élan and aggression as they had displayed at Prestonpans they would surely have inflicted a defeat on the government forces hastily assembling at Finchley Common. It also has to be remembered that two of the defending battalions, St Clair's Royals and Lord John Murray's Highlanders, were composed mainly of Scots and had threatened to join their compatriots if they came within twenty miles of one another.[13] With morale high and boosted by earlier successes, there is enough evidence to suppose that the Battle of Finchley would have resulted in another victory in the field for the Jacobite army.

It is at this point that speculation becomes unprofitable. Winning the battle would not have won the war and the casualties would have been high enough to denude an already small Scottish Jacobite army. Unless the English Jacobites rose in any quantity – at that stage an unlikely scenario – there was no possibility of rapid reinforcement and any subsequent dilution of its resources would have left the Jacobite army badly exposed. It would also have been necessary to secure the city of London, no easy task for lightly armed troops, and while there is evidence to suggest that the French were on the point of taking advantage of the encouraging situation by planning an invasion, the government still had two substantial armies in the field to counter that threat. One of those forces, Cumberland's, would soon have arrived in the capital equipped with cavalry and artillery, and another set-piece battle would surely have gone the government's way. From a strictly military point of view the numbers did not stack up in favour of a successful outcome for the prince's cause: his army numbered 5000, while Cumberland had 9000 and Wade almost 7000. As Lord Malton explained the strategic situation to his son-in-law, 'they [the Jacobites] are now so near two much superior armies that their destruction seems inevitable.'[14] When the logistical problems of operating over such a lengthy distance were added, plus the Highlanders' traditional dislike of being so far away from home territory, retreat was the only sensible solution – a return to the homeland and safety to regroup and replenish for the next phase of the campaign. By then, too, Murray had received the news that some French help had arrived in Scotland and that Lord John Drummond was busily raising fresh forces. From that perspective retreat was the only sensible option, even though to later generations the assessment might seem unglamorous and perhaps overly cautious.

When the Jacobite decision to head back north became apparent at his headquarters, Cumberland greeted it with typical composure. Having been thwarted at Stone he had laid plans to move his army quickly south, and by ordering them to march at a rate of twenty miles a day he felt confident enough to write from Coventry on 7 December that 'by this movement we have gained a march on the rebels, and had it in our power to be between them and London.'[15] As it turned out, though, Cumberland's provisional defensive plans were never put to the test; the Jacobite retreat meant that the next phase of the operation would be pursuit, and his first move was to send an order to Wade, now at Doncaster, ordering him to march immediately into Lancashire to intercept the retreating Jacobites. Unless this happened, stressed Cumberland, 'these villains may escape back unpunished to our eternal shame.'[16]

Wade received the order on 8 December and swung his army towards Rochdale and Lancashire, but two days later he had only reached Wakefield in West Yorkshire, where it became clear to him that the Jacobite army had cleared Manchester and was already approaching Preston. As all hope of an interception had evaporated, Wade decided to make his way back to Newcastle and left pursuit in the hands of a light cavalry force under the command of James Edward Oglethorpe, squire of Cranham Hall in Essex and founder of the North American colony of Georgia.

Oglethorpe was one of the most unusual commanders (he held the rank of major-general) to find himself caught up in the campaign. Born in London in 1696 the son of a soldier with Jacobite leanings, Oglethorpe was commissioned in the 1st Foot Guards, but his first military experience was gained under Prince Eugene of Savoy in the Hapsburg war against the Turks in the Balkans (1716–18). He fought at the Battle of Petrovaradin, where Eugene's 60,000-strong army defeated a Turkish force three times larger, and was also present at the subsequent siege of Timisoara. A career in imperial service beckoned in the company of his close friend James Keith, who had supported the Jacobite uprising in 1715 and later became a field marshal in the Prussian army, but in 1719 Oglethorpe returned to England to attempt to resurrect his career. Despite warm recommendations, he was refused a commission on account of his family's alleged Jacobite sympathies and he turned to politics, becoming member of parliament for Haslemere in Surrey. This proved to be a turning point. By the end of the following decade he had become interested in penal reform – the result of a close friend's death in the Fleet debtors' prison – and this led him to formulate a much more ambitious scheme to deal with the country's prison population.

Seeing the potential of the territorial holdings in North America which had been under English development since the sixteenth century, he proposed creating a new colony to the south of the Savannah River. This would be settled by former prisoners from England, who at little cost to the government would develop the colony by working as soldier-farmers to protect neighbouring South Carolina from the threat of Spanish invasion from Florida. The new colony would be known as Georgia. Oglethorpe's plan received the enthusiastic backing of the government and the church, as well as from entrepreneurs who saw financial advantages in the low costs and potential profits from cotton. Despite difficulties over the employment of slaves, a policy which Oglethorpe opposed, Georgia prospered, and by 1743 the Spanish threat had disappeared thanks to a victorious campaign which culminated with British victories at the battles of Bloody Marsh and Gully Hole Creek. (These were part of the wider War of Jenkins' Ear, 1739–48, a conflict between Spain and Britain fought largely in North America and the Caribbean and which had morphed by the mid-1740s into the War of the Austrian Succession.)

Flushed with success, Oglethorpe sailed back to England to gather more support and to raise a regiment of light horse to be known as the Georgia Rangers, but instead of returning to his colony he found himself caught up in the Jacobite rebellion. Stung perhaps by the accusations that he was a closet Jacobite, Oglethorpe volunteered his Rangers for service under Wade; the offer was accepted and on 25 October, accompanied by a group of fox-hunting gentlemen known as the Yorkshire Hunters, they joined the government army in Newcastle.

Clad in distinctive green jackets, the Georgia Rangers set off across the Pennines in atrocious conditions yet still managed to reach Preston on 13 December, having covered over a hundred miles in three days. It was a creditable performance given the winter weather and the 'troublesome' route over the high snow-packed fells, which did severe damage to the horses' shoes. Their arrival gave Cumberland much-needed reconnaissance capacity, for keeping in touch with the retreating Jacobites was proving to be a wearisome business.

In fact they were not far away, resting in the town of Lancaster some twenty-six miles to the north, where the prince was anxious to engage Cumberland's forces in order to settle the issue in a pitched battle. He was serious about it too. On 14 December, a windswept day full of rain and sleet, he set out south from the town to reconnoitre a possible battleground, accompanied by O'Sullivan, Murray, Lochiel and a small cavalry escort. Two potential sites were found on open hilly ground but it proved impossible to decide between the two places, and the issue was complicated when the party ran into and captured eight troopers of Oglethorpe's Georgia Rangers, who gave them the misleading information that Wade had finally joined forces with Cumberland at Preston.

This intelligence persuaded the Jacobite commanders to continue their march north towards Kendal, but in the game of bluff and double bluff that accompanied this phase of the rebellion they were not to know that Cumberland would have been hard pushed to fight a fixed battle: his force at Preston was lacking infantry, being composed mainly of cavalry and mounted infantry (foot soldiers who travelled on horseback instead of marching). Nor did Prince Charles realise that his opponent was now facing other problems. On 15 December Cumberland received from his father an order to return to London, as intelligence had arrived that a huge French army had landed at Hastings and that all available forces were needed to repel it. Now recovered from his illness and in charge of the reserve forces, Ligonier was given the same order and also wrote to Cumberland advising him to comply immediately: 'The alarm is so great that nothing less than your presence will satisfy the king or the people. I fear this snatches the rebels out of your Royal Highness's hands, but if these fears are well grounded I don't know how to blame them.'[17] Cumberland made preparations for an immediate return to London but it was a false alarm – the French plans had been postponed when it became known that the Jacobite army was in retreat and no invasion had taken place – but the incident enabled the Jacobites to continue their withdrawal. Cumberland meanwhile kept up his pursuit, greatly angered that the prince's army had been allowed to slip away during the twenty-four hours' delay.

Bad luck now joined the winter weather in influencing events. The Georgia Rangers had not recovered sufficiently from their strenuous ride across the Pennines and were in no physical condition to carry out their allotted task as the reconnaissance force for the pursuing government army. They had in fact done well to remain in contact with the Jacobite columns as they struggled over the heights of Shap Fell in Borrowdale, but on the night of 17 December Oglethorpe had to succumb to the snow and the terrain. As his men and horses struggled against the conditions, and unaware that he was closing on the Jacobite rearguard, Oglethorpe ordered his men to leave the main route to take shelter in the nearby village of Orton. Under the circumstances it was the correct decision – his force was too tired and hungry to mount an immediate attack – but with night falling Oglethorpe was unable to remain in contact with the main body of government troops. When Cumberland realised that the Jacobites were still negotiating the road over Shap Fell, he sent orders to Oglethorpe to attack immediately, but in the confusion the orders failed to get through and when they did arrive the moment had passed.

Cumberland was not amused by what he saw as a dereliction of duty and Oglethorpe was treated to a dressing down in front of his men. He was later to face trial by court martial. Although he was acquitted, his military career was finished apart from a brief Indian summer in the late 1750s serving in the army of Frederick the Great with his old friend James Keith. Later in life Oglethorpe enjoyed the friendship of Dr Samuel Johnson and his biographer James Boswell, before dying at his home in Essex in July 1785.

As for the pursuit of the Jacobite army, the damage had been done. Under leaden skies and heavy rain the Jacobite rearguard, now under Murray's command, had made better progress as they moved slowly through Borrowdale with the army's ammunition carts and artillery pieces. Better still from their point of view, the Jacobites had received infantry reinforcements – and they would need them, for Cumberland planned one final push to catch the Jacobite rearguard before the deteriorating winter weather made further operations impossible. According to witnesses he had 'jumped round the room for joy' when orders arrived from London countermanding the previous instruction to move south and he was determined to make up for lost time. Showing initiative and an ability to overcome the disappointment of the confusion at Orton, Cumberland regrouped and set off in pursuit of the rebels with a mounted force consisting of Bland's Dragoons, Kingston's Light Horse, the Georgia Rangers, the Yorkshire Hunters and a troop of imperial dragoons who formed his life guard.[18] Two factors coincided to help them. The atrocious weather and the difficult conditions underfoot had slowed down Murray's rearguard with their wagons and artillery, while at the same time there was evidence of pro-government support in Penrith and Kendal, where the sight of the retreating Jacobite army had emboldened local resistance.

In the half-light of the short winter's day, the last military engagement on English soil between the rival forces took place on 18 December. Fought outside the village of Clifton, three miles to the south-east of Penrith, it was less a battle than a skirmish, and like so many similar encounters it had a confused opening and an unsatisfactory conclusion. The opening rounds were sparked in the early light when the men of the Glengarry regiment and John Roy Stuart's Edinburgh Regiment noticed horsemen on the summit of Thrimby Hill, about halfway between Shap and

Penrith, as they accompanied the wagon train out of Shap village. They could also hear 'a prodigious number of trumpets and kettledrums', suggesting the presence of a large government force.[19] Without further ado the Glengarry men threw off their plaids and rushed up the hillside, where a short and sharp fight took place with some three hundred troopers of Bland's and the Georgia Rangers before the government forces promptly broke off the engagement, leaving behind a substantial assortment of trumpets and drums. One government soldier was taken prisoner but he did not survive, having been cut down by the Glengarry men.

Although this was little more than a brief encounter, it gave Cumberland's force the evidence they needed, and the pursuit continued into the afternoon towards Clifton Moor. Here the landscape began to change to a pattern of small fields and enclosures, and this topography determined the nature of the fighting that followed. Having ordered the wagon train to continue to Penrith, Murray drew up his forces in battle order with the Appin Stewarts and Macphersons on his left while on the right of the road he positioned the Glengarry and Edinburgh regiments to enfilade their opponents from a well-protected position with an open field of fire. Confronted by the Jacobites in fixed positions, Cumberland ordered three hundred dragoons to dismount for an armed assault on foot, putting the detachment under the command of Lieutenant-Colonel Sir Philip Honeywood, an experienced cavalryman and another veteran of Dettingen. His force consisted of men drawn from Bland's, Lord Mark Kerr's Dragoons and Cobham's Dragoons, with Montagu's and Kingston's held in reserve.[20] The Georgia Rangers and Ligonier's 'Black Horse' provided mounted flanking cover on either side of the government line.[21] It was not until late afternoon, in fast-fading light, that both sides were in position; the first move was initiated by the

Appin Stewarts and Macphersons, who advanced through the hedges to engage with the troopers of Bland's. The government soldiers opened fire at about a hundred yards distance, far too soon and much too far away to do much damage, and as the light began failing they started to withdraw with the Highlanders in pursuit. The action ended in chaos when the dismounted troopers removed their top boots, the better to leave the field in the winter darkness.

The Jacobites had succeeded in overwhelming their government opponents on a field which one witness described as 'dark and weird'. Murray was able to withdraw his forces in reasonable order towards Penrith and casualties on both sides were small. Ten government soldiers were buried in the churchyard, although the losses may have been four or five times that number. No more than a dozen Highlanders were killed or taken prisoner; amongst the latter was George Hamilton of Redhouse, an acquaintance of Cumberland who told him that he was sorry to see him in such bad company. In sporting terms Clifton was a draw, but its main point was that Murray had been able to slip away, while Cumberland's men were forced to spend the night in the wet and the dark. Not so their commander; Cumberland sought refuge in a nearby house owned by a Quaker called Thomas Savage, who found him 'a man of parts, very friendly and no pride in him'.[22]

The engagement at Clifton was not just the last military action against the Jacobite army in England; it also eased the tensions that had been building up in London as a result of the advance to Derby and the concurrent fear of French invasion. Not that the latter scare had entirely evaporated. In response to Newcastle's request Ligonier had marched his regiments south on 14 December, and instructions had been given to the lords lieutenant of the counties on the Channel coast to prepare themselves for imminent

French invasion from the ports of Ostend and Dunkirk, where ships and 15,000 troops had been assembling under the command of the Duc de Richelieu, marshal of France. The intention was to attack across the Channel at its narrowest point and land on the coast of Kent and Sussex, but on 18 December the plans were rudely interrupted by the news that the Jacobite army had begun its retreat from Derby. In itself this was not a body blow to Richelieu's project, but it does seem ironic that Prince Charles's constant calls for support were only met when his army was in full retreat back into Scotland. Although the French continued to build up forces in their Channel ports, the Royal Navy's control of the eastern Channel was a decisive factor; throughout December and into January the following year, ships from Admiral Edward Vernon's North Sea Fleet, headquartered on the Downs, were able to intercept and destroy a substantial number of French transports and their escorts. On 1 February Richelieu abandoned the invasion plans, a decision which effectively ended Louis XV's support for Prince Charles.

Unfortunately the affair ended badly for Vernon, who had made his name and become a national figure during the fighting against the Spanish in the Caribbean, notably his triumph at Porto Bello in 1739. Recalled to home waters in 1742, Vernon's constant criticisms about the defence of the Channel and the publication of his heated correspondence with the Admiralty led to him being struck off the flag list in the following year .

It was not quite the end of the Jacobite threat in England. On reaching Carlisle Prince Charles held a council meeting, where there was another quarrel about the next move. For reasons that had more to do with symbolism than military necessity, Charles, backed by O'Sullivan, proposed leaving a small garrison in the castle to signify his determination to return to England and also to guard the main route north across the bridge over the River Eden. Murray opposed the idea, as he could see no need for it; he argued that Cumberland would simply bring up heavy artillery to reduce the castle and that in any case the Jacobite army would be relatively safe once it was back in Scotland. It was another unnecessary disagreement when time was short and once again it was resolved by compromise. A small garrison of a hundred Irish infantrymen and 250 men of the Manchester Regiment was left behind in Carlisle Castle in the expectation that they could hold it until offered terms by Cumberland. The inevitable followed. Shortly before Christmas Cumberland's force arrived. Six heavy eighteen-pounder artillery pieces were ordered to be pulled up from Whitehaven, while gunners and 200 barrels of gunpowder were sent over from Wade's headquarters in Newcastle under the command of Brevet-Major William Belford.

Belford was one of a new breed of professional soldier which emerged following the formation of the Royal Regiment of Artillery in 1726. Gunners, as they became known, were not under the control of the commander-in-chief but of the Ordnance Department and had their own headquarters at Woolwich, which also housed the Royal Military Academy, the new gunnery training school. They were also unusual in that commissions could not be bought but were gained by merit: little is known about Belford's background other than that he was born in London and, having been commissioned in the junior rank of matross, he quickly rose to lieutenant-fireworker and was promoted full captain by 1742.[23] Like others in Cumberland's army, Belford had fought at Dettingen and Fontenoy; unlike most of his fellow officers, though, he owed his promotion not to personal contacts but to his skill and professionalism in handling the men and guns under his command.

On 28 December the task began of reducing the castle. Two days later a white flag appeared, and the small garrison under Townley's command surrendered and went into captivity. They faced an uncertain future, Cumberland having already told Newcastle that 'they [the rebels] have no claim to the king's mercy and I sincerely hope will meet with none.'[24] It had taken less than a day for the six artillery pieces to reduce Carlisle, and with the garrison's surrender all Jacobite resistance in England was finally at an end.

Now the Jacobite army had crossed the border, the next stage for the government was to reorganise its forces. As Cumberland remained in command of the pursuit forces before being recalled south to deal with the continuing invasion scare, there was an urgent need to find someone to take charge of the government forces in Scotland. With Wade having already declined the post, the choice fell on the most senior available officer, the cavalry commander Henry Hawley, who had previous experience of confronting the Jacobites, having fought at the Battle of Sheriffmuir in 1715. He had also served in Europe under Marlborough and more recently at Dettingen and Fontenoy, where he had demonstrated considerable personal courage; however, not only was his military career sullied by his unyielding attitude towards military discipline – he was known as 'Hangman Hawley' – but he had a poor opinion of the Jacobite soldiers and little time for their military abilities, believing mistakenly that Highlanders would always break under a determined cavalry charge. It was perhaps indicative of his leanings that his first order on arriving in Edinburgh on 6 January 1746 was for the construction of gibbets in the port of Leith.

The forces available to Hawley in Lowland Scotland were not inconsiderable – twelve regiments of infantry, five regiments of dragoons and various formations of militia from Edinburgh, Glasgow and Paisley, some 8000 men in total. Further away and as yet untested, he could also call on the support of various Argyllshire militia forces in the west under the command of John Campbell of Mamore (also known as 'Colonel Jack'), a kinsman of the Duke of Argyll, while to the north in Inverness another force composed mainly of pro-government Campbells had been raised by Lord President Duncan Forbes and John Campbell, Earl of Loudoun, who had arrived in the town on 14 October. The latter had already seen action at Prestonpans, where he had been Cope's adjutant-general, but that ignominy notwithstanding he was an experienced soldier who had served with Cumberland in Flanders. Under his command he had a regiment of Highland infantrymen, and by the end of the year this had been augmented by eighteen Independent Companies, each one notionally a hundred strong, drawn from 'well-affected clans' raised at the behest of Forbes of Culloden.[25] Loudoun's presence in Inverness was also a useful counterweight to the second Jacobite army, which had come into being under Lord John Drummond's command with his headquarters at Perth.

Hawley's immediate necessity was to consolidate the position of the government forces in Lowland Scotland and attempt to engage the Jacobite army which had reached Stirling on 8 January. Although the castle remained secure under General Blakeney's command, the Jacobites now had heavy artillery in the shape of six artillery pieces – two eighteen-pounders, two twelve-pounders and two nine-pounders – which had been shipped in to Montrose from France and which they were attempting to bring up to Stirling with the intention of besieging the castle. With some difficulty two of the pieces were hauled across the Forth at the Falls of Frew while, showing great ingenuity, the others were placed on a captured brig and transported down river from Alloa. What followed was a mixture of farce and enterprise as a series of actions took place between the Jacobite convoy and the Royal Navy sloops HMS *Vulture* and HMS *Pearl*. In the narrow waters, though, the two ships ran aground, fire was exchanged and the end result was that the Jacobite gunners 'got the better of the Royal Navy'.[26] It mattered not; the siege guns were never fired against Stirling Castle, for the emphasis of the campaign had once again turned to the land and to Hawley's next move.

With Edinburgh secured and Stirling still unscathed, Hawley was free to advance towards the Jacobite army and on 13 January felt sufficiently confident to tell Cumberland that his first move would involve 'driving the rascally scum out of Stirling'.[27] To make good his promise he had already ordered his first forces to move out of Edinburgh under the command of Major-General John Huske, a Foot Guards officer who had experience of operating against the Jacobites as a secret agent after infiltrating their movement in Europe in the wake of the 1715 rebellion. Having transferred to the line infantry – Herbert's Foot (later the Royal Welch Fusiliers) – he commanded an infantry brigade at Dettingen, where a fellow officer wrote admiringly that he 'behaved quite gloriously and quite cool, was shot through the foot at the time that our colonel fell, yet continued his post'.[28] If military experience had been the sole arbiter for his prospects, Huske should have commanded the army in Scotland, but he lacked influence and did not receive suitable promotion until much later in his career. His force consisted of around 4000 men in four infantry regiments, two regiments of dragoons and the Glasgow Militia; a few days later they were reinforced by Campbell's Argyll Militia from Dumbarton. On the way westwards Huske surprised a Jacobite raiding force – elements of Murray's army and Lord

Elcho's cavalry – near the town of Linlithgow on 14 January, but nothing came of the encounter.

Hawley had followed with the rest of the forces on the previous day, and he remained supremely confident, having told Cumberland before leaving that the rebels would 'go off' at his approach. He was not to know that the Jacobite army had in fact expanded, with fresh recruits from the Highland clans and an infusion of new blood in the shape of two new regiments from the north and north-east led by Lord Lewis Gordon and Lord Cromartie, as well as the recently arrived professional soldiers of the Royal Ecossais and the Irish Brigade. Their tactics were simple: to continue the siege of Stirling Castle and to prepare for battle against Hawley. On 16 January Prince Charles drew up his forces in battle order on the high ground of Plean Muir, south-east of Stirling towards the town of Falkirk. At that stage the Jacobite high command was keener to engage in battle than Hawley, who slipped away with his staff to enjoy a leisurely evening at nearby Callendar House; his host was Lady Kilmarnock, wife of Lord Kilmarnock, a cavalry commander in the nearby Jacobite army. While she clearly did not share her husband's political sympathies, there is no truth in the later canard that Hawley almost missed the battle thanks to the leisurely and vinous nature of her ladyship's hospitality, though it made a good story at the time. Whatever its origins, however, it was certainly true that Hawley's delay in getting to grips with the situation played into the hands of the Jacobites.

Disappointed that the government army had not offered battle, Murray decided to make the first move, drawing up his regiments and marching them on to a ridge of high moorland to the south-west known as Falkirk Muir. As he had done in Cheshire earlier, he engaged in a feint by ordering Drummond's Irish contingent to march along the main road from Bannockburn to Stirling, a move made under the gaze of the government army. Throughout the morning of 17 January, meanwhile, Hawley maintained his belief that the Jacobites would never dare venture an act of aggression against his army, and such insouciance continued to guide his thinking. Too late, by early afternoon it was clear that the Jacobites were moving towards the summit of the moor, where the high ground gave them a decided advantage. By then it was impossible for the government forces to react.

When Hawley ordered his dragoons to attack the Jacobite right later in the afternoon they were repulsed by the disciplined firepower of the Macdonalds, who were anxious to follow up by falling on their enemy. In the confusion the dragoons turned and fled, crashing through the foot regiments as they retired from the field, and for a brief moment it seemed that a Highland charge would scatter Hawley's army. Huske's foot regiments on the government right held their ground under the command of James Cholmondeley, who then attempted to organise a counter-attack, but by that time darkness was falling and the weather had deteriorated, with heavy rain and a high wind adding to the confusion. Both sides made attempts to rally their men, but chaos now reigned on the sloping battlefield and the Jacobite army was unable to capitalise on its earlier success.

As night fell the Jacobites entered Falkirk, but Hawley and the main part of his army was not to be found, having made their way back towards Linlithgow and then all the way to Edinburgh. They were lucky that the weather was so atrocious and that the Jacobite command was in disarray, otherwise this simple defeat could have turned into a rout. Amongst those swept along the road to Edinburgh in the panic-stricken stream of government forces were the men of Blakeney's Regiment,[29] whose regimental colour was in the hands of Eyre Coote, an eighteen-year-old ensign from Kilmallock in County Limerick. It was his first battle and almost his last: in the ensuing court martial at Perth on 15 February, he and three other officers faced a trial for cowardice. Coote was however given the lesser sentence of suspension ('broke') from the service; his crime must have been considered reasonably innocuous as in 1748 he was listed as a cornet in the Earl of Rothes's Dragoons (later the 6th Inniskillings) and his military career remained intact.

The same could be said of Hawley, who emerged from the defeat with his name unsullied. Although he admitted to Cumberland that he was broken-hearted by the defeat, which he claimed was the fault of cowards amongst his force, he quickly recovered his bluster and two days after the battle felt sufficiently confident to tell Newcastle that he could 'charge himself with no neglect nor fault' and was not 'at all cast down'.[30] His immediate career was saved by the steadfastness of the regiments under Huske's command, but in any case he was due to be replaced. Hawley stayed on as second-in-command, protesting that any remaining vanity in his character had been cured by the lesson of 'that unfortunate day ... 'twas a rough remedy, but I hope t'will do me good'.[31] There was in fact only one man who could restore order and morale, and that was Hawley's successor, the Duke of Cumberland.

3

THE END OF A BAD BUSINESS

Having left London on 25 January, Cumberland arrived in Edinburgh five days later. Shortly afterwards he addressed his forces about the task facing them. He made no bones about his seriousness of purpose, reminding them that they were 'free soldiers of a free people' and that it was their duty 'to crush the insolence of a set of thieves and plunderers who have learned from their fathers to disturb every government they have lived under'.[1] Such words set the tone for the forthcoming operation: the men under his command had already fought for their religion and King George II in Flanders, now they had to extirpate rebels who had risen presumptuously and unlawfully against that same monarch using the identical justification that their forebears had used in the past, namely the restoration of the Stuart dynasty.

As a first step, Cumberland announced that he would march immediately to Stirling to raise the siege and release the garrison. From correspondence between General Guest in Edinburgh and General Blakeney in Stirling, Cumberland knew that the latter was in good spirits and remained confident that he could resist the siege, having destroyed the main arch in the bridge over the Forth and ordered caltrops, or crows' feet, devices equipped with sharpened metal spikes, to be planted in the main crossing places to slow down the opposition's horses. Even if the Jacobites did have the temerity to attack, continued Blakeney, he promised to give them 'a warm reception'.[2] On the morning of 31 January Cumberland set off on the first stage of his mission, taking the blessings of the people of Edinburgh and a sufficiently large force 'to drive them [the Jacobite army] off the face of the earth'.[3]

It was a promising start to the campaign, but when the government army reached Falkirk they found that the Jacobite army had already left Stirling, having begun their withdrawal on the same day that Cumberland had set out from Edinburgh. It was supposed to have been an orderly and disciplined operation, with the prince taking the bulk of the clan army back towards Inverness by way of Badenoch while the cavalry led by Lord Ogilvy headed towards the Mounth, the high north–south route over the eastern Grampians, and Lord George Murray took the east coast route through Dundee and Aberdeen, but no sooner had the retreat been ordered than it descended into chaos following another unseemly row between the prince and Murray.

Once again strategy was the cause. Sensing that this was his last, best chance of engaging and perhaps beating Cumberland's army, the prince asked Murray to prepare a battle plan, only to receive the dusty reply that the army was being weakened by desertions and that their only option was to retreat and regroup in the Highlands. Given the tenor of the response and the implication that it was an ultimatum, the prince had to follow Murray's advice and without further ado the march north began. Jacobite guns were spiked in Stirling and preparations were made to dispose the powder and ammunition, which were stored in St Ninian's Church. Unfortunately during the operation an accidental spark caused the store to explode and the church was blown up – hardly the best augury for a move that was already becoming distinctly shambolic.

Whatever else had happened, though, the Jacobite decision to head north forced Cumberland to respond to meet the new strategic situation. After leaving Edinburgh his hopes had rested on the Jacobites' willingness to offer him battle in the neighbourhood of the Forth valley, as he believed that he could defeat them in one decisive action. With that option gone he ordered Loudoun to be prepared to harass the Jacobites as soon as they got close to Inverness while he pursued them north from Perth. At that stage Cumberland's main fear was that the Jacobite army would disperse once they reached the central Highlands and would scatter into the remote straths and glens of their homelands, making pursuit extremely difficult. The government army would then be sucked into what would now be called a low-intensity conflict, fighting against a largely hidden enemy which enjoyed the support of the local population. Cumberland was anxious to avoid that possibility, but he told Newcastle that if a guerrilla war of that kind developed he would be obliged to employ more robust tactics, promising to send pursuit parties into the Highlands 'to burn and destroy that nest of robbers'.

From the beginning of this next stage of war in Scotland Cumberland stated his intention to use the mailed fist and a new harshness crept into his troops' attitude towards the local population. While waiting for the central arch of the bridge at Stirling to be repaired, he turned a blind eye to plundering in the neighbourhood of St Ninian's Church, and this ruthlessness continued as the army made its way north through the towns of fertile Strathearn.[4]

On 6 February Cumberland reached Perth, where he decided to remain for a fortnight. His intention was both to consolidate his own army, which had been reinforced by four Hessian regiments, and to send out raiding or reconnaissance parties into the surrounding countryside of Atholl, whose men had largely supported the Jacobite rebellion. Blair Castle, the home of the Duke of Atholl, was occupied by forces commanded by Sir Andrew Agnew of Lochnaw; a veteran of the fighting in Flanders, Lochnaw had served there as one of Cumberland's brigade commanders and was well known for his irascibility and dry wit, all expressed in broad Scots. At one point during the Battle of Dettingen the French cavalry managed to fight their way into his regiment's lines, a detail which King George II did not miss. 'I saw the Cuirassiers get in among your men this morning, colonel,' observed the king once the fighting was over. 'Ou aye, yer Majestee,' retorted Agnew. 'But they didna get oot again.'[5] Cumberland had made an astute choice of commander: Agnew, a Lowland Scot with an estate in Wigtownshire, was not just pugnacious but had little respect or liking for Highlanders.

Castle Menzies, also nearby, was occupied by another force under Lieutenant-Colonel Francis Leighton of Blakeney's Regiment. In both cases the commanders' orders were to hold the strongholds and if necessary to use harsh punishments against suspected rebels in the local population, including the enactment of the death penalty without any need for a court martial. It seemed brutal, but even at that stage of the campaign the mood in Cumberland's army did not favour the showing of mercy to the rebels. One of Cumberland's aides was Colonel Joseph Yorke, a young Foot Guards officer; Yorke's father was the Earl of Hardwicke, the Lord Chancellor, with whom he exchanged a regular and lively correspondence throughout the campaign. Something of a martinet who could appear overbearing and self-important, even to his friends, Yorke was firmly of the opinion that 'lenity is construed cowardice, and that's a fault soldiers ought never to bear the reproach of', and allied to this was a lifelong fear that through support of the Jacobite cause France would always be able to gain political leverage in Britain.[6]

Having placed checks on the neighbourhood of Perth, the traditional gateway to the Highlands, Cumberland decided to move his army north-eastwards to Aberdeen. He reached the city at the end of February and established his headquarters there, settling most of his troops in the newly built Robert Gordon's Hospital while he took up residence in Provost Skene's House in nearby Guestrow. Reinforcements and equipment soon started arriving in the city and the presence of the government army on the east coast put a stop to the French use of Montrose as an entrepôt for reinforcements and military supplies. At the same time Cumberland declined to accept the services of the Hessian infantry which had turned up in Perth – both because he doubted their abilities and because he could not agree with their commander, Prince Friedrich of Hesse, on the question of granting parole to captured Jacobites.

Not that Cumberland was idle in Aberdeen. As he had done in Perth, he sent out fighting patrols south into the surrounding areas of the Mearns, Strathmore and the Braes of Angus, both to impose government authority in a traditionally Jacobite-supporting neighbourhood and to act offensively in the lands towards Speyside, where Lord John Drummond had established his own headquarters near Fochabers. To counter that threat Bland was ordered to move four infantry battalions and two regiments of cavalry to the towns of Oldmeldrum, Inverurie, Udny and Fyvie, which covered the routes to the north-west. It was also in

Aberdeen that a new bayonet drill was perfected in an attempt to protect the government soldiers from the effects of the much-feared Highland charge. Basically, this involved striking with the bayonet not at the man directly in front but the one on the right, just as his sword arm was being raised. The tactics required trust, synchronisation and above all strict training.

While Cumberland was to all intents and purposes confined at his new headquarters in Aberdeen, the Jacobite army was engaged in improving its position. In the middle of February Prince Charles was at Moy Hall, eight miles south of Inverness; this was the home of Lady Anne Mackintosh, a prominent Jacobite supporter whose husband Aeneas was serving in the government army. Word was sent to Loudoun in Inverness, and he thought to take advantage of the unexpected presence of the prince by marching south on the night of 16 February and mounting a *coup de main* with a force of 1500 men. What followed was one of the most bizarre episodes of the entire rebellion. The inhabitants of Moy soon learned that government soldiers were heading towards them, allowing Lady Anne and the prince to escape. Meanwhile Loudoun's force was ambushed by a handful of men (some accounts say only five in number) led by Donald Fraser, the local blacksmith, who started shouting orders and firing their weapons to give the impression that they were a larger force of Highlanders. In the darkness Loudoun's men took fright and started running back down the road to Inverness, causing a general panic in which everyone was swept up. A couple of hundred were so distraught that they deserted there and then, and the 'Rout of Moy' (as it became known) encouraged Loudoun to believe that he could no longer hold Inverness. Three days later he was in Easter Ross on the other side of the Cromarty Firth, and was therefore no longer a factor in Cumberland's plans.

To the south there were further Jacobite gains when Fort Augustus fell on 4 March and Fort William came under siege. To cap it all, Jacobite forces under the Duke of Perth pursued Loudoun onto the northern side of the Dornoch Firth, employing local fishing boats in a masterly amphibious operation which forced his opponent to retreat west towards Skye. Suddenly, by the end of March, it seemed as if Murray's policy might be working and that the Jacobite army could continue to prosecute a guerrilla war in the Highlands for some time to come.

Cumberland was well aware of that possibility. Discommoded by Loudoun's flight from Inverness, he was now worried that if Fort William fell the Jacobites would have further access to the coast, which would allow the import of additional French support through the sea lochs of Argyll. He was also worried by the growing Jacobite support in the lands bounding Speyside. On the night of 21 March a small force of Jacobites had surprised a government contingent in the town of Keith, and while casualties were low it persuaded Bland that a recent move he had ordered into nearby Strathbogie could lead to his men being overwhelmed. As a result additional government forces were sent into the area under the command of the Earl of Albemarle, whose arrival proved to be a steadying influence. Cumberland laughed off the incident as 'negligence' on the army's part, but he also noticed that the evidence of recent Jacobite successes was giving heart to the local population. He complained that further south, in the town of Forfar, Jacobite officers had been concealed from arrest, and that throughout the Jacobite-supporting north-east people were constantly 'giving impotent marks of their ill will' despite the presence of a sizeable government army. Like many soldiers operating in what was to them a strange and apparently unknowable country, Cumberland's ignorance of the Scots and their local predilections was always in danger of turning into condescension, bordering on contempt.[7]

Under the circumstances his best bet was to remain in Aberdeen, which was not only easy to defend but had access to the North Sea and through whose harbour supplies were regularly brought in by the Royal Navy. In the previous year the east coast of Scotland had been an asset to the Jacobites: its main harbours – Arbroath, Montrose, Stonehaven and Peterhead – had been vital for importing French supplies, while the entire coastal littoral, being mainly Episcopalian, had been supportive of the Jacobite cause. One might ask why Murray had not held Aberdeen instead of heading off immediately to Inverness to take part in the operations against Loudoun's forces. The loss of the east coast ports ended the French supply route; the final two French ships reached Aberdeen in the last week of February, shortly before Cumberland's arrival.

By that time too the Royal Navy had started a blockade of the coast with a flotilla under the overall command of Rear-Admiral John Byng, who had recently carried out a similar task in the eastern Channel off the coast of Flanders. From his flagship HMS *Gloucester*, a fifty-gun Fourth Rate fighting ship, Byng's tasks were to prevent French ships entering Scottish coastal waters and to operate in support of Cumberland's army. It was no easy task – many of the ships were small and winter storms made for a dangerous environment in which to operate – but command of the seas along the east coast between the Moray Firth and the Firth of Tay was a vital ingredient in government policy during the winter months. On 3 January 1746 Byng was replaced by Commodore Thomas Smith RN, another experienced sailor who had made a name for himself a few years earlier by compelling a French captain to lower his pennant in respect to King George

II after a storm forced his corvette to seek shelter in Plymouth Sound. In his new command Smith was equally forthright in his approach: while operating in the inshore waters of the north-west Highlands, his ships carried parties of soldiers with orders 'to burn the houses and destroy the effects of all such as were out in the rebellion'.

With Cumberland's army garrisoned in Aberdeen the way was open for Murray to move against the government outposts in Atholl, and its main strongpoints at Blair Castle and Castle Menzies. If these could be captured Cumberland would be obliged to send forces south to restore the strategic equilibrium, and in pursuit of that objective on 17 March Murray mounted an operation using his own Atholl men and Macphersons of Cluny. What later came to be known as the Atholl Raid got off to a good start. Lightly guarded outposts in the western areas at Bun Rannoch, Kynachan, Blairfettie and Lude fell easily enough, but Blair Castle foiled all attempts to besiege it into submission – its walls were simply too thick, while Murray lacked heavy artillery and specialist sappers. Amongst the castle's defenders was young Robert Melville, a clergyman's son who had given up his medical studies at Edinburgh University to join the army, becoming an ensign in Sempill's Regiment, which been raised in 1689 by one of his ancestors, the Earl of Leven. He remained in the army after the campaign and continued his interests in ordnance by inventing a new type of naval gun known as the 'carronade'.

Although the Atholl Raid provided evidence for Murray's contention that guerrilla tactics were the best option, it meant that March ended with the Jacobite army spread across the Highlands in Atholl, Badenoch and Lochaber, while there were few troops in the north-east to prevent Cumberland marching on Inverness. In fact, the only barrier facing the government army was the obstacle of the River Spey, the second longest and the fastest flowing of Scotland's rivers. Running in a north-easterly direction towards the Moray Firth from the Corrieyairack Forest south of Fort Augustus, it is a formidable hurdle, especially in the early spring when snow-melt puts it in spate. The river's physical condition was a governing factor in the timetable Cumberland had to follow in his pursuit of the enemy, and it was not until 8 April that its waters had subsided sufficiently to make a crossing possible.

By then the government army numbered around 9000 men, representing a total of fourteen infantry battalions and three regiments of horse, plus supporting artillery. Two days later the town of Banff was reached and the army swung westwards along the coastal road through Portsoy and Cullen to reach the lower Spey on 12 April. By then the first Jacobite parties had been sighted at Fochabers, but not in any strength – a force of 1500 was under the joint command of the Duke of Perth and Lord John Drummond – and they quickly retreated with only a few desultory shots being fired. Once suitable fording places had been found, the government army crossed to the western bank on 13 April and headed towards Elgin and Forres. With support from the sea Cumberland had no re-supply problems, and from the ships he also had the benefit of intelligence about the movements of the Jacobite army in the coastal area.

Wisely, the Jacobite commanders had decided not to offer battle along the Spey – the advantages of attempting to surprise the government army during the river crossings were outweighed by the disparity in numbers – and the period between 8 and 14 April was spent gathering in the clan regiments from their outposts across the Highland area. With Cumberland heading inexorably towards Inverness, where the bulk of the Jacobite baggage and supplies had been quartered, a battle was in the offing; by 14 April it was clear that it would be fought on the coastal littoral between Inverness and the town of Nairn, where Cumberland's army had halted after four days of hard marching. In fact a battle could not now be avoided: in the Jacobite army food, especially oatmeal, was in short supply and the prince had almost run out of funds to pay his army, a shipment of gold having been captured by HMS *Sheerness* after the French ship *Prince Charles* ran aground in the Kyle of Tongue.[8] Time, money and opportunity were finally running out and on 15 April Cumberland contacted Newcastle informing him that 'the affair would not be very long'.[9]

That same day the Jacobite army had continued assembling near the grounds of Culloden House on the south-western edge of Drummossie Moor, an open and unprepossessing stretch of land six miles to the east of Inverness. The Duke of Perth and Lord John Drummond brought in the men who had been shadowing the government army as it crossed the Spey; Lord George Murray returned with his men from his Atholl raid; Lochiel and his Camerons arrived from Achnacarry and Glengarry's men from the operations further north. There were even some deserters from Loudoun's Independent Companies.

The choice of battlefield was made by the prince, and from the outset it caused controversy amongst the Jacobite commanders. Drummossie Moor is a flat and featureless area of bogland bounded on its eastern limits by the River Nairn with the hills of Inverness-shire rising beyond. Murray certainly did not like what he saw, referring to the strip of land to the south-east of Culloden House as 'not proper for highlanders'; he would have preferred moving the Jacobite army to 'stronger ground' higher up on the other side of the river but was overruled.[10] It did not help Murray's case that O'Sullivan, whose star was still in the ascendant, favoured the chosen ground. Later historians have also disagreed over the suitability of Drummossie Moor, one comparing it to a 'shooting range, flat and open' while another (a former soldier) thought 'it fitted the rebel army's requirements in every respect' as the open ground was perfect for executing their much feared Highland charge.[11] In fact, the Jacobites had no choice but to make a stand, because their strategy had already been framed for them by the time they reached Drummossie Moor. Having decided to fight a pitched battle, they simply had to defend Inverness; their supplies and logistical support were in the town, and if these fell into Cumberland's hands their campaign would peter out and collapse. Besides, the road from Nairn to Inverness ran to the north of Culloden and that meant that beyond peradventure it had to be defended.

Unfortunately, the open boggy moor was also ideal for Cumberland's small but mobile army, now camped at Balblair outside Nairn, where additional rations and brandy had been distributed to the men to celebrate their commander's twenty-fifth birthday. Since the majority of the men already had experience of combat from the operations in Flanders, they were as prepared for battle as professional soldiers could ever be. However, as 15 April drew to a close it became clear to Jacobite commanders that the government army was not going to make a move but would remain at Balblair to allow the soldiers a chance to recoup their energies with ample food, drink and a night's rest.

For the Jacobite soldiers there was to be no similar respite. Drawn up in their battle lines near Culloden House, they had not been fed and were now to be denied a battle, all very dispiriting for men who were probably reaching the end of their tether. The weather too was deteriorating, with a strong north-easterly wind causing squalls of rain to scud in from the Moray Firth.[12] With spirits plummeting, a fillip was needed – and it came in a startling suggestion from Lord George Murray, who proposed a surprise night attack on the camp at Balblair. He underscored his argument with the not unreasonable suggestion that the government army would probably be incapacitated by the alcohol consumed in honour of Cumberland's birthday. The idea was met with acclaim, particularly amongst the clan regiments, who were anxious for action and generally favoured the indirect approach. The alternative was another night waiting in the open with empty bellies, whereas the possibility of ambushing Cumberland's men was too good to miss and at least provided an opportunity to play to the strengths of the Highland way of fighting.

There was much to recommend in the idea, not least the disposal of the government army; the infantry had been kept at Balblair while the cavalry was camped at Auldearn further to the east. Surprise too would play a part, as would the darkness of a wet and windy night. But even under the best meteorological and physical conditions a night march was not to be undertaken lightly. Careful staff work was needed to plan the best route and then to keep to it, making sure that obstacles did not become insuperable and that men maintained the agreed timetable in order to cover the ten miles to their objective. It was also inconceivable that the government camp would be left unguarded or that outer pickets had not been placed to check possible intruders into their operational area. The plan was essentially to advance on Balblair in three columns, with Murray's Highlanders marching to the south bank of the River Nairn and attacking from the rear, while the rest of the force advanced on the northern bank to make a frontal assault with the attack going in at 2 a.m. However there was no time for detailed planning, and Murray's later comment summed up the mixture of optimism and derring-do that accompanied the column of some 1200 men as it set out after dark: 'There was no need for orders ... everyone knew what to do.'[13] The problem was that they did not really know what to do, and as a result the operation quickly ran into difficulties.

Marching in darkness over rough ground is never easy, and when obstacles such as walls and ditches are entered into the equation it is all too easy for things to go awry. Men soon found that they could not keep up the necessary pace in the dark; they had to slow down again as they moved through Kilravock Wood with its walled enclosures, and the patches of boggy ground along the route produced another impediment. Lack of accurate intelligence also played a role; it was found that the local guides did not possess detailed knowledge about the ground over which the men were marching. Quite early in the march it became obvious that the force, especially the regular French-Irish infantrymen, could not keep to the timetable to reach the start line for the main assault. Shortly before the agreed time Murray halted his column, still three or four miles short of Balblair, and decided that an attack was now impossible and retreat was the only sensible option. Unfortunately it took time for the decision to percolate through to the Duke of Perth's force, which had got within hearing distance of the government camp; accompanied by much rancour, the Jacobite force slowly made its way back to Culloden as dawn was breaking.

The day of battle had finally arrived and the contrast between the rival armies could not have been more marked. Cumberland's army had been fed and rested and the red-coated soldiers were expectant and confident; the Jacobite army was hungry and exhausted after marching back and forth over rough ground in the dead of night and their soldiers were obviously dispirited. As light began breaking the government army was first on the move, with drums beating the assembly, and shortly after 5 a.m. it began marching towards Drummossie Moor in evenly spaced columns, following (in reverse) roughly the direction taken by the Jacobite force the previous night. An advance guard of Campbell of Mamore's Argyll Militia scouted ahead of the main force, together with a troop of Kingston's Horse. As news of the approach reached Culloden House, the Jacobite army started making its own preparations, returning to the positions the men had occupied the previous day when a battle had seemed imminent.

The contested terrain over which the battle would be fought was a stretch of bleak moorland bounded by two permanent obstacles – the stonewalled enclosure of the Culwhiniac Park, which ran down to the River Nairn, and to the north-west the walls of Culloden Park, abutting the Lord President's house. Most of the ground was covered by rough tufted grass and heather, much of it was boggy with surface water, and rough pasture covered the flanks. James Grainger, a surgeon's mate in Pulteney's, one of the advancing infantry regiments, later described the landscape in apt soldier's terms: 'the ground on which they stood was plain, and the field seemed adapted in every way to decide the fate of the Rebellion.'[14] He could have added that the weather conditions were appalling. The wind, a cold north-easterly, continued to blow across the moor bringing with it showers of rain and sleet, numbing hands and soaking clothes. The conditions also made life difficult for men using muskets; Fusilier Edward Linn of Campbell's North British Fusiliers was not alone in tucking his weapon under his wide lapels in an attempt to keep it dry.[15] At least that was an equalising factor – or it should have been, if the Jacobite army was preparing to fight with full bellies – but for most of the men in the prince's army their last meal had been eaten some time ago. Time was moving on. By 11 a.m. the rival armies were in sight of one another as the red-coated columns marched on to the moor, drums beating and regimental colours flying in the sharp wind.

The army marched in three columns, each of five battalions, and their drill was perfect. On the left was a fourth column of three regiments of horse; on the right came the artillery train under the command of Colonel William Belford, whose gunners had done so well at Carlisle. Big shire horses hauled the three-pounder artillery pieces and the wagons carrying the ammunition, powder and portable Coehorn mortars, while the baggage train was brought up in the rear. The positioning was deliberate and economical, allowing the force to move quickly into the standard battlefield formation three ranks deep to face an enemy line which was often only thirty yards away.

Each man was equipped with a flintlock musket, a formidable weapon replete with socket bayonet but one which had to be used properly and with the utmost discipline. Twenty-one words of command were needed to prime, load and fire the weapon, and as a result infantry regiments put much effort into the weapon training and close-order drills necessary to manoeuvre regiments on the battlefield. Once in action regiments formed up and, in theory at least, fought in exactly the same patterns as they had practised on the parade ground. As a result close-order drill was regarded not just as a means of disciplining the men but also of ensuring their survival in combat. Even though the standards of drilling were probably uneven – James Wolfe had 'a very mean opinion of the infantry in general' – it had clearly been practised to a high standard by the infantry battalions at Culloden. One infantryman marching on to the moor that day later wrote with pride about the action of forming into line, 'which was done with great beauty of discipline and order'.[16]

The order to move into line came shortly before noon, once

Barrell's had reached the Leanach steading buildings which were to be the army's left marker. It was a simple yet precise manoeuvre which had been perfected as laid down in General Bland's famous *Treatise*: the columns moved forward to form three lines, each second battalion moving to the left of the first battalion and the fourth battalion moving up to the left of the third, leaving the fifth battalion to form the last line. The manoeuvre took ten minutes to complete and it left the government army in the following order of battle facing the enemy left to right:

Front line (Albemarle): 2nd Royals, Cholmondeley's, Price's, Campbell's Royal North British Fusiliers, Munro's, Barrell's
    Second line (Huske): Howard's, Fleming's, Bligh's, Sempill's, Conway's, Wolfe's
    Third line (Mordaunt): Pulteney's, Battereau's, Blakeney's flanked by Kingston's Horse[17]

Cobham's Horse took up position on the right and Lord Mark Kerr's Dragoons on the left, close to the Culwhiniac enclosure, where they were supported by five infantry companies of Loudoun's Highlanders and Argyll Militia under the command of Captain Colin Campbell of Ballimore. Into each of the five spaces between the front-line infantry battalions Belford inserted two three-pounder guns, which would open the battle for the government army once the time came. As the serried ranks watched and waited Cumberland rode by them, raising his hat in salute, and was greeted with cries of 'Billy' and 'Flanders'; with him went his staff, mostly younger officers and all favourites who had been under his command at Fontenoy or Dettingen – Wolfe, Yorke and Sir George Howard, scion of a distinguished military family who was later accused of exercising undue harshness in the operations after the battle. The newest member of this charmed circle was Henry Seymour Conway, cousin of the author and wit Horace Walpole, with whom he maintained a spirited correspondence; he received his lieutenant-colonelcy from Cumberland on the eve of battle. Cumberland also had the support of experienced and battle-hardened senior commanders such as Bland, Hawley, Huske and Mordaunt, the last of whom commanded the reserve and like many other soldiers of that period was also a member of parliament. All the while the men rested on their weapons and stared across the open moor in the direction of their enemy, who were taking up position opposite them less than half a mile away, forming into a long line with the horse regiments drawn up behind them.

Both sides then made last-minute adjustments. Cumberland moved his cavalry around both flanks to give them an open field when the moment arrived, and on the right Bland ordered Lord Mark Kerr's Horse and Campbell of Ballimore's infantry to take possession of the Culwhiniac enclosure, which inexplicably had been ignored by the Jacobite commanders earlier in the day and it remained unoccupied. In response to this move Murray ordered Lord Lewis Gordon's infantry to turn to face south from the second line on the right, but by then the government army had accepted a priceless opportunity to use the position to enfilade the Jacobite lines from the protection of the enclosure's northern wall. Others in the Jacobite army were equally unhappy. To the anger of Clan Donald, the Macdonald regiments had not been given their traditional place on the right of the line, having been forced to cede it at Murray's request to the men of Atholl. Touchily, they took the left of the line – Glengarry, Clanranald and Keppoch – and awaited developments.

Cumberland made the first move shortly before 1 p.m. when he ordered Albemarle's son and heir Lord Bury to ride to the front of the lines to reconnoitre the ground between the two armies. This young Bury did with commendable aplomb, riding boldly forwards to inspect a line of stones which could have protected the enemy artillery. They did not, being merely an old wall, but the appearance of the richly red-coated young officer was enough to spark the battle. From the centre of the Jacobite line came the roar of cannon fire, followed by a small cloud of smoke blown back in the wind. The shot flew over Bury and the government lines, landing in the rear where 'it did little execution'. It did however provoke an immediate response from Belford's gunners, who quickly showed that they were superior in both training and equipment to anything the Jacobites had to offer. The results were quickly apparent. The first shots careered into the Jacobite lines, causing random casualties; then Belford ordered his gunners to raise their elevation to fire towards the rear where the prince and his party were posted. For around half an hour (or perhaps less; the accounts differ) the Jacobite army endured this short season in hell, all the while imploring their officers to begin the charge. But for whatever reason there was a delay. Nominally the command should have been given by the prince, but even when word reached Murray it took half an hour for him to act on the order – a result of the confusion caused by poor communication and his natural antipathy for O'Sullivan.

At last the Jacobite line began its advance, with Clan Chattan in the van followed by the regiments on the Jacobite right – Atholl, Cameron and Appin. Those on the left – Macdonald, Glenbucket and Perth – had a longer run-in and as a result the front was not unified as the charge progressed over the uneven ground; many of the rebel soldiers simply discarded their matchlocks and flintlock pistols and went in with their broadswords. Their first target was Barrell's and Munro's on the government army's left, and to the watching Joseph Yorke the onrush of the Highlanders seemed to form three 'wedges' which bore down at great pace on the government army's first line. 'After firing very irregularly at a considerable distance,' he wrote afterwards, 'they rushed furiously in upon them, thinking to carry all before them, as they had done on former occasions.'[18] As the front-line battalions steadied themselves to receive the charge, Belford ordered his gunners to switch to grapeshot, and this had a devastating effect. The ammunition consisted of a bag or canister of tightly packed balls and assorted nails and bolts which spread out on being fired, providing an effect akin to a giant shotgun. Many were killed before they even reached the government army's positions.

Under the impact of the initial collision on the extreme left Barrell's buckled as the sword-wielding clansmen broke into the front line, but they did not collapse entirely. Munro's also held firm, reinforcements coming from Ligonier's and Wolfe's on the second line which wheeled round from the government army's left, while Bligh's and Sempill's completed a similar manoeuvre on the right. Not only had the charge been stopped but, thanks to Huske's diligence in realigning the infantry positions, the attacking clansmen found that they were now surrounded on three sides by red-coated infantrymen. During the enfilading fire some 700 Jacobites were shot down almost immediately, causing terrible losses in a relatively small army.[19] This was the tipping point, and as the firing gave way to equally fierce hand-to-hand fighting the infantrymen did dreadful damage with their bayonets. As the clansmen faltered, Cumberland noted with satisfaction, 'in their rage that they could not make any impression upon the battalions, they threw stones at them for at least a minute before their total rout began.'[20]

The charge of the Macdonald clans on the Jacobite left had also failed to make any impression. With the front-line regiments, Pulteney's and 2nd Royals, holding firm there was no chance that the attack would succeed, not least because the Macdonalds had been forced to cover over half a mile before they reached their objective, a huge task for tired and hungry men. Thanks to the ferocity of the grapeshot and musket fire they also faltered three times and were reduced to facing their opponents swords drawn but with all impetus gone, a prey to the muskets and bayonets of the infantrymen ahead of them. Writing to his wife after the battle, Fusilier Edward Linn described the effects of his regiment's fire in terse but effective words: 'We kept a continual closs [barrage], firing upon them with our small-arms . . . we gave them a closs with grape-shot which galled them very much.'[21] And later, men in the government army would remember the Highlanders vainly holding up their plaids against their faces as if they were facing hail instead of a storm of bullets and assorted pieces of old iron which cut through their ranks, killing and disembowelling.

As the Clan Donald regiments started running from the field they passed through the steady ranks of Brigadier Walter Stapleton's Irish picquets,[22] who now also had to face the charge of Cobham's Horse and Kingston's Horse as they swept in from the right flank to chase and cut down the fleeing foot soldiers. On the Jacobite right similar scenes were being enacted, as Campbell of Ballimore's infantry continued firing into the flanks while the government cavalry 'rode in among the fugitives and hacked them terribly with their broad swords'.[23]

Cumberland's victory was already as complete as any field commander could have desired. The government army was left master of the field; their opponents had been soundly defeated, casting aside their weapons and running for their lives from the moor to leave it to the smoke and the wind and the rain. Within an hour of lining up for battle, the subalterns in the government regiments were ordering their men to 'Rest on your Arms!' Muskets were lowered and the government soldiers looked over the moor at the charnel house they had created. Even the veterans of Flanders were dumbfounded by the scene – a heaving mass of dead and dying piled up in the tufts of heather, the air heavy with the moans and shrieks of the wounded. 'I never saw a field thicker of dead,' was Fusilier Linn's terse but apt comment.[24] Casualties in the government ranks were 50 killed and 259 wounded, while Jacobite casualties have been estimated to be in the region of 1500 and were probably even higher.[25]

There are several reasons for Cumberland's overarching success at Culloden. Some are obvious, others less so. His army enjoyed superiority in manpower and firepower. They outnumbered the Jacobite army roughly two to one and they were much better prepared and trained; in the Brown Bess musket they had a proven battle-winner and their artillery completely outclassed their opponents' equipment, being modern and manned by professional gunners. They were also fit for purpose, having been rested, well fed and decently quartered the night before the battle. This was especially true of the regiments on the government army's left, which faced the first brunt of the Jacobite attack. Barrell's had felt the full force of a Highland charge at Falkirk and had remained undaunted while others had turned and run. Munro's also behaved well, as did the battalions in the second line, which responded quickly and efficiently to Huske's order to realign the defensive wall. Elsewhere in the line, Cumberland noted, 'the Royals and Pulteney's hardly took their Firelocks from the shoulders', while the Campbells' enfilading fire from the Culwhiniac enclosure allowed the government dragoons to complete the victory with a fury that the watching James Wolfe called 'great slaughter'.[26] Discipline also came into the equation – not through the unthinking application of the lash, which was used to keep men in order in King George II's army, but the self-confidence that had been bred into the men during their stay in Aberdeen.

Leadership and sound staff work also played key roles. Cumberland arrived on the battlefield with a deserved reputation from his experiences in Flanders and he enjoyed the support of his soldiers. Partly this was due to the loyalty they naturally felt for his father, King George II, but they were also inspired by him and valued his presence in their ranks before and during the battle. Wolfe, often an acerbic witness, asserted that the small army was 'ready to undertake anything, having so brave a man at the head of them'.[27] Indeed, so popular was Cumberland that after the battle he was forced to issue an order forbidding his soldiers to stare in admiration at him while on parade.[28] In the wider history of the British Army Cumberland was not one of the great captains, but Culloden was definitely 'the crowning point of his career' and if the soldiers in his army did not exactly feel affection for him they certainly felt gratitude.[29] Soldiers admire a winner, especially if they owe their lives to his leadership abilities and to his grace under pressure, all of which Cumberland demonstrated on the day of battle.

The administration within Cumberland's army was also good. On the logistical side the men were well fed and equipped, there was an efficient baggage train and because men slept and ate in close proximity to those beside whom they would fight, there was a good sense of unit cohesion within the infantry battalions and the three regiments of cavalry. On the supply side, as has been noted, the support of the Royal Navy in the North Sea was invaluable.

Cumberland was also well served by the officers under his command. Lord Bury had set the tone before the battle by riding along the front line in sight of the Jacobite army, and had later shown no little personal courage after a Highlander, feigning surrender, attempted to shoot him at close range having mistaken him for Cumberland. Bury's enemies within the army included Wolfe, who derided him as a man of privilege who had 'a way of trifling with us poor soldiers that gives many honest, poor men high disgust', but there was more to him than accident of birth.[30] While it is true that Bury owed much to royal preferment and his friendship with Cumberland – through his mother he was descended from King Charles II – he had a good head for organisation, a skill he had learned from his father Albemarle, who had been given command of the first line of the government army during the battle. No doubt it was to his advantage that he had been educated at Westminster, the school which Cumberland had briefly attended and which enjoyed close links with the royal family, having received its charter from Queen Elizabeth in 1560 and more recently having received endowments from Cumberland's father and grandfather.

The other line commanders, Huske and Mordaunt, were equally professional in their approach to soldiering. Both had performed well at Falkirk, rallying the scattered infantrymen and preventing a total rout, and at Culloden Huske had contributed enormously to the victory by his skilful deployment of the second line to seal off the Jacobite attack on the left flank. But for his lower rank Huske might have been appointed commander in Scotland after Culloden; instead he had to yield to Hawley, who had almost lost the battle of Falkirk. Wolfe, who served as Hawley's aide-de-camp, claimed of his chief that the 'troops dread his severity, hate the man, and hold his military knowledge in contempt',[31] but properly handled Hawley was a reasonably competent and loyal soldier who repaid the trust placed in him by Cumberland. At Culloden, under the duke's direction, he used the cavalry on both flanks to good effect to harass and outflank the Jacobite lines and gave the vital order to Bland to pull down the northern walls of the Culwhiniac enclosure, allowing the dragoons to be introduced to the battlefield on the Jacobite right. Age might also have influenced Hawley's occasionally querulous approach: at the time of the battle he was in his sixties and by then was probably a better second-in-command than leader. Cumberland and his commanders nevertheless deserve credit for gaining a tidy and economical military victory.

Battles can be lost as well as won and it is difficult to avoid the conclusion that the Jacobite army and its commanders contributed a great deal to their own downfall. It began at the very top. On the day itself Prince Charles was the overall battlefield commander and in his first experience of combat command he was found wanting. Not only had he chosen the battlefield, but he had failed to reconnoitre it – although, given his lack of military experience, it is doubtful if he would have gained much information even if he had walked the area. Not only did he fail to notice that the rough ground would cause problems for his charging Highlanders but he also had little inkling of the dangers posed to his flanks by the walled enclosures. Then, at O'Sullivan's bidding, he moved his command post to a position known as Culchunaig, which was to the right of the rear of the Jacobite lines. This had the drawback of leaving him unsighted when the battle began, a serious disadvantage for any field commander. As a result he could not see the damage being done to his lines by the government artillery, and when the regiments on the right eventually charged he was unaware of the problems caused by Clan Chattan's unevenly paced attack and the failure of Clan Donald on his left. Then, in the final stages of the battle when Cumberland's horse began their flanking movements, he failed to spot the danger and had to be led away from Culchunaig for his own safety. Others in his army noticed his retreat and to all intents the move signalled the beginning of the end of the action on the moor.

Of those failings, the most serious was the delay in ordering the charge at a time when the Jacobite army's front line was being cut down in swathes by the government artillery – in their tightly packed groups the front-line soldiers provided an irresistible target for Belford's gunners and they took full advantage. Quite apart from the death and destruction, the feeling of impotence did nothing for morale as the clansmen waited in vain for the order. For an army which depended on the shock of the much-feared Highland charge, which would have seen the clan soldiers, broadsword in hand, career into the static lines of government infantrymen, it was a mystifying failure. Either Prince Charles froze at the moment of decision or the chain of command failed, partly through the prince's indecision and partly through bad luck – one of the runners entrusted with the order was decapitated by a cannon-ball and the order had to be repeated through Brigadier Stapleton. Even then there was confusion and vacillation, with the men of Atholl setting off precipitately on the right while Clan Chattan veered in the same direction. At the same time Clan Donald hesitated on the left; both Keppoch and Clanranald fell before their men's attack finally gained any momentum and it finally petered out. Throughout the period of heaviest fighting Prince Charles was in an agony of uncertainty, and although he showed considerable personal courage while trying to rally his men it soon became clear that he had lost what grip he had ever had on the battle. According to Lord Elcho, when the prince was finally led from the field by Colonel Robert O'Shea, commander of Fitzjames's Horse, he was 'in a deplorable state', probably numbed by the defeat and the growing carnage around him.[32] At the same time Elcho was allegedly less circumspect, shouting out: 'There goes a damned Italian coward.'

In the sense that Prince Charles failed to exercise any control over the battle and was unable to 'read' it as events unfolded, he must bear the brunt of the blame for the defeat, but he was not alone in shouldering that burden. He was badly let down by his subordinate commanders. O'Sullivan was a competent and shrewd staff officer but he was not an experienced combat soldier, while Murray, for all his personal courage and military ability, was neither a team player nor a completely trustworthy individual, as he had already demonstrated in his dealings with the prince. Other unit commanders such as Brigadier Walter Stapleton and Lord Ogilvy proved their competence and courage during the battle, the former by covering the Jacobite left at the time of the government breakthrough and the latter by handling his regiment well despite being given contradictory orders about their positioning on the left flank. However, neither was in the same league as Cumberland's subordinate officers, and that was one of the big differences between the two armies and the way in which they were led. Under Cumberland's command were officers and men who had fought at Dettingen and Fontenoy. Apart from the Irish picquets and the soldiers in French service, Prince Charles had very few who could equal them.

But even if there had been parity in the quality of command, the battle had effectively been lost before it began due to a steady and insistent multiplication of forced and unforced errors. The Jacobite army had to engage the government army in order to safeguard their logistical base at Inverness, otherwise they would have no option but to retreat into the West Highlands; the ground was not of their choosing and had not been inspected beforehand; there was a serious discrepancy in numbers and the levels of equipment which gave Cumberland's men a decided advantage; there were divisions within the Jacobite ranks over clan precedence, and constant squabbling amongst key senior commanders; many of the men were hungry and exhausted; and, finally, there had been the disastrous and totally unnecessary night march to Nairn on the eve of battle. Combine those issues, add on other debilitating factors such as the atrocious weather and the wonder is not that the battle was lost so quickly but that it was allowed to be fought in the first place.

4

Bruise those Bad Seeds
Spread about this Country

By late afternoon on 16 April Cumberland's army had emerged triumphant at the battle which came to be known as Culloden. It had been a relatively cheap and easy victory, but it would have been very difficult for King George II's younger son to claim that the rebellion against his father had been quashed. Prince Charles and most of his senior commanders remained alive and on the loose, while large numbers of the Jacobite army had managed to escape from the moor; in theory at least they were free to take up their arms again and fight another day.

Some of them had struggled to escape the battlefield, but the vast majority of the prince's army simply dispersed or made their way south through Badenoch towards Ruthven Barracks, which had been designated as the main rendezvous point. Others attempted to get back to their homes. Lord Ogilvy's Forfarshire Regiment marched in good order to Ruthven and then headed east over the hills to Glen Clova, where the men disbanded five days later. After hiding in the hills Ogilvy took ship to Norway and thereafter made his way to France, where King Louis XV commissioned him to raise a new Scottish regiment for service in the French army.[1]

For the Irish and French soldiers there was the possibility of surrender and parole as they were considered to be prisoners of war and not rebels; as a result, most of the men of the Royal Ecossais and the Irish picquets were well treated, although Brigadier Stapleton died of his wounds a few days later. However, the same leniency was not offered to other members of the Jacobite army – the Highland clansmen, the Lowland Scots volunteers and the English deserters who suddenly found themselves beyond the law. For many of them the mere fact of falling into government hands meant summary execution, as the wounded were bayoneted on Drummossie Moor and those attempting to escape were cut down by the dragoons – 'knapping of noddles' as one observer drolly put it.[2] Even idle spectators of the battle were not spared, many government soldiers giving vent to a violent bloodlust in the hours which followed the end of the fighting. In the months ahead, bloodshed would become the norm as the government army continued its pursuit of Jacobite soldiers and their supporters, mounting what would later be called a counter-insurgency campaign against the largely civilian population of the Scottish Highlands.

The conduct of Cumberland's army after Culloden has received a good deal of attention over the years, all of it negative, and at the time its behaviour was well documented by observers on both sides. There can be no argument that atrocities were committed by government soldiers, and that these were frequently condoned by senior officers in the interests of crushing the Jacobite cause and gaining a measure of revenge against those who had fomented the rebellion. Before the battle Cumberland had engaged in a lengthy correspondence with Newcastle in which he had requested guidance about the measures to be taken against those involved in the uprising, both to punish them and to ensure that rebellion never broke out again. The advice was woolly at best and contradictory at worst. Cumberland was authorised to 'to do whatever is necessary for suppressing this unnatural rebellion', but no general rule could be given other than for him to remember that he was not to 'give any just cause of complaint to a country [Scotland] so ill disposed to the king'.

Faced by such an unhelpful directive, Cumberland responded that he 'could have wished the king's order had been fuller. Yet I'll take the hint.'[3] Other officers, such as Hawley and Yorke, were in favour of harsh measures from the outset, not least because they believed that the relative leniency practised after the 1715 rebellion had merely encouraged the Jacobites to rise again thirty years later. As a result Cumberland was left in the uncomfortable situation of wanting to pursue a policy of forceful retribution while understanding that without firm orders he might be guilty of acting outside the law. Like many commanders in his position, he wanted specific guidance on what his soldiers could and could not do, but this was not forthcoming.

At the time, while tempers were still inflamed from the violence on the battlefield, much was made of an infamous Jacobite forgery insisting that no quarter was to be given to government soldiers, and the leaking of this counterfeit order was used to vindicate much of the initial casual violence. Several copies of the order exist, some of which were supposed to have been signed by Lord George Murray, but all are fakes. Nor is there any evidence to suggest that these forgeries were created on Cumberland's orders after the event to excuse the violence meted out to the defeated

Jacobites – as was suggested in some enemy papers retrieved from the battlefield.[4] As Cumberland's most recent biographer concludes, 'there is nothing in his character to support an accusation that he was capable of deliberately fabricating false rebel orders', for the very good reason that, having already come to the conclusion that harsh measures were needed to deal with the defeated Jacobite army, the duke had no need to descend to such measures.[5] That being said, there is a dreadful ambiguity in one order issued by Cumberland on 17 April:

A captain and fifty foot to march directly and visit all the cottages in the neighbourhood of the field of battle, and to search for rebels. The officers and men will take notice that the public orders of the rebels was to give no quarter.[6]

The wording of the final sentence can be read in two ways. Either it was an unspoken order to give no quarter to those rebels discovered in the cottages, or it was a warning to take additional care in dealing with desperate men who might be unwilling to surrender and would fight to the last. On balance, and taking into account the widely held belief that official Jacobite policy was to refuse quarter when dealing with the wounded in the government army, the inference must be that Cumberland was already minded to use stern measures against the perpetrators of the rebellion and was warning the captain accordingly. If so, he clearly believed that he was acting within his rights, and also in his father's best interests in promoting a policy of aggressive pacification. That belief led to a number of misunderstandings; as they multiplied, the problem was exacerbated in the months after the battle.

To gain some understanding of Cumberland's behaviour in the aftermath of Culloden it is necessary to return to the moment when the battle ended and to see the problem in terms of the times and from the viewpoints of both sides. The aftermath of the battle also fell into two distinct phases. The first came after the formal fighting had come to an end and it dawned on the government soldiers what they had done – they had gained an easy victory in the field, but their enemy was still a threat. As the last Jacobite soldiers fled from the moor, the government infantrymen stood down briefly and waited for an order to advance along the line to take possession of the battlefield. This was a moment of triumph for Cumberland and he accepted it, riding along the lines and shouting words of thanks to the men who had given him victory. In return the infantrymen cheered him loudly, chanting the familiar refrain of 'Billy!' and 'Flanders!' Then, after he had passed by the serried ranks, the men advanced by beat of drum, halting only when they reached the point where the Jacobite army had faced them. As they rested their arms and stood at ease, biscuits and cheese were brought up from the supply train. It was at this point that the first atrocities took place.

All around the groups of resting red-coated soldiers lay Jacobite corpses and the twitching remains of those who were wounded or on the point of dying. For those unfortunates, death at the end of a bayonet was an all too common fate as the government soldiers took their revenge on an enemy who had been locked in battle against them only an hour or so earlier. As the fighting had been conducted at close quarters and was therefore extremely personal, there was little sympathy for the wounded, many of whom paid the price for being helpless and unable to defend themselves. Such slaughter was not done in the heat of battle but in cold blood, and there is evidence to suggest that both Hawley and Bland were amongst the officers who encouraged their men to finish off the wounded. If any further incitement were needed it was usually fuelled by racist abuse which contributed to the dehumanisation of the enemy, with officers characterising the Jacobites as 'vermin' or 'popish savages' beyond the pale of civilised society. In one well-attested incident at Culloden House twelve wounded Jacobites were shot by a party of government soldiers who had earlier promised to have them treated by a surgeon. Later, King George II asked Duncan Forbes of Culloden if this story were true; he received the bleak reply that Forbes wished he could deny it.[7]

In modern warfare there is no excuse for soldiers to be left wounded on the battlefield and casualty evacuation is a refined art in most enlightened armies, so much so that by the beginning of the twenty-first century even badly wounded soldiers expect to survive if they are treated quickly and effectively, usually within the first hour. However, at the time of Culloden there was limited interest in tending the wounded other than offering what might be called basic first aid, enhanced by the amputation of shattered limbs. Surgeons were unable to offer much in the way of treatment or cure, especially when abdominal wounds were concerned and when the resulting sepsis could not be treated. There was also an unspoken belief that wounded soldiers were a hindrance, and that they used up scarce resources, such as transport, that might be needed for military purposes. If the wounded could reach treatment centres they would be cared for to the best of the surgeons' abilities, but otherwise 'natural triage' would take its course.[8] None of this excuses the killings, but it does help to explain why the Jacobite wounded had no protection and could expect no mercy from government soldiers who were subject to the same official indifference. As it was, it took another three days before search parties went on to the moor to collect or bury the government casualties.

The second phase was the execution of the reprisals which was more systematic and was carried out under Cumberland's direction. While the rump of the surviving Jacobite army was making its way southwards, the government army began moving towards Inverness, where Cumberland took as his lodgings the house in Church Street belonging to the Dowager Lady Mackintosh – mother-in-law of the fiery Lady Anne Mackintosh of Moy. The town was to be his headquarters for the next five weeks as the initial moves were made to subdue the residue of the forces loyal to the Jacobite cause. In fact the first step had already been taken in February, when Cumberland had issued a general order that following the defeat of the Jacobite army, clan or regimental leaders would be detained in custody while the rank and file could present themselves to a magistrate to surrender their arms, upon which they would be given an official certificate permitting them to 'return unmolested to their home until His Majesty's pleasure is known'.[9] The position was quite clear: an amnesty was being offered but it was conditional and would only hold good if the individual agreed to lay down his arms – a risky undertaking given the tenor of the times and one which would compromise his place within the clan structure. In any case, the guarantee only ran for six weeks and already some Jacobite commanders – amongst them Clanranald, Lochiel, Cluny, Glenbucket and John Roy Stuart – had made it clear that they wanted to continue fighting, thereby putting themselves and their followers in breach of the amnesty.

Meanwhile there was the task of pacification and punishment to be carried out, and Cumberland's men set to work with a will. On the day following the battle, courts martial were held for government deserters captured in the Jacobite army and thirty-six of their number went to the gallows, the inevitable punishment for any soldier who had turned coat. On the same day a detachment of Pulteney's under Lieutenant-Colonel Thomas Cockayne was dispatched to Moy Hall to arrest Lady Anne Mackintosh, while Mordaunt took another force west to the Fraser estates at Aird, where Lord Lovat's castle of Beaufort on the banks of the River Beauly was burned down and cattle and other possessions were confiscated. It was here that Prince Charles had sheltered after the battle, and Cumberland was keen to apprehend him before he could escape back to France. In pursuit of that aim a force of cavalry was assembled under Lieutenant-Colonel the Earl of Ancrum with orders from Cumberland to ride into the Jacobite stronghold of the north-east, where any house found with illegal arms would be 'burnt to ashes'.

The eldest son of the Marquess of Lothian, whom he would succeed in 1767, William Henry Kerr, Earl of Ancrum was a professional soldier who had served in the Foot Guards and had been wounded in the head during the Battle of Fontenoy. He was another young officer who enjoyed Cumberland's patronage, and a month earlier he had repaid that interest by taking a small force of horse and infantry into the wilds of Strathdon to capture and destroy a store of Spanish arms and munitions which was being held at remote Corgarff Castle. The action took place in bitter winter weather, proving that government soldiers could operate in mountainous terrain whatever the season, and its success led Cumberland to report that 'during the whole expedition he [Ancrum] has behaved with the greatest prudence and caution, and much like an officer.'[10]

At Culloden Ancrum had been in command of the cavalry forces on the left of the government line, and in that role he has to bear some responsibility for the savage way in which the troopers pursued the fleeing Jacobite soldiers, 'with so good an effect that a very considerable number were killed'.[11] The execution was done in the heat of battle as the dragoons swept through the Culwhiniac enclosure in pursuit of the fleeing Jacobite foot soldiers, harrying them as if they were prey, and in that red mist Ancrum would have been powerless. On a softer note, at one point he attempted to spare the life of Gillies MacBean of Clan Chattan, who fought bravely to the end only to die of his wounds; but Ancrum was at heart a loyal army officer who reasoned that the Jacobites had to be punished for the effrontery of their rebellion and that instead of offering mercy he would 'go on a very different way'.[12] It cannot have improved his equilibrium that his brother, Lord Robert Kerr, was the commander of the grenadier company in Barrell's Regiment and had been killed in the opening stages of the battle as the first line received the full force of the Jacobite charge. Kerr was one of 17 killed and 108 wounded in Barrell's, the highest number of casualties in any regiment in the government army.

Whatever the reasoning behind Ancrum's robust response, his force took firm measures against anyone suspected of maintaining support for the Jacobite cause: on 1 August in Aberdeen, 'this infamous town' according to Ancrum's report, the windows of over two hundred houses were smashed by men of Fleming's Regiment following the refusal of the inhabitants to display lighted candles in honour of the birthday of King George II. As he told Cumberland, it was the only way to deal with people who had supported the claims of the Stuarts: 'nothing will make them do their duty but starving them or in some other shape forcing them to it, I have quite lost the little humanity I had for 'em, I mean even for those who pretend to be well affected.'[13]

In that respect the behaviour of Ancrum's men in Aberdeen typified that of the government army as Cumberland continued the second phase of his post-battle operations, namely retribution against those who had taken part in the rebellion. In the third

week of May he began moving the bulk of his army – one regiment of horse (Kingston's) and eleven infantry battalions (Howard's, Barrell's, Wolfe's, Price's, Bligh's, Campbell's North British
Fusiliers, Cholmondeley's, Munro's, and three newly arrived
battalions which had arrived in Inverness by sea as reinforcements
after the battle) – south to Fort Augustus. By this time the remnants of the Jacobite army were in disarray. Up to three thousand
of their number had mustered at Ruthven on the day following
the battle but without firm leadership there was confusion about
their next move. A handful of diehards wanted to continue the
campaign and plans were laid to rendezvous at Achnacarry in the
middle of May, but only around six hundred, mainly Camerons
and Macdonalds, turned up. The harsh reality was that without
Prince Charles at the helm the rebellion had petered out and the
spark could not be rekindled. For the rest of the summer he and a
small number of aides were on the run in the western Highlands
and islands, fugitives in the country which the previous summer
they had hoped to win for the Jacobite cause.

As a result, and with a shattered army and its leadership in
chaos, fleeing for their lives, Cumberland took measures which he
felt to be appropriate to the circumstances. By moving to the south
of the Great Glen he had stationed his army in a position from
which he could threaten the heartlands which had supported the
Jacobite cause – or, as Cumberland told Newcastle, he was now in
a situation to 'teach them an important truth for them to know,
by showing them that they can retire to no mountain so barren or
remote where he cannot in person lead and subsist a sufficient force
from His Majesty's army'.[14] The message was obvious. With the
amnesty coming to an end and very few weapons having been surrendered, the emphasis of Cumberland's operations changed from
pacification to punishment. The arrival of the government soldiers

in Fort Augustus was a statement of intent in that it demonstrated to the local population that they were capable of mounting operations anywhere in the West Highlands. An important element in the clansmen's military mystique was their undoubted hardiness and fleetness of foot as hill-men, yet red-coated Lowland soldiers were now showing that they too could operate with ease in areas previously deemed inaccessible to soldiers with no previous experience of the region's steep mountains and remote glens.

Before Cumberland left Inverness he had received a deputation from Duncan Forbes of Culloden. Forbes urged him to act with clemency towards the Jacobite foot soldiers, as 'unnecessary severities create pity, and pity from unnecessary severities is the most dangerous nurse to disaffection, especially if continued for any time.'[15] While the Lord President was not against the idea of punishing the Jacobite leadership, and if necessary favoured deportation of whole clans, he did not condone the arbitrary persecution of the Jacobite rank and file.

For his pains, Forbes was allegedly dismissed by Cumberland as 'that old woman who talked to me about humanity'.[16] (The comment has been often quoted but is probably untrue, having been reported by a hostile source, Robert Forbes, a non-juring bishop who had been imprisoned in Stirling Castle as a Jacobite supporter.) By the time that the government forces had set up camp at Fort Augustus in the middle of May it seems that Cumberland had already decided to use a heavy hand against the people of the West Highlands, or as the *Scots Magazine* put it so graphically, 'to lay the rod more heavily upon them, by carrying fire and sword through their country, and driving off their cattle'.[17] And that is precisely what Cumberland's first four raiding parties did when they engaged on their first pacification missions at the end of May.

Lieutenant-Colonel Edward Cornwallis of Bligh's Regiment set the tone when he led 300 infantrymen into Lochaber and set fire to Lochiel's house at Achnacarry, while further west in Knoydart Lord George Sackville, third son of the Duke of Dorset, carried out similar depredations in the territory between Fort Augustus and Glenelg. Both commanders were of similar age, being in their early thirties, and both came from aristocratic backgrounds, and both were intelligent and cultivated men. As was the case with so many battalion commanders in Cumberland's army, they had fought in Flanders, where they had caught the eye of their captain-general; a career soldier, Sackville had joined the army in 1737 after an education which included Westminster School and Trinity College Dublin, and had quickly emerged as one of Cumberland's protégés. First commissioned in Bragg's Regiment of Foot, later the 28th, he served with distinction at Dettingen and Fontenoy where he was commended by Cumberland for his bravery in battle. At the time of the Jacobite uprising he was ordered to return to Britain to take over command of Bligh's (later the 20th Foot) but he arrived late and missed the fighting at Culloden. Cornwallis's twin brother was a future Archbishop of Canterbury and he himself had spent five years in the diplomatic service, but as Private Michael Hughes, a volunteer in Bligh's, recorded, no one under his command was minded to show any mercy to the defeated enemy:

> The order was to set fire to his [Lochiel's] mansion house, but the best of his movables were carried off before the soldiers came; however his fine chairs, tables and all his cabinet goods were set afire and burnt with his house. His fine fruit garden, above a mile long, was pulled to pieces and laid waste. A beautiful summer-house that stood in the pleasure-garden was also set on fire, and everything valuable was burnt or destroyed.[18]

Sackville, too, showed no mercy, ordering the destruction of the home in Lochaber of Donald Macdonald of Tirnadris, a Jacobite officer who had been second-in-command of the Keppoch regiment, that fact being enough to condemn him. Sackville had arrived with the reinforcements which had reached Scotland after the battle and he showed that he was as enthusiastic as his fellow officers about carrying fire and sword into the western Highlands. Nor were the coastal areas and inshore islands neglected: parties of soldiers under the command of Captain John Fergusson RN were carried on board the fourteen-gun converted sloops HMS *Furnace* and HMS *Terror* to harry the islands of Canna and Raasay and sailed up Loch Nevis to land parties to burn the house of Macdonald of Barisdale. All these operations followed a common pattern – the houses of prominent local families were burned down, property was confiscated and cattle and sheep were driven off. Fort Augustus became a giant market where it was estimated that at least 20,000 cattle were sold, as well as huge numbers of sheep and goats. In many cases violence was used even against people who had certificates of immunity, and summary execution and rape were not uncommon as the government troops continued their work throughout the summer of 1746.

Not every commander behaved without thinking about the adverse implications of his actions. When Loudoun was ordered to move his forces from Skye and return to Fort Augustus, he was instructed 'to drive the cattle, burn the ploughs and destroy what you can belonging to all such as are or have been in the rebellion, and burning the houses of the chiefs', but although he carried out his orders to the letter he was equally scrupulous in dealing with those who had chosen to surrender.[19] His courteous behaviour and frequent intercessions would also be important in the later healing process within the ruling elite in the Highland areas. He was particularly attentive to Lady Anne Mackintosh while she was under arrest, despite the fact that she had humiliated him during the Rout of Moy, and their subsequent close friendship led to exaggerated and untrue rumours that they were lovers.[20]

Even so, with his Campbell family name Loudoun was always going to be under suspicion throughout the Highlands. As agents for the Scottish Crown before 1603 and as pillars of the Whig establishment in the eighteenth century, the house of Argyll, with its immense power and large territorial holdings, was pre-eminent in the Scottish Highlands, and as a result the name of Campbell was viewed, especially by the neighbouring clans, with hostility bordering on fear. In the eyes of many Highlanders, to be a Campbell was to carry the mark of Cain; as the position was explained by the highly respected nineteenth-century historian Donald Gregory, they were a 'race that craves ever to fish in drumlie [muddy or murky] waters'.[21]

This does Loudoun less than justice, for he was first and foremost a government servant from the Scottish Lowlands who just happened to have a name which was anathema throughout the Highlands, especially in those areas which largely supported the Stuarts and the Jacobite cause. Although Loudoun commanded a Highland regiment in the government army – and even though his name was Campbell – his family home was at Galston in Ayrshire and his mother was a Dalrymple, daughter of the Earl of Stair, formerly commander-in-chief and a member of one of the great Lowland families. Having been commissioned into the Royal North British Dragoons (later the Royal Scots Greys), Loudoun was a career soldier and a confirmed Whig who had had supported the Hanoverian cause from the outset of the rebellion. As for his use of Highland dress, his command of the pro-government Highland forces obliged him to wear a kilt, but he admitted to friends that he 'longed to have on britches'.[22]

The other prominent Campbell in the government army, John Campbell of Mamore, was rather different from Loudoun, despite possessing the same name. A cousin of the Duke of Argyll, he too was a professional soldier who had served at Dettingen and was close to Cumberland. After Culloden Campbell directed operations in Sunart and Morvern using men of the Argyll Militia, and he tended towards leniency except where Campbell interests were concerned, the payment of rent to Clan Campbell being as much a political as a financial transaction. However, on occasions he ordered the return of cattle, and his men frequently interceded to protect women and children.

Both men deserved their reputations for humanity and consideration to others, but the belief that the Scots in Cumberland's army tended to be more lenient in their treatment of the defeated Jacobites than were commanders from English or Irish backgrounds, was not always justified. It has a satisfying ring, but being a Scot was not enough to make these two commanding officers stay their hands. Being Campbells and Whigs and natural supporters of the Hanoverian succession, both had reason to dislike the clans which had supported the Stuarts, especially traditional Campbell enemies such as Clan Donald and Clan Cameron, but both men were also inclined to the view that punitive measures were not always the best way to deal with the aftermath of the rebellion. Besides, there were other Scottish officers who felt quite differently about the rebels and saw no reason why they should not be forced to pay for their effrontery in rising against the king.

Notable (or infamous) amongst these were Major James (or

William) Lockhart of Cholmondeley's and Captain Caroline Frederick Scott of Guise's, both Lowland Scots; the names of both became associated with the reprisals after Culloden. Not much is known about the personal life of the former, other than that he was a career soldier from Lanarkshire who was responsible for several atrocities in Glenmoriston and Strathglass, including the rape of several women. At the time, though, his name was well enough known in Cumberland's army thanks to a widely repeated story which in fact did him little credit. At some point during the earlier Battle of Falkirk, in an incident which remains unexplained, he seems to have lost his uniform jacket, which was later found on the back of one of the Jacobite deserters hanged at Inverness.

Scott also revelled in his notoriety, so much so that one modern historian of the campaign has likened his arbitrary brutality to the behaviour of 'a medieval condottiere or a commander of the Waffen SS', while an earlier historian simply wrote him off as 'the much detested Captain Carolina [sic] Scott'.[23] In fact Scott was a professional soldier from Edinburgh who owed his unusual Christian name to his godmother Princess Caroline of Ansbach, wife of King George II. The son of a diplomat, he was commissioned in the Royal North British Dragoons before transferring to Guise's in 1741. He, too, had seen service in Europe, in his case in Gibraltar where he appears to have worked as a military engineer. If so, that experience had come to his aid in March when he was in overall command of the defences at Fort William during a Jacobite siege directed by Mirabel de Gordon, who had been in charge of a similar attempt at Stirling castle earlier in the year. For his successful defence Scott was mentioned in one of the dispatches from Newcastle to Cumberland: 'His Majesty looks upon the raising of the siege of Fort William to have been greatly owing to the courage and good conduct of Captain Scott, whose behaviour has given him great satisfaction.'[24]

Another senior army officer, Lord Bury, was equally impressed, describing Scott as 'a very pretty man and diligent officer', and there is little doubt that the Lowland Scot was held in high regard by his contemporaries. He emerged from the campaign with his reputation as a soldier enhanced, and had caught the eye of his superiors to the extent that within six years he would be promoted first to major and then to lieutenant-colonel in command of the 29th Foot (later the Worcestershire Regiment). By 1752 he was also an aide-de-camp to Cumberland and had been transferred to the army of the Honourable East India Company, charged with drawing up new plans for the defences of another Fort William, this time the company's headquarters or 'factory' in Calcutta.[25] Only his premature death from fever the following year would prevent his further promotion in the Company's service. And yet, in Scottish, especially Highland, history Scott has been excoriated as a monstrous figure, one of the 'butchers' who visited revenge and rapine on the people of the West Highlands in the reprisals after Culloden. A hard-nosed soldier, Scott was no angel; however, the worst charges against him – such as the drowning of three men in a mill flume at Lochoy after they had arrived in Fort William to surrender – are based on circumstantial, perhaps even prejudiced, evidence.[26] Other stories tell of his role in the destruction of the house of Alexander Cameron of Glen Nevis, not far from Fort William, but this was no worse than what had taken place at Achnacarry. What is known is that Scott entertained a visceral dislike of Highlanders and their way of life; he seems to have pursued a personal vendetta against Prince Charles, pushing himself and his men throughout the summer months as they scoured Morar, Knoydart and Appin searching for the prince without success. On 23 July, according to the headquarters report on his return, Scott arrived in Fort William 'vastly fatigued and almost naked', but without the prince or any tangible evidence of his whereabouts.[27]

With good reason, the prince's 'Flight in the Heather' is considered to be one of the great epics of the Jacobite campaign. After leaving the battlefield with a few loyal companions, Prince Charles spent most of the rest of the year on the run in the Highlands and western islands – where, to the credit of the local population, no one yielded to the temptation of the £30,000 price tag (£2 million in modern money) which had been put on his head. On several occasions he narrowly avoided capture by the pursuing government troops, and at one stage he was disguised as an Irish maidservant called 'Betty Burke'. Towards the end of September 1746 the fugitives received news that two French frigates had arrived at Loch-nan-Uamh in Arisaig to collect the prince and his party, and early in the morning of 20 September Charles sailed for France accompanied by Lochiel, Lochgarry and Colonel John Roy Stewart. Ten days later, having evaded a British naval squadron off Brittany, *L'Heureux* landed the prince at Roscoff, where both ships fired a twenty-one-gun salute in honour of the occasion.

Their departure signalled the end of the rebellion: the Jacobite leadership had been fractured, and with the son of its titular head back in France, there was little chance that supporters would rally again to the cause. By then Cumberland had also left Scotland, having surrendered his command during the summer and arrived in London on 25 July to be given a hero's welcome. In addition to receiving the thanks of parliament and a grant of £25,000 a year over and above his civil list salary, he was honoured by a service of thanksgiving in St Paul's Cathedral which included the first performance of Handel's 'See the conquering hero comes' from the oratorio *Judas Maccabeus*. Further approbation came from a group of young bloods in London who created the Cumberland Society 'in his honour in grateful remembrance of the Service done our King and Country by His Royal Highness the Duke of Cumberland in extinguishing the Rebellion at the Battle of Culloden'. Its membership was restricted to the duke's age, with new members being elected on each birthday (15 April), and its first president was the Marquess of Granby, who had served in the royal army during the campaign.[28]

Cumberland departed Scotland never to return; as commander-in-chief he left behind Albemarle, who was not best pleased by the appointment, complaining that he had been 'kept in the worst country existing'.[29] Command of the forces in the Highlands was put in the capable hands of William Blakeney, who was also promoted lieutenant-general. The process of punishment and retribution continued into the following year, and there was no easing up until the autumn, when the government introduced a new amnesty for those who had supported the rebellion but had not taken up arms or joined the Jacobite army.

By then the emphasis of the reckoning had changed from outright punishment of individuals and families to embrace measures aimed at curbing Highland society in order to prevent a recrudescence of Jacobite sympathies. In other words, the government wanted to identify and then root out the main causes of disaffection and to prevent their recurrence, so that in the longer term Highlanders would give up their Jacobite sympathies and become loyal subjects of the House of Hanover. Before leaving Scotland, Cumberland had been in extensive correspondence with Newcastle in order to comment on some of the proposed measures, and it is instructive to read his many observations on the draft legislation.[30] He was not merely rubber-stamping government proposals but making astute comments on them, based on his own knowledge of Scotland or arising from his discussions with lawyers such as Duncan Forbes of Culloden or Highland landlords such as Alexander Macdonald of Sleat.

Altogether there were six bills which addressed the need to deal with the main problems affecting the Highland areas and the people who lived there and who had supported the Stuart claim to the throne. In essence the new legislation was designed to undermine the power of the Highland landowners and weaken the strength of the clan system so that it could never again pose a military threat. Disarmament was also part of the process, as was the prohibition of traditional Highland forms of dress.

Given the extent of the powers demanded by parliament, all six bills were controversial in Scotland, especially those dealing with dress and weapons. Under the terms of the Abolition and Proscription of the Highland Dress Bill it became a punishable offence (six months' imprisonment, followed by transportation if repeated) for any Highlander, man or boy, to 'wear or put on the clothes commonly called Highland clothes (that is to say) the Plaid, Philabeg, or little Kilt, Trowse [trews], Shoulder-belts, or any part whatever of what peculiarly belongs to the Highland Garb; and that no tartan or party-coloured plaid of stuff shall be used for Great Coats or upper coats'.[31] The only exceptions were men enlisted in the service of a Highland regiment. In a note on the proposed bill, Cumberland pointed out that tartan dress constituted a uniform and should therefore be abolished as part of the demilitarisation of the Highlands. Further to that aim, the existing Disarming Act was strengthened to add heavier punishments, including conscription or transportation or both, for anyone discovered concealing weapons.

Within the legislation an attempt to remove clan names was dropped as being impractical, for the good reason that an earlier law proscribing the name of the Macgregors had failed because in their own lands the clan had paid no attention to the prohibition Both these acts, however, which were passed in 1746 and 1747 respectively, otherwise hit effectively at the fabric of Highland society and were symbolic as well as solidly practical measures aimed at curbing the clans' sense of themselves as independent organisms. The Heritable Jurisdictions (Scotland) Act moreover abolished the traditional rights of jurisdiction afforded to a Scottish clan chief, effectively ending the practice of 'ward-holding' by stripping him of his right to call men to arms. Other penal laws included legislation to suppress 'all meeting houses and conventicles for religious worship in Scotland where the King and the Royal Family shall not be prayed for by name', a blow against non-juring members of the Scottish Episcopalian Church, while under the terms of the Act anent Estates of Traitors, 1746, Highland estates whose owners had been involved in the rebellion were forfeited to the Crown. As a result thirteen Highland estates were inalienably annexed and managed by a commission one of whose aims was to promote 'the Protestant Religion, good Government, Industry and Manufactures and the Principles of Duty and Loyalty to His Majesty'. The administration of the forfeited estates was undertaken by a committee of Edinburgh lawyers, and the money raised from rents received was used 'for the better civilising and improving the Highlands of Scotland, and preventing disorders there for the future'.[32]

Most of the legislation remained in place until the laws were repealed in the 1780s, by which time the Jacobite threat had more or less disappeared and 'rebel' leaders were considered to have mended their ways. Even so, the fact remains that the passing of those penal laws was regarded as a hostile act against the people of the Scottish Highlands, and the measures were greatly disliked. Their imposition also helps to underline how seriously the government took the threat, not just from the Jacobites but also from their main supporters, France.

At the same time existing laws on treason were used to punish those who had supported Prince Charles during the rebellion, but far from resolving the problem they simply exposed the limitations of using the army in support of the civil powers. For the soldiers on the ground it proved to be an almost impossible task to find and prepare evidence, make the necessary arrests and then provide the prison space before the trials took place. While officers had been conditioned to refer to the Jacobites as traitors and criminals, they were ill-placed to deal with the requirements of criminal procedure and in some instances simply rode roughshod over the law. On one occasion Bland, by then in charge of the Stirling and Edinburgh military districts, complained that it was 'ridiculous to talk of law to a parcel of savages, who never observed any but lived at large, preying on everything that came their way like many lions and tigers'.[33] All too often the inclination of the army was to impose a punishment at the scene of any alleged crime without making arrests or gathering evidence. Nor was it always feasible, when soldiers were operating in remote areas where civilian courts either did not exist or were too far away, to round up large numbers and then to arrange their transportation to larger centres of population to allow them to be legally processed.

In spite of those difficulties, though, there was a systematic attempt to use the criminal justice system to punish the Jacobites, and it marked the end of the second phase of the subjugation of the Highlands in the aftermath of Culloden. Altogether, 3472

Jacobite suspects were arrested and placed in captivity. Of that number 120 were executed, some 3.5 per cent of the total; thirty-six were deserters from Cumberland's army who were shot or hanged after courts martial, the usual punishment for desertion. Most of the Jacobite suspects were held in England in prisons at Lancaster, York and Lincoln, while of those incarcerated in London 157 unfortunates were housed in appalling conditions on board the prison ship *Pamela* at Woolwich. Of these, forty-nine survived the ordeal only to be transported to Barbados in spring 1747.[34] Equally unlucky were twenty-four members of the Manchester Regiment who were executed at various locations in England during the summer of 1746. All of them faced a traitor's death of being hung, drawn and quartered. Nine, including Colonel Francis Townley, were executed at Kennington in London, where they met their fate with great courage and dignity. When Townley, the first to die, had been cut down from the gallows barely conscious, the executioner 'cut off his head, took out his bowels, and flung them into the fire that was burning near the gallows'.[35] The captured Jacobite peers also faced a wretched fate: having been tried by their fellow nobles, they were beheaded on Tower Green – Lord Balmerino and Lord Kilmarnock on 18 August 1746 and Lord Lovat on 9 April 1747. Only Lord Cromarty was reprieved following a dramatic intervention by his wife, who swooned in front of King George II.

To prevent public disorder no trials or executions took place in Scotland and it has to be recorded that several of those who received a death sentence, such as sixteen-year-old George Barclay of Lord Ogilvy's Forfarshire Regiment, won reprieves on account of their age. In some cases lots were also drawn to decide which prisoner should be executed and many of those were pardoned due to other factors such as mental fragility. For the remainder the main sentence was deportation to the Caribbean (936) or banishment (222). A handful (76) received pardons and 1287 were eventually released unpunished. Many died in prison – the official figure is eighty-eight, but given the conditions and the fact that several had been wounded at Culloden, it must have been higher – and a lucky thirty-eight managed to escape.[36]

Because Cumberland was the army commander who had defeated the rebellion, he was also the figure primarily associated with the reprisals and as a result his name passed into history as 'Butcher' Cumberland. (It was not just in Scotland that this name was used: according to Horace Walpole, when 'it was lately proposed in the City of London to present him with the freedom of some company, one of the aldermen said aloud, "Then let it be of the *Butchers*"!'[37] From the standpoint of a later age the soubriquet is not unexpected. As one of Cumberland's officers admitted, a hard line was taken with suspected rebels: 'Those who are found in arms are ordered to be immediately put to death, and the houses of those who abscond are plundered and burnt, their cattle drove, their ploughs and other tackle destroyed.'[38] Although the number of those killed at Culloden was not particularly high, the slaughter of the wounded and the summary executions of Jacobites during the reprisal operations smacked of revenge and were carried out illegally by soldiers who believed that they were simply doing their duty.

Perversely, the recorder of the above comment, Lieutenant-Colonel Charles Whitefoord, was one of the more chivalrous and caring officers in Cumberland's army. A cousin of the Earl of Stair, he had begun his career in the Royal Navy before transferring to the army and was a serving Royal Marine officer in Edinburgh when the rebellion broke out. He distinguished himself as a volunteer at Prestonpans, where he gallantly refused to abandon his position with the artillery after his gunners had fled, and was saved from summary execution by Alexander Stewart of Invernahyle, a Jacobite officer in the Appin Regiment. In the aftermath of Culloden Whitefoord repaid the debt by using his influence with Cumberland to save the life of Stewart of Invernahyle and his family. In later life Stewart related the story to the novelist Walter Scott, for whom it was 'one of those anecdotes which soften the features even of civil war ... equally honourable to the memory of both parties'.[39] Later, in his novel *Waverley*, Scott used Whitefoord as the model for his character Colonel Talbot.

By the standards of the day the death toll during the reprisals was relatively low, but it rankled that so much of Scotland was under military control. In August 1746 Albemarle moved his headquarters to Edinburgh and his command was divided into four military districts – the first stretching from Inverness to Fort Augustus, the second from Strathspey to Aberdeenshire and the third from Perth to Fort William, while the fourth embraced Stirling and Edinburgh itself. From a chain of outposts and forts, columns of soldiers patrolled the outlying areas, making arrests, harrying the local population and all too often rounding up or killing livestock as they carried out their orders; amongst their officers were some of Cumberland's closest associates and familiars – Bland, Hawley, Huske, Wolfe, Cornwallis, Ancrum, Sackville and Howard. Wolfe in particular had shown scant regard for the rules of war, writing at one point that 'as few Highlanders were made prisoners as possible'.[40] Most of these officers had been replaced by the following year, but the memory of their presence and their soldiers' depredations cast a long shadow over Highland history, and for that Cumberland was blamed.

It mattered not that Cumberland was equally hard on his own men. Floggings for plundering were a regular occurrence in his army and Bland's *Treatise* warned that soldiers would never be able to maintain their discipline if they descended into criminality by disobeying orders. In one instance, six infantrymen were ordered to be punished with up to 1500 lashes each after they were found guilty of unlawful plundering.[41] It also did not matter that Cumberland left Scotland within three months of the battle; he was saddled with a reputation for organised savagery that marked his whole career and tarnished the good reputation he had won at Dettingen and Fontenoy.

On one level that reputation is justified. Because the questions he asked Newcastle in February 1745 never received a satisfactory answer, Cumberland felt vindicated in using extreme violence 'to bruise those bad seeds spread about this country so as they may never shoot again'.[42] There is ample evidence to suggest that Cumberland felt that the previous Jacobite uprising in 1715 had never been properly punished and that that was sufficient reason to extirpate those who had risen again thirty years later; he wanted 1746 to be the last time that the Jacobite cause threatened his father's throne, and in that hope he was largely successful, even though it came at a terrible human cost. During the reprisal operations the Highlands of Scotland became occupied territory policed by troops with no liking either for the place or its inhabitants, whom they excoriated as 'savages' or 'vermin'. Taking their lead from their commander-in-chief, they quickly came to look on the Highlanders as a subhuman species which deserved to be destroyed. Some senior officers (Hawley and Yorke have already been mentioned in this respect) even complained that Cumberland had been too lenient and that many more of the rebels deserved to be punished by execution or transportation.

Peace enforcement operations are never easy and soldiers fresh from battle are not always best placed to mount them, not least because they carry with them too much baggage in the way of derision or even hatred for their defeated enemy. So it was in the Highlands during the summer of 1746 and into the following year. Although the British army in Scotland received reinforcement battalions when some of those who fought at Culloden returned to Flanders, the bulk of the men involved in patrolling the Highlands had taken part in the battle and were contemptuous of their opponents. All too often that disdain turned into violence as they lost sight of the truth that in counter-insurgency operations the population is the prize to be won and not lost if the area is to be pacified. By giving free rein to his troops, and by leaving them and their commanders without clear orders during punitive or peace enforcement operations, Cumberland forgot or ignored one of the rules of command, namely that it is more difficult to train soldiers in the exercise of restraint than it is to encourage them to close with and kill their enemy. On that score the pejorative nickname of 'Butcher' does not sit over-heavily on Cumberland's shoulders.

In time his name also came to be associated with the legislation aimed at curbing the Highland way of life, and which contributed in time to the break-up of the clan system through the weakening of the Gaelic-speaking culture which bound together clan society. This accusation does not represent the whole story. While it was true that Cumberland had commented extensively and enthusiastically on the government's measures to disarm the Highlanders and to prevent them wearing their traditional dress, which he considered to be a uniform and not an ethnic garment, the laws proved difficult to enforce; in most cases attempts at prosecution amounted to little more than a series of humiliations which were widely resented and added to the growing sense of grievance. As one recent historian has put it, the truth was that 'it remained hard to disarm clansmen who did not want to be disarmed.'[43] In that sense the disarming and disclothing legislation was more of an irritant than a realistic means of curbing Jacobite support. (During the period of prohibition several leading Highland landed gentry, including the Macdonalds of Sleat, had portraits painted showing them in tartan dress, but they of course were either Whigs or supporters of the Hanoverian dynasty.) Even so, the collective memory of those events intensified anti-English feeling (or at least anti-government feeling) in the Highlands and Cumberland's name was usually associated with the process, so much so that many Highlanders took to calling the weed common ragwort 'Stinking Billy'. More productive in the longer term was the forfeiture of property and the ending of heritable jurisdictions, which ended once and for all ancient and long-outmoded practices of Scottish feudalism. In both cases the government provided assistance in the form of compensation for most of those affected, with landowners being paid substantial funds to accept the new order.

In the aftermath of Culloden one other factor had spurred on Cumberland: he was determined to resolve matters in Scotland so that he could return the British battalions to Flanders. This was an important consideration; the War of the Austrian Succession was still being fought and the French army had gradually gained the upper hand in the Low Countries. Following a string of victories in the Austrian Netherlands and the partial withdrawal of British troops in 1746, Saxe had renewed his campaign against the allied Pragmatic army, capturing Antwerp as well as clearing the territory between Brussels and the River Meuse.[44] In October 1746, in an attempt to retrieve the situation, the Austrian general Prince

Charles of Lorraine and General Sir John Ligonier, commander of the British forces, engaged Saxe at Rocoux, where the French army gained a notable victory by crushing the Dutch on the left of the allied front line. Saxe's second major victory, it allowed the French to capture Liège, thereby putting the United Provinces to the north under threat of a French attack.

While these events were unfolding, Cumberland remained in London, but it was inconceivable that the hero of the hour should not return to his former command in Europe.

5

LEARNING THE LESSONS THE HARD WAY

During the War of the Austrian Succession the fighting in Flanders and the Jacobite uprising were regarded in London as being one and the same thing – both were aspects of a continuing conflict with France, a major rival and a constant threat to British interests throughout the eighteenth century. As a result, those events underscored the necessity both of having an army that was suitable for taking the war to the enemy, and of coming to terms with the changing demands of land warfare at a time when the Royal Navy was considered to be the country's first line of defence.

War, the great bringer of change, meant that lessons had to be learned, and this was often a fraught process. The great battles – Dettingen and Fontenoy, as well as Culloden – had reinforced the necessity of discipline and the devastating effect of sustained volley fire from well-trained infantrymen. Logistics and the close support of warships were also important, but it was now obvious that the army had to be flexible enough both to mount regular operations against a major continental rival and to be capable of coping with irregular operations against any remaining Jacobite threat in Scotland – or indeed in any other part of Britain.

Those were the pressing needs which Cumberland took with him when he returned to London en route to renewing his responsibilities as captain-general in Flanders. As he knew only too well from his recent military experience, there was much work to be done if, having learned the lessons from the Jacobite campaign, the army was to be reformed to meet the new challenges that lay ahead. Another factor also intruded: the need to create an 'American Army' capable of operating against French and native American forces in North America, as it was already clear that a future conflict with France would also be fought on the other side of the Atlantic – in Canada, on the eastern seaboard and in the Caribbean.[1] Soldiers fighting there would have to be capable of operating in physical extremes ranging from the bitter winter cold of Nova Scotia to the heat and stinks of the West Indies. In short, Cumberland was faced by the need to introduce reforms which would create an army able to defend the British homeland from internal and external attack, while mounting coalition operations in Europe and meeting the challenge of fighting in North America.

Generals are frequently berated for a tendency to continually fight the last war. But in Cumberland's case he had to take cognisance of what he had experienced during the Jacobite campaign, for as Newcastle told friends the Scots might be a nuisance but 'we must consider that they are within our island.'[2] This was no shallow understatement; there was a pressing need to ensure that there should never again be a Jacobite revival. To this end, in the period following the Jacobite defeat at Culloden, the Highlands of Scotland had become occupied territory under the control of the British Army, whose soldiers were not only responsible for general policing but also for implementing the new legislation aimed at reducing the region's existing autonomy and suppressing possible future subversion. This was a completely new role for them, one which required fresh thinking.

In the autumn of 1747, the operational tempo in Scotland was eased after a fresh pardon was issued to all those who had supported the Jacobite rebellion without taking up arms or fighting in Prince Charles's army. But this did not mark a significant slackening of overall pressure on the clans. While the measure reduced the need to mount frequent counter-insurgency operations, the army remained a visible and unpopular presence north of the Highland line, operating mainly in a law enforcement role. To support the deployment of up to eight infantry regiments, the programme of road and bridge building begun by Wade was continued and enhanced; between 1746 and 1767 some 750 miles of roads would be constructed under the direction of the Irish-born military engineer Major William Caulfield, a grandson of Viscount Charlemont and erstwhile quartermaster to Sir John Cope. All this progress aided military communications and improved the infrastructure of the Highlands, but the programme was also a powerful manifestation of the benefits of what became known as 'heavenly Hanoverianism' – a self-conscious attempt by the Scottish intelligentsia and upper classes to embrace the advantages of the union with England and to equate cultural and economic progress with absolute loyalty to the house of Hanover. This was accompanied by a tendency to refer not to Scotland but to what was increasingly spoken of as 'North Britain'.[3]

In this brave new world there was no more pungent symbol of royal power than the construction of Fort George at Ardersier outside Inverness. Built within two decades of Culloden, it was conceived as the main garrison fortress in the Highlands, and had accommodation for two infantry battalions and additional staff officers (some 2000 men) and an awesome armament of over eighty artillery pieces. By the time it opened in 1769 the Jacobite threat had all but vanished, but the huge edifice survives as a reminder of the government's determination to crush Jacobite sympathies in the Highlands and to deter its inhabitants from ever again rising in rebellion against the Crown. The message was clear: the British government had it within its power to put down any attempted uprising, and the people of the Highlands must either conform to the new order or accept an enforced change to the way they led their lives.

The army, the instrument of government power, had not always been a popular institution, north or south of the border. Partly due to the memory of the rule of Cromwell's major-generals during the 1650s, it had been held in low esteem for most of its existence and the concept of a standing force was widely feared as a possible threat to the civil liberties of ordinary people. In fact that very existence was precarious. Each year parliament debated the terms of the Mutiny Act – the legislation which permitted a standing army – and on each occasion there was extensive discussion on the annual defence estimates, which had already been pared to avoid the impression of creating a military machine. Inevitably at every level of society this concern about the precise role of the army bred tensions which were evident throughout the eighteenth century and were exacerbated in time of peace when its infantry regiments were effectively used as a police force.

Recruitment had always caused difficulties, being unpopular and resented in the wider civilian community. Military matters, moreover, were low on the government's agenda. The result was that many infantry regiments were undermanned, badly trained and generally not fit for purpose. The deployment in Flanders had shown up serious deficiencies in the army's organisation, not least in its expeditionary capabilities and its capacity to operate in continental Europe. This was in marked contrast to the successes enjoyed by the great Duke of Marlborough at the beginning of the eighteenth century during the War of the Spanish Succession (1701–14), where his victories at Blenheim, Ramillies, Oudenarde and Malplaquet destroyed the myth of French invincibility and reinforced his reputation as Britain's greatest soldier.

There was also some nervousness about the structure of the army. Its infantry regiments owed their allegiance to the monarch, but they were in effect proprietary businesses owned by their commanding colonel and managed for him by civilian agents, described as 'insignificant figures mere *commis* [deputies] to the senior officers who chose them'.[4] Line infantry regiments were known by their colonel's name, and all officers invested in the regiment by purchasing their commissions or by raising recruits in return for rank. Additional sums were found from any surpluses from the funds provided by government for feeding and equipping the rank and file. The system was regarded as a means of foiling government parsimony and indifference, but as a recent historian of the politics of the British Army has argued, 'it was also of course an excuse for peculation, corruption, and misappropriation.'[5] As a result, the army was both an instrument of state and a private business concern which varied in size and readiness according to the government's needs.

In the wake of Culloden, however, the presence of the army was broadly welcomed by a public which had been greatly alarmed by the possibility of a Jacobite success and the imposition of Catholic rule should the Stuarts have returned to the throne. Its determination to control the Highlands gave the army tremendous authority and bolstered its national standing across Britain. The victory also reinforced Cumberland's personal authority by giving him a voice in determining Britain's defence policy both at home and abroad at a time when the only initiatives for reform tended to come not from parliament but from the Crown.[6] Much of that allure rubbed off on those who had served with him in Scotland, some of whom had pertinent ideas about what should be done to reform the country by involving the army in the process.

Amongst the most influential of Cumberland's senior officers was Humphrey Bland, who succeeded Albemarle as commander-in-chief in Scotland on 17 September 1747 following a short posting to Flanders, where he served as second-in-command to Hawley. He retained the Scottish command until 1756, when illness forced him to retire temporarily, while during that period he also held the colonelcy of the 1st Dragoon Guards and in 1749 occupied the post of governor of Gibraltar.

Bland was one of the most interesting and unconventional army officers of his day. The earlier publication of his drill book had given him enormous prestige and this had brought him to royal attention. It also gave him considerable authority within the army, and he seems to have had the happy knack of making friends with people who were themselves persons of influence. However, Bland had little time or sympathy for the Highlands and its inhabitants, whom he thought backward, primitive and, above all, priest-ridden, so much so that in the immediate aftermath of Culloden he had been particularly zealous in ordering the arrest of Catholic and Episcopalian clergy. At one point he circulated an order to his officers claiming that the Catholic and Episcopalian churches had instilled 'into the minds of the people Popish principles, contempt of the law, and disobedience to his Majesty's mild and merciful government' and that therefore their activities had to be curbed.[7] As a corollary of this enthusiasm for crushing all signs of popery, Bland was intensely interested in the promotion of Presbyterianism as a means of reforming the Highlands. His fascination was both practical and bookish. While acting as commander-in-chief Bland made constant reference in his correspondence to the previous occupation of the Scottish Highlands in the wake of Oliver Cromwell's invasion in 1650, when for the first time since the fourteenth century Scotland had been conquered and a political union with its southern neighbour had been imposed.

Cromwell had made the move to protect his own position and to prevent any recrudescence of support for the Stuart cause, especially in the Highlands where backing for the Jacobites was as strong as it was in Bland's time. In 1652 those fears had been realised when the Earl of Glencairn mounted a pro-Jacobite rebellion in support of the future King Charles II and Cromwell was forced to deal with the Highland problem, first through General Robert Lilburne and then through General George Monck, both tried and tested parliamentary soldiers. The Cromwellian tactics were simple but effective: the Lowlands were kept quiet and secure while the Highlands were cut off to prevent attacks being made from them. At the same time small mobile garrisons were stationed at key points in the upland areas to prevent any insurrection from spreading. English forces then spent the summer months sweeping up isolated pockets of resistance, tightening the net around the main lines of communication and, as Monck told Cromwell, 'reducing the Highlands' – shorthand for bringing it under strict control and crushing the remaining Jacobite centres of resistance.[8] Bland's only cavil was that the Cromwellian occupation had been too short and that once Monck's forces, never more than 18,000 in number, left Scotland at the time of the Restoration, the Highlanders had reverted to their 'natural barbarity'.[9]

Throughout 1747 Cromwell's name kept cropping up in Bland's correspondence with Newcastle, and the idea of using Presbyterian influence backed by military power to pacify the Highlands was central to discussions he had with many of Edinburgh's leading politicians and jurists (often one and the same thing) during his two periods in command in Scotland. One of his closest confidants was Andrew Fletcher, Lord Milton, whose uncle was Andrew Fletcher of Saltoun, a political theorist commonly known as 'The Patriot' on account of his opposition to the Act of Union of 1707. Milton had been appointed Lord Justice Clerk in 1735 and used his position to become one of the most powerful figures in Scottish politics, so much so that it was said of him that he had 'the charge of superintending elections, which he considered as his master-piece'.[10] In his role as the senior judge responsible for overseeing the country's criminal judiciary, Milton was especially active in the wake of the Jacobite rebellion. To him fell the responsibility of preparing evidence for trials, smoothing relations between military and civil authorities and organising the ships for prison-ers sentenced to transportation. As a long-standing opponent of Jacobitism it was a task which gave him much satisfaction; it also brought him increasingly to the attention of the government, who warmed to his no-nonsense approach in dealing with the remain-ing Jacobite threat.

Bland, too, felt that he had found a fellow spirit in Milton and was soon a regular visitor at his elegant residence, Brunstane House, which stood on the eastern outskirts of Edinburgh. Out of their convivial and earnest discussions came a paper entitled 'Proposals for Civilising the Highlands' which appeared in December 1747; while its ideas were never fully implemented, the paper was influ-ential in determining the direction of government policy at the time. Earlier, in a letter to Newcastle of 17 April, Milton had given a strong hint about the methods which he and Bland recommended should form the basis of government policy.

It is to be wished that some effectual measures were laid down and followed out to establish the peace of the Highlands upon a solid and lasting foundation, by effectually punishing or banishing those we ought to get rid of, and by effectually disarming such as his Majesty may think proper to pardon, and civilising them by introducing Agriculture, Fisherys, and Manufactures, and thereby by degrees extirpateing their barbarity, with their chief marks of distinction, their language and dress, and preventing their idleness, the present source of their poverty, Theft and Rebellion, which would cut off that branch of the Pretender's hopes, and that handle the French have to distress us, whenever they judge it most for their purpose; and at the same time would make that barbarous part of the Island, hitherto a noxious load upon the whole, become hereafter our support and strength, by the produce of our Fisherys and Manufactures, and the great supply of men for our Fleet and Armys, to which the Genius of the Highlanders naturally lead them.[11]

In dealing with the Highlands after Culloden, Bland and Milton were agreed that the only way to handle the clan system was to undermine or destroy the authority of the traditional chiefs and the power they wielded over their own people. That would entail reforming land ownership so that tenants were no longer obliged to provide military service in return for rents, and improving the economy so that people could understand that stability was preferable to the uncertainties of rebellion. In extreme cases the new order would be strengthened by importing settlers from the Lowlands of Scotland and from England, many of whom might be military veterans such as out-pensioners from the Royal Hospital at Chelsea whose loyalty was already proven. As these men were already in receipt of government pensions, the funds could be used in their future employment in Scotland. In all cases such immigrants would be English speakers and Protestants who would 'suffer no Mass or Nonjuring Meetings within their bounds'.[12] Bland went further, arguing that the peace would only be kept on a lasting basis if the army created garrisons throughout the Highland area just as Monck had done in the previous century. His hope was that not only would these outposts be a tangible demonstration of government resolve, they would in turn attract to their vicinity civilians whose industry and manufacturing abilities would be of benefit in improving the local infrastructure and creating new wealth. Both Bland and Milton were adamant that unless drastic measures of this kind were instituted, the Highlands would again revert to their 'natural barbarity' and its inhabitants would never be loyal to King George II and his heirs and successors.[13]

Others, including Cumberland, believed that the process of reform would take over a generation to implement, so 'deeply ingrained' was the tendency of Highlanders to support Jacobitism by turning to violence and insurrection.[14] At the heart of their thinking was an argument that the army could be used as an instrument of reform to rid the Highlands of ignorance, violence and instability, and that in carrying out that task it would act as a civilising influence for the benefit of all.

Among those who supported the concept of using the army proactively in the Highlands was James Wolfe, who had ended the Culloden campaign at Inversnaid on the eastern bank of Loch Lomond. Unlike Bland, who enjoyed the company of Presbyterian society in Lowland Scotland, especially in Edinburgh, Wolfe had little time for the country or its people. Although he was to be based on and off in Scotland for the next seven years he described it as 'a country not at all to my taste', and in one disgruntled letter to his father called the 'Scotch excessively dirty and lazy'.[15] His circumstances at the time might have coloured his attitude. Wolfe had performed well during the campaign and still enjoyed Cumberland's patronage but his career had reached a point of stasis, largely as a result of his failure to be promoted to the rank of major and his lack of funds for purchasing the command of an infantry battalion. At the end of 1746 he returned to Flanders; the following year he served in Sir John Mordaunt's brigade at the Battle of Lauffeld (see below), where he was badly wounded and had to be returned to Britain.

This focus on the army as an instrument of change having benefited Cumberland's position as captain-general, he returned to Flanders in the new year of 1747 to resume the fighting against the forces of Marshal de Saxe. His new ally in the coalition army was his brother-in-law Prince William IV of Orange, but from the outset there was disagreement between the two men over Cumberland's proposal to attempt to oust the French from Antwerp. Instead of adopting this plan, a joint British-Hano-verian-Dutch army of 90,000 confronted the French outside Maastricht at Lauffeld (or Lafelt or Val), where Cumberland's chances were compromised from the outset. Not only was he facing a larger army of 125,000 but it soon became clear that Saxe was able to outmanoeuvre him. Against the advice of General Ligonier, who commanded the coalition cavalry, Cumberland failed to fully fortify and defend a line of small villages including Vlytingen and Lauffeld, which sat on the slope of a small plateau to the north of the battlefield. This gave Saxe an unexpected opportunity to threaten the Pragmatic army, and he was not slow to take it.

When the fighting began on the morning of 2 July, the French moved towards the villages and, finding them lightly defended, brought up artillery to reinforce the forthcoming infantry assault. Although Cumberland organised a counter-attack it achieved nothing; French weight of numbers and firepower eventually told, and the allied army soon broke under the strain of the enemy assault. Amongst those attacking were the battalions of the Irish Brigade which had fought so well at Fontenoy, and only a determined intervention by Ligonier's cavalry force prevented the retreat from turning into a rout. By the end of the day Cumberland had been soundly defeated; once more Saxe had shown the greater initiative and acuity. But the British captain-general was by no means wholly disgraced, having again demonstrated considerable personal courage under fire. Casualties in the French army were higher (9357 killed or wounded), thanks largely to the superior firepower of the British infantrymen who expended 50,000 rounds of ammunition during the course of the battle. In any case the war was entering its closing stages; the French were anxious to start peace negotiations, and these were eventually concluded at Aix-la-Chapelle in October 1748, the last action being the inconclusive siege of Bergen-op-Zoom which had fallen the previous month.

The end of the War of the Austrian Succession brought little material benefit to Britain. But it did allow Cumberland to return to London, where despite the defeat his military reputation remained intact, especially amongst his own supporters in the army. Before leaving Flanders he was also able to offer reassurance to Newcastle that rumours of a revival of Jacobite sympathies need not be taken seriously. This followed an alarmist speech within the Cabinet made by Lord Chesterfield, who warned that in many parts of England Jacobite sympathisers had been holding meetings and that there was every likelihood that France was again hoping to capitalise on any unrest. Cumberland thought otherwise:

> By the sum total of Lord Chesterfield's speech I perceive that he states the badness of our situation worse than it really is: I allow that the distresses of England and those of the [Dutch] Republic are great, that the spirit of Jacobitism which has shew'd itself in England is very disagreeable and that Scotland is as willing to rebel as ever, tho' I should believe rather too weak in numbers to dare to attempt it without a powerful assistance from France.[16]

Such was the extent of Cumberland's experience in these matters that Newcastle was relieved to learn from him that there was no need to base additional troops in Scotland to counter the perceived threat. However, once he was back in England Cumberland was soon embroiled in a completely different kind of battle.

Cumberland's elder brother Frederick Lewis (baptised Friedrich Ludwig), Prince of Wales, had been born and brought up in Hanover until 1728, when he moved to Britain following the accession to the throne of his father George II. Perhaps it was because he had been nurtured in the care of his grand-uncle Ernest Augustus, Prince-Bishop of Osnabrück, and considered himself a Hanoverian outsider, or perhaps it was a difference in personalities, but Frederick never enjoyed a close relationship with his parents, whose favourite was their British-born second son. On arrival in London Frederick quickly established an alternative court, first at Carlton House and then at Norfolk House, both in St James's, and until his unexpectedly early death in 1751 he was more or less at war with his parents, so much so that it was recorded that on state occasions 'the King would appear neither to see or know that the Prince was in the room' while the Queen, his mother, 'never gave him one single word in public or private'.[17] To compound the problem Frederick was also at odds with his younger brother, who naturally enjoyed considerable public popularity on account of his leadership in putting down the Jacobite rebellion. Both brothers attracted their own adherents and quite soon there were two different camps – Frederick was admired for his patronage of the arts, while Cumberland could bask in his military achievements and attracted to his circle a number of similarly minded army officers.

It did not help that the two brothers dabbled in politics, in both cases to the detriment of their reputations. On entering the House of Lords in 1739 Frederick had allied himself to the Tories, although his adherence seemed to be more about increasing his personal financial allowances than any firm commitment to the party. As King George II entered his sixties and it seemed his son might before long succeed him, Frederick was in a good position to attract political alliances – although one of his closest supporters, the Rev. Francis Ayscough, claimed that he enjoyed 'neither Power, Influence, or Credit' and that anyone in receipt of his political patronage would soon be undone in public life.[18] The prospect of Frederick becoming king was also undermined by the common knowledge that his father had toyed with the idea of handing the British throne to Cumberland while Frederick ruled in Hanover; that too was a disincentive to potential supporters. Frederick had many powerful Tory acquaintances – he was close, for example, to John Perceval, 2nd Earl of Egmont, who worked as his main political advisor and with whom he shared interests in foreign affairs and defence. (Sadly for posterity, after Frederick's sudden death on 20 March 1751, papers relating to their correspondence were burned on the orders of his wife, the former Princess Augusta of Saxe-Gotha.) Far from being a king in waiting surrounded by a powerful political clique, however, he was in reality an isolated figure.

Cumberland also showed that he was prepared to be proactive in the political scene as a member of the House of Lords. In this sphere he was particularly keen to involve himself in defence policy, although this move allowed the Prince of Wales to attempt to discredit his brother as a militarist and a threat to constitutional rule. Unfortunately for Cumberland his own imperious behaviour in the upper chamber did not add lustre to his reputation, and in London there was soon an undercurrent of dissatisfaction with the kind of policies he espoused with regard to the army. In 1749 he sponsored changes to the Army Act which made disobeying orders a capital offence; this led Horace Walpole to claim that Cumberland 'loves blood like a leech' and that 'his savage temper increases every day'.[19] It all caused a great deal of upset to King George II, who could not understand why his favourite son had suddenly become so unpopular and claimed that the feeling must have been propagated by the Scots or the Jacobites.

At the same time Cumberland did not help his case, generating anger within the army when he decided to disband Bragg's Regiment, one of the infantry battalions brought back from Flanders to deal with the Jacobite rebellion. Although 'Old Bragg's' had enjoyed a good reputation in the past, the regiment had not performed well during the campaign and Cumberland wanted to make an example of it due to its 'infamous condition'.[20] At the same time he wanted to retain the services of Conway's Regiment, which was in danger of being disbanded. Cumberland's interference caused offence on two grounds: Bragg's was part of the so-called 'old corps' and therefore a senior regiment; not only was Conway's much junior but its colonel, Henry Seymour Conway, had fought at Culloden and was a favourite of Cumberland. Cupidity was also involved: the officers in Bragg's had paid more for their commissions than those in Conway's and they had a financial incentive for combining in common cause to prevent the disbandment. At the same time Cumberland was foolish enough to admit that he scarcely knew Major-General Philip Bragg, whose career had been spent largely in Ireland. Within a very short space of time the man who had saved the country at Culloden was being condemned within military circles for generating 'the hatred of men of all ranks and condition', and for his liking for harsh discipline and arbitrary punishment.[21]

At the same time Frederick was voicing concern about his brother's position as captain-general, which he saw as representing a threat to his own position as crown prince. To that end Frederick and his supporters did their best to discredit Cumberland as a threat to the constitution. This they did by reawakening fears about Cromwell's major-generals and by claiming that Cumberland's ambitions extended to usurping the Prince of Wales and seizing the throne. A series of scurrilous pamphlets, most likely written by Lord Egmont, justified those claims by comparing Cumberland to John of Gaunt and Richard 'Crookback' Duke of York, characterising him as 'one of the proudest, haughtiest jackanapes that ever lived'.[22] For those on Frederick's side the inference was clear: Cumberland's deployment of the army in Scotland presaged the way he would use it in support of his claims to the throne, and for that reason he had to be halted before his position became over-mighty.

It was a bitterly contested animosity, characterised by the case of Lieutenant-Colonel the Hon. George Townshend, a brilliant if emotionally unsteady young officer who had served under

Cumberland at Culloden and Lauffeld but had become increasingly antagonistic towards his erstwhile patron. The young man was close to his mother Lady Townshend, 'a woman known for her wit and promiscuity, her dislike of Cumberland, and her sympathy for the Jacobite cause', and although he had been placed on Cumberland's staff partly to counter her influence, by 1749 he had conceived a huge dislike of the victor of Culloden due to their differences over the correct use of the militia.[23] Having joined the Prince of Wales's party and been elected member of parliament for Norfolk, Townshend resigned his commission, took up the cause of the militia as a counterweight to the regular army and used his undoubted gifts as a caricaturist to lampoon Cumberland. This he did unremittingly and mercilessly: of one cartoon of the captain-general, Horace Walpole was moved to tell his friend Horace Mann, envoy to Tuscany, that Townshend's 'genius for caricature is astonishing . . . I need say nothing of the lump of fat crowned with laurel at the altar [Cumberland]'.[24] The breach was widened in 1751 with the publication of a pamphlet entitled 'A Brief Narrative of the late Campaigns in Germany and Flanders' which was particularly critical of Cumberland's military leadership. Needless to say, the subject of the attack believed that Townshend had connived in its production.[25]

Townshend's impetuosity and his 'insuperable urge to ridicule' Cumberland made him a dangerous political opponent, but those traits temporarily hindered his progress and his immediate achievement may have been the efforts he put into espousing the revival of the militia as a national defence force. After years of neglect the reform of the militia had become a burning issue in the early 1750s: Cumberland had little time for the militia, claiming that it was no substitute for regular troops as under the law it was unable to be deployed abroad. He had not been impressed by the conduct of the militias in the north of England during the Jacobite rebellion and it had been the lack of adequate home defence that had constrained him against his wishes to agree to return the regular infantry battalions from Flanders. To him the regular forces should have primacy, but as Townshend opposed that kind of thinking the debate over reform of the militia only served to deepen the gulf between the duke and his erstwhile protégé.

Throughout the late 1740s and into the 1750s the question of army reform remained a genuine political issue, inspiring heated debate. Many politicians supported Townshend's aim of producing a new force for home defence, while at the same time Cumberland and his allies were determined to reorganise and reform the army. The two issues were related, but there were differences of opinion about the best policy to follow. By this time, fears about the existence of a standing army had largely been assuaged by the fact that regular regiments of infantry and cavalry had been responsible for defeating the Jacobite rebellion and that therefore a standing army had to be tolerated. However, Townshend and his supporters were opposed to any reorganisation or expansion of regular forces which owed their loyalty to the Crown and which the monarch could use as a means of patronage to reward his supporters. That made the militia a viable alternative as a supplementary force for home defence which would then allow the regulars to serve abroad. There was also the undoubted fact that a reformed and enlarged militia would be cheaper to maintain than a reformed and enlarged standing army.

Even so, despite Townshend's campaign the government was tepid about the proposals and in 1745 and 1752 Militia Bills failed to gain any support in the House of Commons. It was not until later in the decade, in 1757, that a bill was finally enacted to create a part-time force whereby each year every parish in England and Wales had to draw up lists of adult males, and to hold a ballot to choose those who would serve in the militia. While this embodied the ancient English principle of a citizen's duty to defend the realm, it was effectively a form of conscription and quickly became unpopular.

At the conclusion of a conflict, the government will generally take the opportunity to reduce expenditure on the army and the navy, and 1748 was no exception. Following the Treaty of Aix-la-Chapelle, which had concluded the War of the Austrian Succession, the army disbanded ten infantry regiments, leaving three regiments of foot guards and forty-nine line infantry regiments. The cavalry was left with three regiments of horse guards and fourteen regiments of dragoons or dragoon guards. The strength of the army was fixed at 30,000, two-thirds of whom would serve at home while one-third was earmarked for service in the colonies, mainly in North America, Gibraltar and Minorca.

The reductions in strength could have been a recipe for chaos – soldiers rarely like change and the cuts were unpopular – but Cumberland proved to be equal to the task of restoring order and imposing a sense of discipline within the service. Already known as something of a martinet, he decided that the army needed to be reorganised along strict and coherent lines to give it a sense of shape and to instil fresh pride amongst the officers and men. Fortunately he enjoyed the support of King George II and his top-to-bottom reform programme proved to be inclusive and radical. It was backed by an insistence on basing each decision on disciplinary factors at all levels, but as Horace Walpole noted Cumberland was 'as intent on establishing the form of spatter-dashes [gaiters] and cockades as on taking a town or securing an advantageous situation'.[26]

His most important innovation, and in many respects the true monument of his time as captain-general, was the reform of the regimental system, a process which straddled the Battle of Culloden. Despite the vociferous opposition to the notion of a standing army which had continued apace during the years of Robert Walpole's 'long peace' – the period following the end of Marlborough's campaigns and the War of Jenkins' Ear of 1739 – the army had continued to grow in size. However, to some critics such as the Earl of Granard who had served as a lieutenant-general, it had also been 'growing old in idleness and routine' and was badly in need of change. Sensibly, Cumberland and his father had started with the regiments, recognising that the proprietary system of ownership by colonels was detrimental to good order and uniformity. The first change had already come in 1743, three years before Culloden, when it was ordered that each 'marching regiment' of infantry should carry a King's Colour, the Union flag, as well as a Second Colour consisting of the regiment's facings (uniform lining, usually blue, buff, green or white) and a Union flag in the upper canton.

A second royal warrant, issued four years later, dealt with clothing matters and refined the order for colours to insist that in 'the centre for each colours is to be painted or embroidered in gold Roman characters the number of the rank of the Regiment within a wreath of roses and thistles'. This did not apply to the regiments of foot guards and horse guards, which were considered part of the king's household, but it was the first attempt to standardise the regimental system by removing the colonel's right to name the regiment and include his own heraldic devices upon its colours. It also made clear that regiments owed their loyalty to the monarch, another safeguard for those who feared the notion of a standing army. However, probably because the army was involved in Flanders and in post-Culloden operations at home this order was largely ignored, and it took a third royal warrant of 1 July 1751 to insist that henceforth regiments were to be known only by their numbers and not by any other name. On this point the warrant was quite clear:

No Colonel to put his Arms, Crest, Device or Livery on any part of the Appointments of the Regiment under his Command.

No part of the Cloathing [sic] or Ornaments of the Regiments to be Allowed after the following Regulations are put into Execution, but by Us, or our Captain General's Permission.[27]

To give one example of how this new order worked, the Royals (or St Clair's), whose 2nd battalion had fought at Culloden, became the 1st Royal Regiment of Foot under a new Order of Precedence to reflect its lineage as the oldest of the line infantry regiments. It was a neat and orderly system which removed the confusion of colonels' names and settled the matter of precedence in the order of battle. It was also logical. As the army expanded, new regiments could be added when the need arose and would simply be given the next available regimental number. At the same time the first Army List came into being to record the names and service of all commissioned officers.[28] Only one necessary change was not executed: Cumberland had long been an opponent of the purchase of officers' commissions, arguing that it was a bar to promotion on merit, but he failed to make any headway; not only was 'merchandising' too established a system to brook any change but many politicians believed that lingering fears about a standing army would be obviated by the fact that its officers came from a class, normally the nobility or landed gentry, which was guaranteed to remain loyal to the Crown. This was the argument put forward in the House of Commons in December 1744 by Prime Minister Henry Pelham: 'Has it not always with great reason been urged that our liberties are in no danger from our standing army because it is commanded by men of the best families and fortunes amongst us?'[29] The practice of purchasing commissions was not abolished until 1871.

One other reform was introduced. Following promptings from experienced middle-ranking officers such as James Wolfe, regimental orders were changed to improve the performance of infantrymen in the firing line on the battlefield. At that time of the Battle of Culloden the British Army followed a practice known as platoon firing, or platooning as it was also called. Under this system an infantry battalion was divided into a number of platoons or fire units which provided three distinct firings when they were lined up in ranks. Once in action these platoons fired their weapons in a numbered sequence to produce a steady spread of musketry along the battalion's line of fire while allowing the first platoons to reload. In theory this should have resulted in a wall of well-directed fire, but the practice was usually rather different. Once the first volleys had been fired, the remaining fire tended to be more random as men reloaded their weapons and simply blasted off at the enemy, impervious to the orders of their officers or the beat of drum. When Wolfe had temporary command of the 20th Foot in 1749 he introduced a simpler system based on the formation of company columns which enabled the fire to be better controlled. At the same time Wolfe made changes to bayonet drill, ordering that his men should handle their muskets from the hip, a change that enabled the bayonet to be used as an offensive weapon in the charge. Wolfe's tactical innovations were later incorporated in his publication *Instructions to Young Officers*, published posthumously in 1768.

The new regulations would be needed sooner than many anticipated. It soon became clear that another conflict with France was
in the offing, and all the signs pointed to it being sparked in the
North American colonies, where existing enmity between the
rival communities was always liable to lead to a wider outbreak in
hostilities between Britain and France. In the summer of 1745, a
force of New England militia commanded by William Pepperell,
a wealthy Massachusetts merchant, and backed by ships of the
Royal Navy had succeeded in capturing the powerful French fortress of Louisbourg on Cape Breton Island (known to the French
as Ile Royale). This was a significant achievement as the position
was vital for French communications in Canada and had been
recently reinforced at huge expense. In the following summer
further raids took place when forces under William Johnson, com-
missioner for Indian affairs, penetrated into Canada in support of
Iroquois land claims, thus prompting retaliatory French attacks on
New York. Both moves had obviously discommoded the French in
North America, but to the anger of Pepperell and his fellow New
Englanders the Treaty of Aix-la-Chapelle gave back Louisbourg
to France in return for the Indian city of Madras, which had been
captured by the French in 1746.

On one level it was a good deal. India was central to the surrogate warfare being fought between Britain and France in the
guise of their local trading companies, while Madras was one of
the key points for supremacy on the Coromandel Coast and the
neighbouring Carnatic. On another level, though, it appeared
to the North American colonists to be an unequal exchange.
Distant Madras seemed to be 'an insignificant factory' with no
strategic importance, whereas Louisbourg was one of the key
points in North America, a fortified seaport which guarded the
Cabot Strait and the approaches to the mouth of the St Lawrence

River. Situated on the south-eastern coast of Cape Breton Island, Louisbourg was the Dunkirk of North America; whoever held it possessed the key to the sea routes into Canada and the populous colony of New France, which at the height of French influence extended from Newfoundland to the Rocky Mountains and from Hudson Bay to the Gulf of Mexico. It had been founded by the French in 1713 as Havre à l'Anglois and had quickly emerged as a thriving trading port and fishing harbour. A huge fortress had been built on the seaward side, and in time this became the largest European military fortification in North America.

The move seemed moreover to be a sign of weakness at a point when the boundaries between the British and French communities, especially on the peninsula of Nova Scotia, were still being contested. Under the terms of the Treaty of Utrecht, which ended the War of the Spanish Succession, Britain had taken possession of the territory known as Acadia in 1713, but the British were outnumbered by the French Acadians, who had intermarried with the local native American Mi'kmaq people and resented British rule. As Sir John Fortescue, the historian of the British Army, baldly stated the matter: 'The French in Canada instantly took the alarm, and after their unscrupulous manner incited the Indians to murder the settlers, sparing no pains meanwhile to alienate the hearts of the Acadians from the British.'[30] In an attempt to redress the balance, and in so doing to address the growing problem of dealing with soldiers released from the army in the aftermath of the recent war in Flanders, the British government hit on the expedient of making provision for them by offering them land in Nova Scotia (fifty acres per man with an additional ten acres for each child) as well as free passage and an immunity from taxation that lasted for ten years. In return they would be expected to form a militia for the defence of the British holdings, the idea being to create a bulwark to the threat posed by the fortress at Louisbourg. There was also the added bonus that because the settlers were all Protestants, they would be a useful counter-balance to the French Catholic population in Nova Scotia.

Four thousand souls accepted the challenge and in the spring of 1749 set sail for the colony, which had been placed under the control of a new governor, Edward Cornwallis, fresh from his counter-insurgency operations in the West Highlands of Scotland. In that time he had come far, having been given command of the 24th Foot and been made a groom of the bedchamber in King George II's court. With his instincts for discipline and good order, and his experience as an army officer in the field, Cornwallis was a good choice and he was still a youngish man in his late thirties. Following his earlier diplomatic experience and his preference at court, Cornwallis must have regarded this latest appointment as a promotion and a step in the right direction, because he made sure that the commission would last no more than three years – long enough to make things happen yet not so long that it would impede other ambitions. Having landed in Nova Scotia on 21 June on board the sixth-rate frigate HMS *Sphinx*, with the rest of the expedition sailing in five days later, he showed further good sense by deciding to rename the settlement at the harbour of his point of arrival. Henceforth, he declared, Chebucto would be known as Halifax in honour of George Montagu-Dunk, 2nd Earl of Halifax, who was President of the Board of Trade and Plantations and therefore the politician responsible for overseeing Cornwallis and his activities.

However, from the outset there was trouble. The Mi'kmaq people regarded the new settlement as a violation of an earlier treaty which had been agreed in 1726, and a succession of attacks was soon launched against Halifax and other neighbouring settlements at Chignecto Bay and Canso. Cornwallis's initial inclination was to attempt reconciliation at a meeting held in September but the Mi'kmaq leaders promptly rebuffed his advances, telling him: 'The place where you are, where you are building dwellings, where you are now building a fort, where you want, as it were, to enthrone yourself, this land of which you want to make yourself absolute master, this land belongs to me.'[31]

With no authority to continue negotiations, and unwilling to surrender the territory gained in the new settlements, Cornwallis responded to the wave of Mi'kmaq attacks that followed by using tactics similar to those employed in the Scottish Highlands after Culloden. This involved the creation of substantial Protestant communities protected by military power and waging war against the Mi'kmaq people. At his disposal were two infantry battalions from Ireland (the 29th and 45th) and three companies of New England Rangers, a brutal paramilitary force of 'picked Indians [mostly Mohawk] and other men fit for ranging the woods' under the command of Captain John Gorham, who had been responsible for the earlier defence of Annapolis Royal, the capital of Nova Scotia prior to the establishment of Halifax.

Cornwallis used these forces to project British power in Nova Scotia by establishing new forts in the largest Acadian communities, which were located at Windsor (Fort Edward), Grand Pre (Fort Vieux Logis) and Chignecto (Fort Lawrence). The idea was to squeeze out the Acadians and Mi'kmaq people forcing them to leave Nova Scotia for Cape Breton Island unless they accepted British hegemony by signing an oath of absolute allegiance to King George II and his successors.[32] If they did not comply their lands would be confiscated. To ram home the point that the British would not be dissuaded from achieving their objectives, Cornwallis put his name to a declaration on 1 October offering ten pounds for every Mi'kmaq scalp brought in to Halifax, ordering his forces to 'Annoy, distress, take or destroy the Savages commonly called Mic-macks [sic], wherever they are found'.[33]

Scalping had been used before by the native Americans and Acadians and it was prevalent on both sides, but its association with Cornwallis would leave a stain on his name and Britain's reputation.[34] Cornwallis, though, remained defiant about his tactics in the frontier war which broke out in late 1749, often referred to as Father Le Loutre's War after the name of one of the French priests who directed the Mi'kmaq operations. In Cornwallis's view the opposition did not represent a formal enemy but were merely rebels who had broken the terms of the earlier peace agreement of 1726 and could therefore be treated outside the normal rules of war. His thinking on that point was not dissimilar to what had been expressed by Cumberland and his cohorts after Culloden.

Finance, too, was a problem. Cornwallis had been ordered by the Board of Trade to keep within the agreed budget of £39,000 for the first year's operations, yet by the middle of 1750 this had risen to £170,000 and he was under constant pressure from London to reduce expenditure. Briefly stated, Cornwallis's problem was that he had to use the available funds to complete the settlement of Halifax – shiploads of new Protestant settlers, some of them from the Low Countries and Germany, arrived on a monthly basis throughout 1750 – but at the same time he had to wage war against the Mi'kmaq.[35] Much of the additional expenditure was earmarked for Gorham's Rangers, who did most of the fighting, and as the year progressed into 1751 the correspondence between Cornwallis and Thomas Hay, Viscount Dupplin, one of the trade commissioners, became increasingly heated as the Board tried to prevent additional and perhaps unnecessary expenditure on military operations. Dupplin, a stickler for detail, had a reputation for his grasp of fiscal affairs, and he and his fellow commissioners were relentless in dispatching a succession of exhortations to Cornwallis to make further economies.[36] At the same time they were anxious to see an end to the war against the local people and in the interests of future harmony urged him to show restraint.

For Cornwallis the two demands were incompatible. His requests for further military assistance were largely met, less so for an increase in naval support, but he bridled at the constant demands for reductions in expenditure, arguing that the problem of dealing with the 'savages' (his word) could be resolved only by force. When matters came to a head in the spring of 1751 he informed his masters in London that to 'flatter Your Lordships with hopes of savings' would be 'dissimulation of the worst kind' on his part and that he would not attempt to do so.[37]

The argument continued throughout the summer until September, when Cornwallis's health broke and he asked to be relieved of his duties halfway through his anticipated tour of duty. Much to the relief of all parties, his request was granted and he left Halifax for London the following October. The war he had started dragged on until 1755 when British forces under the command of Lieutenant-Colonel Robert Monckton won a decisive victory at the Battle of Fort Beauséjour. Monckton went on to oversee the deportation of the bulk of the Acadian population to Cape Breton and Prince Edward islands; he also renamed the site of his victory Fort Cumberland in honour of his former commander in Flanders, with whom he had served at Fontenoy.

In the sense that the Acadians had been finally removed from Nova Scotia and the Mi'kmaq people had been subdued, Cornwallis's policy had been vindicated, but only by dint of escalating the violence against the local people. By then, too, Britain was about to become involved in a wider struggle with the French over their rival rights of possession in North America and elsewhere in the globe. This would be known to history as the Seven Years War.

6

Over the Mountains and Over the Main

In the assertive and uncompromising words of Winston Churchill, the Seven Years War was fought 'to humble the House of Bourbon, to make the Union Jack supreme in every ocean, to conquer, to command, and never count the cost, whether in blood or gold'.[1] It is not an inaccurate summary, but as with any pithy historical précis it conceals as much as it reveals. In many respects the conflict was a continuation of the earlier three dynastic wars which had overwhelmed Europe in the period between 1689 and 1748, and which in so doing had plunged England (and, after 1707, Britain) and France into a series of expensive and indecisive conflicts. While these had been costly in lives, they had done very little to change the contemporary European balance of power, other than to make territorial readjustments in the peace treaties which interspersed the conflicts.

There had also been confrontations between the British and the French in other parts of the globe where they had colonial holdings, notably in North America and India, with both areas providing bargaining chips in the various truces and treaties, but compared to the fighting in Europe these were considered sideshows in London and Paris. In contrast, the fighting which erupted in the mid-1750s was to be both continental and colonial and it was to bring to a head (if only for a short while) the rivalry between the two countries. The first flashpoint came in Nova Scotia in the aftermath of Edward Cornwallis's operations, which had not only resulted in the defeat of the Acadians and their Mi'kmaq allies but had also heightened existing territorial rivalries between the British and the French settlers across the whole Canadian area.

To all intents the confrontation was a proxy war between the two parent countries. As a condition of the Treaty of Aix-la-Chapelle, a boundaries committee had met regularly in Paris with the aim of fixing the borders between the two communities in Nova Scotia. But it had dragged its heels, and as Newcastle told Albemarle in October 1754, Britain and France were virtually at war without any declaration having been made:

> Every year since the peace [Aix-la-Chapelle, 1748] troops have been sent from Europe to the Mississippi and Canada, Indians have been collected, with which Force they have actually hostilely invaded our possession, drove us from our Forts and are making a chain from Canada to the ocean by the Mississippi to cut off all our colonies from commerce with the Indians, and building forts on the back of our possessions on ground actually belonging to the Crown of Great Britain, all this done in full peace without saying one word of it to us and in breach of the agreement that nothing of the kind should be done until the Commission had reported on the boundaries.[2]

It was a not unreasonable summary of the problem. Throughout the seventeenth century and into the eighteenth, both Britain and France, as well as Spain, had been building up spheres of interest in North America to further their commercial ambitions, often entering into treaties with local native American peoples – notably the French with the Iroquois. By the middle of the eighteenth century a period of fresh French expansionism had begun. On 1 July 1752 the new French governor of New France, Ange de Menneville, Marquis Duquesne, arrived in Quebec and immediately began planning an aggressive forward policy against the British settlers by taking possession of the headwaters of the River Ohio. This would give the French access to the River Allegheny , a vital tributary, and the move was accomplished quickly and efficiently by building a string of forts between Lake Erie and the Ohio valley.

As the southward march continued it brought the French closer to the British-controlled territories of Virginia and Pennsylvania. Not unnaturally this hostile move presented a challenge which the ambitious and hard-working lieutenant-governor of Virginia, Robert Dinwiddie, could not ignore; to do nothing would be effectively to acknowledge the legality of the French action, and being an ardent defender of British interests he was not a man to sit and watch. Having taken soundings with the government in London, Dinwiddie sent a stern warning to the French that if they persisted in their advance in the Ohio valley he would have to take appropriate action 'to require your peaceable departure'.[3] The message was dispatched by hand to the French commander, Jacques Legardeur de Saint-Pierre, at his forward operating base at the newly built Fort le Boeuf in north-west Pennsylvania (present-day Waterford). It arrived in the depths of winter, just after sunset on 11 December 1753, and along with his six escorts the young man carrying the dispatch showed all the signs of having ridden through some pretty rough country. His name was George Washington, a twenty-one-year-old officer in the Virginia militia and the well-connected son of a wealthy cotton planter.

Legardeur de Saint-Pierre received Washington politely enough, but said that he would forward the ultimatum to Duquesne and for the time being would remain in charge of the territory he had annexed. Dinwiddie's next action was to send a small force of Virginia militia to build Fort Prince George at the forks of the Ohio River, where the Allegheny and Monongahela rivers merge, another aggressive move that was bound to encourage the French to retaliate. Their response duly came at the beginning of 1754 when the fort was overcome by a larger French force and promptly renamed Fort Duquesne (present-day Pittsburgh) after the new governor. The scene was now set for further confrontation: first Cornwallis had trodden on French sensitivities by encroaching on their holdings in Acadia and now Duquesne had responded in kind against the British in the Ohio valley.

Having been held overnight by Legardeur de Saint-Pierre and then released, Washington made his way with some difficulty back to Williamsburg in Virginia to report the French intransigence. Dinwiddie's response was to act swiftly before Fort Duquesne was reinforced; Washington was ordered to attack and capture the French position during the early summer of 1754. Commanding a force of 300 militiamen – totally inadequate for the task – he set out at the beginning of April, but was destined never to reach his destination. Following a short but sharp skirmish with a joint French and native American patrol, during which the French commander Joseph Coulon Jumonville was killed, Washington and his party were forced to regroup at nearby Great Meadows (now in Fayette County, Pennsylvania, about thirty-seven miles south of Pittsburgh) where they retreated into a small fort – little more than a reinforced stockade – christened by Washington Fort Necessity.

The idea was to use it as a staging post for mounting a later attack on Fort Duquesne, but that plan never came to fruition. On 3 July a superior French force backed by native American scouts approached Fort Necessity. Following a succession of confused engagements, Washington's Virginians retreated back into the stockade, where a heavy downpour of rain added to their problems by soaking their supply of gunpowder. At this point the two sides parleyed, with Washington agreeing to surrender, although by signing the capitulation he had unwittingly accepted responsibility for Jumonville's death. The following day he moved his small force back into Virginia.

Unbeknownst to him at the time, the first shots had been fired in a conflict which would spread across the globe and involve most of the great powers of the age, with fighting taking place in three continents and the world's great oceans. Called in North America the French and Indian War, the wider conflict known as the Seven Years War would also involve many soldiers who had taken part in the Jacobite campaign in the previous decade.

In London Washington's surrender was regarded as a setback which had to be avenged. Cumberland therefore ordered the creation of a small force consisting of two infantry regiments. One of these, the 48th Foot, had fought at Falkirk and Culloden as Conway's Regiment and had taken part in the subsequent counter-insurgency operations in the Highlands; the other, the 44th Foot, had fought at Prestonpans under the command of Sir Peter Halkett of Pitfirrane, now its colonel.

The entire force was under the command of Major-General Edward Braddock, another of Cumberland's protégés who had just finished an assignment as acting governor of Gibraltar. Except for a period as a regimental officer in the Coldstream Guards, Braddock had little military experience – he did not take part in the Jacobite campaign and seems to have seen limited operational service in Flanders – and apart from Halkett the only senior officer with any relevant military background was the commanding officer of the 44th, Lieutenant-Colonel Thomas Gage, son of Viscount Gage, who had served at Culloden as an aide to Albemarle and had taken part in the counter-insurgency operations after the battle.

Braddock's orders were somewhat vague. He was to sail to North America, where he was to put New England on a war footing and raise sufficient forces from the colonial militias and local native American tribes to recapture Fort Duquesne, thereby denying the French access to the Mississippi and their holdings at New Orleans; or, as Cumberland bluntly framed the order: 'the French shall be drove from their Posts upon the Ohio.'[4] Then, having achieved those objectives, Braddock was to push the French back into Canada before mounting subsequent attacks upon their outposts of Fort Niagara, Crown Point on Lake Chamblois (Champlain) and Fort Beauséjour in Nova Scotia. As happened so often in the history of British colonial warfare, a campaign was being planned from maps in discreet offices in far-off London where distances, not to say waterways and ravines, were depicted in a neat and orderly fashion that bore no relation to topographical reality. It was moreover an immense task for such a small force and such an inexperienced commander; Braddock himself seems to have been overwhelmed by it even before he set sail, telling friends 'we are sent like sacrifices to the altar.'[5] Braddock sailed for North America in December 1754 and arrived at Hampton, Virginia on 20 February 1755.

His troubles began almost immediately. Far from welcoming him as a saviour and offering him every co-operation, the colonial administrations were lukewarm in their response, and were vague and uninterested when he discussed the need for funds and sufficient troops to mount a campaign against the French and their local allies. It was not until the middle of April that he managed to persuade the colonial governors of Massachusetts Bay, Virginia, New York, Maryland and Pennsylvania to support his plans for marching on Fort Duquesne; even then they remained elusive about supplying sufficient funding and manpower for the operation. Braddock added to the problem by being inflexible and impatient with the governors and their staffs, telling them what must be done instead of consulting them – a common failing with British Army officers throughout this period. Instead of listening to them and winning their confidence, he was brusque to the point of rudeness and betrayed contempt for the militia forces while placing an over-reliance on the two regular regiments of infantry which had accompanied him. According to one observer, Benjamin Franklin, a local businessman and colonial official who seems to have acted as a go-between, Braddock also alienated local native Americans 'who might have been of great use to his army as guides, scouts etc. if he had treated them kindly, but he slighted and neglected them, and they gradually left him'.[6] Fewer than a hundred of their number had joined him, mainly from the Delaware tribe; they were reluctant volunteers and were hardly enthused by Braddock's abrupt manners.

By acting in this off-hand way Braddock was neither doing himself any favours nor was he helping the British cause. His orders from London, while vaguely drafted, were perfectly reasonable and within the letter of the law: the colonial assemblies were bound by existing legislation to raise funds for their own defence and to provide support for forces dispatched by London. However, from the outset Braddock's imperious style caused unnecessary complications, and it was not until early summer that most of the main issues were resolved. Even so, one other variable had to be factored in: the terrain of Pennsylvania was challenging, being largely a forest wilderness through which tracks would have to be cut for the main force and their transport. The distance to Fort Duquesne was over a hundred miles, a target that would have troubled regular forces and wagoned transport, let alone the improvised army which Braddock had to assemble. Given the harshness and unknown character of the topography the support of native American scouts would have been essential, but as Franklin noted, these melted away even before the expedition set out.

To put the matter into perspective, Braddock was faced with a demanding task, one which under normal circumstances would have required a great deal of preparation. From a purely military point of view, he had been ordered to recapture Fort Duquesne as a prelude to expelling the French from Ohio Territory, and as a soldier he understood the requirement to produce the relevant forces for the operation. That meant raising and training a joint British-colonial force composed of regular and militia soldiers and then providing the logistics to take them across a hundred miles of wilderness which might or might not be contested by enemy fighters, some of whom would almost certainly be native American allies of the French. Braddock had moreover to arrive at his objective with sufficient men and equipment to be capable of mounting a successful siege. To this was added the political element: he had to work in tandem with the colonial administrations and attempt to forge an understanding with potentially friendly native American leaders, as Cornwallis had done in Nova Scotia.

Within those limits Braddock did what he could to create and prepare a suitable force during the late summer of 1754 and the spring of 1755. His base was Fort Cumberland at Wills Creek on the confluence with the Potomac River, which had been expanded as the final staging post for the expedition. On arrival in North America both the 44th Foot and 48th Foot consisted of around 500 officers and men; these were augmented by local militiamen, mainly Virginians, and by April 1755 the two regiments consisted of 700 effectives. The remainder of the infantry was provided by nine independent Virginian companies with whom Braddock was not overly impressed, remarking that their quality was 'indifferent'. Also under Braddock's command was a party of sailors under Lieutenant Charles Spendelow, whose task would be to provide rafts for river crossings. The naval party was under the overall command of Commodore Augustus Keppel, Albemarle's second son, who had taken part in the naval operations during the Jacobite rebellion, operating patrols off the Irish coast. There was also a siege train commanded by Captain Robert Hind, Royal Artillery, consisting of four 12-pounder cannon, six 6-pounder cannon, four 8-inch brass howitzers and fifteen Coehorn portable mortars.[7] In all Braddock eventually commanded a force numbering 2000 infantrymen, a reasonable number, but logistics remained the main problem. From the outset there was a serious shortfall in the number of transport wagons and horses, and this was only made good after Franklin supplied the force with 150 wagons, 259 horses and a number of drivers.[8]

The slow-moving nature of the preparations and the endless delays at Fort Cumberland have helped to promote the image of Braddock as yet another unimaginative British colonial general who tried to organise his campaign on a European model and paid later for his pig-headedness and failure to adapt to local circumstances. While that stereotype has a satisfying ring it is somewhat different from the reality. Compared to other officers of his generation who had gained valuable combat experience during the campaigns in Flanders and Scotland, Braddock had his deficiencies, but that did not prevent him from doing his best to fulfil Cumberland's orders. From the outset he recognised the problems imposed by the local topography and weather conditions and introduced a number of reforms to obviate them. These included lightening the men's loads by removing unnecessary equipment such as shoulder and waist belts and small swords, providing lightweight cloth for waistcoats and breeches and ordering men to place water-filled leather bladders under their hats to guard against sunstroke. An attempt was also made to introduce new tactics to meet the demands of the wilderness terrain – the main column was eventually divided into two sections. But it was all too little and too late. Basically, if Braddock was guilty of any shortcoming he was culpable of doing what was second nature to any British infantry officer of his training and background: he had put together a force which was comfortingly familiar to him, having 'forged a miniature European army with which to fight other Europeans – the French'.[9] That meant guarding the column and transport with superior firepower and relying on the infantrymen's well-drilled discipline to see off any enemy attack and ensure the security of his ordnance, the main siege weapons.

When Braddock began his march to Fort Duquesne on 30 May he must have been relatively confident, in spite of the qualms he had felt on arrival the previous year. Not only did he possess superior firepower and a numerical advantage over his opponents but he had prepared reasonably well, and he took comfort in the fact that some of his men in the 48th Foot had experience of fighting in the mountainous terrain of western Scotland following the operations after Culloden. Once they were in position out-side Fort Duquesne there was no reason why his force would not be well placed to institute a siege and bring it to a successful conclusion.

The main problem would be getting there, and almost imme-diately Braddock ran into difficulties. With no suitable track through the forests, his pioneers were soon hard at work felling trees and where necessary constructing crude bridges over the gullies and streams that bisected the area, but this was hopelessly time-consuming and it quickly became clear that in attempting to move such a large and unwieldy force Braddock was sacrific-ing time and pace. After nine days' struggle his men had only marched twenty-five miles, and a drastic reappraisal of tactics was required. In order to speed things up Braddock divided his force, sending a flying column to push ahead under the command of Peter Halkett and Thomas Gage, who at least had experience of commanding infantry forces in equally trying topography. He also decided to hold back the ordnance for the siege operations on the grounds that in the event of any engagement with the enemy, cannon would be relatively useless in the dense woodland.

Even so, dividing any force always carries risks, and so it proved. Almost immediately Braddock's column began to founder in its new configuration, and by 14 June his principal staff officer, George Washington, was writing to his cousin complaining that the sheer weight of numbers might produce an 'insurmountable obstacle' for the expedition.[10] By then too the first French scouts were shadowing the British force; they soon noticed that the extended line made it vulnerable to attack as the men trundled on, making an average of only three miles a day. All the while supplies were running low, and by the beginning of July the expedition was reaching the point of no return.

It was at this crucial point that first contact was made with the enemy, when the advance guard under Gage and Halkett collided with a French force on the morning of 9 July, having crossed a ford of the River Monongahela some eight miles short of Fort Duquesne. Later in life, Washington said that despite the ever-present dangers and the hardships endured by the men, the river crossing was one of the finest sights he had ever witnessed:

Every man was attired in his best uniform; burnished arms shone bright silver in the glistening rays of the noonday, as with colours waving proudly above their heads and inspiring bursts of martial music, the steady files, with disciplined precision and glistening in scarlet and gold, advanced to their position.[11]

The advance guard was made up of 100 grenadiers of the 44th Foot under Gage's command with the main body following behind, but no sooner had they entered a wooded ravine than they encountered the French, who immediately opened fire. British discipline stood firm as Gage's grenadiers wheeled into line, firing off an accurate volley which killed the French commander Liénard de Beaujeu and several of his soldiers. Another volley and a determined bayonet charge might have scattered the French, but Gage hesitated and started withdrawing his men into the main body of the force, a move that allowed the French to regroup. It was then that Braddock misread the situation. Hearing the firing, he ordered his column forward and the result was chaos. Far from helping Gage's men, the main force became enmeshed with the advance guard; in the resulting melee the French and their Indian allies were able to take cover in the surrounding woodland and fire at will at the exposed British soldiers and their officers, who responded with hasty but untargeted volleys. As the British casualties mounted, especially amongst the officers, discipline gave way and the line began to waver. There was none of the controlled firepower and steady discipline in the line that Cumberland had instilled amongst his infantrymen at Culloden against a similarly lightly armed enemy. Many of the men at Monongahela had served at that earlier battle and would have been used to confronting irregular forces, but on this occasion their lack of self-control was their undoing.[12]

Braddock was no coward and attempted to rally his men, riding up and down the lines shouting encouragement, but he was soon wounded and disabled. The incapacitation of their commander was the last straw: left without a leader the lines began to disintegrate, and as individual fear was replaced by general panic, men began to stream away from the wooded ravine and the smoke and the terrifying whoops of the native Americans. The field now belonged to a much smaller force numbering just 854, 104 of whom were French and 150 were French-Canadian militiamen. The rest were native Americans who had used their knowledge of the terrain and their skill at field craft to outwit Braddock's stolid infantrymen and inflict heavy losses on them. During the fighting sixty-three British or colonial officers were killed or wounded, while the casualties amongst the NCOs and men were 914.

Much to their surprise the French and their allies had won a notable victory, one which was not only disastrous for the British but had repercussions on the outcome of the operation: if Braddock had been permitted to begin his siege his superior artillery would have brought about a successful conclusion. In other words, the defenders had had no other option but to move to engage Braddock and negate his heavy ordnance and superior firepower before he was able to begin a formal siege.

Four days later Braddock died from his wounds; his last words were reported to have been, 'we shall know better another time.' That was probably true, but he was still blamed for the disaster, and that led to the loss of his reputation – tellingly, some critics have likened the collapse of his forces to the behaviour of the infantry battalions at Prestonpans, even though only one, the 44th, had been present at that battle.[13] Halkett, its commander, was amongst the casualties; the only officer to emerge with any credit was Gage, who had done very little to deserve any encomium other than by demonstrating personal courage during the initial engagement with the enemy.

Gage also defended himself successfully against a libellous attack made on his leadership in a local newspaper and, generally speaking, his military career was left unsullied by his participation in Braddock's defeat. He was also sufficiently astute to ally himself with a new reforming mood which swept through the British Army, largely as a result of the experience of the fighting on the Monongahela River.

Although Braddock had not done anything specifically wrong in handling his force, but had simply followed the military doctrine of the age, it was impossible to ignore the lesson that both troops and their tactics had to adapt themselves to the vastly different physical conditions of the American wilderness. The result was the creation of the light infantry – men capable of showing individual initiative in scouting, skirmishing, field craft and marksmanship, acting in much the same way as the native Americans had demonstrated in the French-led army.

One of the first manifestations of the new doctrine was the creation of the 62nd Foot (Royal Americans), a regiment composed of four battalions of light infantry, many of whose members were of German or Swiss origin.[14] Its creation was followed by the raising of the 80th, 85th and 90th Regiments, all of which espoused light infantry tactics. Of these the 80th was formed by Gage, which at least showed that he had learned something from his experience on the Monongahela.

A contemporary instruction characterised the new light infantrymen as soldiers trained 'to load and fire, lying on the ground and kneeling ... to march in Order, slow and fast, in all sorts of Ground'.[15] In time it became commonplace to add light companies or 'light bobs' to all infantry regiments to protect the left flank (the right being the preserve of the grenadiers), although it has to be said that training in this new art of warfare was often rudimentary and carried out mainly in the breach. It was not until much later that the light infantry concept finally took root in the British Army, when an 'experimental corps of riflemen' was founded in 1800.

In the aftermath of their unlooked-for victory the French took advantage of the situation to consolidate their possession of Fort Duquesne, but they too were not immune to lack of initiative. Instead of regrouping to finish off the British force they turned their attention to looting, while the native Americans indulged their bloodlust by scalping the wounded. This allowed the surviving rump of Braddock's force to withdraw in reasonable order.

At the end of the summer Braddock's command was taken over by William Shirley, the governor of Massachusetts who had been responsible for capturing the fortress of Louisbourg during the previous war with France – after which, despite having little military experience, he had been commissioned in the rank of major-general. In that role he was determined to see action, and in the month following Monongahela he raised a force of 1500 which he led up the Mohawk valley seeking Frenchmen to kill, his eventual aim being to attack French-held Fort Niagara at the western end of Lake Ontario. Five years earlier Shirley had been a member of the British delegation at the boundaries commission in Paris, and he was well aware of the need to prevent the kind of territorial aggrandisement which the French were practising in the Ohio valley. He had already warned London about such dangers, informing them of the need to unite the North American colonies to meet the French threat, and was convinced that a general war was in the offing. There was also a personal score to settle: his eldest son William had been killed at Monongahela while serving as Braddock's military secretary.

As it turned out, the resulting expedition was something of a farce. Not only did Shirley fail to make contact with the French at Fort Niagara, when he approached the position he decided that the odds were stacked against him as French military reinforcements had already arrived in the area. As a result of his dithering little was gained, and he returned to Albany having achieved nothing other than an ineffectual attempt to reinforce Fort Oswego (in present-day Upper New York State) as a staging post for a later operation.

All the while, the political situation in Europe's capitals was worsening. In a series of moves likened to a diplomatic quadrille, a new series of partnerships was gradually being formed which saw Britain lined up alongside Prussia against a triple alliance consisting of the major powers of Austria, France and Russia, as well as Sweden and Saxony. This new alignment ended Britain's traditional friendship with Austria, although Newcastle, now prime minister following the death of his brother Pelham, hoped that it would better preserve the balance of power in central Europe and prevent a fresh outbreak of hostilities between Britain and France. It did not turn out that way; as 1756 began, the world was nearing a flashpoint which would see a determined French-inspired attempt to cripple Prussia in continental Europe and curb Britain's colonial ambitions across the globe.

Fighting did not break out in Europe until late August, when in an attempt to cement great power status King Frederick II (the Great) of Prussia launched a pre-emptive strike against Austria by attacking south into Saxony and occupying Dresden in an attempt to bring the campaign to a rapid and successful conclusion. It was a gamble, and it failed, for although Frederick's forces took possession of Saxony they made no headway in Bohemia. Although to a certain extent the Seven Years War was a repeat of earlier pan-European conflicts, there was one marked difference. Normally colonial conflicts were a by-product of European wars, but in 1756 the potential for an outbreak of fighting between Britain and France was already simmering in North America. Now this needed to be resolved by military means. To meet the challenge both countries appointed new commanders-in-chief to take the fighting on to its next stage. On 11 May Marquis Louis Joseph de Montcalm arrived with reinforcements to take command of all French forces in Canada, while Britain responded by replacing the hapless Shirley with John Campbell, Earl of Loudoun, who owed his advancement to Cumberland. Despite his earlier problems in Scotland during the Jacobite rebellion, especially at the Rout of Moy before Culloden and the ineffectual defence of Inverness, Loudoun had ended the campaign on a high note, largely on account of the good sense and humanity he had brought to the counter-insurgency operations in the western Highlands in 1746. Indeed he had received high praise from his superiors, not least because he had 'kept all that part of Scotland in awe, prevented numbers from joining the rebels, and greatly impeded all their measures'.[16] Having promoted his protégé to the rank of lieutenant-general, Cumberland clearly hoped that he would bring the same good sense and orderliness to his work in directing the campaign against the French in North America. As an added spur, Loudoun was granted the colonelcy of the new Royal American Regiment and appointed to the sinecure of governor-general of Virginia, both lucrative appointments which made him ever more beholden to Cumberland and his main political allies in London.

This mattered, because Newcastle's term as prime minister had started unhappily, and more than ever Westminster was suffused with rumours about his alleged shortcomings. Too late, Newcastle began to realise that the confrontations with France in North America were a prelude to a wider conflict and that the changing alliances within Europe had done nothing to ease the situation. Far from settling matters, the new European order had simply destroyed the old system of checks and balances and had left Britain at the mercy of both France and Austria. In this febrile atmosphere, with Newcastle's ministry becoming increasingly unpopular, Cumberland wanted to declare war on France immediately, and he saw an opportunity for landing an early blow in North America. Loudoun's commission thus took on particular importance. As captain-general, Cumberland had been forced to accept responsibility for the Braddock fiasco; he was anxious to make amends, both for his own benefit and for the sake of new political allies such as Henry Fox, the up-and-coming Secretary for War who had also supported the Braddock expedition and was shortly to become Newcastle's main associate in the House of Commons. (As an aristocrat Newcastle sat in the House of Lords and needed a leader in the Commons.)

In other respects, namely military competence and attention to detail, Loudoun was not without his virtues. Short, stocky and sandy-haired, he looked like an archetypal Scot, and while he added to that impression by possessing a short fuse – 'a rough

Scotch lord, hot and irascible' was one contemporary description – he was shrewd and businesslike and possessed a strong sense of his own social and political worth.[17] Although history has not been kind to him, his appointment by Cumberland was not just about the imposition of political patronage. As Loudoun had proved after Culloden, he was a good manager of men and understood the problems of waging a counter-insurgency war in uncultivated areas in which political nous was as important as military judgement. Above all he was disciplined and trustworthy, and he had a reliable second-in-command in Major-General James Abercromby, a solid if unimaginative officer known to his troops as 'Granny' who had learned his soldiering while serving in the Royals and who was also part of Cumberland's circle of influence.

Unfortunately for both men there were endless delays in deciding the extent of their commission, and it soon became clear that neither would be able to cross the Atlantic until late spring. The decision to replace Shirley with Loudoun had been taken on 7 January 1756, but due to legal wrangles the commission was not finalised until 6 May, when it was agreed that the new man would be armed with 'every power civil and military'. But even when the orders were finalised they were nebulous and unfocused, just as had been those given to Braddock. Worse, the administrative delays meant that Loudoun did not arrive in New York until 22 July, after contrary winds had delayed his passage on board the frigate HMS *Nightingale*. Abercromby had already arrived, bringing with him two new infantry regiments, the 35th Foot and the 42nd Highland Regiment, but before then the French had stolen a march on their British rivals.

Montcalm had arrived in Canada earlier in the spring, also bringing with him two infantry regiments as reinforcements, and he had immediately thrown himself into a new campaign. By then France and Britain were officially at war, the declaration having been made on 17 May shortly before the two new British commanders crossed the Atlantic. An experienced soldier who had begun his military career aged nine, Montcalm was determined to act quickly and decisively against the British before reinforcements arrived; just as Braddock had become enmeshed in local political difficulties, however, so too did Montcalm discover that his ability to act unilaterally was circumscribed by his difficult relationship with his superior officer. Duquesne's replacement, Pierre de Rigaud de Vaudreuil de Cavagnial, Marquis de Vaudreuil, the Canadian-born governor-general of New France, had come to embrace the idea of employing guerrilla-type tactics, a concept that was anathema to Montcalm. Vaudreuil was also vain and adept at political intrigue and came quickly to view Montcalm as a dangerous rival who had to be hindered rather than helped. It did not help matters that Montcalm was not only hotheaded and opinionated, but he also had a poor opinion of the local militias, who preferred waging irregular operations to following the precepts of the European doctrine of land warfare.

Given that challenging background, Montcalm's first move could have been fraught with problems, but its execution was flawless. His interest was immediately attracted by the possibility of capturing the British fortifications at Fort Oswego on the south-eastern shore of Lake Ontario, which also covered the approaches to the Mohawk River. The position had also interested Shirley, but apart from raising a small garrison including regulars of the 50th and 51st Foot and militiamen from Massachusetts, the fortifications were incomplete and many of the men had been weakened by illness. Montcalm saw his chance and in mid-August he took it, leading a force of some 3000 troops, French regulars, local militias and native American scouts which he moved along the lake's coastline by shallow-draught boats. Upon reaching his target he ordered the construction of siege trenches on the exposed eastern side of the fortifications, and having brought up nine artillery pieces he was able to direct fire into the fortifications almost unhindered. The death by decapitation of the British garrison commander, James Mercer, proved to be a decisive blow, and in the morning of 12 August the white flag was run up and the 1700-strong garrison surrendered. In the aftermath the position was looted, while many of the surrendered soldiers were subjected to scalping and other indignities by the French-officered native American scouts.

In addition to discomfiting the British, the French capture of Fort Oswego opened up a direct route from the lakes towards their holdings in Louisiana. Loudoun seemed to grasp this unpalatable fact, but although he ordered up the 44th Foot as reinforcement it was too late to do anything other than guard the approaches to the Mohawk valley, and he was fortunate that Montcalm did not capitalise on his success by attacking other British positions in the area of the lakes. The loss of Fort Oswego was nevertheless a blow to British prestige which could not easily be explained or excused. Much of the blame was heaped on Shirley, who was sent back to London shortly after Loudoun's arrival to answer charges of military mismanagement and financial cupidity – although, thanks to his links with Cumberland, he avoided court martial and was instead promoted lieutenant-general and awarded the lucrative governorship of the Bahamas. His removal assisted Loudoun, who was now free to pursue his own policies within the remit that he had received in London, that is to put the colonies on a war footing ready to oppose the threat of French attacks from the north.

The preferred solution adopted by the colonial assemblies was to guard the border with a chain of forts linked by regular foot patrols. Some of those structures were proper fortifications which guarded key points; others were blockhouses; others still were no more than elementary stockades offering little in the way of protection. On the map they looked orderly and impressive, but as most were twenty miles or more apart they were difficult to defend and offered tempting individual targets to the opposition. Even Washington was not impressed, describing the system as of 'no Singular Service to our Country'.[18]

Montcalm was equally contemptuous and saw in the fortifications not a barrier but an opportunity. He already knew what had been achieved at Oswego and judged that a repeat performance would further undermine local confidence among the British in their North American colonies. It was a fair estimation of the situation: the loss of Oswego had not only caused a crisis of confidence in distant London but had added immeasurably to the problems facing Loudoun in New York.

On arrival Loudoun quickly sensed that the tactical situation in North America was not dissimilar to the one he had faced in the western Highlands after Culloden. The land along the frontier had to be secured so that fighting patrols could control it and prevent incursions by the French and their allies – just as Cumberland's regiments had done at Fort Augustus and the lands of Lochaber in the summer of 1746. That meant that the chain of forts along the frontiers of Virginia, Pennsylvania and Maryland had to have both defensive and offensive capabilities. However, that entailed manning them with regular soldiers, and from the outset Loudoun found that he had difficulties with the colonial administrations similar to those experienced by Braddock.

Two problems combined to make his task almost impossible to achieve. The first was the nature of Loudoun's commission, under whose terms he had been entrusted with plenipotentiary powers and an agreed plan of action while being allowed no budget for fighting the campaign other than the funds that he could raise from the colonial administrations. As with Braddock these were not immediately forthcoming, and requests were met with ill grace. The second difficulty was Loudoun's own personality. Not only could he appear rigid and unbending, but he betrayed a distinct lack of sympathy for the colonists, making it apparent that he found them uncouth, unhelpful and pusillanimous. For their part many of the colonists reciprocated the bad feeling by withdrawing co-operation and declaring in private that Loudoun was a greater threat to their liberties and general happiness than any French general.[19] Matters came to a head in August when he ordered one of the Royal American Regiment's battalions to be quartered in Philadelphia and met with a stark refusal from the local population.

Facing an impasse, Loudoun threatened to use force to break it, a tactic which only exacerbated an already hostile situation by seeming to underline British superiority in the colonies, and the year ended in mutual suspicion and recrimination. By then the situation in London was also unravelling, almost as if events in Europe and Britain were mirroring the chaos and blunders in North America. If 1756 had been bad for Braddock and Shirley (and perhaps also for Loudoun), it had been doubly worse for the Newcastle administration, especially for Cumberland and Fox. The pair had not only laid the plans for the operations on the other side of the Atlantic, for the failure of which they had been blamed, but were also facing a similar reverse of fortunes in Europe following the outbreak of general hostilities earlier in the summer. Even before war had been declared, France seemed to sense Britain's military and naval unpreparedness and lack of direction by reviving earlier plans for a cross-Channel invasion and initiating a massive mobilisation which included raising a sizeable fleet at Toulon. Unfortunately this latter move was disregarded in London, largely thanks to the inability of Newcastle's government to determine France's intentions. Were they building up their naval forces for an invasion or were they planning to send reinforcements to North America?

Too late it became clear to Newcastle that the movement at Toulon was aimed at threatening the island of Minorca, a British possession since 1713 and together with Gibraltar a key to Britain's Mediterranean policy. As Britain and France drifted towards war, a French expedition to attack Minorca was dispatched in April 1756 under the Duc de Richelieu and Admiral la Galissonnière. It was their intention to make a rapid attack before reinforcements could reach the garrison and in this they succeeded, landing 15,000 men who laid siege to Port Mahon. When the danger finally became apparent the Royal Navy responded in the worst possible way. A small and badly equipped squadron of ten ships was tardily put together under the command of Vice-Admiral John Byng and told to make its way into the Mediterranean to prevent the French from carrying out the attack.

Byng had come far since his command of the warships supporting Cumberland off the northern Scottish coast. Promoted to flag rank, he had been in charge of the naval forces which supported Austrian troops in the Riviera and had grown rich from prize money, but he was also a diffident man whose retiring personality was matched by a natural querulousness in command. It was not the best background for what happened next. Having arrived in the Mediterranean he found that a French force had already landed on Minorca and that the British garrison was under attack. Although Byng engaged the French squadron the battle ended in stalemate; fearing that Gibraltar might be threatened, he with-drew, leaving Minorca to its fate.

The decision not only doomed the British garrison, which eventually surrendered at the end of June, it also spelled doom for Byng. When the news reached London, there was an outcry followed by calls for someone to take the blame for the debacle. That someone was Byng, who was charged with negligence and a refusal to engage the enemy under the Twelfth Article of War. He was tried by court martial and eventually found guilty, even though it was clear that he had been dispatched on an impossible mission and had done his best under difficult circumstances. The president of the court martial was Vice-Admiral Thomas Smith, who had served under Byng during the Culloden campaign; by a further coincidence the commander of the Minorca gar-rison was William Blakeney, who by showing the same shrewd cussedness that he had demonstrated at Stirling Castle in 1745 had managed to hold out for seventy days against the besieging French army in the hope that the British relief force would arrive on the island. In many people's eyes Blakeney's sturdy defence contrasted with Byng's diffidence to the detriment of the latter, and his evidence helped to condemn the admiral. No blame was attached to Blakeney, but a different fate awaited Byng. Against most expectations he was sentenced to death, and amidst pro-tests and appeals he was shot by firing squad on the quarterdeck of HMS *Monarque* at midday on 14 March 1757.

By then Newcastle's government had fallen and William Pitt had become the new leader of the administration, a change that was to have ramifications in the way the war was persecuted not only in Europe but also in North America. 'England has long been in labour,' noted Frederick the Great, 'but at last she has brought forth a man.' Known to history as Pitt the Elder to distinguish

him from his son of the same name, Pitt had been educated at
Eton and Trinity College Oxford and had entered politics in 1735,
but did not achieve high office until 1746 when he was appointed
Paymaster-General. At the same time he began to gain attention as
a powerful orator and skilled parliamentarian who had a mind of
his own, so much so that he incurred the enmity of King George
II through his abrasive rhetoric and refusal to support the system
of subsidies for fighting in Europe. The Seven Years War gave Pitt
his opportunity, and at the end of 1756 he emerged as the one
political leader capable of waging a successful war against France,
particularly in North America where the British badly needed a
coherent plan.

Throughout the winter of 1756–7 Loudoun had done his best
to convince the colonial assemblies to provide more financial support, and he was also able to lay the foundations for creating an
efficient army for the defence of the colonies. The supply system
had been rationalised by establishing a centralised commissariat
backed up by efficient transportation and the imposition of an
embargo to prevent trading with the French. Loudoun had also
devised an audacious plan to strike at the centre of French power
in North America, the city of Quebec, which had been in French
hands since the early seventeenth century. The key to any successful attack on the city, which was situated at a point where the St
Lawrence River narrows, was the ability to mount an amphibious
operation, and that meant taking advantage of the brief summer
period when the river was free of ice. For the British that entailed
gaining naval superiority, and in turn it meant taking possession of
the fortress of Louisbourg, which had, of course, been returned to
the French at the Treaty of Aix-la-Chapelle. To carry out that task
and then to attack Quebec Loudoun insisted that the force should
consist primarily of regular troops, leaving the colonial militias to

guard the frontiers. Fortunately Pitt was thinking along similar lines and promised to provide a further 6000 regular soldiers for the campaign, which he wanted to begin that summer.

That left Loudoun in a strong position. He already enjoyed Cumberland's patronage and now he had Pitt's support for the new venture. Newly energised, he spent the early summer building up a naval and military force which he believed capable of taking Louisbourg and then striking at the heart of French power further up the St Lawrence River. When he set out on 20 June he commanded a fleet of over one hundred transport ships and an army some 6000 strong, making it what one historian has described as 'the best-planned, -manned, -equipped and -coordinated campaign in the history of British North America'.[20]

So it was, but no sooner had it set out than disaster returned to the frontier where Fort William Henry, a newly constructed post guarding the approaches to the Hudson valley, came under attack by a huge force of 6000 French regulars and some 2000 native American allies, the latter drawn to the area by stories of plunder as a result of the earlier fighting at Fort Oswego and the Monongahela. All that stood against them was a small garrison of 1500 colonial militiamen and regular soldiers, mainly from the 35th Foot, under the regiment's commander Lieutenant-Colonel George Monro, a Scot of some age (he was fifty-seven) who nevertheless had very little direct military experience.

To the credit of Montcalm, who conducted the siege operations at Fort William Henry, he attempted to maintain European standards of warfare, inviting Monro to surrender in the face of overwhelming odds. With equal credit the defenders refused, putting their faith in the hope that they might be relieved by forces under Loudoun's third-in-command, Major-General Daniel Webb, a veteran of Dettingen and Fontenoy who was however known to be querulous and weak-willed. For almost a week the siege dragged on, both sides taking casualties from artillery fire until it became clear that further resistance was pointless. On 9 August Monro and Montcalm worked out an agreement of honest surrender which would allow the defenders to leave the fort with all the honours of war and their reputations intact. It was not to be. The native Americans under Montcalm's command cared little about European standards of honour and promptly set about scalping and tomahawking many of the survivors. Despite French attempts to restore order and save lives, around two hundred soldiers and camp followers were slaughtered before they even left the garrison. (The incident was vividly portrayed in James Fenimore Cooper's novel *The Last of the Mohicans* and in the film of the same title in 1992 starring Daniel Day-Lewis.)

Inevitably the massacre had consequences for all the participants. Montcalm was appalled by the behaviour of his native American allies; he feared that it would encourage the British to retaliate, and that the repercussions would be deleterious to the French cause. For their part the British were outraged by both Montcalm's inability to control his men and the outburst of what they regarded as native savagery. As for their American colonial allies, they felt humiliated and regarded the episode as another example of British military incompetence. Even the native American leaders felt betrayed by their French allies, who had tried to prevent them from plundering and accepting the rightful returns (in their eyes) of a military victory. The real loser, though, was Loudoun, who had played no direct role in the siege of Fort William Henry but was still affected by its outcome. Monro, who had behaved decently throughout the episode, survived, but died of a heart attack three months later and was buried in Albany.

By the end of June Loudoun's invasion force had reached

Halifax, where he awaited the arrival of a fleet including twelve ships of the line and assorted frigates under the command of Vice-Admiral Francis Holburne. Delays in the Atlantic passage, however, meant that it did not arrive until 12 July, by which time the French had reinforced Louisbourg with a more powerful fleet. Holburne was no coward – and as a member of Byng's court martial, he knew only too well the consequences of refusing to engage the enemy – but he understood the consequences of being outnumbered and outgunned. On 4 August, his fears were confirmed by the return of a scouting vessel whose captain revealed that the French fleet numbered eighteen ships of the line, forcing Holburne to advise his fellow Scot Loudoun that 'against such a force he saw little probability of success.'[21] There was no other option but to retire before the winter set in. After transporting Loudoun's force back to New York, where the news of the loss of Fort William Henry was received, Holburne returned to Louisbourg in a vain attempt to lure out the French fleet, but the venture came to nothing when much of his own fleet was destroyed in a hurricane in the middle of September.

Having failed to make any headway in his plan to drive the French out of Canada, Loudoun was faced with the unpleasant realisation that they now held the upper hand and that he himself would have to bear the responsibility for this reversal. Meanwhile, although he could not have known it at the time – transatlantic communications being slow and cumbersome and subject to the whims of the weather – the first cracks had appeared in the charmed circle which Cumberland had created in the aftermath of his victory at Culloden a dozen years earlier.

7

The World at War: North America

Cumberland had begun the war as the country's most successful soldier, a man whose views were eagerly sought by politicians and who, as the king's son, enjoyed considerable political power; the allure of his victory at Culloden moreover still held him in good stead. He was also remarkably broad-minded about policy. While his instincts and his family's connection with Hanover led him to favour a continental strategy in the fighting against France, he was not averse to supporting an aggressive military policy in North America.

Following the reception of the news of Washington's defeat, Cumberland had been enthusiastic about sending Braddock to avenge the setback. He had also been instrumental in fixing Loudoun's appointment and hoped that his old comrade-in-arms would manage to reverse Britain's fortunes by driving the French out of Canada. There is evidence to suggest that he was upset, even angered by these blows, taking them as a personal affront – especially when his candidates and favourites were involved. On hearing about Byng's failure at Minorca, following as it did in the wake of the defeat on the Monongahela, Cumberland exclaimed: 'We are undone! Sea and land are cowards! I am ashamed of my profession!'[1]

These setbacks also caused a good deal of public anger, with calls for revenge, and it was in this mood that Cumberland was dispatched to Europe to lend military support to Britain's main ally, Prussia. At the beginning of 1757, shortly after first accepting office as the leader of the House of Commons, Pitt announced proposals for the deployment in Europe of a 60,000 strong 'Army of Observation' for the defence of Hanover and in support of the alliance with Prussia. Composed mainly of German combat troops, command of this force was given to Cumberland, but his instructions were vague and governed by the need to exercise caution – his father's orders were to preserve the Army of Observation and at all costs to keep it within two days' march of the French.

Almost immediately matters started unravelling. On arriving at his headquarters at Bielefeld in the Spring of 1757, Cumberland dithered about his next move. His Prussian allies wanted him to move towards Wesel on the Rhine, where Frederick had assembled a German army to guard against the possibility of a French offensive, but Cumberland was wary of taking any step which might leave Hanover exposed to attack.

His dilatoriness was his undoing. Led by Marshal Louis-Cesar Letellier d'Estrées, the French Army of Westphalia crossed the River Weser in the second week of July and moved towards Hameln, where Cumberland had deployed his army on high ground to the south-west, close to the village of Hastenbeck. Having crossed the Weser both to the north and the south of that position, d'Estrées caught Cumberland in a pincer movement, and when the fighting began on 26 July he was able to turn the Hanoverian left flank, a move which eventually forced Cumberland to order a retreat to the north. Amidst the confusion Cumberland failed to provide sufficient troops to protect the high ground on nearby Obensberg Hill and this weakness was exploited by D'Estrées' able subordinate commander, the elderly François de Chevert, commander of the Picardy Brigade, who pushed his men forward on to the slopes and quickly overwhelmed the flimsy defences.

At this point the employment of French cavalry could have been decisive, an observation later made by Napoleon in one of his critiques of French generalship.[2] Believing that the day was lost, Cumberland ordered a withdrawal from the field and did not halt until his army had reached Verden, south of Bremen. This prevented Frederick from marching, as he had planned to do, on Vienna. Coming on top of an earlier defeat of Prussian forces at Kolin near Prague on 18 June, it was a serious setback for the coalition.

Hastenbeck spelled the end for Cumberland. The defeat left Hanover open to invasion by France, although this did not happen immediately as D'Estrées was sacked after falling from favour in one of the many baffling and inexplicable intrigues at court which were such a deleterious feature of Louis XV's reign. Even so, when news of the defeat reached London King George II instructed his son to seek terms with the French, offering to pull Hanover out of the war in return for its neutrality but he was already playing a double game. Under pressure from his ministers, who did not want to upset Prussia, the king then changed his mind, but it was too late. Cumberland had already entered into negotiations with the French at Klosterzeven on 10 September, and had agreed to terms which allowed them to occupy the areas under their control while the Hanoverian army was effectively neutralised. In vain did George attempt to countermand the agreement, which he regarded as a dishonourable capitulation.

Even though the king had played a major part in bringing about this latest change of heart, he blamed Cumberland and ordered him home in disgrace, telling him that 'he had ruined his country and his army, and had hurt, or lost, his own reputation'.[3] As a result of his father's apoplectic reaction, Cumberland resigned from all his military commissions, including the position of captain-general, and at the end of the year was replaced by John Ligonier, by then a full general and Master of the Ordnance.

The promotion came as a welcome surprise to the elderly soldier: twelve years earlier he had been forced to make way for Cumberland after commanding the government forces in England at the time of the Jacobite invasion. Left in command of the reserve forces, the experienced Ligonier missed out on the subsequent campaign in Scotland and the glory which had come with it. He would not have been human had he not noted with satisfaction the difference between Cumberland's reception as a conquering hero after Culloden and his disgrace after Hastenbeck. (Some idea of the intensity of George II's wrath can be found in a letter from Newcastle describing how the king raged that Cumberland was a 'rascally son; His Blood was tainted.'[4]) Even though Ligonier was in his seventy-seventh year, he enjoyed robust physical and mental health and was liked and respected not only by the king and Pitt but also by his fellow senior officers in the army, many of whom would owe their subsequent advancement to his ability to spot and reward talent.

As for Cumberland, he never commanded again and three years later, on 21 August 1760, he was felled by a stroke. He survived, but the mishap ended his military ambitions and he stood down from public life. It was a sad ending to a career which had promised so much. Although he had owed his early preference to the fact that he was the king's youngest son, he was nonetheless a natural soldier. Above all he possessed great personal courage and was well respected by the men under his command. At Dettingen his 'great bravery and resolution' had been well attested, and he showed considerable forbearance in coping with a wound in his leg which left him incapacitated throughout his life and may have contributed to his later substantial weight gain.[5] Had it not been for Dutch lethargy and faulty intelligence, Fontenoy should have been his finest hour – Cumberland had the beating of Saxe – but at least it taught him the important lesson that concentrated and accurate artillery and musket fire could be a battle winner. Once again, too, his bravery under fire was beyond doubt, and if it is a commander's duty to show resolution and self-confidence, not to say courage and unflappability, when things are going badly then Cumberland had little to prove in that respect; one witness recorded that 'he rallied the troops when broken and made a stand which saved the army from being entirely cut to pieces'.[6]

Those lessons were learned, and there is little doubt that by the time of the Jacobite campaign he was a more rounded soldier than he had been two years earlier. However, in stark contrast, his military reputation after Culloden never reached the same heights, and in the later fighting in the Low Countries it became clear that Cumberland was not really capable of managing large armies in the field. By the time of his defeat at Hastenbeck he was a shadow of his former self (though not in girth), and his early retirement from military life leaves a question mark over the lasting reputation of the 'martial boy' whose greatest moment as a soldier came not in the lowlands of Flanders but on a bleak April day on the open wastes of Drummossie Moor within sight of the Scottish mountains.

Cumberland's demise also ended Loudoun's career in North America: at the beginning of 1758 he was sacked on the orders of Pitt, who had engendered a 'fierce contempt' for him, and was replaced by his deputy Abercromby.[7] This was purely a stop-gap arrangement: not only was Loudoun's successor not up to the job but Pitt was determined to regain the initiative in North America with a new plan which involved a two-pronged assault on the French holdings. (It was in fact very similar to what Loudoun had already proposed, but it would entail larger numbers of troops, nearly 14,000 in all.) The first operation would take Louisbourg before an advance on Quebec and Montreal, while a second series of operations would capture the French forts on the great lakes at Duquesne, St Frederic, Crown Point and Carillon – the latter known to the British as Ticonderoga – all with a view to opening up the southern route into Canada.

To achieve that aim Pitt consulted Ligonier about suitable new commanders; the veteran general came up with the names of four men who, whilst not widely known outside the army, had already achieved promising reputations. For the first operation Pitt chose as commander Jeffrey Amherst, a favourite of Ligonier who had served as an aide-de-camp at Dettingen and Fontenoy and was an efficient soldier with solid experience of logistics and intelligence gathering. His second-in-command would be James Wolfe, already known as a skilled and battle-hardened soldier who had served at Culloden and for a time had enjoyed Cumberland's patronage until the duke lost patience with his constant and usually indiscreet demands for promotion.

For the second operation, the choice to take Fort Duquesne fell on John Forbes, another Culloden veteran and previously Ligonier's aide-de-camp, having begun his career in the Royal North British Dragoons (Scots Greys), while the thirty-three-year-old

George Augustus, Viscount Howe, another Cumberland protégé, was given responsibility for assisting Abercromby in the
attack on Fort Carillon. All had relatively little experience as field
commanders, but all were trusted by Ligonier, who valued their
abilities as planners and enablers. Amherst was probably lucky to
be chosen, given that he had served under Cumberland at Hastenbeck, but he had managed to survive that particular obloquy,
emerging with his reputation largely unscathed thanks to his
mastery of logistics and his capacity for sound administration. He
was also relatively young, being just over forty at the time of his
appointment; moreover, he was reasonably well-liked within the
army and had not made any obvious enemies.

Wolfe, his second-in-command, was equally fortunate as he had
been involved recently in a military fiasco. After several years of
failure to secure command of an infantry regiment, during which
time he generally made a nuisance of himself, he had dropped out
of Cumberland's inner circle and become dependent once more
on his old Culloden ally Sir John Mordaunt, whom he described
as a man of 'civility, good breeding and good honour'.[8] Wolfe's
estimation was probably also improved by the fact that a few
years earlier he had fallen in love with Mordaunt's niece Elizabeth
Lawson, although nothing had come of the relationship.

Through this new connection Wolfe had been appointed in
the summer of 1757 to Mordaunt's staff as quartermaster to assist
in the planning for a daring attack on the French naval port of
Rochefort on the Atlantic coast. This was one of many projects
which were being discussed at a time when nothing seemed to be
going right for Britain in the war against France, and it had the
added attraction of producing a counter-threat to French invasion
plans. Mordaunt warmed to the inclusion of Wolfe in his team
largely because he had taken notice of his younger colleague's

revisionist work on infantry tactics and wanted to see them put into practice. It was also deemed useful that Wolfe had recent experience as a quartermaster, having been appointed to the post of Quartermaster-General in Ireland in March 1757.

Mordaunt enjoyed the support of Ligonier and King George II, who was anxious to strike a blow against the French following his youngest son's failure at Hastenbeck. With such powerful backing, the new commander was given considerable leeway in selecting his staff who would help him with planning the expedition; in addition to Wolfe he chose two other Culloden veterans, Edward Cornwallis and Seymour Conway, both of whom had enjoyed Cumberland's patronage and were in need of a new benefactor to rekindle their military careers. Following his return from Nova Scotia Cornwallis had turned to politics, becoming an avid supporter of the Newcastle administration while keeping his army commission and taking part in Byng's expedition to Minorca. The fact that he had been one of those who had advised the admiral not to attempt to relieve the garrison and to retire with his fleet could have jeopardised Cornwallis's career, but at the subsequent court of inquiry he was absolved of any blame and his prospects seem not to have suffered.

Both men were central to Mordaunt's plans, with Conway acting as second-in-command of the expedition, and both had been appointed not just because of their reputations but also because of their connections at court.

It was a good team, but even before the operation began there were doubts about the wisdom of mounting what was little more than a tip-and-run raid on the French coast, at the time the preferred option of taking the war to France. Although such raids enjoyed some minor success by discomfiting local commanders and their garrisons, they did nothing to divert resources from the main scene of the action on the Rhine. Opponents scornfully wrote off the tactics as 'breaking windows with guineas', and even participants such as Wolfe and Conway were dismissive of their ability to accomplish any long-term result. When the Rochefort operation was being planned both Conway and Cornwallis expressed concern that a direct result on the port was doomed to failure. They both had good reason to advise caution: such intelligence as existed was out of date and little was known about the size and quality of the French garrison. Even Ligonier, who was bullish about the operation, conceded that 'a great deal must be left to fortune', and the two naval commanders Admiral Sir Edward Hawke and Vice-Admiral Sir Charles Knowles were equally unhappy about the prospects.[9]

After numerous delays the force sailed from the Isle of Wight on 6 September and arrived off Rochefort a fortnight later. For what was in essence a raiding force it was quite substantial – thirty-one warships, forty-nine transports and ten infantry battalions – but it soon became apparent that it was quite inadequate for mounting a serious assault on a sizeable and heavily defended French fortress. Although Mordaunt managed to seize the Ile d'Aix at the mouth of the River Charente, it was clear to the sailors in the party that any landing was impractical due to the shallow waters of the estuary and the dangers posed by the prevailing westerly winds. Other possibilities were considered, including a night attack – an option favoured by Conway – but with the end of summer approaching Hawke and Knowles were unhappy about keeping their ships in an isolated position. On 1 October the decision was taken to abandon the expedition and to return home.

Coming on top of the earlier setbacks – Braddock's at Monongahela and Cumberland's at Hastenbeck – this latest reversal was an added blow to British pride, and King George II was furious.

Mordaunt was acquitted at the subsequent court martial, but he never served again in a senior capacity before his death in 1780. Conway and Cornwallis had their names struck off the Army's list of staff officers for 1758; only Wolfe managed to escape censure. (In response to Ligonier's comment that at least Conway had tried to convince his colleagues to take part in a subsidiary attack on Fort Fouras, George II responded: 'Yes ... *après dîner la moutarde.*')[10]

In October, despite his involvement in the Rochefort raid, Wolfe was promoted to the brevet rank of colonel and given command of the 2nd battalion of the 20th Foot, an important step up the ladder which, as he told his father, 'at this time is more to be prized than any other, because it carries with it a favourable appearance as to my conduct upon this late expedition'.[11] This was the breakthrough he had been seeking and he was determined to put it to good effect, having gained his first experience of taking part in combined operations. Being a restlessly intelligent man, it would have been unusual if he had not noted the problems in getting soldiers and equipment ashore to mount attacks on prearranged targets, and a letter to his old friend William Rickson showed that he had learned from the failure:

> I have found that an admiral should endeavour to run into an enemy's port immediately after he appears before it; that he should anchor the transport ships and frigates as close as can be to land; that he should reconnoitre and observe it as quick as possible, and lose no time in getting the troops on shore; that previous directions should be given in respect of landing the troops, and a proper disposition made for the boats of all sorts, appointing leaders and fit persons for conducting the various divisions.[12]

As Wolfe was to demonstrate in Canada, the experience of amphibious operations would stand him in good stead. The following year his brevet rank became substantive and on 21 April 1758 he took over command of the 67th Foot. This was the moment when Ligonier decided to promote him to the local rank of brigadier-general and to post him to join Amherst in North America, a rapid and not inconsiderable change in his fortunes.

The campaigning season in North America opened in the summer of 1758 with Abercromby still in charge to lead the assault on Fort Carillon, where the relatively small French garrison was under Montcalm's command. From the outset, though, it seemed as if this expedition was going to be dogged by the same bad luck which had attended the earlier forays in Ohio territory. At the beginning of July Abercromby assembled his force beside the wreckage of Fort William Henry, where they boarded a huge fleet of whalers and shallow draft barges (*bateaux*) to transport them to Fort Carillon. All went smoothly, but when the advance guard began the approach march to the fort it was ambushed by a French force, and in the confusion Lord Howe was killed by a stray (or well-aimed) musket ball. Although Howe was the only casualty, his death cast 'a great damp on the army'; even in the short time he had been in North America he had made an impression on everyone on account of his energy and commitment.[13] Worse was to follow: Abercromby seemed incapable of imposing order on the survivors, and a day was wasted before they regrouped to prepare for an assault on the fort, which lay only two miles distant from the place of ambush.

All this activity and the subsequent delay played into Montcalm's hands. Not only had he been alerted to the British presence but he was able to strengthen the defences of the fort. It was a chance he did not let slip: trees were chopped down on the landward side across the promontory, about a mile from the fort, to give an open field of fire and at the same time the timber was used to create new defences. However, thanks to British naval supremacy in the Atlantic, where Hawke had destroyed a French supply fleet in the Basque Roads on 4 April, the British forces had received reinforcements and the French were badly outnumbered. At his disposal at Fort Carillon Montcalm could only call on the services of some 3500 infantrymen, and even before the expedition set out his sole remaining option was to strengthen his defences against the threat posed by the British artillery, which would be a key factor in any siege. The British commander also possessed superiority in his infantry forces, which had been slowly building up as a result of Pitt's determination to pursue a more active strategy against the French. In addition to two battalions of the Royal American Regiment, he had five battalions of line infantry – the 27th, 44th, 46th, 55th and the recently arrived 42nd Highlanders, the first Scottish Highland regiment to serve in North America. There were also militia companies from Connecticut, Massachusetts, New York, New Jersey and Rhode Island, as well as Rogers Rangers, a scouting force raised by an irascible frontiersman called Robert Rogers, a soldier of Irish origin who gained great celebrity on account of his skills at field craft.

This brought the total up to 15,390 effectives, the single biggest British force to be put into the field in North America. Of these only 6337 were British regular soldiers; the rest were New England militiamen who were described by John Forbes in a letter to the War Office as 'an extream [sic] bad Collection of broken Innkeepers, Horse Jockeys & Indian traders, and . . . the Men under them are a direct Copy of their Officers, nor can it be otherwise, as they are a gathering from the scum of the worst people in every Country'.[14]

However, Abercromby was well served by his field commanders, amongst whom were Thomas Gage and William Haviland, an experienced regimental officer who had served as Blakeney's aide during the Jacobite campaign. Both were veterans of Culloden and the subsequent pacification operations and both were experienced in handling light infantry forces in frontier warfare. The regular infantry battalions and their officers were also sound. In command of the 42nd was Lieutenant-Colonel Francis Grant, a favourite nephew of Simon Fraser, Lord Lovat, the prominent Jacobite supporter who had been one of four Scottish peers executed in the aftermath of the rebellion. Grant had been commissioned in the regiment at its founding in 1739 and had fought with it at Fontenoy before it returned to England as a home defence force on the Kent coast during the Jacobite rebellion. Like most officers in the regiment, Grant had a Highland background but was a government supporter and Hanoverian loyalist who had had little difficulty in opposing Prince Charles Edward Stuart's rebellion.

His regiment landed in New York in June 1756 and made an immediate impression on the local people, who 'flocked from all quarters to see the strangers' as they marched in their kilts through Albany. The 42nd wore a uniform based on Scottish Highland dress – 'a scarlet jacket and waistcoat with buff facings and white lace', together with 'a tartan plaid of twelve yards plaited round the middle of the body, the upper part being fixed on the left shoulder ready to be thrown loose, and wrapped over both shoulders and firelock in weather' – but they were fully integrated into the British military establishment at a time when regiments of their type were a novelty.[15] At the time, too, they were very different from the clan soldiers who had served in the Jacobite army, being composed of men who – like their commander – were staunchly pro-Hanoverian and opposed to the claims of the House of Stuart.

Many of the rank and file were also 'of a higher station in society than that from which soldiers in general were raised; cadets of gentlemen's families, sons of gentlemen farmers, and tacksmen [lease-holders], either immediately or distantly descended from gentlemen's families – men who felt themselves responsible for their conduct to high-minded and honourable families, as well as to a country for which they cherished a devoted affection.'[16]

It was one of the better regiments under Abercromby's command, and it soon became clear that the general would need all the experience at his disposal. Following the initial skirmish he sent forward Lieutenant Matthew Clerk, the expedition's military engineer, to reconnoitre the approaches to Fort Carillon, but this was done in a perfunctory and amateurish way, with the result that Clerk came back to report that the defences were incomplete and could be taken by storm using only infantrymen. The opposite was true, but as Abercromby accepted the intelligence at face value and did not make any attempt to verify Clerk's findings, the decision was taken to begin the assault the following day, 8 July, before Montcalm received expected reinforcements. With little further discussion, Abercromby's council of war agreed to draw up the men in the traditional three lines and to march them up to the enemy's lines, where they would begin the assault once in range of the breastworks. Light infantry soldiers would lead the vanguard, but this innovation was negated by the fact that the attack would be made as if it were being carried out on the plains of Flanders and not in the wilderness and rough ground of North America. It was as if nothing had been learned since the debacle at Monongahela.

Due to further problems in co-ordinating the attacks, the advance was conducted in a piecemeal manner under the midday sun with the 44th and 55th in the centre, the 27th and 60th on the right and the 42nd and 46th on the left. Of these the 27th had fought at Culloden as Blakeney's while the 44th had fought at Prestonpans and in Flanders as Lee's Regiment, but this would be the first action for the 46th and 55th Regiments. Although the 42nd Highlanders had not taken part in offensive operations during the Jacobite rebellion – their loyalty was still in question – the regiment had fought with distinction at Fontenoy under Cumberland. Following that battle a French pamphlet extolled the Highlanders' courage, describing a moment towards the end of the fighting 'when the Highland furies rushed in upon us with more violence than ever did a sea driven by a tempest'.[17] The light troops under Abercromby's command were also experienced skirmishers, especially the Royal Americans, and the colonial militia forces were not as unworthy as Forbes had described them, needing only discipline and a workable plan to keep them in good order.

On the day, though, those military necessities were not forthcoming. Following the initial assault by the light companies and militia from New York and Massachusetts, the first lines of regulars began to engage the French positions at around 1 p.m., attacking from right to left, but the assault quickly began to falter under withering French musket fire from the hastily improvised barricades. Without the supporting artillery, whose fire would have suppressed the French defences, the attacking infantry presented easy targets to the French riflemen. In a letter to his father, Lieutenant William Grant, an officer in the 42nd, said that 'It was exceedingly heavy and without intercession insomuch as the oldest soldier never saw so furious and incessant a fire. The fire at Fontenoy was nothing to it. I saw both.'[18] Even when some British artillery pieces did appear on the scene, carried upon barges along the nearby La Chute River which abutted the southern promontory, they were quickly suppressed by French fire from Fort Carillon.

By early afternoon it was clear that the attack had failed; even though a party of the 42nd – led by Captain John Campbell of Strachur, who had served under Cumberland in Europe and had been wounded at Culloden – succeeded in forcing their way over the French breastworks, the ferocity of the defenders obliged Abercromby to order the retreat. During the battle, which had to be counted as a defeat, the 42nd lost 8 officers and 306 soldiers killed and 17 officers and 316 soldiers wounded, the highest casualties sustained by the British line infantry regiments present at the engagement. As a result of its conduct during the battle it was awarded royal patronage, becoming the 42nd Royal Highland Regiment later in the year. Ticonderoga, as the British called the battle, resulted in heavy casualties, according to Abercromby's report 547 killed, 1356 wounded and 77 missing, although the figures might well have been higher.

In the wake of the defeat Abercromby pulled his forces back to their starting point and then attempted to put himself in a good light by informing Pitt that he had retreated in order to avoid presenting the French with an opportunity to advance into British-held territory. The reality was that Montcalm would have been unable to do anything of the sort; on the contrary, if Abercromby had stayed put and retrenched his forces on the promontory, with his superior numbers and the arrival of artillery he could have instituted a formal siege of the French fort and the chance of success would have been very high.

Abercromby would remain in America until September, when Pitt ordered him to return to London to explain himself. He must have made a good impression, because Ticonderoga was not his undoing: he was promoted lieutenant-general and in 1772, six years before his death, became a full general, not an unreasonable outcome for a man who was not a natural soldier.

As for Montcalm, he prudently waited for two days before doing anything, convinced that the British retreat was a feint and that Abercromby would be back. When he was shown evidence of the haste and disorganisation of the British withdrawal, he ordered a victory mass to be celebrated and then erected a wooden cross on the site of the breastworks which had assisted him in winning a battle that his opponent should never have lost. It was the last piece of good news for the French that year: the failure to capture Fort Carillon had not stopped the British plans to take control of the lakes and the territory of Ohio by driving out the French from their defensive position at Fort Duquesne, the target of Brigadier-General Forbes's planned expedition.

There was also an urgent need to retrieve British honour after the setback at Fort Carillon and this imperative encouraged Abercromby to give permission for a second operation to be mounted against Fort Frontenac, a French trading post and defensive position at the mouth of the Cataraqui River where the St Lawrence River leaves Lake Ontario. (Later this was the location of the industrial town of Kingston, Ontario.) The operation was not part of Pitt's original planning and no mention had ever been made of Frontenac, but it did represent a significant challenge – and fortunately there was a man capable of meeting it.

Lieutenant-Colonel John Bradstreet was very different from the other commanders who had ended up fighting in North America, having had no military experience in Europe and being short of influential patrons in the army. The son of an army officer in the 40th Foot who had married an Acadian girl, he was born in Annapolis Royal in Nova Scotia in 1714 and christened Jean Baptiste. Having changed his name he was commissioned in his father's old regiment and began taking whatever chances came his way. His participation in the capture of Louisbourg in 1745 brought him to the attention of William Shirley and for a time he enjoyed the support of Loudoun, who recognised his considerable logistical abilities as well as his capacity to get on with native Americans. Even when that patronage was removed with the replacement of Loudoun, Bradstreet transferred his loyalties to Abercromby and quickly involved himself in the operation against Fort Carillon and the subsequent withdrawal. Even Wolfe, no mean judge of men, was impressed by his abilities, singling out Bradstreet as an 'extraordinary man' who had done his best under trying circumstances.

By then Bradstreet had become convinced that British policy in Ohio territory could only be underpinned by securing Fort Frontenac, a vital cog for French trading operations at the eastern end of Lake Ontario and in the upper Mohawk valley. Before leaving Canada Loudoun had given his blessing to such an operation, which Bradstreet had promised to fund through the sale of furs and other captured French booty so that it was not a drain on the local defence budget. Loudoun's removal from office seemed to have scuppered the idea, but Bradstreet did not give up and set about selling the idea to the normally cautious Abercromby. Under normal circumstances he would have rejected such a risky proposal, but the times were out of joint and Abercromby was willing to buy the idea on the grounds that a quick success could help not only to make good the setback at Fort Carillon but also perhaps to improve his own standing.[19]

Luckily, as a result of his recent fiasco Abercromby had sufficient troops at his disposal and 3600 were allotted to Bradstreet for an operation that would begin almost immediately, in August. As fewer than two hundred were British regulars, the rest being militiamen plus a handful of local Onondaga scouts, it was a hazardous undertaking, but Bradstreet was full of confidence. Not only had the French fort become something of an infatuation but he also believed that a successful operation would further his own ambitions – it was one thing to be praised as an enabler, but he clearly wanted his own independent field command, preferably one that would bring success. Greed, too, perhaps played a part: he was frequently accused of profiteering and Frontenac was a busy trading post. However, in the summer of 1758 the most important impetus for Bradstreet was the glory to be gained by striking a blow against the French in Ohio.

Having won Abercromby's agreement, Bradstreet lost no time in transporting his force up the Mohawk valley towards Oswego, which was reached on 21 August. As they were accompanied by only a few small artillery pieces, surprise was of the essence, and miraculously they managed to stay out of French eyes as the fleet of whalers and barges crossed the lake towards Fort Frontenac. Good luck stayed with them after they landed on the promontory where the Cataraqui River debouches into the lake, and after a short and sharp engagement the surprisingly small French garrison surrendered on 27 August.

It soon became apparent that the fort was a prize worth having. The storehouses were full of pelts, all manner of clothing, vast quantities of food and ample supplies of weapons and ammunition. Outside the fort nine sloops lay at anchor in the bay, their presence a reminder of how lucky Bradstreet had been during the crossing as their guns would have made short work of his fleet of small unarmed boats. As for the fort, the most valuable items were seized and the rest, including the buildings, were destroyed. At one stroke Bradstreet had weakened the French position in the Great Lakes and reduced the chances of maintaining their other positions in Ohio territory. By any military standards it was a timely coup; on his return, Bradstreet immediately set about encouraging Abercromby to capitalise on the success by taking possession of the whole of the region.

Clearly such an expedition was beyond British capabilities. But after the setback at Fort Carillon Bradstreet was enraged by the lack of support, and was sufficiently hot-headed to produce an anonymous pamphlet extolling his own role and excoriating Abercromby for his lack of vim and enterprise.[20] The message did not fall on deaf ears, being picked up and acted upon by Captain Charles Lee of the 44th Foot, who came from an influential family in Chester in England and who had been severely wounded during the operations at Fort Carillon. Well educated and highly intelligent, though never one to suffer fools gladly, Lee was one of the few British officers who had any regard for the local tribes; he not only lived openly with the daughter of a Seneca chieftain but had been accepted into her tribe, which had given him the name of *Ounewaterika*, meaning 'boiling water, or one whose spirits are never asleep'.[21] From his sickbed Lee had read Bradstreet's pamphlet and was outraged that nothing was being done to capitalise on the success at Fort Frontenac. Not the kind of man to keep his displeasure to himself – he had already attacked a doctor trying to treat him – Lee wrote a letter to his sister, clearly meant for publication, claiming that Abercromby was a 'poltroon' unworthy of command: 'If our Booby in Chief had only acted with the spirit and prudence of an old Woman, their whole Country must inevitably have this year been reduc'd.' Lee's criticisms probably played a role in persuading Pitt to order Abercromby to return to London in the autumn, and it also gave the young captain a not undeserved reputation for unconventional political behaviour.[22]

Later in his life Lee resigned his commission and fought on the American side as a senior commander in the War of Independence, but he was undone when a lifelong failure to keep his temper under control led to his dismissal by Congress towards the end of the conflict. As for Bradstreet, he did rather better, being praised by Pitt for his 'Success in the difficult Enterprize against Cadaraqui, which he had planned with so much Judgement, and executed with equal Activity and Resolution'.[23] He was also promoted full colonel and later to the rank of major-general – a not insignificant elevation for an officer with Acadian blood – although for reasons which are not entirely clear, but may have to do with professional jealousy, this preferment brought him the lasting enmity of Thomas Gage.

The capture of Fort Frontenac led to no letting up in the plans to seize the other French strongholds. While these stirring events were taking place on Lake Ontario, Forbes was moving slowly, even ponderously, towards Fort Duquesne. Like the other British commanders, Forbes had been restrained by the need to build up supplies and complete the raising of his forces. These included 1400 men of the 1st Highland Battalion, raised by Archibald Montgomerie, an Ayrshire aristocrat who became 11th Earl of Eglinton in 1769; he was described by contemporaries as a hard-drinking boor with no intellectual aspirations. His regiment was later numbered the 77th Foot but was better known as Montgomerie's Highlanders and had served under Forbes in the Fort Duquesne campaign. There were also 400 men of the Royal Americans, together with around forty gunners and 5000 provincial militiamen under the command of George Washington – although Forbes surprisingly did not rate Washington, claiming in his correspondence about his map-reading abilities that he was 'noways like a soldier'.[24]

Above all Forbes was determined to learn from Braddock's mistakes, even if that meant eating humble pie by studying the ways in which the local native people made war. Although he castigated them as 'rogues', he decided early on that 'in this country, wee must comply and learn the Art of Warr, from Ennemy Indians or anything else who have seen the Country & Warr carried on in itt'.[25] Forbes deserves credit for the way in which he attempted to enter into working agreements with Ohio territory tribes such as the Cherokee, Delaware, Mingo and Shawnee, which had previously been averse to co-operating with the British. In this respect he had received unexpected support from Abercromby, but Bradstreet's victory at Fort Frontenac also proved advantageous: not only did it add to British prestige but the drying up of French trade adversely affected the local native American economy.

Forbes's other change of tack was to choose a different route from the one taken by Braddock. Instead of heading directly towards Fort Duquesne, he decided to take a more westerly route through Pennsylvania by cutting through the Alleghenies and creating secure points or blockhouses every forty miles. Inevitably this caused further delays, while there were never-ending problems in handling the various tribes, who proved to be fractious and avaricious in their dealings with him. It did not help that Forbes was incapacitated by dysentery and could only travel on a kind of sledge pulled by two horses. Thus hindered, he decided that his best option was to order a vanguard of Montgomerie's Highlanders to push ahead under the command of Major James Grant of Ballindalloch, another veteran of Fontenoy who had begun his army career in the Royals and who shared Forbes's beliefs about learning from the local native people.

Grant, however, was also rash and impetuous, and this failing led him to ignore Forbes's order only to scout ahead of the main force. Instead he pushed quickly towards the enemy position and attempted to bring the French to battle some forty miles short of the fort, believing that the garrison was smaller than anticipated. This was not the case, and in the ensuing clash the French and their native scouts made good use of the surrounding forest as cover from which they fired heavy fusillades into Forbes's column. In the one-sided melee that followed the British and American force suffered 342 casualties, of whom 232 were from Montgomerie's Highlanders; they included Grant, who was taken prisoner. This seemed to be Monongahela all over again – with the added drawback that Forbes believed it had undone all of the good work created by the victory at Fort Frontenac by 'alienating and altering the disposition of the Indians, at this critical time, who (tho' fickle and wavering), yet were seemingly well disposed to embrace our alliance and protection'.[26]

That mattered, as with the help of the governors of New Jersey and Pennsylvania Forbes was attempting to formalise a treaty which would guarantee territorial and hunting rights in the Ohio valley and western Alleghenies in return for the support of thirteen native American tribes, including the Delaware and the Shawnee.

Any hint of a French resurgence would have affected the negotiations, but the terms were concluded at Easton in Pennsylvania on 26 October, leaving Forbes with a small window of opportunity before the onset of winter. Although he was becoming increasingly weak, he was determined to make a last push before the snows arrived. Fortune proved to be on his side. While assembling his forces at Loyalhanna Creek on the Kiskiminetas River in Westmoreland County on 2 November, he received the welcome news that the French had begun withdrawing from Fort Duquesne and, thanks to the agreement at Easton, could no longer count on the support of the native Americans. Seizing the moment, Forbes ordered an immediate advance on the fort; when his men reached it three weeks later it was found to have been abandoned and the buildings destroyed. As the British marched up to the remains, though, they were confronted by the dreadful sight of a number of dead and decapitated Highlanders, their heads impaled on stakes on top of the fort walls, with their kilts displayed below. It was a gruesome end to what had been a successful campaign.

For Forbes there was nothing to be done but to return to Philadelphia, where he hoped to receive medical treatment before going home to London. Before leaving the wilderness he wrote to Pitt on 27 November, informing him the fort was in British hands and telling him that he had 'used the freedom of giving your name to Fort Du Quesne [sic], as I hope it was in some measure the being actuated by your spirits that now makes us masters of the place'.[27]

The fort was quickly rebuilt, but Forbes did not long survive his triumph. He succumbed to his illness in March 1759 and was buried in Philadelphia with full military honours, far away from his native Edinburgh. His lasting monument, though, was not just his military success in securing the Ohio valley by taking control of Fort Duquesne, but his equally important diplomatic initiative settling Britain's affairs with the native American population in the area. Amongst his final correspondence were letters addressed to Amherst, Abercromby's successor, begging him to place a priority on his dealings with them and 'not to think triflingly of the Indians or their friendship'.[28]

As the year came to an end, Pitt's plan had largely been implemented: while the Ohio forts were being reduced, news had arrived of the capture of the fortress at Louisbourg, following a daring assault by British forces under Amherst and Wolfe. This was the first prong of Pitt's strategy and, thanks to the forcefulness and determination of British leadership on land and the arrival of a superior British fleet under the command of Admiral Edward Boscawen in his 100-gun flagship HMS *Royal George*, it had succeeded brilliantly.

The operation had begun on 8 June under the tactical command of Wolfe and the senior brigadier Charles Lawrence, a veteran of service in Nova Scotia who had served under Cornwallis and was experienced in the local conditions, having played a part in the first capture of Louisbourg in 1745. Under their command the two brigadiers had twelve companies of grenadiers, a composite battalion of light infantry and American Rangers, a battalion of Montgomerie's Highlanders and another infantry battalion of Scottish Highlanders which had been raised in Inverness the previous year by Simon Fraser, eldest son of Lord Lovat but himself an avowed supporter of the Crown. Known as the 2nd Highland Battalion, it was eventually numbered the 78th Foot but was universally known as Fraser's Highlanders.

Both regiments were very different from the 42nd Royal Highlanders, which had a strong Perthshire connection, and they are also not to be confused with the establishment of other Highland regiments later in the century. Although Fraser was the scion of a leading Inverness-shire landowning family, very few of his recruits were Highland born and bred. They wore tartan and were dressed in the Highland military manner, but only 126 lived on the attainted Lovat estates while the rest, some 800, were recruited from all over Scotland, mostly from the cities of Dundee and Glasgow and the eastern counties of Angus and Aberdeenshire. Although most of the officers were Gaelic speakers, they were mainly Hanoverian supporters who had served in the armies of Protestant rulers in Europe and were natural opponents of Jacobitism.[29] There were exceptions, notably Donald Macdonald, a scion of Clanranald, who had served with the Jacobite army in the Royal Ecossais at Culloden yet also saw action at Louisbourg with Fraser's Highlanders. Whatever their background, though, Wolfe had no particular admiration for any of them, having made his feelings clear to Captain William Rickson in a letter from Scotland dated 9 June 1751 while Rickson was serving in Nova Scotia and the idea of using Highland infantrymen was first being mooted as the solution to Britain's recruitment problems:

I should imagine that two or three independent Highland companies might be of use; they are hardy, intrepid, accustomed to a rough country and no great mischief if they fall. How can you better employ a secret enemy than by making his end conducive to the common good? If this sentiment should take wind what an execrable and bloody being should I be considered here in the midst of Popery and Jacobitism![30]

Louisbourg was to be the first major battle for these men, and they were to prove their worth in conditions which Wolfe later described as 'a rash and ill-advised attempt to land'. Not only was there heavy surf running as the men attempted to come ashore, but as at Fort Carillon the initial fire from the defenders was prolonged and accurate, so much so that the casualties were forty-six killed and fifty-nine wounded. Wolfe, though, seemed to be equal to the task of making landfall, directing the light infantrymen with a cane before leading them in a determined bayonet charge on the French flank. This forced the enemy to fall back, and within four days of the landings the French were back inside the fortress facing a formal siege.

By then Amherst had arrived from London, but Wolfe continued to direct operations, which followed a well-honed and well-understood pattern. The fortress covered a sheltered harbour in which five heavily armed French ships of the line rode at anchor as a deterrent to Admiral Boscawen's fleet, but while they were a formidable obstacle Louisbourg was not impregnable. Its garrison numbered 6000 soldiers and was well set up with various types of artillery pieces, but it faced an equally determined enemy who had parity in firepower and possessed the advantage of support from Boscawen's heavy naval guns. It was moreover a fact of life in contemporary siege warfare that the defenders could do little other than hold out for as long as possible, while the attackers had the advantage of varying their tactics to make life more difficult for those inside.

That was exactly what Wolfe did. Having driven the French from their own outlying works, he ordered the construction of trench systems and gun positions and then took possession of a spur known as Lighthouse Point, which dominated the harbour entrance. This provided a commanding position. Bad weather made it difficult to get the artillery ashore; it was not until 19 June that the gunners were able to open fire, albeit initially from extreme range; it took another fortnight for them to get closer, and it was not until the first week of July that it became possible to fire mortar bombs into the fortress. When this was done, however, it caused considerable damage and started fires within the walls.

The first tipping point came on 21 July, when an incendiary mortar round hit the seventy-four-gun French ship of the line, *L'Entreprenant*, at anchor in the harbour and set it ablaze. A strong offshore wind fanned the fire and shortly afterwards the ship's magazine exploded, setting fire to two smaller vessels. Not only did this cause considerable alarm to the garrison by demonstrating the superiority of British firepower – the fire and explosion produced an awesome spectacle – but it deprived the French of the most powerful ship in the Louisbourg fleet. By the same token the incident gave added encouragement to the British outside the walls, and the following day the sinking of the ships was followed by direct hits on the King's Bastion on the landward side of the defences, setting fire to nearby buildings and causing an immediate slump in the defenders' morale. With three French ships destroyed Boscawen decided to act quickly: taking advantage of a thick sea fog, his fleet entered the harbour on the night of 25 July and captured the sixty-four-gun *Bienfaisant*, while another group of sailors boarded the smaller *Prudent* and set it on fire. At one stroke the French naval screen had been neutralised within sight of the garrison inside the fortress and Louisbourg was defenceless from the sea.

It was the beginning of the end. As heavy artillery continued to bombard the fortress, other buildings caught fire; the following day the French commander Chevalier Augustin de Drucour, a naval officer, decided that he could hold out no longer and should sue for terms – the usual arrangement when resisting a siege was no longer tenable for a garrison. According to the etiquette of the day, Drucour had done all he could to survive and had satisfied the demands of military mutual respect to the extent that he should have been granted an honourable surrender. That would have allowed his garrison to keep their personal arms and colours and to have been paroled as non-combatants.

Amherst however was in no mood to act the gentleman. He remembered what had happened at Fort William Henry, where British personnel had been slaughtered after surrendering, and – just as Montcalm feared would happen as a result of that outrage – wanted revenge. Honourable terms were refused: arms and colours would be surrendered and the garrison would become prisoners-of-war and be sent to Britain, while the fortress's civilians would be returned to France. Suddenly, the war in North America was losing its amateur status. Things were getting much more serious.

8

Paths of Glory

According to Pitt's original plans the capture of Louisbourg should have been the prelude to an immediate advance on Quebec to take advantage of possible French disarray. Amherst, however, disapproved of any precipitate action. Even though it was only the end of July, he believed that it was too late in the season for an advance up the St Lawrence before the arrival of winter, when the waterway would be impassable for up to five months. An amphibious operation that year was therefore impossible.[1] There was another reason for delay: the receipt of the news of the failure of the operation against Fort Carillon and Amherst's subsequent decision to leave for New York.

While he was absent, Amherst sent Wolfe with three battalions of infantry to Miramichi Bay on the Gaspe peninsula at the mouth of the St Lawrence on what was essentially a brutal search and destroy operation against the French fishing settlements in the area. Mounted to punish the residents for their refusal to swear allegiance to the British Crown, the operation had echoes of what had taken place in the West Highlands after Culloden, and once again the philosophy and the practice were the same. Houses were burned down, property including furs and livestock were seized and over a hundred men were arrested. Although Wolfe claimed that the work was beneath his dignity, he still ordered his men to carry it out with care if not with compassion, and wrote with satisfaction that 'these miserable people will in all probability be forced to abandon their settlements and retire to Quebec.'[2]

Other than alienating the local population, which included Acadians displaced after Cornwallis's earlier culling in Nova Scotia, nothing was achieved by the operation and the hiatus coincided with the postponement of further planning for an assault on Quebec. It also left the restless Wolfe with very little to do, a state of affairs anathema to an ambitious soldier. Feeling, not without reason, that he was at a loose end, Wolfe decided to make his own luck. In September, while Amherst was absent, he took ship for England pleading ill health – a justifiable excuse, for he had never been a particularly fit specimen and was now suffering variously from rheumatism, scurvy and bladder problems. However, these physical drawbacks seemed not to impede him unduly, and on arrival in England he quickly established himself in London with the aim of furthering his own career. Just as he had demonstrated in his dealings with Cumberland after Culloden, Wolfe was no shrinking violet when it came to self-promotion.

At first he pinned his hopes on Lord George Sackville, his commander after Culloden, a man who had himself been reliant on Cumberland's patronage. In the period after 1748 Sackville's career had prospered, with the command of two cavalry regiments; by the time that Wolfe arrived back in England, he was a major-general and was in command of British forces sent to assist Prince Ferdinand of Brunswick in the fresh campaign against French forces in central Germany that would form a major element of European hostilities in the Seven Years War. Wolfe had always admired Sackville and immediately pinned his hopes on getting a command from him, preferably of a cavalry regiment. He was aiming high, but there would have been no justification for such an appointment, and in the light of subsequent events it would have been a disaster: Sackville would be court-martialled the following year after a quarrel with Prince Ferdinand.

However, Wolfe's efforts did attract Ligonier's attention. The commander-in-chief was not amused by the obvious self-promotion and told him in no uncertain terms that not only was he not authorised to be in London, but there would be no place for him in the forces under Sackville's command. Perhaps to ease the blow, for the old soldier had a soft spot for him, Wolfe was asked to give Ligonier a briefing on the events at Louisbourg. Crucially, Pitt also attended the meeting.

Wolfe needed no second bidding. He had already been busy hinting that he was the real victor and that Amherst had been overly cautious in his approach to the battle, and it did not take long for him to write to Pitt that if there were to be fresh operations in 1759 he had 'no objection to serving in America, and particularly in the river St Lawrence, if any operations are to be carried on there'.[3] At the time of speaking he must have known that Pitt was determined to complete his plans for the conquest of Canada by attacking Quebec, but it clearly did no harm to press his claims for an independent command while he was visiting London. So it proved: before the year was out Wolfe had been given 'river command' with the local rank of major-general, and had been handed instructions to invade Canada from Louisbourg by way of the Lower St Lawrence River.[4] Although King George II was sceptical about the appointment he offered no objection, as by then he had come to approve Pitt's plans to expel the French from Canada and was prepared to back any move which brought that hope to fruition. For the king the capture of Louisbourg had been a good harbinger and he believed that now was the time to capitalise on that much-vaunted success. It may have been during this time that he made his much-quoted remark about Wolfe's alleged mental instability: 'Mad is he? Then I hope he will bite some of my other generals.'[5]

Now, too, was the time to put flesh on the bones of Pitt's war plan. Broadly this was to continue to support Britain's allies in Europe, to use the navy to put pressure on France in the Channel, the North Sea, the Mediterranean and the Indian Ocean, and to expand the army for operations in Germany, the West Indies and Canada. This would require money and manpower; correspondingly, for the coming year, 1759, parliament authorised an increase of expenditure to £13 million, an enormous sum, and approved plans to raise the size of the army to 101,000, a decision that would require the militia to be mobilised for home defence. At the same time construction of warships became a priority.

Wolfe meanwhile was hard at work, his first task being to appoint his own staff and his principal subordinate officers. As any commander would do in that position, he chose from those who were well-known to him and whom he trusted. His quartermaster was Guy Carleton, who had started his career in Sempill's (one of the Culloden regiments) and had attracted Wolfe's interest at the time of the Louisbourg expedition, while his adjutant-general was Isaac Barré, an Irishman who had served with Wolfe both at Louisbourg and during the raid on Rochefort. In time both would prosper as soldiers through their connection with Wolfe, just as he had done well for himself as a result of Cumberland's patronage.

His other appointments were solid but unspectacular, his two aides – Tom Bell and Hervey Smith – being young officers who had also served with him at Louisbourg. Not only did he have to contend with Amherst, however, who cannot have been best pleased by Pitt's sudden decision to give the young brigadier command of the Quebec operation, but he had little luck with his three brigade commanders. To all intents and purposes they were foisted on him without much consultation, and his relationship with them turned out to be frosty at best and downright hostile at worst.

The officers in question – Robert Monckton, James Murray and George Townshend – were all scions of the aristocracy, never a recommendation as far as Wolfe was concerned, but they were experienced soldiers. Monckton, a viscount's son, was already battle-hardened, having served under Cornwallis in Nova Scotia; a product of Westminster, he had also been a member of Cumberland's army at Dettingen and Fontenoy. Murray, too, had proved his capabilities at both Rochefort and Louisbourg; he was also close to Wolfe's old patron Sir John Mordaunt and had spoken up for him after the failure of the Rochefort expedition. Murray was a younger son of Lord Elibank and his family had Jacobite connections – his brother Charles had served in the Jacobite army during the rebellion – but this drawback was countered by his own illustrious military career. Townshend was very much Pitt's choice; Cumberland's former political opponent was now himself a senior soldier.

Although these brigadiers had decent reputations, all three brought with them a good deal of professional and personal baggage which made them less than ideal subordinates. Monckton, who acted as Wolfe's second-in-command, was generally considered to be little more than a decent plodder, Murray had an uncertain temper and tended to be abrasive, while Townshend was not only mercurial but possessed a vindictive personality and a sharp tongue which he used to good effect against anyone crossing him. Nor was he slow to use his new boss as a model for his talent as a caricaturist.

Wolfe and his staff left England from Spithead on 14 February and did not make landfall until they arrived at Halifax at the end of April. It would be June before his first dispatches reached London. On arrival in North America the first surprise awaiting him was that the 12,000 expected soldiers had not materialised. Instead he had around 8500 effectives, leaving his ten infantry battalions under strength. That said, they were all regular battalions and experienced in North American warfare: Monckton's brigade consisted of the 15th, 43rd, 58th and 78th (Fraser's) Highlanders, Townshend's of the 28th, 47th, the 60th and the 2nd Royal Americans, Murray's of the 35th, 48th and the 3rd Royal Americans.[6] In addition there were three companies each of light infantry and grenadiers, specialist soldiers who fought separately from their parent battalions, as well as six companies of American Rangers whom Wolfe called 'the worst soldiers in the universe'.[7]

The second surprise was the unwelcome presence of ice in the St Lawrence River, which had obliged the British fleet to stay clear of Louisbourg and to make for Halifax. There, to Wolfe's annoyance, he found the naval squadron commanded by Rear-Admiral Philip Durell still at anchor. Wolfe was not impressed, not least because Durell's caution had allowed the French to send in reinforcements consisting of seventeen transports and three frigates; these were under the command of Colonel Louis-Antoine de Bougainville, who would emerge as an important aide to Montcalm in the weeks ahead. Clearly it would be impossible to keep to Pitt's timetable for a start in mid-May, and matters were not improved by the onset of thick sea fogs.

While these forces were assembling, Amherst was working

slowly and methodically to raise and equip the forces required to invade Canada from New England. For the first time the colonial governments had responded reasonably amicably to Pitt's request to provide forces 'for invading Canada by way of Crown Point, and carrying the War into the Heart of the Enemy's possessions'.[8] Several reasons have been posited for this change of heart – from a sudden rush of patriotism to a rise in anti-French feelings – but the most likely explanation is that on this occasion the colonial administrations had faith in Pitt's promise that they would receive financial compensation for their efforts. Whatever the motivation, unlike earlier episodes when Loudoun and Abercromby had had to fight tooth and nail for subsidies and manpower, there was a new willingness to support Pitt's requests and find the wherewithal to eject the French from Canada.

Amherst's first move was to send 5000 men north to take Fort Niagara. Under the command of Brigadier-General John Prideaux, another veteran of Dettingen, who had arrived to take Howe's place as the main regional land commander, this force moved slowly up the Mohawk and reached their first staging post at Oswego at the end of June; there they found around one thousand Iroquois warriors waiting to join the British. Largely this was a direct result of the previous year's negotiations at Easton, although the about-turn in policy was also an outcome of inter-tribal rivalries and a perception that British influence was becoming paramount in Ohio territory. Yet another factor was the presence of Sir William Johnson, a remarkable Irishman from County Meath who owned land in the Mohawk valley. Johnson enjoyed considerable influence amongst the local native American people, both through his own sympathies and interests – he had been given the Iroquois name of *Warraghiyagey* ('he who does much business') – and through his work as superintendent of Indian affairs. He was certainly instrumental in encouraging the warriors to join Prideaux's force, and when the siege of Fort Niagara began he used his influence to dissuade the local Senecas from continuing their alliance with the French.[9]

This was quite a turnaround in other ways, for the generally accepted British point of view – Brigadier-General Forbes apart – was still to have little to do with the native Americans. Whereas the French valued them as allies and admired their field craft and fighting skills – one senior officer admitted that 'one can no more do without them than without cavalry in open country' – the British reaction was that they were more trouble than they were worth.[10] Braddock, Loudoun and Abercromby had all been chary of employing men from the local tribes and Amherst had raised that dislike to contempt. Earlier in the year he had written to Pitt expressing his scorn for the Stockbridge Mahican tribe:

> They are a lazy rum-drinking people and little good, but if ever they are of use to us it will be when we can act offensively; the French are more afraid of them than they need to be, numbers will encrease [sic] their terror and may have a good effect.[11]

This was prejudice speaking, but Amherst did at least acknowledge the fighting qualities and shock tactics which the native Americans could bring to any battle with the French. In that sense the assistance of the Senecas was much needed, because Fort Niagara was not an easy objective. Not only was it extremely well built, being protected by extensive outworks, ramparts and ditches, but it was also commanded by an experienced military engineer, Captain Pierre Pouchot, who had been responsible for organising the defences at Oswego. His Achilles heel lay in the fact that he had detached 2500 men to reinforce Fort Machault in the Ohio valley and had fewer than five hundred men inside Fort Niagara: the last thing he needed was to see his Seneca allies give up on him.

By 17 July Prideaux's men had pushed their trench system down the peninsula towards the outer defences and were ready to pour shells into the fort. It was at this crucial point that Pouchot was almost saved by the return of his men from Fort Machault, but this unexpected move was thwarted by the initiative of Lieutenant-Colonel Eyre Massey of the 46th Regiment, who had ordered his men to create a defensive breastwork along the approach road at a position called La Belle Famille. Massey's first patron had been General William Blakeney, with whom he had served during Admiral Vernon's abortive attack on Porto Bello in 1741; an Irishman from County Limerick, he had served as an ensign in Blakeney's Regiment at Culloden, where he had been wounded. Like Wolfe, he had caught the eye of Cumberland, who recommended his promotion, setting him on his path to his eventual rank of major.

Serving alongside Massey in Amherst's army was Captain Allan Maclean of Torloisk from the island of Mull. Maclean had served in the Jacobite army at Culloden; after fleeing to the Netherlands he joined the Dutch Scots Brigade and fought in the war against France. Taken prisoner at the Battle of Bergen-op-Zoom, he returned to Britain in 1750, and following a parole granted by King George II was eventually commissioned in the Royal American Regiment, serving in the 4th battalion at Fort Carillon. At Fort Niagara he was to be seriously wounded. Later in his career he raised a two-battalion infantry regiment under the title Royal Highland Emigrants; taken on to the British military establishment in 1775 as the 84th Foot, its colonel was Eyre Coote, the young ensign who had fought so ingloriously at the Battle of Falkirk.[12] (By then, of course, Coote had more than redeemed himself through his military leadership in India and his decisive victory at Wandiwash.) Maclean and other former Jacobites who ended up in military service in North America were exceptions to the rule expounded by Wolfe that they were simply savages with no military experience. Although Wolfe's lack of regard for the Scots had been demonstrated by his actions in the West Highlands after Culloden and his private comments while serving in the country, he was clearly prepared to suppress his feelings when taking military ability into account, describing Fraser's Highlanders in May 1758 as 'very useful Serviceable soldiers'.[13]

Even though Prideaux was killed during the siege operations at Fort Niagara – felled by a shell fragment from one of his own Coehorn mortars – William Johnson was able to take his place and the position fell on 25 July when the garrison surrendered, thereby giving the British control over western Ohio and bringing Montreal within striking distance. To consolidate this gain Amherst replaced Johnson with Thomas Gage, who had cemented his own position in North America by making an advantageous marriage to Margaret Kemble, the eldest daughter of a wealthy and politically important family in the province of New Jersey. Amherst wanted Gage to begin preparations for an immediate move towards Montreal and the Upper St Lawrence valley to assist the advance which he hoped Wolfe would be beginning, or might even have already begun – one of the problems all field commanders faced throughout the campaign was maintaining communications over such vast distances, and especially with London. But Gage was not minded to make any precipitate move without knowing the strength of the French forces which might or might not be blocking his path. No one could doubt Gage's

The face that launched the 1745 Jacobite rebellion: Prince Charles Edward Stuart, also known as 'Bonnie Prince Charlie' or 'The Young Pretender'. (© Scottish National Gallery, Edinburgh / Mondadori Portfolio / Electa/Giorgio Lotti / Bridgeman Images)

The defeat of the government army at Prestonpans outside Edinburgh was a huge fillip for the Jacobites. This humorous print satirises the flight of Sir John Cope, although in fact he did not desert his troops. (Mary Evans / Library of Congress)

Soldier, politician and playwright Henry Seymour Conway commanded a regiment at Culloden and went on to enjoy a spectacular military career, rising to the rank of field marshal. (© National Portrait Gallery, London)

The 'Martial Boy': the Duke of Cumberland in his role as the Captain-General. His handling of the government army at Culloden crushed Jacobite hopes and paved the way for further military success in North America. (© National Portrait Gallery, London)

'An Incident in the Rebellion of 1745' by David Morier. The painting shows government soldiers at Culloden, in this case an officer, sergeant and privates of Barrel's Regiment, in hand-to-hand combat with Highlanders. (Royal Collection Trust © Her Majesty Queen Elizabeth II, 2015 / Bridgeman Images)

The last British king to lead soldiers in battle – at Dettingen in 1743 – King George II survived the Jacobite attempt to oust him from the throne and lived to see the defeat of the French in Canada.

'We shall know better another time.' General Edward Braddock's last words after the defeat of a British force at Monongahela in July 1755. These were the opening shots in the Seven Years War in North America.

'Good soldier but no warrior': Thomas Gage served at Culloden and later in North America where he was one of the first British officers to recognise that the colonists were capable of organising a revolt against British rule. (Yale Center for British Art, Paul Mellon Collection, USA / Bridgeman Images)

From disgrace at the Battle of Falkirk to triumph at the Battle of Wandiwash: Eyre Coote laid the foundations for the expansion of British power in India and the later creation of the British Raj. (© National Portrait Gallery, London)

The Marquess of Granby relieving a sick soldier – Edward Penny's painting reveals Granby as a man of charity. Many soldiers used the money to open public houses, hence the popularity of the name throughout England. (National Army Museum, London / Bridgeman Images)

Highland Furies: the 42nd Royal Highlanders in action at the Battle of Ticonderoga in 1758, in which they played a leading role despite it being a British defeat. Later the regiment was better known as the Black Watch. (© The Black Watch Museum)

The north view of Fort Royal on the island of Guadeloupe, which was captured by British forces in 1759. Together with Martinique and Cuba, it gave Britain a powerful colonial holding in the Caribbean. (Courtesy of the Council of the National Army Museum)

British infantry defeat French cavalry at the Battle of Minden on 1 August 1759, a unique occurrence in the history of the British Army. Six British infantry regiments took part in the battle and their successors still wear red roses in their caps on Minden Day. (Courtesy of the Council of the National Army Museum)

Condemned as the 'Coward of Minden' due to his refusal to obey an order to bring up the cavalry, George Sackville revived his career as Lord Germain, Secretary of State for the American Colonies during the War of Independence. (Courtesy of the Council of the National Army Museum)

The fall of the fortress at Louisbourg in June 1758 paved the way for the invasion of Canada and the defeat of French forces at Quebec the following year.
(© McCord Museum)

The capture of Quebec or the Battle of the Plains of Abraham. During the amphibious phase of the operation British troops were landed at a cove west of the city and scrambled up the cliffs to do battle with the French. (Courtesy of the Council of the National Army Museum)

Benjamin West's portrayal of the death of General James Wolfe at Quebec became one of the great icons of empire. The positioning of Wolfe as a dying Christ figure brought down from the cross underlines the sense of Pietà. (National Gallery of Canada / Phillips, Fine Art Auctioneers, New York, USA / Bridgeman Images)

'A rough Scotch lord, hot and irascible', John Campbell, Earl of Loudoun owed his advancement to Cumberland's patronage but he came to grief commanding British forces in North America. (Allan Ramsay, National Galleries of Scotland)

John Ligonier was a French-born Huguenot who had been permitted to purchase a commission in the British Army in 1703. He lived to the age of eighty-nine and succeeded Cumberland as the army's commander-in-chief. (Courtesy of the Council of the National Army Museum)

William Pitt the Elder: Britain's prime minister and the architect of victory during the Seven Years War. (© National Portrait Gallery, London)

James Wolfe's victory at Quebec laid the foundation for the capture of Canada and the creation of Britain's empire in North America. His *Instructions to Young Officers* of 1768 revolutionised British battlefield tactics. (© National Trust Images)

courage in battle – he had fought bravely while leading the light infantry screen at Monongahela – but he was otherwise unusually timid and averse to taking risks. Because he was an able and sensible administrator that might not have mattered, but when his immediate commander, Amherst, was equally over-cautious and querulous it was not a recipe for decisive action.

As it was turning out, though, Amherst had other matters on his mind during the summer of 1759. He too had been tardy in setting out to seize his first objectives at Crown Point and Ticonderoga. One reason had been the slow arrival of the provincial militias under his command; another was a succession of delays in arranging his quartermastering. But these problems could have been overcome if Amherst had been decisive. With 10,000 men in his army, including seven regular infantry battalions, he was reasonably well equipped and should have anticipated a successful campaign, but the lack of available intelligence encouraged his natural caution. He also seems to have been puzzled by the French response to his movements. At Fort Carillon the defenders had put up only token resistance before spiking their guns and exploding the magazine. There was a similar outcome at Fort Saint-Frédéric near Crown Point, which was also blown up by the garrison, and it was here that Amherst received the news of the fall of Fort Niagara on 4 August. Suddenly all French resistance in the Lake Champlain region seemed to be collapsing – from deserters he received the equally welcome information that the French had moved as far as the Ile-aux-Noix, a heavily fortified island eighty miles away on the other side of the lake on the River Richelieu which helped to guard the approaches to Montreal. A bold strike north could have put British forces into the Upper St Lawrence, where they would have been ready to march on Quebec from the west, but Amherst was disinclined to act. Not only was his natural caution at work but he was also concerned about French naval activity on the lake, especially about the suspected presence of an armed schooner which would have posed a huge threat to his own fleet of unarmed troop-carrying *bateaux*. Nor did he have any information as to Wolfe's whereabouts, and being a natural worrier he concluded that no news had to be bad news.

Faced by such uncertainty, Amherst decided to consolidate his gains and ordered his men to set about the reconstruction of the forts at Ticonderoga and Crown Point, reasoning that it was too late in the season to advance to Quebec and that it was better to be safe than sorry. After all, without any intelligence to the contrary, Wolfe might already have been defeated and Montcalm might also be reorganising his forces to strike south towards Lake Champlain and its chain of forts.

In fact, following an unpromising beginning Wolfe's expedition was making some progress. Like Amherst he had made a slow start to his campaign and was at least a month behind schedule, not having left Louisbourg until 4 June. His aim was to advance up the St Lawrence as far as the Ile d'Orléans, a large island twenty miles long and five miles wide, that bisected the river about three miles below Quebec, and this was achieved by 28 June. Thanks to his large fleet the operation was accomplished with little difficulty. Not only did Wolfe have at his disposal 140 vessels, including 23 ships of the line and 13 frigates, but these came under the command of an experienced naval commander, Vice-Admiral Sir Charles Saunders, described by Wolfe as 'a brave zealous officer', a man who had taken part in Admiral Anson's earlier circumnavigation of the globe.[14] In return Saunders seems to have understood the need to forge a working relationship with the younger general, who could be excitable and temperamental if he felt that he was being thwarted in any way. When Wolfe began criticising Durell for his lethargy, arguing that they were in 'a devilish scrape, and that they should be call'd to a severe account for not being in the chops of the River early enough to prevent supplies going to Quebec', Saunders calmly ordered the squadron to make haste to enter the tidal river. To assist navigation Saunders also moved his flag from HMS *Neptune* into the smaller and more dexterous sixty-four-gun HMS *Stirling Castle*, a necessary precaution in order to navigate the narrow and unfamiliar waters of the St Lawrence.[15]

Quebec proved to be a difficult objective, being heavily defended and protected by its lofty position on a high promontory formed on one side by the St Lawrence and on the other by the smaller St Charles River. It was therefore vital that Wolfe and Saunders should agree about the positioning of the fleet in advance of land-ing the ground forces. On entering the Quebec basin Saunders decided to place his ships in the south channel between Pointe-Lévy and Pointe d'Orléans, which would provide the first staging post. It was a logical move, but the position was horribly exposed and on the night of 28 June the French took advantage. Instead of preparing to oppose any landing they launched a fleet of seven fireships in an attempt to disrupt the British. As they crackled and fizzed their way down river, the ships were an impressive sight, but they had been fired too soon and the British crews were able to parry them with little difficulty, using rowing boats to tow them to the shore. A watching army officer, Captain John Knox, confided to his journal that the sight produced 'the grandest fireworks (if I may be allowed to call them so) that can possibly be conceived many circumstances having contributed to their awful, yet won-derful, appearance, and afforded a scene infinitely superior to any adequate description'.[16]

However, these were mere diversions. Wolfe was still faced by the need to decide what he should do next to begin the investment of Quebec. Given its precipitous position some three hundred feet above the river, the logical approach was to get his army onto the Beauport shore to the north; but Montcalm had strongly fortified the area, making use of the difficult terrain to create a formidable obstacle for any attacking force. It was an imposing sight, and Wolfe and his fellow commanders must have been slightly over-awed by the scene that unfolded through their telescopes. High above the St Charles River at the head of a rocky cliff, Quebec resembled a huge fortress, heavily fortified with external trenches and breastworks running down to the cliff edge above the North Channel, the whole area being thickly dotted with trees and shrubs of all varieties. To the rear the houses in the settlement of Beauport had been barricaded and provided with additional for-tification, making them a potentially formidable obstacle. Further along the shore of the North Channel beyond the houses lay a screen of woods which ran on towards the Montmorency River. It was along this six-mile stretch overlooking the river that the French had placed their main defensive forces. Wolfe's landing and encampment were exactly opposite the Ile d'Orléans, and just as the British soldiers could see the position occupied by their opponents, so could the French observe them as the stores were unloaded and the artillery pieces were moved into position.

Inside Quebec Montcalm had taken over command of the French forces and, bolstered by his experience at Fort Carillon, he fully expected the British to attack him from the south. So too did his immediate superior, the governor Vaudreuil, who had confi-dently informed Paris that Quebec was impregnable and that 'we shall die in the ruins of Canada, our native land, before we surren-der to the English.'[17] Although both men had been nonplussed by the arrival of the British fleet, having considered the St Lawrence to be unnavigable to large warships in its upper reaches, they still believed that they had sufficient forces, while they enjoyed the tactical benefit of defending a position protected by steep cliffs which would be difficult to attack. Not only did the defenders possess all the advantages in terms of ground held, but they also had open fields of fire while those attacking had little cover and had to ascend steep cliffs. Only the recently arrived Bougainville counselled caution, arguing that while the British forces would be unlikely to 'make any attempt against it [Quebec], they might have the madness to do so'.[18]

Wolfe was certainly not insane, and an initial survey convinced him that an outright assault on Quebec was out of the question due to the strength and disposition of the French forces along the Beauport shore. He was also in the possession of detailed maps and sketches of the military dispositions within the citadel prepared for him by his chief engineer, Major Patrick Mackellar, who came from Argyll and had previous experience of soldiering in Minorca and Canada. Normally Wolfe had little time for military engineers – he had blamed them for the slow pace of the siege of Louisbourg – but Mackellar was different; he had been inside Quebec while a prisoner and had pronounced it 'formidably entrenched within'. In a letter written to his uncle Walter outlining his rationale for the forthcoming campaign, Wolfe had promised that if he found the enemy 'strong, audacious and well commanded, I shall proceed with the utmost caution and circumspection'.[19]

But Wolfe was also impatient, headstrong and liable to act impetuously. To set matters in train he ordered the bombardment of Quebec and the French positions, but given the topographical difficulties this did not, and could not, achieve immediate results. It proved difficult for Saunders to position his warships ready for the bombardment due to the unexpected presence of an underwater shelf on the Beauport bank, while the harassing French gunboats also proved troublesome by making tip-and-run attacks on the British fleet. An unexpected storm exacerbated the situation by disrupting anchorages; suddenly unmoored, the ships careered into each other, causing some structural damage. None of this was designed to calm Wolfe's temper, and in his journal he was soon complaining about the direction of Saunders's warships and 'their prodigious distance from the enemy – amazing backwardness in these matters on the side of the Fleet'.[20]

The onus was now on Wolfe to act sooner rather than later. He had to take account of the seasons: although it was only the beginning of July, he had little more than two months at his disposal before the arrival of winter and with it the icing up of the St Lawrence, which would force Saunders's fleet to withdraw. His first move was to order Monckton's brigade to take Pointe-Levy, the high ground on the southern shore directly opposite Quebec, which gave him the opportunity to bombard the fortified town. Unaccountably its open position had been ignored by Montcalm, who had done nothing to occupy it even though he had noted the danger. The second move was to make his forward camp on the northern shore below the Falls of Montmorency using Murray's and Townshend's brigades. As his long stop Wolfe left behind a small detachment of marines on the Ile d'Orléans.

But still the phoney war continued. As July wore on the only action involved occasional skirmishes between the rival forces on the Beauport shore and the bombardment from Monckton's batteries on Pointe-Levy , which began on 12 July and caused considerable damage to the upper town of Quebec. At the height of this aerial assault, 300 mortar bombs a day fell on this largely residential quarter, helping to set the scene for what followed next.

While crossing the Atlantic Wolfe had mused long and hard

about the forthcoming campaign, and in one revealing letter written to Amherst on 6 March he had outlined his thinking about what should be done if he encountered unexpected resistance. In view of his behaviour after Culloden and his conduct the previous year at Miramachi Bay it is worth quoting at length:

> If, by accident in the river, by the enemy's resistance, by sickness or slaughter in the army, or from any other cause, we find that Quebec is not likely to fall into our hands (persevering however to the last moment), I propose to set the town on fire with shells, to destroy the harvest, houses and cattle, both above and below, to send off as many Canadians as possible to Europe and to leave famine and desolation behind me; belle résolution & très chrétienne! But we must teach these scoundrels to make war in a more gentlemanlike manner.[21]

It was no idle threat, and as Quebec was a fortified city Wolfe was within his rights to make it, even though to a later age it smacks of the tactics of terror and has been condemned in those terms by later Canadian historians. At the time Wolfe was exasperated by the lack of progress, while he had been enraged by the conduct of the fighting, namely the continuing tendency of native American skirmishers in alliance with the French to scalp his soldiers – in his view the perpetrators were the 'most contemptible, cowardly scoundrels in creation'.

Wolfe had already warned his opponents what lay in store for them if they continued their opposition by issuing two proclamations in which he threatened to 'burn and lay waste the country', but these had produced little effect other than to harden opposition. Now he was determined to put those threats into action. On 23 July an order was given for fighting patrols to 'burn and lay waste the country for the future, sparing only churches or houses dedicated to divine worship'. Women and children were supposed to be exempt but they were still rounded up, one patrol bringing back around 300 women after a raid on the village of Trembleau. And in one ghastly incident recorded by Knox, British troops set fire to a farmhouse thought to be uninhabited, only to be horrified at the sound of screams from the inside as the flames took hold, engulfing the inhabitants. A rescue attempt failed.[22] Later, once the campaign was over, one unnamed officer estimated that during the siege of Quebec '535 houses were burnt down, among which is the whole eastern part of the lower town (save 6 or 8 houses) which make a very dismal appearance. We also destroyed upwards of fourteen hundred fine farm-houses in the country &c.'[23]

Once again, such behaviour was surprisingly similar to the tactics used after Culloden, and Wolfe would not have been shocked by having to employ them. He also knew that the skirmishing between his own men and the French was equally brutal; scalping was a fact of life, albeit one which Wolfe abhorred and deplored and was determined to punish – 'we cut them to pieces whenever we found them, in return for a thousand acts of cruelty and barbarity', he had written of his army's handling of the Mi'kmaqs during the siege of Louisbourg the previous year.[24] But he understood, too, that such terror tactics could be counter-productive and urged moderation on his men, emphasising the need to spare women and children. From the available evidence it seems that his main aim was to elicit a reaction from the French commanders, who were exasperating him by failing to make any first move to engage his forces in a pitched battle. When they attempted to discomfit him by sending down another fleet of fireships on 28 July, Wolfe wrote angrily to Montcalm saying that fire would be met with fire: 'If you presume to send down any more fire-rafts, they shall be made fast to the two transports in which the Canadian prisoners are confined in order that they may perish by your own base invention.'[25] As before, the threat might not conform to the rules of war, but Wolfe was uncomfortably aware that time was running out and that his opponents still held the advantage in terms of position and superior numbers. Clearly a bold stroke was required, and at the end of July Wolfe decided to make it.

Faced by the stalemate, his mind turned to the possibility of landing forces up river from Quebec and attacking it from another quarter. To test that plan he ordered Guy Carleton to take 600 men to Pointe-aux-Trembles, some twenty-five miles above the town, to mount what was in essence a reconnaissance mission. Wolfe trusted 'grave Carleton', as he called him in his correspondence, and had ignored King George II's opposition to having him appointed to his staff, but the purpose of the mission was far from clear. The possibility of capturing French operational papers had been mentioned but was not acted upon, and when Carleton returned he only brought back with him a small group of women, children and old men who were all well treated, presumably for propaganda purposes.

Wolfe then turned his attention back to the Beauport shore and the French position between the Montmorency and St Charles rivers. Other than that he intended to make a frontal assault on Montcalm's positions it is difficult to discern Wolfe's purpose; the plans were constantly evolving, so much so that an opportunistic raid was transformed into a major assault involving the bulk of his army. All he told Pitt in a later dispatch was that he 'resolved to take the first opportunity which presented itself of attacking the enemy, though posted to great advantage, and everywhere prepared to receive us'.[26]

The bare bones of the situation looked like this: Montcalm's headquarters was located on a cliff-top overlooking the North Channel opposite the Ile d'Orléans; Wolfe resolved to assault this position from both sides, with Monckton's brigade making an amphibious landing on a strand some two hundred yards long in order to seize a French redoubt which contained two gun emplacements. At the same time Murray and Townshend would prepare their brigades to cross a ford on the Montmorency and advance under the protection of the cliffs. The operation was to be preceded by a huge artillery bombardment from Saunders's warships and the established shore batteries, but this was only to be a prelude to a frontal assault designed to bring Montcalm to battle. During the attack Wolfe showed his customary coolness under fire while directing operations from the transport *Russell*, which together with the *Three Sisters* was run aground to continue firing on the French positions, but it soon became apparent that the tide was lower than expected, obliging the warships to stay offshore and limiting their firepower. Although this hindered the landings, it allowed Wolfe to undertake closer reconnaissance of the intended target. As his ship approached shore Wolfe could see that the redoubt was much closer to Montcalm's position than he had envisaged; being within French musket range, this meant that they were unlikely to leave their positions to mount the desired counter-attack, but would simply open fire on the opposition. In other words, Wolfe's men were about to be landed in a potential killing ground.

By then it was late afternoon; the British assault force had been cooped up in their boats for several hours and were desperate to see some action. First ashore were the grenadiers and two hundred Royal Americans, who showed little discipline and immediately mounted a wild charge against the French redoubt. At the same time they came under heavy fire from the French infantry on the cliffs above, who according to one witness 'pour'd their small shot like showers of hail which caus'd our brave grenadiers to fall very fast'.[27]

At that point a torrential downpour and thunderstorm made any thought of continuing the attack academic, and it was clear that the assault would have to be called off to prevent further casualties. To add to the confusion, Monckton's second wave – the 15th and Fraser's Highlanders – had started landing and Townshend's brigade had crossed the Montmorency ford. They too had to be stopped, and although Wolfe originally sensed confusion in the French ranks which could have been exploited, a general retreat was sounded. With the tide rising this turned out to be a chancy business, especially as the Montmorency had to be forded again, a process delayed by the refusal of Fraser's Highlanders to attempt the crossing until all their men had been accounted for. Only their suddenly soaked powder stopped the French firing on the retreating soldiers and prevented worse casualties.

By any standards it had been a serious setback. Not only had nothing been achieved but the British had lost heavily, with 443 officers and men killed or wounded, largely as a result of the determination of the French defences and the wild behaviour of the grenadiers. Earlier in his career Wolfe's reputation had been grounded on the need to maintain discipline on the battlefield – he even advocated the use of instant execution to maintain order – but this had been entirely lacking among the grenadiers and the Royal Americans in the first assault. As Townshend noted in his journal, 'the cause of this disaster, as in so many other cases, was the burning thirst for battle on the part of the troops, officers and men like, such as one sees in men, who, never having been on active service before, are impatient to find themselves engaged.'[28]

Someone had to take the blame for the fiasco, and while Wolfe did not shrink from self-criticism in his dispatch to Pitt, his main targets were his immediate subordinates, who responded by saying that they had not been sufficiently consulted. In the aftermath Murray complained that Wolfe's orders had demonstrated 'little stability, stratagem or fixed intention', while later in the summer Townshend wrote to his wife: 'General Wolfe's Health is but very bad. His Generalship in my poor opinion – is not a bit better; this only between us.' Even the normally loyal Carleton was moved to voice his disappointment.[29]

All was not lost, however, and in his cool and analytical way Wolfe was determined to move on, telling Monckton that 'the loss is not great' and that the failure had not dissuaded him from continuing the policy of trying to coax Montcalm into battle. Despite the disapproval of his subordinate officers Wolfe's army had not faltered, a result of the discipline he inculcated and perhaps also of his soldiers' admiration for their tall, lanky, red-haired commander, who looked ungainly but who was clearly fearless and soldierly under fire. The willingness of a senior officer to take risks and to share the dangers faced by his men is always a vital factor in warfare, and in that respect Wolfe was not found wanting. The men also remained well-supplied and still trusted their superior officers, both important factors in maintaining an army's morale. Considering that they were operating deep in enemy territory and knew that their only hope of withdrawal lay with the navy, they were in remarkably good spirits as the summer wore on, bringing with it wet and windy weather.

Little happened in August other than a three-week operation mounted by Murray's brigade which took them some thirty miles up river of Quebec. This achieved little materially and failed in its aim to gain any intelligence about Amherst's movement, but

Murray's presence encouraged Montcalm to realign his forces by moving 1600 men, mainly cavalry commanded by Bougainville, to meet the challenge posed by the presence of a large and determined enemy force. If there was a cloud on the horizon it came in the shape of Wolfe's poor health. On 19 August he retired to his bed in the farmhouse he occupied at Montmorency and was clearly a sick man. His illness was described as a 'slow fever', but as he had never enjoyed robust health, it is difficult to discern the exact cause of his physical collapse. Stress probably exacerbated his existing problems, manifesting itself in an increasingly short temper. He quarrelled with Saunders, remained on bad terms with Townshend and was infuriated by Murray's lengthy absence up river. To his surgeon he made a simple and heartfelt request: 'I know you cannot cure my complaint, but patch me up so that I may be able to do my duty for the next three days and I shall be content.'[30] At this low ebb, and perhaps worried that he was either dying or on the point of failure he decided to consult his brigadiers, asking them to be 'so good as to meet, and consult together for the public utility and advantage, and to consider the best method of attacking the Enemy'.[31]

In his communication dated 30 August Wolfe offered three alternative plans. All of them were variations on the earlier move to assault the French positions on the Beauport shore, and all of them involved engagement on ground known to be advantageous to the defenders. On receipt of the proposals Monckton, the senior brigadier, called a meeting of his colleagues and their response was unanimous. Not only did they find Wolfe's proposals flawed and unworkable, they also believed that implementation of the plan would lead to disaster. But all was not negativity. While arguing that another attack on the Beauport position would be calamitous, they put forward an alternative proposal to make a different assault, also on the northern shore but up river from Quebec, somewhere near Cap Rouge; there, they argued, 'the Marquis de Montcalm must fight us on our own terms. We are betwixt him and his provisions.' To underscore the unanimity of this new thinking the papers were shown to Saunders, a necessary precaution not only to retain unity of command but also to involve the navy in what would be a hazardous amphibious operation. Saunders added his agreement and the following day the papers were sent back to Wolfe, who gave them his approval. He then sent a dispatch to Pitt summing up the tactical situation, which he described as 'such a choice of difficulties, that I own myself at a loss how to determine'.[32]

It was an honest appraisal which did not make light of the difficulties and hinted at the possibility of failure. Wolfe had however left himself with no option but to be totally candid, for time was not on his side. Not only was he seriously ill and possibly dying, but Saunders had given notice that he would have to 'very soon send home the great ships' in advance of approaching winter. Moreover, the agreed plan was sketchy, yet Wolfe refused to discuss it any further. All the senior commanders understood the intention but at that point none of them, perhaps not even Wolfe himself, had any inkling of the execution.

It was an astonishing situation. In advance of a major operation and a landing which might lead to a decisive battle, Wolfe was unwilling to consult either his brigadiers or Saunders and the naval commanders. His physical incapacity may have been one reason for his silence, while he may have been guided by the need to maintain tight security within his camp. His natural reticence may also have been a factor, although given his history as a commander this seems unlikely. At the siege of Louisbourg he had made his intentions clear from the outset and seemed to revel 'in

what was to all intents and purposes an independent command';
now his conduct was the exact opposite. As one of his officers put
it: 'Every step he takes is wholly his own, I'm told he asks no one's
opinion, and wants no advice.'[33]

Whatever the reasons for his behaviour – he may genuinely
not have decided his next step – what is known can be pieced
together from his own and Saunders's correspondence with the
War Office and the Admiralty. On 3 September the operation
began with the evacuation of the camp at Montmorency, and the
following day the army lined up to embark on the ships which
would take them up river. Completed without incident, this stage
was watched by the men of the French army and their allies, who
like Wolfe's men had very little idea of what was taking place.
The flotilla then made its way past Quebec towards Cap Rouge,
where they awaited Wolfe's command. At some point during this
phase of the operation Wolfe decided what would happen next.
He spent much of the time on the deck of HMS *Sutherland* scan-
ning the northern shore, and it is possible that he also listened to
advice from Captain Robert Stobo, a Scot serving in the Virginia
militia who had spent time in Quebec as a prisoner and knew the
lie of the land. Whatever the reasoning behind his decision, by 12
September Wolfe had determined to land his forces at a position
known as the Anse au Foulon some two miles above Quebec,
where the cliffs gave way to a precipitous path which led up to
the flat ground known as the Plains of Abraham.

Fortuitously the area was only guarded by a token force of
militia. That evening the order was finally given to his brigadiers,
who were also told that they and their men would be transported
down river on the ebb tide and that they were 'to act as silently as
the nature of the service will admit of'. At the same time Saunders
would make a diversion towards the Beauport shore to confuse

Montcalm into thinking that the attack would come from that direction.

Under a quarter moon the first sections of light infantrymen landed at Anse du Foulon shortly before dawn, led by Lieutenant-Colonel William Howe of the 58th Foot, and they quickly scrambled up the 175-foot escarpment. A heavily built man known to his family as 'the Savage', William Howe was the brother of Lord Howe, who had been killed at Ticonderoga the previous year, and his own military career had begun in Scotland during the pacification operations after Culloden. He was also brave and athletic and it was due to his efforts that a way was found up the track to the top of the cliff.

Behind Howe and his light infantrymen came the 3600 men of the main force, led by Wolfe and his brigade commanders. As dawn began to break, Wolfe was in a position to order his men into line for the battle that surely lay ahead, according to instructions which he had issued in advance of the landings: 'The first body that gets ashore is to march directly to the enemy and drive them from any little posts they may occupy. The battalions must form on the upper ground with expedition and be ready to charge whatever presents itself.'[34]

This simple but urgent order entailed the entire force facing up with the right of the line resting on the edge of the heights above the St Lawrence River, while the left moved out towards a thickly wooded area on the flank. From the right Wolfe's battalions were lined up as follows: the 35th Foot, the Louisberg Grenadiers (consisting of the grenadier companies of the other regiments), the 28th Foot, 43rd Foot, 47th Foot, Fraser's Highlanders and the 58th Foot. One light gun had been dragged up the cliff and placed between the 47th and the Highlanders. The 15th Foot was formed at a right angle to the line on the left to protect the flank.

Two battalions formed a reserve, the 3rd/60th and the 48th Foot. Two companies of the 58th guarded the access up the cliff and the 2nd/60th protected the rear against any incursion by a French reserve force. In addition, there was a battalion of light infantry and a unit of Rangers. Monckton and Murray commanded the line and Townshend the reserves, while Wolfe positioned himself with the 28th on the right of the line. The single line stretched over almost a mile, and as dawn gave way to the light of day it began to rain. To counter the effects and to give his men some shelter from French, Canadian and native American snipers, Wolfe ordered the packed ranks to lie on their weapons to keep them dry. All he had to do now was to wait for the French reaction.

In some respects the position was not dissimilar to that on Drummossie Moor over a dozen years earlier – two smallish armies about to confront one another across open ground – and the air of déjà vu was reinforced when Montcalm appeared. At his side was his aide the Chevalier de Johnstone, who as James Johnstone had served in the Jacobite army at Culloden and who had later fled to France to enter French service. It is not an exaggeration to say that Montcalm was astounded by Wolfe's move. Not only had he dismissed the Anse du Foulon as a potential landing place, but he continued to believe that the Beauport shore would remain the British target. Even so, his position was not hopeless. At that stage he did not have to engage Wolfe's army, and he could have avoided battle while waiting for Bougainville to arrive from the west. This would have placed Wolfe between two forces, his only escape a parlous retreat back to the boats on the river below.

However, Montcalm had been schooled in European warfare with its belief in the primacy of set-piece battles, and he feared that inaction on his part would pass the initiative back to Wolfe: 'If we give him time to establish himself,' he told an artillery officer called Montbelliard, 'we shall never be able to attack him with the sort of troops we have.'[35] Both sides were in fact evenly matched, at about 4500 apiece, but Wolfe's men were well-trained regular troops while Montcalm had at his disposal mainly militia-men and levies, distinctly inferior to the twelve infantry battalions facing them. Only a rapid attack could discomfit them, and that was exactly what Wolfe wanted to happen.

At around ten o'clock Montcalm gave the order for his line to advance towards the British positions. Almost immediately the attacking force was in disarray, the French regulars in the centre maintaining a steady advance while the militias on the flanks burst into a ragged charge before halting over a hundred yards from the British line and firing their weapons without thought of discipline or cohesion. All the while the red-coated British battalions held their fire until the enemy was within fifty yards, when they opened fire by battalion as they had been trained to do by Wolfe. As Captain John Knox of the 43rd described it in his journal, it was as 'close and heavy a discharge, as I ever saw performed at a private field of exercise, insomuch that better troops than we encountered could not possibly withstand it'.[36] As Wolfe had forecast in his infantry manual, the effect was devastating, and when the French began to break and run the battalions fired a second round before beginning the pursuit with bayonet or, in the case of Fraser's Highlanders, with drawn claymores – the big heavy swords which had done so much damage against government forces during the Jacobite rebellion. In the company of the 28th Foot and the Louis-berg Grenadiers, Wolfe joined in the charge along the edge of the battlefield as the action degenerated into rout.

It was during this last phase of the battle that Wolfe was hit by a sniper's bullet. While urging on his men he was struck in the lower abdomen and the chest. Mortally wounded, he was carried to the rear, where he was able to remain conscious just long enough to learn that the French were in disarray and the field was his. Earlier in the battle he had been shot in the wrist, but this was the final blow. Monckton too had been wounded – shot through the lungs – and there was now a pressing need to bring order to the battlefield, where the earlier cohesion of Wolfe's command was steadily disintegrating. With Murray still in the van of the Highlanders' charge, command fell to Townshend, who promptly showed that he was equal to the task by calling off the pursuit of the fleeing French and restoring order to the frenzied battalions. It was none too soon, as shortly before midday Bougainville's force arrived on the field with two hundred cavalrymen. A tricky moment was saved by Townshend's prompt orders to bring up two battalions of infantry, whereupon Bougainville withdrew his force to the west to reassess the situation.

The battle for possession of the Plains of Abraham was over. Montcalm had retired to Quebec mortally wounded by an unlucky shell-burst, and Wolfe was the hero of the hour.

9

WINNING THE WEST:
CANADA AND THE CARIBBEAN

By dying in his moment of victory Wolfe achieved the fame he had craved throughout his short military career. Indeed, it can be said that everything he did during his last hours of life pointed to this particular outcome – recklessly exposing himself to enemy fire as he inspected his lines before battle, and showing scant regard for his safety by boldly leading from the front. In death, he was immortalised as the victor of Quebec, the hero who would be forever young, and because the news of the triumph arrived at the same time as the announcement of his death the two events became irrevocably intertwined. Within a dozen years his place in the pantheon was assured when the British-American artist Benjamin West exhibited his painting *The Death of General Wolfe* at the Royal Academy. In a classically staged (but historically fanciful) tableau, the dying Wolfe lies cradled in the arms of his adjutant-general Isaac Barré as a messenger arrives with news of victory. The positioning of Wolfe as a dying Christ figure brought down from the cross underlines the sense of Pietà. The painting caused a sensation when it was first exhibited and it was quickly turned into an engraving which sold thousands of copies, becoming in time an important part of the iconography of empire.

As for Wolfe, his body was embalmed and brought back to England, still wearing the new red coat which had made him such a prominent figure on the battlefield and such a good target for enemy marksmen. He was buried in the family vault at the church of St Alfege in Greenwich on 20 November 1759, amidst an atmosphere of widespread national mourning.

In the context of the times Wolfe certainly deserved the adulation. He had won a great victory, and although the French had not yet been expelled from Canada, in the public's mind that triumph was surely imminent (it would be achieved within a year of his victory). As Wolfe was so young at the time of his death, however, it is difficult to give an accurate assessment of his role as a field commander and to decide whether he was a military genius or simply a spirited and talented young officer who managed to ride his luck when he faced the greatest challenge of his career. He was certainly no Marlborough, but one of his peer group, the Marquess of Granby, told Pitt that had Wolfe lived, he would have done 'the greater honour to his country, as he would have been of the utmost service to it, nature having endow'd him with activity, resolution and perseverance, qualities absolutely necessary for executing great plans of operations, all of which he had taken care to improve by great application'.[1] It seems a fair assessment, for by the time of Quebec Wolfe had achieved a great deal, and under normal circumstances would have been destined to do more. Not only was he an experienced and combat-hardened commander with several major battles under his belt from Dettingen onwards, but he was also an educated soldier who understood the importance of ensuring his men's welfare and providing them with the tactics which would help them to overcome difficulties on the battlefield. As his latest biographers have pointed out, his legacy was probably not so much winning the possession of Canada as utilising the disciplined rifle fire and bayonet drill which would make the British infantryman such a feared opponent for the rest of the century and beyond.[2]

Wolfe was also fortunate that his two victories at Louisbourg and Quebec paved the way for the expulsion of French forces from Canada and the eventual triumph of British arms in North America. This was central to Pitt's policies in engineering the defeat of France in the Seven Years War, and as the agent of that military and naval success Wolfe's place in history is unassailable. No general who executes a political leader's wishes is ever going to be accounted a failure, and together with other commanders in the same theatre, notably Amherst and Monckton, Wolfe deserved the accolades.

In this respect his position can be contrasted with that of Cornwallis and Loudoun, who returned from North America with their careers tarnished after the setbacks of 1756 and 1758. Both were passed over for further promotion; they had failed where Wolfe succeeded, a point made by Wolfe when he said of Cornwallis in 1757 that 'there is a storm gathering over the head of my unfortunate friend, such a one as must necessarily crush him.'[3] All three men were veterans of the Culloden campaign and protégés of Cumberland, but the difference was that Cornwallis had dithered at Minorca and Rochefort and Loudoun at Fort William Henry, while Wolfe did the exact opposite at Louisbourg and Quebec. Of course Wolfe also made mistakes: he was pig-headed at Montmorency, where he pushed ahead with the assault on the French lines despite sustaining heavy casualties; he had also hesitated in the run-up to the main battle before Quebec. But at the crucial point when Montcalm decided to attack his lines, he held his nerve and led his army to a notable triumph.

From that standpoint alone his fame was secure. A victory was a victory, even though in this case it was not complete. Although Montcalm had died during the fighting and his forces were in disarray, casualties on both sides had been fairly even and Townshend as the senior British officer was faced with the prospect of laying siege to Quebec before complete victory could be claimed. This he did with a will, ordering his men to dig entrenchments and drag up heavy guns from the river bank while the British forces still retained their advantage. Fortunately for Townshend the French leadership was pusillanimous in the extreme. Bougainville had retreated west towards Montreal and Vaudreuil followed suit, leaving the French militia isolated inside Quebec with little option but to stop fighting. On 18 September the French formally surrendered, and in return Townshend and Saunders offered surprisingly generous terms, allowing the regular soldiers to return to France and the militia to lay down their arms on condition that they swore allegiance to the British Crown. One shadow from Wolfe's strategy fell over the victors: the French in Montreal had full barns from the previous harvest, but thanks to the August reign of terror Quebec's countryside yielded nothing for the British and they had to make to do with the remaining supplies they had brought with them across the Atlantic.

With winter fast approaching Saunders prepared to sail his big warships back to England at the beginning of October, leaving behind two sloops as well as the bulk of Wolfe's army. With him he took Townshend, who handed over to Murray command of a force of around seven thousand men to face the rigours of the Canadian winter. At the same time Monckton retired to

New York for the good of his health, having been more seriously wounded than had been thought during the recent battle. Not long after the fleet left the St Lawrence, news of the fall of Quebec reached Amherst while he was still on Lake Champlain, and with the days growing shorter and colder he decided to order his men into winter quarters at Crown Point. Ahead lay a bitter period for all concerned, even those who had managed to get back to Britain.

It did not take long for Townshend to run into trouble. On his return to London he carried with him a dispatch describing the victory at Quebec which so delighted Pitt that he ordered it to be published immediately in a *Gazette Extraordinary*. Having been in a state of despair – Wolfe's earlier reports had been gloomy and doom-laden – Pitt's mood turned to elation as the entire country rejoiced. However, rumours soon began to circulate suggesting that Townshend had embellished his role in the battle at the expense of Wolfe and that he was guilty of attempting to gain some credit for the victory. As Townshend was known to have been on bad terms with Wolfe – his malicious temperament was also widely recognised – the tittle-tattle was readily believed, not least because it was accompanied by the publication of a number of scurrilous and anonymous pamphlets.[4] Matters came to a head the following November, when a pamphlet was published accusing Townshend of unprofessional behaviour at Quebec. As its author was believed to be Cumberland's former aide the Earl of Albemarle, Townshend challenged him to a duel; only the timely intervention of the Captain of the King's Guard (Captain Timothy Caswell, Coldstream Guards) prevented it taking place.

For a short time thereafter Townshend was in bad odour, but he was saved by his political friendships, not least with the up and coming Earl of Bute whose career had been enhanced following the death of King George II a month earlier. A Scottish aristocrat, Bute had used his position as tutor and mentor to the Prince of Wales (the future King George III) to further his own ambitions at the expense of Pitt. This allowed Townshend to be promoted lieutenant-general and to be sworn in as a privy councillor in the first months of the new king's reign.

Monckton also eventually prospered as a result of his service in North America, although he never forgave Townshend for omitting him from the discussions leading to the French surrender at Quebec. By February 1761, having spent a year in Philadelphia, Monckton had recovered his health and had been promoted major-general in command of the British forces in New York.

At Crown Point, meanwhile, Amherst, the other commander in Canada, had also been busy. Although his advance north had been plodding and unspectacular, by the spring of 1760 his carpenters had constructed the three ships required to give him naval supremacy on Lake Champlain and he was ready to advance on Montreal.

It was not a moment too soon. The winter had allowed the French to regroup under the command of Francis de Gaston, Chevalier de Lévis, Montcalm's former second-in-command. A tough Gascon fighting soldier and veteran of the earlier campaigns in Europe, it seemed to him that the French had the beating of Murray's smaller force, which had spent a difficult winter inside Quebec, suffering around a thousand casualties mainly to disease and malnutrition. Not only was food and fuel in short supply, but the small British force had been bedevilled by ill-discipline. Drunkenness and thieving were rife, sickness – especially scurvy – was rampant and as a result of the depredations morale was at rock bottom

On the other hand, Lévis's men had been revitalised by their own stay in secure winter quarters inside Montreal and were ready for action. In addition to being fitter they were also numerically superior – 7000 regulars to Murray's 4000 – and this gave Lévis the opportunity to act before the snows finally melted. He also hoped that he would be reinforced from France, having asked for an additional 7000 men as well as more artillery and ammunition. In this he was to be disappointed, for only 400 reinforcements were dispatched to Canada; nevertheless, undaunted, Lévis's forces landed outside Quebec on 26 April 1760 and took up position at the British outposts of Lorette and Sainte Foy.

Murray had been expecting a French riposte, and despite the difficulties facing his soldiers had managed to reinforce some of his defensive positions around the city. Before the French arrived he withdrew his infantry screen of eight battalions, with two in reserve, and positioned his forces – including twenty field pieces and two howitzers – on the high ground at Buttes-à-Neveu. Had Murray ordered his men to stay put and maintain a defensive posture he could have used his artillery on the ridge to good effect, but below him he could see Lévis's men moving into an offensive column and he was concerned that the advantage would pass to them. Rather than let that happen he decided to mount an attack which he hoped would be decisive – to destroy the French forces quickly before they could get into position, just as Montcalm had planned to do to Wolfe the previous year.

Initially it seemed to work. Taken by surprise, the French line wavered as Murray's men pressed home their attack. But the slushy snow and mud worked to the disadvantage of the British infantry battalions, and the fighting quickly disintegrated into a series of close-quarter brawls. A French flanking move on the right almost cut off Murray's line of retreat, and after three hours' fighting he was forced to order his depleted force to withdraw back into Quebec. As one soldier in the 15th Foot put it, they retired 'to their former ground; happy would it have been had they never left it.'[5] Although the British regular infantrymen had fought stubbornly, they had lost heavily – 1104 were killed, wounded or missing. Amongst their number were 213 men of the 78th Fraser's Highlanders, the heaviest loss suffered by any battalion in Murray's field force that day.

For the French it should have been a decisive victory, but Lévis was unable to capitalise on it and was left with no option but to begin a siege, hoping all the while that reinforcements would arrive from France. Although he had some advantages, in that his men were familiar with the ground over which they were fighting and he himself had a good understanding of Quebec's defences, he was stymied by the fact that the few artillery pieces he possessed were woefully short of powder and ammunition, so much so that his guns were restricted to firing twenty rounds per day. All hope disappeared in the middle of May when the first of three British warships appeared in the St Lawrence and destroyed the French frigates supporting the siege. Faced by this new threat, and aware that there would be no French naval or ground reinforcements, Lévis lifted the siege and ordered his men to retreat back towards Montreal. Not only did that reverse signal the end of French resistance but it passed the initiative back to the British, who were now in a good position to complete Wolfe's great work of cementing British interests in North America.

The next stage was simplicity itself. Under Amherst's overall command the British campaign plan for 1760 called for a three-pronged attack on Montreal: reinforced from the St Lawrence by a strong naval force, Murray would attack up the river from Quebec, Amherst would make his move from Albany by way of the River Mohawk to Lake Ontario before swinging down the St

Lawrence, and a third force led by Blakeney's former aide William Haviland, now a brigadier-general, would take the direct route north from Crown Point across Lake Champlain and on towards Montreal. On 27 August, backed by a substantial fleet which included thirty-two armed vessels and nine floating batteries, Murray's force of 4000 regulars arrived at Lac St Pierre where the River Richelieu debouches into the St Lawrence and dug in to await the arrival of Amherst and Haviland. He had encountered little opposition and had enjoyed an almost stately progress up river – unlike Haviland and Amherst, who had to fight brisk actions against the French at Ile-aux-Noix, St Jean and Chambly before they reached Montreal on 8 September.

The following day Vandreuil and Lévis took the decision to surrender. Both were aware that further resistance was not only impractical but would cause unnecessary casualties, and although there were disagreements over the terms – once again Amherst was resolved to punish the French by refusing them the honours of war as a result of their complicity in barbarities perpetrated by their native American allies – the campaign in Canada was over and the British were masters of the field.

When, during the surrender negotiations, Vandreuil attempted to postpone the inevitable, Amherst made this perfectly clear. Brushing aside his opponent's efforts, he replied magisterially in fluent French: 'I have come to take Canada, and I will take nothing less.'[6] From the Carolina border to the St Lawrence River, 'Wolfe's dream of an English-speaking North America ... was now a reality.'[7]

Although the support, power and reach of the Royal Navy in the north Atlantic were vital to the success of the land forces – and would prove to be equally so in the Caribbean – the capture of Canada and the expulsion of the French is one of the British Army's major achievements, and it helped to restore the reputation gained under Marlborough earlier in the century. The campaign had begun modestly enough, with several setbacks, but once the government had taken a grip on the need to reinforce the North American garrison, to provide it with sufficient funds and equipment and to promote ambitious and well-grounded leaders, the tide began to swing in its favour, the crowning glory being Wolfe's capture of Quebec. Although it took time for some British officers to appreciate the military virtues of the American colonial forces – and while they were often a mixed blessing – they, too, played their part in the eventual triumph of the so-called 'American Army' in Canada, as they would later do in the Caribbean.

By any reckoning, through meticulous planning Amherst had won a convincing victory in 1760: under his composed and effective guidance the three British armies had converged on Montreal and forced the French to surrender without unnecessary bloodshed. Thanks were also due to Pitt for his far-sightedness in producing the funds for the military and naval operations and in gaining the support of the American provincial governments. Credit should also be given to Ligonier, who as commander-in-chief encouraged the use of combined operations in North America and sanctioned the appointments of Amherst, Wolfe, Howe and Forbes. Although almost into his eighties, his energy and commitment remained unyielding, and despite a bout of illness in 1760 he retained a youthfulness which was an inspiration to his subordinates. With his political connections and his undoubted gifts in diplomacy, Ligonier had emerged as an important prop in Pitt's direction of the war.

The next stage did not run so smoothly. For reasons which are difficult to unravel, Amherst did not particularly enjoy life in North America, and even before the fall of Montreal had been pestering Pitt for an order to return home – despite the fact that his career was firmly rooted in the continent, where in addition to being commander-in-chief he was titular governor of Virginia and colonel of the Royal American Regiment, all of which brought him a sizeable income. One reason was domestic – his wife Jane Dalison, whom he had married in 1753, was showing the first signs of the mental instability which led to her death five years later, and she longed to return to England. Another reason was personal to Amherst. As a soldier and administrator he entertained little respect for the colonials, especially for their troops, telling a fellow officer that 'if left to themselves [they] would eat fryed [sic] Pork and lay in their tents all day long'.[8] While he was careful to keep his opinions to himself and his closest confidants, his dislike must have coloured his attitude to his posting, and it shows in his letters and journals. More serious were his feelings about the native Americans, whom he treated with a contempt that bordered on outright racial hatred. In common with many of his fellow officers he found little merit in the local tribes, describing them routinely as vermin or as savages beyond redemption. In particular he was, like Wolfe, deeply offended by their practice of scalping and murdering prisoners; at one point he wrote of the local Cherokee people that they were 'more nearly allied to the Brute than to the Human Condition', fit only to be hunted down by dogs.[9] Language of that kind had been used routinely to describe the Jacobite forces during the Culloden campaign fifteen years earlier, and while Amherst had not served in the government army in Scotland he had been a member of Cumberland's inner circle long enough to understand that the expression of hostile racist sentiments was tolerable and even to be expected in the lexicon of senior British officers.

The coming of white Europeans to the eastern seaboard of

North America had been a culture shock for all concerned and a clash of very different civilisations. From the outset, native Americans were regarded by the Europeans as being both savage and exotic, while for their part many of the tribes on the eastern seaboard welcomed the incomers only as potential trading partners and military allies. There were, of course, differences in approach. Despite the cultural and linguistic barriers, the French tended to court the locals and attempted to enter into alliances with them despite doubts about their military abilities. During the recently ended conflict many of the native American peoples had sided with the French, who showed a more laissez-faire attitude and often married the local womenfolk. There had also been discussions amongst British commanders about using native American warriors, while some local tribes were sympathetic to British interests, especially where trade was concerned – most notably the Iroquois people, who lived along the Great Lakes and were suspicious of French expansionism. However, fraternisation was usually a matter of striking the best local deal, and as a result misunderstandings were commonplace.

Pictorial evidence of the time, such as George Townshend's unflattering sketches of native Americans, reinforced existing prejudices and the written evidence is equally compelling. Amherst routinely described native Americans as 'subhuman' and beyond the 'rules of law' (although on occasions he could also write about them with touching sentimentality, almost as if he were describing pet animals or children). So deeply ingrained was this feeling of racial superiority that in one letter he admitted that he would gladly 'extirpate this execrable race', although to put this observation into context it has to be admitted that Amherst was writing after he had received news about the slaughter of soldiers in isolated garrisons and the grisly scalping of women and children. In one horrific incident witnessed by Captain John Knox of the 43rd Foot, a missing soldier was eventually found in the woods, 'killed and scalped; one of his arms was cut off; his bowels were taken out and cut into shreds, almost innumerable, with a long skewer thrust through his upper lip, nostrils and the crown of his head; the bloodhounds carried away his heart'.[10] Having witnessed the cruelty, Knox added that the Indians (as he and many others called native Americans) made 'undesirable allies'; clearly, in the aftermath of the French surrender, war in the wilderness areas of Canada and North America was not for the squeamish.

The matter had also been complicated by an outbreak of violence in the state of South Carolina, where tensions between the local population and the previously peaceable Cherokee people erupted into open warfare in early 1760. Unable to contain the uprising, state governor William Henry Lyttelton contacted Amherst and asked him to send reinforcements. According to Lyttelton the behaviour of the Cherokees in the spring of 1760 had alarmed all the southern colonies, and that accounted for his request for assistance. The resulting force was drawn from the British garrison at Fort Duquesne and consisted of a small number of colonials, plus 1200 regular soldiers in two battalions – the 2nd Royals and the 77th Highlanders, both of which had served in North America since 1758. The Royals had been one of the government regiments at Culloden and had also taken part in the subsequent pacification operations in the western Highlands, while some of the 700 men in the 77th Highlanders had either fought in Prince Charles's army at Culloden or had been recruited from areas with strong Jacobite sympathies. (One example of this tendency will stand for many: serving in Fraser's Highlanders at Quebec was Patrick Grant, also known as Black Peter of Craskie, one of the 'Seven Men of Moriston' who had given shelter to Prince Charles during the summer of

1746. He would have been well acquainted with the government army's brutality in the West Highlands after Culloden.[11])

In command of the operation was Colonel Alexander Montgomery; an Irishman with a taste for violence, he received orders to proceed as quickly as possible into the country of the Cherokees, and after 'chastising' them to return to New York, to prepare for Amherst's expedition against Montreal. By the middle of June Montgomery's force had reached the vicinity of the Cherokee town Little Keowee; here he left his baggage train under guard while detaching the light companies of the Royals and the Highlanders to destroy the surrounding area. Montgomery's next step was to march on to the town of Estatoe, where the main force of Cherokees had assembled and where he hoped to surprise them. However, on their arrival at Estatoe, they found the enemy had fled. Montgomery then retired to Fort Prince George; finding that the recent operation had had no effect, he paid a second visit to Little Keowee, where he met with more resistance and suffered casualties – 2 officers and 20 men killed, 26 officers and 68 men wounded. Having completed their work, Montgomery's force returned to Fort Prince George.

Meanwhile, the rest of the Cherokees had not been idle. They laid siege to Fort Loudon, a small fort on the border with Virginia, defended by 200 men and possessing only a small stock of provisions and ammunition. The garrison was too weak to take on the enemy in open battle and was eventually compelled by starvation to surrender with the full honours of war, namely on condition of being permitted to return to Charleston carrying their colours and weapons. However, as happened on so many occasions, the Cherokee warriors observed the convention only as far as it was in their interests to do so and attacked the garrison on its march. In the resulting massacre all the officers were killed except for

Captain John Stuart, a Charleston merchant and member of the South Carolina militia who had emigrated from Inverness after the Jacobite rebellion. Later in life, and as a result of the compassion shown to him by Cherokee leader *Attakullakulla* (Little Carpenter), he used the experience to further the interests of friendship with the Cherokee people.

The Royals already had direct experience of punitive operations, and in response to the Cherokee offensive, according to the regimental historian 'their instructions were to kill all the males they could and to burn their settlements'.[12] Under the command of Major Frederick Hamilton, the 2nd battalion carried out its task with grim efficiency. Villages were put to the torch and Cherokee men were rounded up and slaughtered. All resistance was crushed; not even the Cherokees' 'horrid gestures and ear-piercing yells' – which, according to one account, the soldiers in the Royals found 'more terrible than the slogan of the Gaels' – prevented the force from carrying out its bloody business. In the modern world such operations would be counted as atrocities, but from the outset the relationship between the colonists and the native Americans had been fraught with tensions which led to frequent and uncontrolled outbreaks of violence on both sides. In some places and during some periods a live-and-let-live policy prevailed, but as the colonists began expanding their territories there were too many cases of both sides cheating the other during commercial dealings, with the result that violence was endemic. In the Royals' case the native Americans proved to be particularly resilient, and it took a total of three operations before the Cherokees of South Carolina were finally crushed by superior firepower. The losses in the Royals were thirty-nine officers and men killed, plus a small number wounded.

In the greater scheme of things, the Cherokee War did not

achieve much and the fighting petered out with neither side gaining any advantage. Montgomery was replaced by his second-in-command, Major James Grant of Ballindalloch, who with a larger force of 2600 brought the fighting to an end in 1761, when the British regiments withdrew from the south Appalachians having carried out a scorched-earth policy which was eerily similar to the operations in the West Highlands after Culloden.[13] However, a curious by-product of the campaign had a long-term effect on the way in which the British Army was perceived: it cemented the martial allure of the Highland soldiers and played its part in laying the foundation for the later romanticism which surrounded the figure of the kilted Highlander. By the time the Seven Years War came to an end, the British Army in North America numbered 24,000 soldiers, and of those around 4000 were Scots serving in four Highland battalions – two battalions of the 42nd, Fraser's 78th and Montgomerie's 77th. With their belted plaids and weapons, they formed a distinctive grouping within the army, a sense of 'otherness' reinforced by the fact that many of the men were Gaelic speakers with little or no understanding of English.

They lived up to their martial billing too, demonstrating dash and élan in attack; from the outset of their service in North America they had caught the eye in battle, attracting the attention of letter writers, diarists and other commentators. At the battle of Ticonderoga in 1758 the 42nd had suffered massive casualties, but a watching English officer compared their charge to 'roaring lions breaking from their chains' and the phrase stuck.[14] From feats like these came a romantic and well-recorded belief that there was a close affinity between the Highland soldier and the native American warrior. Both seemed to be noble savages, both were skilled in field craft, both appeared strange and other-worldly in their dress and behaviour, both possessed a barbaric allure on the field of battle and both seemed to be at ease in the wilderness of the Appalachian mountains. At least one British commander in North America was sufficiently moved by the similarities between the two very different peoples to describe them as 'cousins'.[15] It is also noteworthy that soldiers like James Grant of Ballindalloch, later a leading Highland member of parliament, had a sentimental attachment to the Cherokee people, though this fellow feeling did not extend to any support for the abolition of slavery. The phenomenon is still hotly debated; yet, while many of the comparisons are fanciful, it is probably quite true that, as soldiers, both the Highlanders and the native American warrior felt equally at home in the rugged landscape of the Carolinas and Virginia.[16]

At the same time the Scottish Highland soldiers had reinforced an unassailable reputation for their swiftness and ferocity in attack; according to one contemporary account written in a letter from the battlefront, the enemy had come to believe that the Highlanders enjoyed superhuman properties:

By private accounts, it appears that the French had formed the most frightful and absurd notions of the Sauvages d'Ecosse. They believed that they would neither take nor give quarter, and that they were so nimble, that, as no man could catch them, so nobody could escape them; that no man had a chance against their broadsword; and that, with a ferocity natural to savages they made no prisoners, and spared neither man, woman nor child: and as they were always in the forefront of every action in which they were engaged, it is probable that these notions had no small influence on the nerves of the militia, and perhaps regulars of Guadeloupe. It was always believed by the enemy that the Highlanders amounted to several thousands. This erroneous enumeration of a corps only eight hundred strong, was said to proceed from the frequency of their attacks and annoyance of the outposts of the enemy who 'saw men in the same garb who attacked them yesterday from one direction, again appear today to advance from another, and in this manner ever harassing their advanced position to allow them no rest.'[17]

The reality was slightly different. Like the rest of the army, apart from their tartan plaids the men were dressed in the same unyielding red uniforms which they had worn in Europe, complete with pipe-clayed belts. The ensemble might have looked smart but it was hardly suitable for local conditions; it was not uncommon for soldiers to tailor their uniforms or to adapt civilian clothes, especially in the wilderness areas. They also had to carry their muzzle-loading muskets and ammunition, knowing that in wet weather they were useless. In action a soldier had to pull the cartridge from his pouch, remove the top by biting, shake powder into the priming pan, put the ball and the wadding into the barrel, press them home with the ramrod, return the ramrod to its position on the musket, fix the plug bayonet and then fire the weapon, which was only accurate over fifty paces. As battlefield tactics depended on the men following the firing procedure like clockwork, it is no wonder that the best regiments insisted on strict discipline.

That said, as the French account about 'the Sauvages d'Ecosse' makes clear, the Highlanders had learned from the experience of the fighting in North America, where some of the best units were the light infantrymen of the Royal American Regiment commanded by the Swiss-born Colonels Frederick Haldimand and Henry Bouquet. Their loose-knit fighting formations and field discipline were impressive, and they led the way in adapting to local conditions by docking their full-skirted red coats and using native American weapons such as tomahawks for close-quarter fighting. In the 42nd Royal Highlanders some soldiers abandoned their kilts and plaids for breeches, especially when they were fighting in rough woodland. They also learned to fire their weapons from a prone position and to fire independently when the need arose. Many of those innovations were adopted by the British regular infantry battalions serving in North America; the Highlanders in particular proved to be adept at this new kind of irregular warfare.

With the fighting against the native American people in the Appalachians having died down for the time being, Amherst was free to organise operations in the West Indies in pursuit of Pitt's policy of attacking French garrisons wherever they existed. In the Caribbean this meant assaulting Guadeloupe, the key to Dominica, as well as the French island of Martinique, which had been captured in 1759 only to fall back into French hands; both were valuable prizes, being important sugar-producing islands and therefore generators of trade (including slaves) and cash. The two battalions of the 42nd were amongst a 13,000 strong force sent back to the area to retake Martinique at the beginning of 1762 under the command of Robert Monckton, who was serving as commander-in-chief of the New York garrison. His second-in-command was William Haviland, and command of the fleet was in the capable hands of Rear-Admiral George Rodney, who had previous experience of amphibious operations at Rochefort and Louisbourg. Unlike the previous assault, when there had been a lack of firepower to support the landings, this time there was sufficient artillery and the French garrison on the island surrendered on 7 February. Under his command Monckton had three battalions which had served at Culloden, namely the 4th (Barrell's), the 27th (Blakeney's) and the 48th (Conway's). These were in addition to the Highland soldiers of the 42nd, who distinguished themselves yet again when they 'rushed forward like furies' in the attack to capture the French artillery battery defending the town and citadel of Fort Royal. During the course of the action the regiment lost two officers and thirteen soldiers killed, while seven officers and seventy-six soldiers were wounded.

In the aftermath of the fighting a new governor was appointed to Guadeloupe: he was Robert Melville, last seen at Blair Castle in the operations before Culloden. Having remained in the army he had served in Flanders and had fought at the battles of Rocoux and Lauffeld. By then a brigadier-general, he took part in the assault on Guadeloupe, where he was badly wounded and later became blind. Melville was a typical British army officer of that period – a clergyman's son, modest, well connected but not wealthy, and utterly committed to his profession. Like so many of his kind he died unmarried, in his case in 1809 when he was the second oldest general in the British Army.

Whilst these operations were taking place, Spain took advantage of the instability in the Caribbean to declare war on Britain in support of the French. As a result a second force was raised under the command of the 3rd Earl of Albemarle (as Lord Bury of Culloden fame had become in 1754 in succession to his father) and was given the task of securing the island of Cuba, another important sugar-producing territory. Albemarle's brothers Augustus and William Keppel also served under his command, while command of the naval task force was given to Vice-Admiral Sir George Pocock, a cousin of the disgraced John Byng and an experienced sailor who had made his name fighting in the Indian theatre of the war.

Arriving off Havana at the beginning of June, Albemarle

decided to lay siege to the massive fortress of El Morro, which guarded the eastern side of the mouth of the harbour. Unfortunately this proved to be a time-consuming business, and it was made no easier by the fact that the guns of Pocock's ships could not be elevated sufficiently to join the bombardment. With stalemate threatening, the matter was resolved when a smaller force of light infantry and marines landed on the western side of the harbour under the command of Lieutenant-Colonel (later General Sir) William Howe, the man who had led Wolfe's troops up the cliff before the battle of Quebec. At the end of July the explosion of a mine allowed El Morro to be stormed and after some fierce close-quarter fighting the fortress fell into British hands. Amongst the attacking party were 200 men of the 2nd Royals under the command of Lieutenant Charles Forbes, who put the remaining garrison to the sword after the Spanish survivors ignored the ceasefire.

It was a timely victory. As always happened in operations in the Caribbean, more casualties were lost to illness and disease than to enemy musket or artillery fire; sickness was now taking a grip in the besieging army and causing unacceptably high casualties. The total number of deaths was 5366, the bulk of these the result of disease (mainly yellow fever, malaria and dysentery), and within weeks the toll would rise to double that number. To give one example of regimental losses, in the 42nd Highlanders eight officers were killed in battle but eighty-two officers and men succumbed to sickness.

However, from a strategic point of view it had been worth it. Havana, the so-called 'key to the New World', was not only a major port exporting tobacco and sugar but was also the historic symbol of Spanish maritime power in the Caribbean. Pitt understood the problems involved in taking the place, but he also knew that it sent an unmistakable message to the Spanish. Havana was not just a prize worth winning – the Royal Navy captured the entire Spanish squadron of eighteen warships – but would also be a crucial bargaining counter in the peace negotiations which began the following year.

After the successful conclusion of the expedition the bulk of Monckton's and Albemarle's army returned to New York, amongst them the 1st battalion of the 42nd Highlanders. With them they took the bulk of the fit men of the Highlanders' 2nd battalion, which had been disbanded as part of the defence cuts which followed the end of the war.

In addition to overseeing the campaign in the Caribbean, Amherst also had to establish a military government which would govern Canada in the aftermath of his victory at Montreal in 1760. This territory included New France and the lands to the west known as *pays d'en haut* ('the upper country'), which was made up of present-day Michigan, Ontario, Ohio, Indiana and Illinois. Until a new civil administration was formed, this required him to divide the area into three administrative districts; these were controlled by James Murray, Thomas Gage and Ralph Burton, the last a Yorkshireman who had commanded the 48th Foot during the Quebec campaign. Altogether they had about 16,000 soldiers under their command, far too few men for such a large area, and with little hope of reinforcement – on cost grounds as much as any other – Amherst had to fall back on other tactics. One was the introduction of settlement programmes centred on the chain of existing forts, just as Humphrey Bland and Lord Milton had proposed in Scotland as a means of pacifying the Highlands after Culloden.

Many of those who petitioned for grants of land had served in the British regiments of the garrison in North America and were not inclined to return home. In the aftermath of the French collapse, most of them petitioned for lands on the two sides of the Hudson River, between Lake George and Lake Champlain, and east of the Green Mountains. Captains were entitled to 3000 acres, lieutenants to 2000, sergeants 200, corporals 100 and privates 50.[18] It was a workable idea which could have encouraged trade and regulated immigration into Canada, but it had a fatal flaw. The presence of local native American peoples, especially in the western territories, meant that tribal lands might be encroached upon, while the growing European settlements seemed to be an abrogation of British promises to withdraw their army at the conclusion of hostilities and to encourage trade. As most of these tribes had supported France it seemed a double betrayal, a feeling aggravated by the British practice of treating the native Americans as a defeated people and not as potential future allies. The discontent was also fanned by Amherst's decision to discontinue the custom of giving presents (or as he called them, 'bribes') to local tribal leaders and to cut back on their supplies of powder and ball. The first issue was a matter of pride and courtesy – the gifts were redistributed to the tribe and were important for maintaining prestige – but the second created real hardship; it restricted hunting for food and furs, thus causing desperate problems for the local native American population.

Inevitably Amherst's policies began to cause resentment in *pays d'en haut*, where most of the native Americans had supported the French. This was exacerbated by the outbreak of epidemics, including smallpox, and by the predictable starvation following food shortages as a result of discontinuing the supplies of ammunition. Far from cowing the local people, however, such hardships prompted a revivalist movement of religious intensity inspired by the teachings of a number of self-proclaimed prophets amongst the Delaware people in the Susquehanna valley. Their message was essentially that the 'Master of Life' or the 'Great Spirit' had been angered by the British presence and had been greatly displeased by the Delawares' adoption of European ways of living, not least their heavy consumption of alcohol. Very quickly the message spread amongst other tribes in Ohio and the Great Lakes; matters came to a head in 1761 with the emergence of a particularly charismatic prophet known as Neolin, who urged the people to consider an uprising as the only means of purging the evil of the British presence. Allied to the existing problems of hunger, illness and social depredation, this was a powder keg waiting to explode. In an attempt to stop that happening, Sir William Johnson summoned a conference in Fort Detroit to address the issues raised by the prophecies. While this papered over the problem, mainly by proposing a partial renewal of gifts, it solved nothing, for the very good reason that Amherst was still bitterly opposed to rewarding the native Americans in return for their friendship. In a warning letter to Johnson he insisted that those attending the conference should be told that 'We have it in our power to reduce them to Reason'. Having such a low opinion of the native Americans' fighting ability, Amherst insisted that any future hostilities would be put down quickly and efficiently, just as the recent Cherokee revolt had been. In his view British soldiers who had meted out a heavy defeat to another European army outside Quebec and Montreal were unlikely to be discomfited by 'a perfidious race of Savages'.[19]

Such an attitude made matters worse, as amongst the British high command it reinforced the notion of white racial superiority. As a result the situation continued to deteriorate, coming to a head on 27 April 1763 at a meeting held ten miles outside Fort

Detroit. It was addressed by a shadowy war leader of the Ottawas called Pontiac, who urged the assembled warriors to attack the weakly defended British garrison as a first step in driving them out of the area. Around 400 warriors agreed to join the uprising, and it began on 7 May with an assault on Fort Detroit, although this was beaten off by the smaller British Army garrison of 125 regulars commanded by Major Henry Gladwin, a veteran of the Indian wars who had served under Braddock at Monongahela. Although the attack failed – probably because news of it had been betrayed to Gladwin – it sparked a wider revolt across the area, with other British outposts being attacked by warriors from six different tribes.

Perhaps the most distressing incident in this phase of the uprising occurred in late June at Fort Pitt, a heavily defended fortification built in 1759 on the site of Fort Duquesne. It was under the command of Captain Simeon Ecuyer of the Royal American Regiment, and although he was well equipped to withstand a siege the garrison had been swollen by refugees from the surrounding area and he knew that he could not hold out indefinitely. When the Delaware leaders asked for a truce to discuss the situation, Ecuyer agreed, and as part of the parley he handed over a gift of provisions and supplies; these, however, included blankets from the garrison's hospital which had been used by smallpox victims. Whether or not this was a deliberate and cynical move is unknown, but the event was witnessed by a visiting trader and was fully recorded.[20] Some weeks later, on 16 July, Amherst told Lieutenant-Colonel Henry Bouquet of the Royal American Regiment that he approved of this method of dealing with the native Americans: 'You will Do well to try to Innoculate the Indians by means of Blanketts, as well as to try Every other method that can serve to Extirpate this Execreble Race.'[21] This chimed with

Amherst's general orders to his commanders to take no prisoners during the revolt and matched his general contempt for the whole native American race.

It was a short jump from such words to subsequent claims that Amherst was an early advocate of biological warfare. It is known that a smallpox epidemic broke out near Fort Pitt in the spring of 1763, while Amherst's letter to Bouquet commending the use of infected blankets as a weapon of war was at one with his general correspondence, which was ripe with racist comments about the native opposition. Given the tenor of the times and the well-known fact that native American attacks on the European community 'aroused Amherst to a frenzy, a frenzy almost hysterical in its impotence', it is relatively easy to proceed to the conclusion that the British were responsible for using smallpox as a weapon during the period of Pontiac's revolt. The plague claimed several hundred victims in the Ohio valley and because its eruption coincided with the distribution of the infected blankets, the charges against Amherst have stuck;[22] down the years he has been accused of everything from genocide to fomenting biological warfare. According to the findings of the most recent research, 'while blame for this outbreak cannot be placed squarely in the British camp, the circumstantial evidence is nevertheless suggestive.'[23]

By way of balance we should remind ourselves that the Delaware people and other native Americans were themselves capable of visiting great cruelties on local settlers and prisoners who fell into their hands, but that does not excuse matters. However, there is no hard evidence to suggest that the act of giving possibly infected blankets sparked the epidemic or that the tactic was official British policy; the best that can be said is that the whole incident is not proven.

Because the attempted truce with the Delaware people had

come to nothing Fort Pitt was immediately besieged, and by the end of June the country between Pennsylvania and the Ohio was laid waste by native Americans who had heeded Pontiac's call to revolt and reacted by attacking remote British forts such as St Joseph, Miamis, Peesquile and Mackinaw. All that was available to Amherst for the relief of Fort Pitt was a scratch force of Highlanders of the 42nd and Montgomerie's 77th, with contingents of the Royal American Regiment under Bouquet's command. Although many of the men were exhausted by their efforts in the Caribbean, they rallied at Bushy Run in Westmoreland County in Pennsylvania on 5 August, and by dint of superior tactics and disciplined musket fire inflicted a defeat which successfully achieved its objective of relieving Fort Pitt. According to Sir John Fortescue, there had been 'few finer performances in its scale than this victory of a handful of English, Highlanders and Germans under the leadership of a Swiss colonel [Henry Bouquet]'.[24]

Pontiac's revolt had come as an unpleasant surprise to the British government, who could not understand why a handful of unsophisticated (for so it seemed) native Americans had managed to tie down a professional British army which had so recently defeated the French and driven them out of North America. It mattered not that Pontiac's uprising had been put down by the end of the year: the very fact that it had taken place meant that the British garrison could not be cut back and soldiers would still be needed in the locality. As a result Amherst was recalled to London in November 1763 and his place was taken by Thomas Gage. This was an outcome which Amherst had long desired, but his return to London was clouded by his wife's mental illness and by the loss of his main patrons. With Ligonier's career in decline and Cumberland having fallen victim to a stroke, it was by no means certain that he would receive support from King George III or the newly formed Bute admin-istration. By this time, too, the Seven Years War had been con-cluded by the Treaty of Paris, but Amherst's career was already entering a sharp decline; although he was ennobled and eventu-ally came back to high command during the American War of Independence, he was never able to capitalise on his leadership at Louisbourg, where Wolfe had picked up all the plaudits. Amherst was one of those unfortunate generals who had started well and had prospered by being one of Cumberland's favourites, but whose name has been overlooked largely as a result of his failure to win one major battle in the field.

10

THE WORLD AT WAR: INDIA

In the late summer of 1756, a small convoy of ships of the Honourable East India Company made its way towards the approaches of Madras, the principal city on the Coromandel Coast, which had been returned to Britain from the brief possession of the French in 1749 as a result of the Treaty of Aix-la-Chapelle. On board was a draft of soldiers to reinforce the 39th Foot, raised in 1689 for service in Ireland as Lisburne's Regiment of Foot. Its colonel was John Aldercron, a Huguenot Irishman who was already in his sixties. Despite the benefits of age and experience, however – he had served in Europe in the Low Countries – Aldercron was clearly not up to the job he was about to assume, being described as 'a prickly, pompous mediocrity with no experience of Indian troops and Indian warfare'.[1]

That being said, the regiment he commanded did have a special place in history. It was the first British line infantry regiment to move to India, where after an uncertain start it would be based for the following two decades, and it remained intensely proud of that fact: later in life, as The Dorset Regiment, its cap badge was adorned with the motto *Primus in Indus*. Commanding the detachment sent to Madras was Captain Eyre Coote, formerly of Blakeney's Regiment (later the 27th Foot), who following the Battle of Falkirk had run away from the field carrying the regimental colours before unwisely arriving in Edinburgh ahead of his defeated regiment. Having survived the inevitable court martial, and following a period of service as a cavalry officer in Germany, he had ended up in the 37th Foot before transferring to the 39th. It was to be the making of Coote, but before taking his story further it is necessary to recount the recent history of Madras, his first destination.

At the time India was largely under the control of the Moghul emperors, Central Asian Turko-Mongols from modern-day Uzbekistan, who claimed direct descent from the warrior emperors Genghis Khan and Timur (Tamerlane). In the late sixteenth and early seventeenth centuries the Moghuls controlled much of the Indian subcontinent, but by the middle of the following century their influence was in decline. The situation was complicated by the presence of two European nations jostling for power under the guise of their powerful trading companies. Britain operated in India through the Honourable East India Company, which had been founded by royal charter in 1600 to trade with the 'East Indies' and had opened its first trading station two years later in the town of Machilipatnam on the Coromandel Coast. To begin with its main rivals were the Dutch, but they were replaced in mid-century by the more formidable challenge of France's Compagnie des Indes Orientales. By the time of Coote's arrival the British presence centred on three main areas or presidencies: Madras (Chennai) and the Coromandel Coast, which guarded the province of the Carnatic; Bombay (Mumbai) on the Malabar

Coast; and Calcutta (Kolkata) in the province of Bengal. Each presidency was governed by an autonomous council consisting mainly of local merchants under the chairmanship of a president or governor.

During the wars of dynastic succession which racked Europe in the first half of the eighteenth century, half-hearted attempts had been made to keep at bay the rivalry between Britain and France in India. Such efforts had been reinforced by various Moghul rulers, who reminded the British and the French that they were allowed to operate in India only on condition that 'they behave themselves peacable and quietly'.[2] The man responsible for challenging that ruling during the War of the Austrian Succession was Joseph François Dupleix; having first arrived in southern India in 1715, he had quickly emerged as a successful trader and colonial administrator with ambitions to turn the French holdings into colonies which would rival New France in distant Canada. His chance came in 1746 with the arrival off the Coromandel Coast of a French fleet under the command of Bertrand-François Mahé de La Bourdonnais, governor of Mauritius, an important French possession in the Indian Ocean. La Bourdonnais' arrival prompted the capture of Madras in September and the subsequent routing of the army of the Carnatic, following an ill-advised attempt by the Nawab of the Carnatic to impose his veto on hostilities. This led to two things: at one stroke France became masters of the Carnatic – an area of southern India which embraces the modern states of Tamil Nadu, south eastern Karnataka, north eastern Kerala and southern Andhra Pradesh – and native Indian soldiers had been revealed as ineffectual in the face of the discipline and superior firepower of European forces. However, at that point Dupleix and La Bourdonnais quarrelled, and with the war in Europe coming to an end the operations in southern India reached stalemate. French prestige rode high, while the standing of the British was the precise opposite. The only glimmer of satisfaction for the East India Company was the clause in the Treaty of Aix-la-Chapelle which exchanged Madras for Louisbourg in Canada.

It was at this nadir of British influence that two men emerged to rescue their country's fortunes and to lay the basis for Britain's subsequent empire in India. The senior of the two was an unlikely hero. Born in Hereford in 1697, Stringer Lawrence had entered the army thirty years later, shortly before Christmas 1727, presumably because he was at a loss what to do next with his life – thirty was relatively old to become an ensign. Commissioned into Clayton's Regiment, he served in Gibraltar and Spain; later, when it became Price's Regiment, he fought at Fontenoy and then again in the front line of the government army at Culloden. At the end of the Jacobite campaign Lawrence reassessed his position, resigning his commission in order to join the army of the East India Company in an effort to improve his financial status – the Company's records show that he was appointed at a salary of £250, with expenses of 'one hundred guineas for his charges out'. Lawrence arrived in Madras with the rank of major at the beginning of 1748, aged fifty, and was described as 'robustly corpulent'. Even so, he was also energetic and astute, and he soon built up a close affinity with the men who would serve under him. No sooner had he arrived than he began transforming the Company's soldiers into an effective fighting force.[3]

The second man could not have been more different. Robert Clive was twenty-eight years Lawrence's junior; born in Market Drayton in 1725, he had led a somewhat aimless life before being indentured into the East India Company as a writer or clerk in 1743. He seems to have been an awkward employee, quick to take offence and slow to fit in, and on at least one occasion his homesickness led him to attempt suicide. Dupleix's machinations against Madras changed everything and put him on an entirely different tack. During the French attack Clive quickly made his way out of the city for Fort St David, where he obtained a commission after making himself useful by working on the local defences. On Lawrence's arrival Clive again made sure that he was noticed, and so began a good working connection between these two very different men – Clive the highly strung amateur soldier and the older, self-effacing and experienced Lawrence. Quite early in the relationship the older man came to the conclusion that his younger charge possessed 'a martial disposition' and that it was his duty to act as a father figure and mentor. Being an ambitious young man, Clive respected Lawrence's advice and encouragement, and it is no exaggeration to claim that between the two men's efforts can be found the beginnings of the British Indian Army.

However, it is also fair to say that their first exercise in military co-operation was not a success. With British forces bolstered by the arrival of a battle fleet in July 1748 under Rear-Admiral Edward Boscawen, it was decided to attack the French holdings at Pondicherry, but although the British outnumbered the French there was confusion in the British chain of command (a good sailor, Boscawen was no soldier). Lawrence was taken prisoner and Boscawen was forced to withdraw his warships without the objective being achieved.

What followed was a turning point for both sides. In place of the previous commercial rivalry between the two companies, which acted as a surrogate for the wider enmity between Britain and France, southern India, particularly the Carnatic, also became a battleground. Most of the credit for this turnaround is usually given to Dupleix, but the British too were no slouches when it came to involving themselves in local intrigues, supporting one local leader against another, withdrawing support on a whim and double-dealing when the moment suited them. As the Company's most recent historian saw the situation on the eve of the Seven Years War: 'For 150 years the Company had been endeavouring to appease the existing political hierarchy; in three years Dupleix had simply usurped it. The English must either follow suit or leave the table.'[4]

However, there was a problem. Between 1749 and 1756 Britain and France were not officially at war and therefore could not do battle against one another in southern India. This meant that the proxy war had to continue, with the result that the ensuing Carnatic War (as it came to be known) was often an inchoate and muddled process. Briefly stated, both sides concentrated their efforts on supporting rival puppet rulers. In 1749 Dupleix threw the weight of France behind Chanda Sahib in his claim for the Nawabship of the Carnatic, while Britain plumped for Mohammed Ali, the son of Chanda's murdered rival. In the following year Dupleix upped the stakes by supporting the claims of Muzaffar Jang – a close ally of Chanda Sahib – for the Nizimate of neighbouring Hyderabad. Britain responded to the challenge by using the army that was being developed by Lawrence and Clive. In September 1751 Trichinopoly, capital of neighbouring Tanjore, was put under siege while Clive marched inland towards the fortified town of Arcot, at the head of a force of 500 men plus three field guns. He took possession of the town and fort without any opposition, thus delivering a blow to French prestige and making a great impression on the local people. Having secured Arcot, Clive then proceeded to hold it against Chanda Sahib's forces.

At the same time Lawrence departed India for leave in London in order to speak to the Company about his conditions of employment. He must have produced a convincing argument, because he returned the following spring with his pay doubled to £500 and with the new rank of commander-in-chief in the Company's service. (As a royal officer in the British Army he retained the rank of major.)[5] He immediately repaid the debt by bringing coherence to the operations at Trichinopoly, where he defeated a French force on the island of Srirangam in the River Cauvery (Kaveri) outside the city walls. With him Lawrence had brought another veteran from Culloden in the shape of John Caillaud, a Huguenot Irishman who had served in Wolfe's Regiment in the second line of Cumberland's army. In common with several other officers from that campaign, Caillaud had been attracted by the adventure of serving in India and having a settled career in the Company's service, in his case first as a captain and then as commander-in-chief in Madras. His niece later described him as 'a man of great fire of character and personal spirit ... and possessed of strong natural talents'.[6] In other words, he was just the sort of leader that was needed in a fast-moving campaign in which officers were required to show initiative in front of their men and to take risks without reference to higher command.

Although Lawrence's initiative did not end the fighting it restored the prestige of Mohammed Ali, who gained some ground not least because his rival Chanda Sahib had been murdered by the Tanjoreans after surrendering. The skirmishing also revealed the improvements which had taken place in the effectiveness of the Company forces. Not only was their sustained firepower superior to the undoubted courage shown by the French native troops but they also benefited from the leadership of experienced officers such as Lawrence and Caillaud.

Dupleix's unexpected recall to France after 'falling a victim to obscure intrigues and jealousies in Versailles'[7] brought this phase of the fighting to an end, but both sides continued to take the opportunity to reinforce their forces with fresh drafts from Europe. With war about to break out again between the two countries, another trial of strength was in the offing; this time it would involve the north-eastern province of Bengal, where the British and French companies also had important trading interests.

At the time the ruler of Bengal was the Nawab Alivardi Khan, who kept a wary eye on the European presence from his new capital at Murshidabad, likening them to bees 'of whose honey you might reap the profit, but if you disturbed their hive they could sting you to death'.[8] Already alarmed by events in the Carnatic, where it seemed that European rivalries were unduly influencing events, he became additionally sensitive when the British and the French started taking steps to reinforce their presence in Bengal. First the French strengthened their defensive positions at Chandernagar, then the British looked to do the same at Fort William, a stronghold already condemned by Boscawen because it 'does not appear to be a place capable of making a long resistance'.[9]

Built by the Company on the banks of the River Hooghly in 1696, the fort was the centre of British commercial activity but it was hopelessly obsolescent, being compared to 'a deserted and ruined Moorish fort'. At the prompting of the Company a newly appointed engineer-general drew up plans for Fort William to be rebuilt as a garrison for one thousand European troops, capable of withstanding modern siege warfare. The engineer in question was Colonel Caroline Frederick Scott, who had served in the government army at Culloden and had attracted a sulphurous reputation for his activities in suppressing the population of the

West Highlands in the aftermath of the battle. Having made such a dire name for himself in the Scottish Highlands, it might have been expected that Scott would simply bulldozer his plans through the governing council, of which he was a member, and an eminent one at that – he was described as 'a gentleman of distinguished abilities and character' – but instead he proved to be circumspect and punctilious in his dealings with Company and Bengali officials alike. Having finalised the plans for the rebuilding of Fort William, he asked that they be forwarded to the Nawab for approval. This happy proposal was vetoed by the Company's agent on the grounds that Alivardi Khan would either turn down the plans without discussion or simply demand an exorbitant bribe. As a result nothing was done, and the matter lapsed in May 1754 when Scott died of fever during a visit to inspect the fortifications at Madras.[10]

Thus the Company got the worst of both worlds. Scott's death robbed them of an experienced and well-respected military engineer whose skills would have undoubtedly improved the defences at Fort William; at the same time the failure to present the plans to the Nawab only heightened the existing tensions between him and the British. Scott's reputation also remained in a curious kind of purgatory, being for ever associated with the cruelties practised by the government army in the operations after Culloden rather than with the kind of forward-thinking military engineering involved in the development of British interests in India. In the opinion of a later observer, had the plans been shown to the Nawab and had permission for the rebuilding been secured, Scott's 'name would almost certainly have ranked high amongst the founders of our Indian Empire'.[11]

By then the Nawab had been succeeded by his nephew Siraj-ud-Daula, who proved to be no less confrontational or suspicious than his predecessor. Shortly after succeeding to the Nawabship, Siraj complained to the Company about their plans to rebuild Fort William and their fortification of the nearby town of Kasimbazar. Unfortunately the Company's officials misread the seriousness of the situation and thought that Siraj would be placated by a bribe, but the new Nawab's blood was up. On 18 June he launched a huge army (rumoured to be 50,000 strong, plus war elephants) against Calcutta, with predictable success. The feeble Company garrison was quickly overwhelmed and all authority collapsed with equal rapidity, around a hundred of the survivors being locked up in the fort's guardroom where many succumbed to the crowded conditions and heat. Among those who died were Colonel Caroline Scott's nephew, Ensign William Scott. In the shocked aftermath, the fate of those imprisoned in the so-called 'Black Hole of Calcutta' became known and this 'infernal scene of horror' was later turned into an exemplar of Indian brutality and frightfulness. This was in no small measure due to the efforts of the new commander in Calcutta, John Zephania Holwell, who survived the ordeal and went on to write a fanciful and lurid account of what had happened in the confines of the tiny detention cell.[12]

Horrifying though this was to people back home in Britain, who were shocked by the barbaric details, it was balanced by some relief that the Company was still in business, albeit operating down river at Fulta, and had not lost financially as a result of the affair. The fact that news from India took many weeks to arrive and was usually out of date or had been overtaken by events once it became public knowledge helped soften the blow. Even so, the Company was under pressure to produce a positive response to the outrage; by October a relief force had been pulled together in Madras under the command of Clive and Vice-Admiral Charles

Watson, who had served earlier as governor of Newfoundland. As the senior royal officer, flying his flag in HMS *Kent*, Watson took precedence over Clive – this was common practice in India – but an accommodation was reached which allowed the Company officer to command the ground forces, which amounted to 900 European soldiers including 250 of the 39th Foot, and 1500 sepoys.

If precedence had been followed, command of the ground forces would have been given to Colonel Aldercron, but it was wisely decided that his appointment would be disastrous due to his well-known lack of military ability. By way of revenge Aldercron forbade any royal forces to be used in the expedition, but he eventually relented and allowed three companies of the 39th to take part. It was a good decision: one of them was commanded by Eyre Coote and a second by James Grant (not to be confused with Major James Grant of Ballindalloch), another army veteran of the Jacobite campaign.

Despite the adverse weather conditions – it was the monsoon season – the expedition set sail in October, the earliest date it could be made ready. Consisting of five transports and four warships (HMS *Cumberland*, HMS *Tiger*, HMS *Salisbury* and HMS *Bridgwater*), it was not a large force, but it was all that could be spared; Watson was under strict instructions to get it back to Madras with all due haste to meet a new but expected French intervention in India. By then Britain and France were drifting to war again, and the Madras Council had intelligence that a French force of nineteen ships and 3000 troops was assembling at Brest ready to sail to India. This meant that Bengal had to be secured quickly, so that Madras could begin preparations for its own defence against the expected onslaught.

On arrival in Bengal shortly before Christmas, the small army prepared to march up the River Hooghly towards Calcutta on 27

December. But first it would have to overcome the obstacle posed by a fort at Budge Budge (Baj-baj) which guarded the route to Calcutta.[13] Although Siraj's forces enjoyed numerical superiority and almost managed to mount a surprise attack in the hours of darkness on 30 December, Clive's men showed steadiness under fire and the position was taken relatively easily. There was also an element of farce when an intoxicated sailor called Strachan made his way on to the fort's bastions and shouted loudly 'This place is mine!'[14] Fortunately it was empty of enemy troops. On Watson's orders the sailor was promptly arrested for this serious breach of discipline, no allowance being made for the fact that he was a Scot and that it was New Year. 'Thus the place was taken without the least honour to anyone,' noted Coote in his diary of the campaign.[15]

Having gained control of this section of the river, Clive was free to take his army north towards Calcutta, and the city fell almost absent-mindedly on 2 January 1757 after a Union flag was seen flying from Fort William signifying the departure of Siraj's army. There was an undignified moment when Watson and Clive squabbled about the right to receive the surrender. Watson believed that Coote, as the senior royal army officer, should have the honour, while Clive countered that he would arrest the young captain if this were to happen; the row permanently soured relations between the two men. Coote was a hot-tempered young man, a stickler for military protocol who bore grudges and was quick to take offence, while Clive could be equally small-minded and obstinate. In this case, though, a compromise was reached and a week later Coote was ordered to take a mixed force of 39th, marines and sepoys to capture the town of Hooghly (Hugli-Chuchura), a former Dutch staging post to the north of Calcutta.

This provided a more difficult obstacle. Following a sharp

artillery engagement on 12 January 1757, however, Coote's men swept into the breach and the defenders quickly retreated. Coote also took the opportunity of plundering the town and burning a large granary in a nearby village to prevent it falling into Siraj's hands. This was common practice in colonial operations, as Wolfe had shown at Quebec, but in this case it had the advantage of prompting an immediate response from the Nawab, who had done his utmost to avoid a battle with the Company's forces.

This time he had no option but to act. Clive had taken up a position to the north between Calcutta and Murshidabad, a move which encouraged Siraj to respond by making his own advance, albeit without the immediate support of artillery. Because Clive could not afford to delay – he was keen to defeat Siraj quickly and then to attack the French trading station at Chandernagar – he determined on a night march before attacking at dawn.

In such ventures, a move in darkness is generally hazardous, and the situation here was not improved by the presence of a thick mist which made visibility doubly difficult. The ground, too, was treacherous, being dominated by swamps and a three-mile-long defensive feature known as the Maratha Ditch which was not only deep but awkward to traverse. As a result there followed 'a most ill-managed battle' notable for confusion on both sides, in which Clive's forces only narrowly avoided defeat thanks to their discipline and superior firepower. When the sun burned away the mist in the early morning of 4 February, they found that they were still within range of Siraj's artillery and in the subsequent engagement suffered 157 casualties killed and wounded. Fortunately Siraj had been badly shaken by the fighting, in which his own casualties had been much higher (an estimated 500), and as a result withdrew his army to Murshidabad; there he decided to enter into negotiations with Watson, offering to restore all privileges to the Company and to allow them to fortify Fort William. This was accepted, but both Watson and Clive doubted if the agreement would hold. Watson held to the view that there was no point in signing a treaty until the Nawab had been 'well thrashed', while Clive wanted to move quickly against Chandernagar even though such an action would never be allowed under the terms of the protocols between the Company and local rulers.

Eventually the matter was unwittingly resolved by Siraj, who wrote two letters in quick succession, the first giving permission for an attack against the French and the second banning any such proposal. In the best traditions of imperial initiative, Clive and Watson decided to act on the first message and moved their forces up to Chandernagar on 13 March. It was on this occasion that Watson wrote his oft-quoted warning that unless Siraj complied with British wishes, he 'would kindle such a flame in the country that all the waters of the Ganges should not be able to extinguish'. In case this threat was misunderstood, he added, 'Remember that he who promises you this, never yet broke his word with you, or with any man whatever.'[16] Having warned the Nawab what to expect, the British promptly opened siege operations against the French. The garrison was ordered to surrender, and the matter was resolved when Watson arrived from Calcutta with three warships and used their guns to batter the position into submission. During the action, in which Coote played a leading role in the fighting for the outer defences, the British captured 500 French, 700 Indians, 183 artillery pieces, three small mortars and a large quantity of ammunition. The Royal Navy lost 130 men killed or wounded (casualties for HMS *Kent* were 19 men killed and 49 wounded; for HMS *Tiger* 13 killed and 50 wounded). The British ground forces lost 35 men killed or wounded, while the French lost 40 men killed and 70 wounded.

Siraj then underscored his duplicitous behaviour by writing to Clive confirming his 'inexpressible pleasure' at the result, while at the same time writing to the French commander Pierre-Mathieu Renault de Saint-Germain expressing his hope that 'these English, who are unfortunate, will be punished for the disturbances they have raised'.[17] The crocodile tears were unnecessary, for Clive had not only achieved his objectives in Bengal but had stolen a march on the French before they had been able to dispatch reinforcements.

The Madras Council was well within its rights to order Clive and his forces to return without delay, but it was clear to him that his great work (as he described it to his father) remained incomplete. Not only did he have no faith in Siraj, but he was uncomfortably aware that the French could still combine with the Bengalis and make common cause against the British. That was certainly on Siraj's mind. In the aftermath of Clive's triumph at Chandernagar he offered his protection to the smaller French settlement at Kasimbazar and made sure that it was replenished with cannon and ammunition. He also made overtures to Charles Joseph Patissier, Marquis de Bussy-Castelnau, the shrewd and capable French commander in neighbouring Bihar, who had served with distinction under Dupleix.

This was what Clive had feared most, and it persuaded him to write to Sir George Pigot, the new governor of Madras, disclosing that he had received information from within the Nawab's court that Siraj was 'universally hated and despised'; bearing that information in mind, he (Clive) was confident that 'there can be neither peace nor security while such a monster reigns.'[18] In fact Clive had already made contact with malcontents who might be persuaded to translate their discontent with Siraj into something stronger. These included a group of Hindu bankers including the influential Jagat Seth, and most importantly, Mir Jafar, the commander-in-chief of the Nawab's army, who was related to Siraj's predecessor Alivardi Khan and presumably had ambitions of his own. Acting as a go-between was a Calcutta merchant called Amir Chand, who made heavy weather of the secret negotiations largely because he was more intent on imposing excessive financial demands for himself.

Intrigues of this kind were not unknown in Indian diplomacy – Dupleix and Bussy-Castelnau were past masters – but they required a good measure of secrecy, tact and patience, and it took time to reach agreement on a plot which would see Siraj deposed and replaced by Mir Jafar who promised Clive that he and his forces would switch sides. It also required a fair amount of duplicity. When it became clear that the plot might founder on Amir Chand's demand for payment of five per cent of Siraj's exchequer, Clive got round the problem by preparing two versions of the agreement, one on red paper which included the payment to Amir Chand and one on white paper which did not. Both were signed by Clive and Watson but only the latter document was genuine.

Even so, Clive was not entirely sure if Mir Jafar would stick to his written promise. He had good reason to be concerned: at the last minute, and with good reason, Siraj suddenly demanded Mir Jafar's absolute loyalty, making him swear on the Koran – although, as a contemporary witness put it, 'they [the two men] parted with smiles in their countenances and treachery in their hearts.'[19]

Duplicity and hidden negotiations could only take Clive so far. He still had to use his army, and he did so on 13 June when he led his men towards Murshidabad, where he planned to do battle with Siraj's numerically superior forces. A week later he halted near the fort at Katwa, which had been captured by an advance column led by Coote. It was here that Mir Jafar would play his hand, but there was no sign of him or his promised army apart from a letter again pledging his loyalty. Thoroughly perplexed, Clive decided to hold a council of war, which was attended by twenty of his senior European officers. They were presented with a stark choice. Clive's army was outnumbered, and without Mir Jafar's support the question was posed whether to attack 'without assistance and on our own bottom' or to wait until some more propitious moment. It was also pointed out that the monsoon season was approaching. Clive was in favour of a postponement, and that was the majority view; but Coote, the senior royal officer present, voted for an immediate attack on the grounds that 'we had hitherto met with nothing but success, which consequently has given great spirits to our men, and I was of opinion that any delay might cast damp.'[20] He also cited the possibility of French intervention and the dangers of making a long retreat back to Calcutta. Six other officers supported Coote.

Suitably emboldened, Clive decided to head north at dawn the next morning, crossing the swollen waters of the River Bhagirathi and heading towards a hunting lodge and mango grove at a place called Plassey (Placis). On arriving at daybreak on 23 June they heard incontrovertible evidence that the enemy was near at hand – gongs, drums and cymbals, and the trampling of horses and elephants.

Siraj had drawn up his army in a shallow semi-circle with Mir Jafar holding the left wing. It consisted of 35,000 infantry of all sorts, armed with matchlocks, swords, pikes and rockets, and 18,000 cavalry, armed with swords or long spears. Interspersed at intervals were fifty-three pieces of artillery, mostly large calibre and many of them antiquated. Clive disposed his smaller army to face them with their backs to the mango grove and the river to their left. A water tank lay slightly to the right of their line and the Nawab's hunting lodge and gardens to their left. Coote and his 39th Foot occupied the centre of the British line together with elements of the Bengal, Bombay and Madras European Regiments. As Coote noted in his journal, the Bengalis had taken possession of what high ground there was, and it was from these eminences that the battle opened with a sharp cannonade which forced the line to move back into the mango grove, 'where we formed behind the ditch that surrounded it'.[21] It was within these confines that the battle would be won. For the rest of the morning the firing continued from both sides in a desultory manner, causing sound and fury but doing no damage as Clive's men were secure behind their defences.

At that stage Clive's plan was to hold the position until nightfall, but at midday there was a huge thunderstorm. Rain swept across the battlefield, soaking the Bengali gunners and their powder but not the British, who were able to raise tarpaulin shelters. Thinking that their opponents were facing the same predicament in not being able to fire their guns, this change of weather gave Siraj's forces the confidence to attack from the water tank towards the mango grove where they were greeted by grapeshot and musket fire. This quickly dispersed the cavalry, and at around one o'clock the first elements of Siraj's army started, in Coote's words, 'to retire on all sides'. It was not quite the end, but it was the beginning of the end. As darkness began to take hold, Coote advanced towards the opposition lines with the support of Major James Kilpatrick, a Company officer from Madras who had led the initial deployment to Bengal. This closed the gap between the two sides, and with Siraj's troops looking 'visibly dispirited' the battle was as good as won.

Clive had triumphed in a battle that has been described as 'more in the nature of a transaction'. Siraj had lost the day and Mir Jafar had not been forced to reveal his treachery.[22] The Bengalis had lost over five hundred casualties, while the Company's losses were four Europeans and fourteen sepoys. Next morning Mir Jafar was proclaimed the new Nawab, while Siraj 'suffered the usual fate of all deposed Indian princes' by being promptly executed. Within the space of two hundred days Bengal had been secured as a British sphere of influence, and the first step had been taken in Britain's consolidation of its new empire in India.

Meanwhile the campaign continued, in a minor key. Coote went on to chase the enemy as far as Daudpur, six miles from the battlefield, where the fading light made further pursuit unwise. It was only a temporary setback. Coote ended the campaign on a reasonably high note after being appointed to an independent command with orders to pursue a fleeing French force which had been dispatched from Kasimbazar but had arrived too late to play any part at Plassey. His force consisted of 750 Europeans and sepoys, plus two artillery pieces, and its route took it 200 miles north towards Bihar through difficult country at the height of the monsoon. Only when the French force escaped into neighbouring Oudh did Coote halt the pursuit and return to Bengal, where he was ordered home on sick leave with the bulk of the 39th Foot. The voyage took eleven months, but Coote used his time in England to good effect.

Unlike the campaign in North America, there had been little or no interference from London in events in Bengal, which had been directed by the Company's representatives on the ground. For example, the government in London had only just begun digesting the news of the fall of Calcutta and the evidence of the notorious Black Hole when, unknown to them, Plassey was won by Clive. This gap in intelligence gave freedom of action to local commanders such as Clive and Lawrence, albeit within the constraints imposed by the Company's councils in Madras and Bengal. But there were similarities between the two campaigns, due to the presence of professional army officers (or royal officers) such as Coote, who were determined to enhance their military careers by playing up their exploits and protecting their privileges. In doing this he resembled James Wolfe, who had used the period after Louisbourg to return to London where he was able to take much of the credit for the capture of the French fortress and to play down the part played by Amherst, his superior. Having arrived in London at much the same time as Wolfe, Coote did much the same thing, although there is no evidence that the two men ever met. When Coote was interviewed by Pitt he was able to present the campaign in Bengal from a soldier's perspective, and he would not have been human had he not taken the opportunity to show his service in a good light and to play down Clive's part. Particularly damning from Clive's point of view would have been the account of the council of war before Plassey and Coote's promotion of the need to do battle without Mir Jafar. Not that Clive had done badly out of the business – he had enriched himself and was appointed president of the Bengal Council – but he did not return to London until 1760. By that time his rival had added to his own laurels.

While Coote was in London he learned that he had been promoted lieutenant-colonel and would command one of two new infantry regiments raised by the government for service in India. His command was the 84th Foot while a second regiment, the 79th Foot, was put under the command of William Draper, who had been educated at Eton and King's College Cambridge before joining the army as an ensign in Conway's Regiment, later the

48th Foot. With them he had served during the Jacobite campaign at the battles of Falkirk and Culloden. Thanks to Cumberland's patronage he transferred to the 1st Foot Guards (later Grenadier Guards) and in 1756 married Caroline Beauclerk (c.1730–69), the younger daughter of Lord William Beauclerk and the niece of the Duke of St Albans. He was also a skilled all-round sportsman and excelled at cricket, having achieved the highest score in an inaugural match between Old Etonians and the rest of England in 1751.[23] Clearly Draper was an ambitious and well-connected officer and the move to India gave him a further opportunity to make his name in the army.

Coote's career was also on the rise. On 14 March 1759 he was appointed commander-in-chief in Bengal in succession to Clive and with equal rank to Stringer Lawrence in Madras. Not unnaturally perhaps, these events were viewed askance by Clive; he supported the rival claims of Major Francis Forde, who had arrived with the 39th but stayed on in India when it returned to Britain. On hearing of Coote's appointment, Clive wrote to Henry Vansittart, his successor in Calcutta, before going on leave, telling him that he should take care in his dealings with the new commander-in-chief:

> I tremble when I think of the consequences of such a mercenary man as Coote commanding here. If you have any regard for your future government for God's sake keep him on the [Coromandel] Coast. There he can only get a drubbing, but here he may ruin the Company's affairs for ever.[24]

Coote, of course, was unaware that this back-stabbing was taking place, but within a few months of his return to India he would give his rival even more to think about.

During the voyage to Bengal he was ordered by the Company to take himself and his regiment south to Madras; for the time being Caillaud, his brother officer from the Jacobite campaign, would take over the Bengal command. This change of plan was occasioned largely by Clive's enmity – but it was to be the making of Coote, who arrived in Madras on 27 October 1759 to find that the French had worked hard to improve their position in southern India. Substantial reinforcements had arrived from Brest in the previous year, including a battle fleet under the command of Vice-Admiral Comte Ann-Antoine d'Aché and six infantry battalions commanded by Comte Thomas Arthur Lally, Baron de Tollendal.

Of the two men d'Aché was an indifferent naval commander with a tendency to be over-cautious and to blame others when things went wrong. But the land forces commander was a very different beast. The son of Sir Gerald Lally, an émigré Irish Jacobite married to Marie Anne de Bressac, a French aristocrat, Lally had entered the French army in 1721 and had distinguished himself at Dettingen and Fontenoy where he commanded the renowned Irish Brigade. In that role he had emerged as an experienced and battle-hardened commander, but he was much more than a mercenary soldier. A confirmed Jacobite like his father, he had joined Prince Charles in his campaign in Scotland in 1745 and served as his aide-de-camp at Falkirk in the following year. He was committed, energetic and intelligent – his friend Voltaire claimed that Lally possessed 'a stubborn fierceness of soul, accompanied by a great gentleness of manners' – but those virtues were often negated by intolerance and a belief that he was always right.[25] He was nonetheless an intriguing personality and his arrival brought fresh hope to the French that they were now in a position to match British naval and military power in south India. The fact that Coote and Lally had been on opposite sides at Falkirk only added spice to the new strategic position.

The new French force quickly showed that it meant business. Although d'Aché's fleet was given a mauling by the British squadron, by then under the command of Vice-Admiral George Pocock following Watson's sudden death in 1757, Lally made good progress on land by laying siege to Cuddalore and Fort St David and quickly forcing their surrender. Madras was now under threat, but because Lally was short of funds and provisions he took his army south into Tanjore. It was the first of several mistaken moves. Not only were his men harassed by Tanjorean irregulars but they caused great offence by going on the rampage and sacking various temples and shrines. As a result Lally was unable to begin the siege of Madras until the end of 1758, by which time Stringer Lawrence had reinforced the place with 2700 sepoys and 1700 Europeans, including the first detachments of Draper's 79th Foot. Lally was also hamstrung by the indecisiveness of d'Aché, whose ships had been on the receiving end of another pounding at Negaptamag on 3 August. Once again the victor was Pocock, who was 'never known to swear, even on board his ship'.[26] As a result of this latest defeat d'Aché eventually took his squadron away from the Coromandel Coast for repairs on the island of Mauritius, where they played no further part in the campaign. Their absence meant that Lally could not continue the siege of Madras; he called it off early in 1759 and could do little else for the rest of the year. It was at this point that Coote arrived and took over command of the Company's forces at Conjeveram.

It was a propitious moment. While the French were facing problems, the British had benefited from the arrival of reinforcements, notably the two new line infantry regiments. Not even the loss of Draper to wounds in the first action could undermine the sense of self-confidence; he was replaced temporarily by his second-in-command Major Cholmondeley Brereton, an aggressive fighting soldier who had spent most of the year attacking French positions and forcing his opponent to fall back on defensive positions at Arcot, Covrepauk, Carangooly and Chittapett (Chet-pet). It assisted his cause that Lally had been forced to withdraw to Pondicherry as a result of illness, leaving his inexperienced second-in-command Chevalier de Soupire with orders not to force the issue by attacking British positions. This self-denying ordinance played into Brereton's hands; de Soupire proved to be a querulous and unenterprising opponent.

Brereton was also aided by the arrival of another royal officer, George Monson, who had been educated at Westminster School and whose career had profited from Cumberland's patronage. The son of Lord Monson of Burton, he had been commissioned in the Foot Guards in 1750 and had strengthened his social and political connections by being appointed a groom of the bedchamber in the Prince of Wales's household. Following his marriage in 1757, Monson decided to pursue his military career by transferring to the 79th and arrived in Madras early in 1759. Well-connected and doggedly courageous, Monson also had the ear of Lord Barrington, the influential Secretary at War, who took a great deal of interest in the careers of promising officers.

On taking over command Coote had the services of both Brereton and Monson, and they recommended that his first target should be Wandiwash (Vandivasi in the state of Tamil Nadu), some sixty miles south-west of Madras; it had already been attacked unsuccessfully by Brereton with the loss of over 300 killed and wounded. Their reasoning for a renewed attempt was prompted by Lally's decision to divide his forces between Arcot and Trichinopoly; Coote agreed that the opportunity was too good to miss and he laid his plans carefully to outwit his opponents. Two smaller forces, one led by Brereton, moved towards targets at Chingleput and Trivatore while Coote took the main force in a feint towards Arcot. That had the desired effect of drawing Lally out, and the year ended with each of the two armies aiming to recover their fortunes by attacking Wandiwash and taking it before the other arrived on the scene. Both sides were reasonably evenly matched, but Lally's army was dispirited as a result of having not been paid, and its morale had also been affected by shortages of food and provender. Not even the arrival of Bussy with reinforcements could alter the situation.

On the other hand, Coote was leading an army which knew that it had the upper hand and trusted its own abilities. Partly this came from the freshness of the two newly arrived foot regiments and the professionalism of their company commanders, but mainly it was due to Coote's leadership qualities. Since his arrival in India Coote had grown in stature and had emerged as a natural leader. That much had become evident during his first independent command in the pursuit phase after Plassey, and it found its truest expression in the first week of January 1760 during the operations leading to the Battle of Wandiwash, when one mistake could have handed back the advantage to the French.

This game of cat and mouse culminated on 22 January with both sides manoeuvring across 'a wide tree-dotted plain, baked hard and dry in the sun' with a low rocky ridge to the north.[27] The prize was Wandiwash Fort, which stood behind the French line of advance in an area dotted with water tanks, three of which lay to the north. It was on this open plain, 'admirable ground for cavalry', that both sides lined up to do battle. At his disposal Lally had 2400 Europeans and 1600 sepoys, together with twenty field pieces and four siege guns. He could also call on a force of

3000 Mahratta cavalry, although this was quickly scattered in the opening stages by British cannon fire. On the other side Coote had 1900 Europeans and 2100 sepoys, plus 1250 native horse and twenty-six field guns. They were positioned in three lines on the eastern side, the 79th on the right and the 84th on the left, with the Madras Europeans between them in the first line. In the second line stood 300 European grenadiers and 200 sepoys on each flank, together with field pieces. The third line was entirely cavalry. That night Coote ordered them all to place green branches in their hats and turbans to serve as identification marks during the turmoil of combat.

Facing them was a single line of French forces – Lally's regiment on the left with some marines protected by a water tank, in the centre a European regiment and on the right the Lorraine Regiment, with 300 cavalry behind them. The line was interspersed with field pieces, and 900 sepoys were ranged on rising ground behind the line. The layout was a classic example of British strength in depth confronting a French column of attack on a narrow front.

Shortly after sunrise the action opened with desultory cannonading by both sides. The first tactical move was made by Lally before midday when he ordered his cavalry to attack the British left flank, but they were driven off by sustained fire from the British field guns. This encouraged Coote to order his own first line to advance to within musket range of the French and then to open fire at sixty yards, using the platoon fire tactics developed by James Wolfe. At the same time the French moved forward to receive them, and the fighting degenerated into savage close-quarter combat with both sides using bayonet, musket butt and anything else that came to hand. This use of overwhelming force had the desired effect and in short order the Lorraine Regiment ceased to be a coherent body, degenerating into a rabble of running men. According to an officer in the 84th which engaged them, 'we had not fired above four rounds before they went to the right about in the utmost confusion.'[28] At that moment came an unlucky occurrence of the kind which can unnerve even the stoutest soldiers. On the French left a chance shot hit a French ammunition cart, which exploded and killed those around it. Amongst them were the marines left behind by d'Aché, and who had not wanted to be on the battlefield in the first place. In panic-stricken confusion they set off for the rear, followed by several hundred equally frightened sepoys.

Not surprisingly, Coote took advantage of the mayhem. Brereton was ordered to move forwards with the 79th and to take the water tanks on the French left. This he did, and as Bussy rallied the French line Coote quickly rushed up sepoy reinforcements and the position was secured. From there the men of the 79th used their protected position to pour fire into the French left, which was by then badly shaken. At this point Monson advanced with the second line, supported by two cannons. It was all too much for Lally's regiment, and although Bussy attempted one final charge his horse was shot from under him and he was taken prisoner. Almost an hour after the battle began it was all over; as Coote noted in his official dispatch, 'their whole army gave way and ran towards their own camp, but finding we pursued them, quitted it and left us entire masters of the field.'[29] To Lally's credit he avoided complete humiliation by rallying his cavalry forces and reorganising them to provide a screen for his infantry as they withdrew, but it was impossible to ignore the fact that he had been on the wrong side of a heavy defeat. He had lost between 600 and 800 men killed, wounded or captured, and these figures were confirmed by the British troops who claimed later that they buried 200 on the battlefield and took 200 wounded and 40 unwounded prisoners. More wounded were left behind during the retreat to Pondicherry. Coote's losses were 53 from the 84th Regiment, 59 from the Madras European Regiment and 80 from the 79th Foot.

The one sour note came from the Company's council in Madras, who claimed that Coote had failed to follow up his victory by taking Pondicherry immediately while the French were at a disadvantage. That too was the defeated Lally's opinion, but being a methodical man Coote was more interested in reducing the smaller French garrisons before turning his attention to the seat of French power in the Carnatic. A year later, on 10 January 1761, following a short but determined siege, Pondicherry surrendered, the fleur-de-lis banners were hauled down, the Union flag was raised and a huge arsenal of 484 field pieces and 12,000 muskets – plus ammunition and powder – fell into British hands. It was the end of French imperial ambitions in India and the beginning of almost a century of British domination. Just as Wolfe had delivered Canada through his victory at Quebec, so too had Coote delivered India at Wandiwash.

Not that the triumph brought him immediate plaudits from his superiors in the Company. Coote was never at ease with officialdom and had a bad relationship with the council in Madras, who remained suspicious of his motives and complained continuously about the costs of running the campaign against the French. For his part Coote could be prickly about his own position and jealously protected his prerogatives as a royal officer. In short he was ill-suited to the needs of diplomacy, and as a result he found it difficult to pander to the needs of a council which he considered to be 'factious, interfering, pompous and often also corrupt'.[30] For their part, the 'nabobs' did not take kindly to Coote's high-handed behaviour and his constant demands, finding him to be shrill, awkward and frequently obstructive.

Only with the soldiers did Coote find complete favour, becoming one of that select band of commanders who were loved and admired in equal measure by their men, not just because they were winners on the battlefield but because they cared deeply for the welfare and well-being of those in their command. One of Coote's junior officers later wrote of him that he was 'the soldier's friend, most dear to the soldiers he commanded for his personal bravery, his great likeability and in his affectionate regard for their honour and interests. Other generals have been approved but Sir Eyre Coote was the beloved of the soldiers of the British Army in India.'[31] The writer knew what he was talking about: an observant soldier with literary ambitions called Innes Munro came under Coote's command later, while serving in the 73rd Highlanders, and according to his judgement it was not for nothing that Coote received from his sepoys the ultimate accolade 'Coote Bahadur' (the bold, or the hero). The compliment was only paid to two other British generals who served in India – Arthur Wellesley, later the Duke of Wellington, and Frederick Sleigh Roberts, later commander-in-chief of the British Army. For Coote, the victor of Wandiwash, a soldier who had begun his army career being excoriated and punished for running away at Falkirk, it was a fitting reward for a military life well led.

In Canada and India Britain had found two men – Wolfe and Coote – who were equal to the task of defeating the French and laying the foundations of a new empire. But it was already clear that despite the triumphs at Quebec and Wandiwash, the war would not be won in the overseas territories alone. On hearing the news of Wolfe's triumph at Quebec, Horace Walpole wrote to the Earl of Halifax observing that English church bells were being 'worn threadbare with ringing for victories', but the harsh reality was that the war was far from over in 1759, the so-called 'year of victories'.[32] On the contrary, after three years of campaigning the triumphs in Canada and India only highlighted the absence of any tangible success in Europe, which for Britain's allies was the main fulcrum of the fighting against France. All that Britain had to show for its efforts in that area was the loss of Minorca in 1756 and the unsuccessful expedition to Rochefort the following year; both seemed to contrast badly with the apparent professionalism shown by Frederick the Great of Prussia, who was being hailed as 'the best Friend and Ally ever Great Britain had'.[33] It is to this theatre of operations that the narrative now returns.

11

THE WORLD AT WAR: EUROPE

It was not only in North America and India that blood was being shed. The fighting in those remote and sweaty places tends to obscure the fact that the Seven Years War was also a conflict with a European dimension, the main continental battles being fought east of the Rhine.

From Britain's point of view this strategic emphasis came about as a result of Pitt's insistence that the American and Indian holdings were the key to the country's trading interests and that their protection had to take priority. Partly, too, the policy arose from the fact that with a home army only 34,000 strong at the beginning of the war, Britain simply did not possess the resources to undertake a major European campaign and had to leave the fighting to its European allies.

Early indications had also demonstrated that the British Army lacked the leadership qualities to take on and defeat the French army; indeed, in the early days of the conflict that failing put at risk Britain's ability to remain in the war. Cumberland's defeat at Hastenbeck in 1757 could have led to the loss of Hanover but for Frederick the Great's stunning victories over the French and their Austrian allies at Rossbach (5 November 1757) and Leuthen (5 December 1757), which not only allowed Silesia to be recaptured but established Prussia as the leading military power in Europe. Just as importantly, those victories tied down 90,000 French soldiers on the Rhine and forced Pitt to rethink how, in conjunction with his German allies, they should be confronted. A year later, in August 1758, he committed an expeditionary force to Hanover in the shape of six regiments of infantry and fourteen squadrons of cavalry under the command of Charles Spencer, the 3rd Duke of Marlborough, a grandson of the great duke and a soldier in his own right having embarked on a military career in 1738 at the relatively late age of thirty two. Although he reached the rank of lieutenant-general – thanks in part to Cumberland's patronage – his only claim to fame had been the command of an unsuccessful expedition against St Malo earlier in 1758, which had resulted in the destruction of a mere handful of small coastal vessels and had caused the French very little anxiety. That being said, the raid certainly brought Marlborough to Pitt's attention as until then the tip-and-run raids against French positions on the European mainland had been the preferred means of prosecuting the conflict, even though they had been shown to be ineffectual and wasteful of resources.

Marlborough's appointment and the deployment of British land forces were not universally popular, especially in the eyes of those who favoured a 'blue water' or maritime foreign policy and were opposed to what they perceived to be a Hanoverian strategy of committing the army to Europe. Pitt's change of heart, however, meant that a new land forces commander had to be found for the British and Hanoverian forces, and in the absence of Cumberland who was still in disgrace after his earlier failures the choice fell on thirty-eight-year-old Prince Ferdinand of Brunswick. An experienced soldier, he appeared to be a winner, having served in the Prussian army at Rossbach; equally importantly, he was of royal blood, being a brother-in-law of Frederick the Great.[1] His greatest drawback was a tendency to be over-secretive, while being exceptionally coy in his dealings with allies and subordinates, but those failings were overlooked: he was self-confident, tough and personally courageous – always a good sign in a soldier. On being appointed commander of His Britannic Majesty's Army (as the Army of Observation had become in 1757), Ferdinand reinforced his independence by demanding and being granted full access to King George II, as well as obtaining the freedom to conduct his own military operations without external political interference. He also requested fresh British reinforcements in the shape of cavalry, artillery and infantry.

Although Ferdinand was the scion of a great German family (Brunswick-Lüneburg), this was no hindrance to commanding British troops, as King George II demanded from all his officers of whatever background absolute loyalty to the house of Hanover. In that role Ferdinand proved to be an ideal coalition commander, having under his command 40,000 Hanoverian and Hessian troops as well as the recently arrived British contingent. Amongst them were three infantry regiments which had fought at Culloden – the 20th Foot, the 25th Foot and the 37th Foot. The others were the 12th, the 23rd and the 51st.[2] They would be remembered and memorialised as the 'Minden Regiments'.

For all Ferdinand's good points as a man and a soldier, he failed to make a favourable impression on his main ally and they on him. Not only did he have a poor opinion of the soldiers in the British Army, finding them ill-disciplined and disrespectful, but he also developed a poor relationship with the general who had been forced by unforeseen circumstances to take over command of the British expeditionary force. Shortly after Marlborough's arrival in Münster in October he succumbed to dysentery and was succeeded by his second-in-command Lord George Sackville. Having been active in the pacification phase after Culloden – during which he had been responsible for some of the worst excesses against the civilian population in Moidart, where his uncertain temper was exacerbated by the pain from wounds in his leg and chest sustained at Fontenoy – he afterwards managed to combine a political career with his life as a soldier and was promoted (in succession to John Ligonier) to the influential position of Lieutenant-General of the Ordnance at the beginning of the Seven Years War. In many respects the Board of Ordnance was the most powerful military office, having both military and civil responsibilities, and its prestige carried grave responsibilities for those who occupied senior positions.

It had been to the benefit of Sackville's career that he enjoyed close links with the Leicester House faction which surrounded the future King George III. Situated on the north side of what is now Leicester Square, the mansion was the London home of the Prince of Wales, and before he succeeded his father was almost an alternative court whose membership included many of the leading politicians of the day, including prime minister Bute. This connection should have given Sackville a key to high office, but his relationship with Bute began to cool following his appointment to serve in Europe – the Leicester House faction was closely identified with the 'blue water' strategy and was opposed to sending British troops to fight on the continent. A contemporary account (written by a hostile witness) describes Sackville as 'a tall man, with a long face, rather strong features, clear blue eyes, a large make, though rather womanly, not too corpulent, and a mixture of quickness and a sort of melancholy in his look, which runs through all the Sackville family'.[3] Opinionated to the point of arrogance and used to getting his own way, Sackville was very much a product of his background and upbringing, but he met his match in the equally well-connected and masterful Ferdinand.

Sackville arrived with the security of his own royal connection and his conceit in being a member of a leading English family – his mother had been a lady-in-waiting to Queen Anne – but Ferdinand trumped him in every respect. Not only did he outrank him, being a field marshal, but he was of royal blood and related through marriage to Frederick the Great. In the final analysis, Ferdinand knew that if he quarrelled with Sackville over the direction of the campaign he would always enjoy the support of King George II, whereas Sackville would not. Although Sackville had been close to the court early in his career, by 1757 the king had lost patience with him following what he regarded as a defection to the Prince of Wales's camp at Leicester House.[4]

Ferdinand's superior royal connection gave him a powerful hand, and he would need it. From the outset, while his relationship with Sackville was polite, it was most certainly not cordial. Matters were not helped by the strategic situation, which had seen the French take the upper hand by going on the offensive to threaten Hanover in order to enlarge the war in Europe. As a result their Army of the Main was now under the command of Victor Francis, Duc de Broglie, who matched Ferdinand for energetic leadership, while command of the Army of Westphalia was in the hands of the equally resourceful Louis Georges Érasme de Contades, 6th Marquis de Contades.

The campaigning season in 1759 had begun in Westphalia with a cat-and-mouse struggle which culminated in the unsatisfactory and inconclusive Battle of Bergen, fought on high ground above the River Main on 13 April. In wet and miserable weather Ferdinand had decided to attack the French positions as the troops were completing their deployment, but with forty-five heavy guns at his disposal Broglie enjoyed artillery superiority, using it to good effect to unsettle the attacking German infantry. By noon it was clear that the Hanoverian attack had failed, and Ferdinand decided to withdraw to the east hoping that Broglie would regard the move as a retreat and order a pursuit. Broglie did not take the bait, however, and when, following renewed artillery exchanges, it became clear that there would be no result from the day's fighting, Ferdinand ordered his army to withdraw to the north, towards the safety of Kassel, the capital of Hesse. The long, winding column made a tempting target as it left the battlefield but inexplicably Broglie did not press his advantage, presumably because he did not want to surrender an advantageous defensive position.

Bergen could be counted as a draw – casualties on both sides were roughly equal and neither gained any advantage – but in the greater scheme of things it was a setback for Ferdinand. Although Broglie had not used the opportunity to attack the retreating column, he had preserved his position and in so doing allowed Contades to cross the Rhine and invade Westphalia. The advantage had passed to the French, and Ferdinand seemed to sense this. Having displayed overweening self-confidence throughout the previous year, he became comatose in his thinking and was suddenly unable to take decisions, so much so that he wrote privately to King George II asking for instructions and warning him that it might be necessary to evacuate the allied army. A similarly phrased letter was sent to Frederick the Great. The response from the British king offered support but also the unhelpful declaration that he left the decision in Ferdinand's own hands.[5] The hesitation affected Ferdinand's subordinates, especially Sackville, who started complaining about the lack of information made available to him and the absence of realisable orders about how he should handle his expanded force. Unsettled by Ferdinand's indecision, Sackville took the opportunity to tell the field marshal that he would not be surprised if the British contingent were withdrawn to meet the growing threat of a French invasion, as had happened during the Jacobite uprising in 1745–6.[6]

At this point, in the middle of July, Contades took a firm grip of the campaign and placed the French forces in a commanding position in the mountains above Herford. By then Kassel had fallen into his hands and he had taken control of a significant swathe of territory including the key towns of Lippstadt, Hameln, Münster and Minden. This provided him with the basis to attack along the River Weser into Hanover; at the same time the French also possessed a numerical advantage, having 54,000 men under the command of Contades compared to the 41,000 available to Ferdinand. The topography also favoured the French: a line of wooded hills separated the two armies and Ferdinand could never be certain about the exact position of his opponent. Given those advantages it was small wonder that Contades repeatedly refused Ferdinand's offer of battle, even when the two armies made contact on 17 July. Instead he preferred to entrench his forces in a seemingly impregnable position to the south-west of the town of Minden, with the Weser on his left flank, high wooded hills on his right and marshy land in front, bisected by a meandering rivulet called the Bastau.

For the next fortnight the rival armies manoeuvred across and around this area, with Contades ever anxious to keep his movements concealed from his opponent until he saw an opportunity to make use of his numerical superiority. The decisive moment came at dawn on 1 August, after Contades decided that the advantage had passed to him following a move by Lieutenant-General Georg August von Wangenheim, who drew up a weakened corps to the north covering the village of Todtenhausen while Ferdinand was still out of sight to the north-west. During the engagement Lord George Sackville commanded the cavalry on the right flank with John Manners, Marquess of Granby as his second-in-command; his forces consisted of the 1st Dragoon Guards (later The Queen's Dragoon Guards), the 3rd Dragoon Guards (later 3rd Carabineers), the Scots Greys (later Royal Scots Dragoon Guards) and the 10th Dragoons (later The Royal Hussars). The allied disposition encouraged Contades to believe that his opponent was dangerously over-stretched, and he decided to take advantage of this perceived weakness. All then depended on Broglie passing through Minden and bringing his corps rapidly into action in an attempt to turn the enemy flank by attacking Wangenheim's position.

This Broglie did punctually and effectively. But then he hesitated to give the order to attack until the rest of the French forces were in their correct positions. The delay allowed a fierce artillery duel to commence, and amidst the confusion the British-Hanoverian infantry on the right flank unexpectedly went into the attack. Backed by three battalions of Hanoverian Guards, the British infantry battalions were formed in two brigades, the 12th, 23rd and 37th under the command of Major-General the Earl of Waldegrave, and the 20th, 25th and 51st commanded by Major-General William Kingsley. Both men were experienced soldiers and veterans of the Battle of Fontenoy as well as of the Jacobite campaign. Kingsley had been commissioned originally in the 3rd Foot Guards (later the Scots Guards), and while commanding the 20th Foot in the aftermath of Culloden had had under his command James Wolfe, who described him as 'a sensible man, and very sociable and polite'.[7] Although Kingsley had taken part in the disastrous expedition against Rochefort, his reputation remained unsullied and he was to add to it immeasurably through his behaviour at Minden.

An equally fine soldier, John Waldegrave was of a somewhat different stamp, being a member of a prominent family of courtiers and diplomats who had managed to shake off an earlier adherence to the Jacobite cause. In common with so many other well-connected army officers of the day, Waldegrave enjoyed Cumberland's patronage and by the time of the Seven Years War he had been promoted to the rank of major-general. He, too, was to prosper further as a result of his command in Germany.

Quite why the infantry advanced so precipitately in the opening rounds of the battle is still open to question. The accepted version is that Waldegrave and Kingsley were given the order that 'when the troops advance they will do so with drums beating'. However, in the heat of battle, when Ferdinand's orders were already far from clear to his subordinate commanders, this was misheard as an order 'to advance with drums beating'.[8] This is plausible, but it does not explain the speed and eagerness with which the battalions attacked, quickly outstripping the second line and turning left to race towards the French centre. Due to the alignment of both armies, which had been drawn up in two shallow arcs, the British infantry went into the attack not against its opponents on the French left but against the cavalry in the centre, a situation unparalleled in warfare at the time. The advance did not draw immediate attention, being shielded by a copse and by the early morning mist, but when the two brigades appeared with Waldegrave's in the van, the French immediately counter-attacked with eleven squadrons of cavalry. When that failed to make any impression against the steady musket fire of the advancing regiments, a second attack was made with twenty-two squadrons but this too was dispersed. A third charge was made, and although it threatened to break the attacking force's flanks it was beaten off by the sustained and disciplined firepower of the British and Hanoverian infantry.

Waldegrave and Kingsley had clearly understood one of the vital lessons of Culloden, namely that disciplined volleys of musket fire could win the day provided that the men were well trained and prepared to stand their ground. In this case the battalions did not form squares as they might have done, but took the riskier option of firing from their extended lines, which provided them with greater firepower but also ran the risk of permitting the attacking cavalry to effect a breakthrough. As to their eagerness to get into action, this is probably explained by the fact that they had done little since being deployed the previous year and were no doubt keen to impress their German opposite numbers. Later, an officer in the 12th Regiment of Foot wrote a short description of the action:

> Our British infantry, headed by Generals Waldegrave and Kingsley, fought with the greatest ardour and intrepidity, sustaining and repelling the repeated attacks of the Enemy with the most romantic bravery. The soldiers, so far from being daunted by their falling comrades, breathed nothing but revenge; for my part, though at the beginning of the Engagement I felt a kind of trepidation, yet I was so animated by the brave example of all around me, that when I received a slight wound by a musket-ball slanting on my left side, it served only to exasperate me the more, and had I then received orders, I could with the greatest pleasure have rushed into the thickest of the Enemy. Interest, honour, glory and emulation, conspired to render the Battle of Thorhausen [Minden] famous to posterity.[9]

As at Culloden, the British lines of infantry were supported by intensive fire from the covering twelve-pounder artillery batteries. One of these was commanded by Forbes Macbean, a minister's son from Inverness who shared his family's anti-Jacobite sentiments and who had joined the army with his two stepbrothers at the time of the uprising. At the siege of Carlisle in December 1745 he had caught the eye of Cumberland, and while he did not accompany the government army in the Culloden campaign in Scotland, he served at Rocoux and Lauffeld and was promoted captain in command of a brigade of heavy artillery in 1759. At Minden it was due to the initiative shown by Macbean and a brother gunner called Foy that the British heavy guns were able to provide continuous support to the attacking infantry, Sir John Fortescue writing admiringly that the French had no answer for their tenacity and forethought:

> As things happened, it fell to Foy and Macbean of the British Artillery to gather the laurels of the pursuit. Hard though they had worked all day, these officers limbered up their guns and moved with astonishing rapidity along the border of the marsh, halting from time to time to pound the retreating masses of the enemy; till at last they unlimbered for good opposite the bridges of the Bastau and punished the fugitives so heavily that they would not be rallied until they had fled far beyond their camp.[10]

Now was the time to launch the British heavy cavalry to support Waldegrave's and Kingsley's men. With the French centre broken and their cavalry forces committed it would have been relatively easy to wrap up their line. On the allied left a French assault had been repulsed, and the British artillery was continuing to cause havoc with heavy and accurate fire along the French positions. It was undeniable that the battle would have been won by a British cavalry charge, but Sackville not only ignored four orders given by Ferdinand but also prevented the Marquess of Granby from taking matters into his own hands. That failure allowed Contades to remove his men from the field, albeit having lost 10,000 casualties, killed, wounded or missing. All the French commander had to say was: 'I never thought to see a single line of infantry break through three lines of cavalry ranked in order of battle, and tumble them to ruin.'[11]

The allied losses were 2600 killed, wounded or missing, the majority being suffered by the right flank regiments. In the 25th Foot the casualties were one sergeant and eighteen men killed, seven officers, four sergeants and 115 soldiers wounded. A week later, the first report of the battle appeared in the *London Gazette*:

The Army was at this time marching with the greatest diligence to attack the Enemy in front; but the Infantry could not get up in time. General Waldegrave, at the head of the British, pressed their march as much as possible; no Troops could show more eagerness to get up than they showed. Many of the men, from the heat of the weather, and overstraining themselves to get on, through morassey [marshy] and very difficult ground, suddenly dropped down on their march.[12]

Minden occupies an honoured place in the history of the British Army. Not only did the attacking infantry battalions display steadiness and discipline while facing the successive heavy cavalry charges but they triumphed in spite of being given the wrong orders. As a result, all six infantry regiments received Minden as a battle honour, and each year Minden Day is still commemorated by the successor regiments with special parades when the officers and soldiers wear red roses in their caps or bonnets. The custom is a reminder that their predecessors plucked wild roses and placed them in their hats as a means of identification before they went into the attack. With good reason the battle was hailed as a unique victory for the infantrymen who stood firm in the face of a determined assault by the French cavalry, and for the skill and discipline of the British gunners who offered their loyal support. But in time it also came to be remembered for Sackville's fatal hesitation, which led Fortescue to write him off as 'a deplorable man' whose courage failed him when it was most needed.[13]

Given Sackville's failure to react during the battle, there were unpleasant repercussions for the British cavalry commander. Even before the fighting began there had been friction between Ferdinand and Sackville over the latter's handling of his army, and during the battle the former had been outraged by the British failure to act in support of the infantry. Inevitably Ferdinand took his revenge. Following the battle he issued general orders in which he alluded to Sackville's conduct by commenting that if Granby had been in command, the allied victory would have been more complete – his actual words were 'if he [Ferdinand] had had the good fortune to have had him [Granby] at the head of the cavalry of the right wing, his presence would have greatly contributed to make the decision of that day more complete and more brilliant.'[14] Sackville's name was deliberately omitted from the papers, but the inference was obvious and no man of honour could survive a slight of that kind. On 13 August Ferdinand wrote to King George II demanding that 'He should be graciously pleased to make a notable change in this army by recalling Lord George Sackville' and that the order should be implemented at once.[15] When Sackville asked for a hearing this was refused; he had no option but to return to England, where he found himself the object of so much public scorn and censure that no one was prepared to defend him when he was dismissed from all his military commands. In despair Sackville demanded a court martial, even though no charges had been brought against him, as he clearly believed that right was on his side.

In fact Sackville's position has never been satisfactorily explained, for much of the evidence was lost, or was misunderstood or misreported in the confusion of the fighting. While it was true that a prompt charge by the cavalry would have scattered the French forces, it was not just the refusal to charge that irked Ferdinand, but Sackville's failure to read the battle as it unfolded. From the outset of the fighting there had been no indication that there would be any problem about the employment of the allied cavalry, which was deployed on the right. To Sackville's right lay the small village of Hahlen, which was in French hands and needed to be cleared by Hanoverian infantry. To his left lay a stretch of woodland which formed an obstacle for advancing cavalry and obscured the view of the battlefront. Assuming that the orders were to clear these obstacles and move towards the open ground in front of Minden, Sackville should have ordered his 3300 horsemen to advance in good order. Meanwhile, also to his left, the infantry brigades were advancing steadily under the overall command of General Friedrich von Spörcken, a veteran of Hastenbeck who had entertained earlier ambitions to replace Cumberland as head of the allied army.

It was at this point that the battle became an unexpected fight between infantry and cavalry as Contades unleashed his squadrons in an attempt to halt the advance of the two British brigades. Ferdinand himself wanted to intervene, and hence sent a galloper with orders to Sackville to support the infantry, but nothing happened and confusion reigned. According to the most coherent account of the battle, 'Sackville assumed that the cavalry were to march to their front, as he had been led to expect', and ordered his forces to move steadily through the woodland. When it became apparent that the infantry was not only holding its own but repulsing the French cavalry, Ferdinand dispatched two further gallopers to Sackville ordering him to move immediately so as to provide much-needed support. But the orders were either ignored or misunderstood, and by ten o'clock in the morning the moment had come and gone. Eventually Sackville rode over to Ferdinand's position, where he asked for the correct meaning of the orders only to receive the dismissive response: 'My Lord, the opportunity is now passed.' By that stage Contades was in full retreat towards Kassel, but a rout could have been a much heavier defeat if Ferdinand's orders had been properly understood and if a workable chain of command had been in position before the battle began.

The general feeling was that Sackville deserved to be punished. By the time he arrived back in London, he found that the public mood was against him and that not even his Leicester House connections could protect him. Not only were the allegations well enough known, thanks to the publication of a number of abusive pamphlets which accused him not only of cowardice but of sodomy (he was widely believed to be homosexual), but the hysteria also generated a demand for the death penalty. This was by no means an unlikely outcome: King George II had already indicated that he would support such a verdict and only three years had passed since Admiral Byng had received a similar sentence. In the end the court martial was something of a fudge: on 5 April 1760 the fourteen generals in judgement handed down a considered sentence which acknowledged that Sackville was 'unfit to serve His Majesty in any military capacity whatever' and was culpable of disobeying Ferdinand's orders, and that therefore the king was justified in dismissing him.[16] To rub home the point that this was a condign punishment, the sentence was ordered to be read out to the army 'so that officers may be convinced that neither high birth nor great employments can shelter offences of such a nature', a practice normally carried out only with capital offences.

More was to follow. Having passed sentence, the king personally removed Sackville's name from his list of privy councillors and to all intents and purposes the military career of 'the coward of Minden' (as he was promptly christened) was over. During the trial Sackville had based much of his defence on the fact that the delay in moving his men forward had not significantly affected the outcome of the battle and that only eight minutes had been lost as a result of his inaction, but this did him little good.[17]

Six months later King George II died. Sackville hoped that his passing would pave the way for a gradual return to public life, but the new king was unhappy about any immediate rehabilitation, telling Bute that 'how much should we not hear again of the unlucky day of Minden if he were in the [military] profession again'.[18] For the next two decades Sackville was never quite able to free himself from the obloquy of his behaviour at Minden, but he was not lost for ever to public life. On the contrary, he became one of those rare people who was able to reinvent himself under a different name and guise. His chance came in 1769 following the death of Lady Elizabeth 'Betty' Germain, an aged cousin of his father who had been widowed for some fifty years and who on her deathbed fulfilled her husband's wishes to leave the bulk of her wealth to a deserving son of the Earl of Dorset. As a result Sackville inherited her property at Drayton House in Northamptonshire, together with suitable funds, provided that he assumed his benefactress's name. The change of name to Germain was granted by act of parliament in the following year, and as Lord Germain Sackville was able to revive his political career by being appointed secretary of state for the American colonies in November 1775 in Lord North's government.

Although he performed ably, revealing himself as a sound administrator with a firm grasp of strategy, this was a poisoned chalice. He remained in the post until 1782, but history has not been kind to his reputation and he is usually included amongst those politicians and soldiers who were reviled for losing the American colonies. His under-secretary, the dramatist Richard Cumberland, came closest to delineating Germain when he wrote that he possessed 'all the requisites of a great minister, unless popularity and good luck are to be numbered amongst them'.[19] Germain died at his home in Sussex in 1785, aged sixty-nine.

As for Ferdinand's second-in-command at Minden, the man who was praised in his post-battle dispatch, John Manners, Marquess of Granby was already a hugely popular public figure, a larger than life, convivial character who was much admired (usually from a safe distance) as a thruster and a gambler and equally reckless in both pursuits. He came from a similar background to Sackville, being the eldest son of the Duke of Rutland, but in his case he had been educated at Eton. He was a very different kind of personality, however, being rash in his behaviour and outgoing and generous with his money. At the beginning of the Jacobite rebellion his father had raised a regiment of irregular horse known as the Leicester Blues and had given command of it to his son. While it never saw any action, being based at the Newcastle garrison, the experience gave Granby a taste for the military life and he successfully volunteered to serve on Cumberland's staff, seeing action during the Duke of Albemarle's operations in Strathbogie in March 1746. After the uprising he retained his commission, served in Flanders with Cumberland and was promoted major-general in

1754. In common with many other officers of the period he also maintained a political career, becoming member of parliament for Cambridge in 1754. Something of Granby's personality can be seen in King George II's rejection of his application to become colonel of the Royal Horse Guards (The Blues) on the grounds that he was 'a sot, a bully, that does nothing but drink and quarrel, a brute'.[20] Nevertheless Granby was an instinctive soldier; having gone to Germany in 1758 in command of a cavalry brigade, he eventually followed the unfortunate Sackville as commander of the British forces in Germany.

In that role he succeeded where Sackville had failed. Not only was he a cavalryman in command of a force in which cavalry was the leading arm, being a natural horseman was also an advantage: he had hunted from an early age and had a sportsman's instincts, with a good knowledge of the lie of the land and an understanding of the power and persuasive force of the cavalry regiments under his command – The Royal Horse Guards, 1st Dragoon Guards, 2nd Dragoon Guards, 3rd Dragoon Guards, 6th Dragoon Guards, 7th Dragoon Guards, 2nd Royal North British Dragoons, 6th Inniskilling Dragoons, 10th Dragoons and 11th Dragoons. This was the heavy cavalry of the time – big men on big horses equipped with weighty cavalry swords, forged straight and made for stabbing rather than slashing. In common with most commanders of elite forces Granby was inordinately fond of his men, and while this encouraged a certain laxity of discipline he did reward them for their services by providing funds for wounded non-commissioned officers to purchase public houses once they had left the army – hence the rash of Marquis of Granby public houses and taverns (using the French spelling) to be found across England. This only added to his popularity, so much so that in 1765 when Edward Penny produced the memorable painting *The*

Marquess of Granby relieving a sick soldier, it was made into a print which outsold the equally popular representation of Wolfe's death at Quebec by Benjamin West.[21]

Granby's time to impress came the following year, on a hot morning at the end of July 1760. A substantial force of French cavalry and artillery (some 20,000 in all) had assembled on a triangle of hilly ground between the rivers Diemel and Weser to the north of Kassel under the command of Lieutenant-General the Chevalier du Muy. It was a key moment for Ferdinand; his forces had been pushed north by a resurgent Broglie, who was intent on recapturing Kassel and regaining the initiative lost at Minden. The day began in a heavy summer mist which hampered visibility; it ended with the rout of du Muy's forces, which had taken shelter behind a long ridge overlooking the Diemel with the town of Warburg to their right and a rounded hill called the Heinburg to their left. Using the mist as cover the allied infantry, including two battalions of British foot guards and the newly raised 87th and 88th Highlanders, attacked the French left flank and quickly overran the artillery positions. A French counter-attack could have averted the threat, but before du Muy could engage his cavalry squadrons, Granby had seized the initiative by leading his force in a brisk forced trot towards the high ground at Desenburg. From there his twenty-two squadrons had the benefit of surprise and shock – and they used both to good advantage, charging into the French lines and bringing with them death and confusion. Given the weight of the charge, most of du Muy's force turned and fled from the field, leaving between 6000 and 8000 casualties killed or wounded. Granby described British losses as 'trifling', but his own role in the Battle of Warburg (as it came to be known) gained him a lasting place in military history. During the charge he famously lost his hat, leaving his head bare;

having been bald-headed since his twenties, he refused to wear a wig and the incident gave rise to the popular expression 'going bald-headed at the enemy'. Needless to say it only added to his soldierly reputation.

Not only did Granby's flair and initiative (not to say courage) help to win the day at Warburg, but it restored the reputation of the British cavalry and reinforced the wisdom of Pitt's decision to wage war against the French in Europe. Ahead lay further allied victories at Vellinghausen (15 July 1761), Wilhelmstahl (25 June 1762) and Brückermühl (21 September 1762) in which Granby and his expeditionary force added further lustre to Britain's military reputation.

Already, however, the direction of the country's war effort was wavering. The death of King George II in October 1760 had been one turning point, his successor George III apostrophising Pitt as 'a true snake in the grass';[22] the emergence of Bute in succession to Pitt, who resigned in October 1761, was another. Both the king and his new prime minister wanted peace, partly due to the prevailing war weariness and partly due to the unpopularity of the campaigns in Europe, which both had opposed. Another impetus for peace had been the unexpected and sudden death of Elizabeth of Russia at the end of 1761, which removed Frederick the Great's main rival and paved the way for peace between the two countries by the Treaty of St Petersburg in May 1762. The new Tsar, Peter III, was an admirer of Frederick the Great and ordered all Prussian territory to be returned while talks began to broker a new accord of peace and friendship between the two countries. (This never came into being as Peter was dethroned in a palace coup in the summer of 1762 and replaced by Catherine II.)

There had been a complication in the summer of 1761 when Charles III of Spain ended his country's neutrality by signing the

Family Compact with France. In the following year he entered the war, thereby creating the possibility that the Franco-Spanish alliance might allow France to regain her losses in North America, but these fears were short-lived. British expeditions were sent to Portugal and to the Caribbean, where the loss of Havana would prove a serious blow to Spanish colonial ambitions. Negotiations with France began in Paris in September 1762; the Spanish intervention in the war was negated by a British proposal that France should cede her remaining North American territory in Louisiana as compensation for Madrid's losses during the fighting. The offer was accepted, although in return Spain had to cede Florida to Britain, which emerged the dominant country in the peace negotiations. Not only had it won the war in North America by effectively expelling the French – the ostensible reason for the outbreak of hostilities in 1756 – but it had also triumphed in India and the Caribbean; in the latter it had conquered the French colonies of Guadeloupe, Martinique, Saint Lucia, Dominica, Grenada, Saint Vincent and the Grenadines, and Tobago. Only In the Mediterranean had it been forced to hand over territory to France, in the shape of the island of Minorca.

Inevitably the negotiations in Paris centred on the possession and exchange of territories, and they provoked bitter divisions in London between those who thought that too much was being offered by Britain and those who wanted peace at any cost. Both countries had suffered financially as a result of the conflict and were anxious to retain any advantage, but there were differences of approach. Bute wanted to extricate Britain from the possibility of any further confrontation with France, while French diplomats regarded the negotiations as another temporary truce whose terms could be overturned at some future date once France had recovered her strength. By any standards Britain should have held the whip hand, having triumphed in India and North America, but despite those advantages the peace-making process was far from straightforward.

The British delegation was led by John Russell, 4th Duke of Bedford, an experienced politician who had served as Lord Lieutenant of Ireland and was deeply opposed to Pitt's continuation of the war. Described as 'a man of excellent parts, though deficient in common sense',[23] Bedford had built his early career on his friendship with Cumberland and but for illness would have served on his staff during the Culloden campaign. Opinionated and strong-willed, he liked getting his own way and all too often preferred following his instincts instead of listening to the advice of his colleagues. While this was balanced by a strong sense of duty it did not make him the ideal leader of the British negotiating team, and so it proved. From the outset Bedford proved to be weak and vacillating in his approach, making it clear to the French that he was prepared to offer concessions in the interests of cementing an immediate deal. He also found it difficult to conceal his Francophilia, arguing that it would be counter-productive to introduce any clause which smacked of punishing France as it would simply lead to fresh confrontation, 'when she has taken breath'.[24] He even doubted the sense of holding on to Canada instead of the wealthy sugar island of Guadeloupe – one was only *quelques arpents de neige*, 'some acres of snow' (as Voltaire had it), while the other was worth £6 million a year in sugar exports. It did not help matters that Bute interfered continually in the process and that his own position was weakened by constant attacks from those loyal to Pitt.

The preliminaries were signed on 3 November 1762 and the Treaty of Paris was concluded on 10 February 1763. As a result Britain consolidated and added to its possessions in North America – Canada, Nova Scotia and Cape Breton were secured, together with Florida and the left bank of the Mississippi River – while in the Caribbean she received the islands of Grenada, St Vincent, Dominica and Tobago. Together with other territorial gains in Africa, India and Europe, these accessions confirmed Britain's position as a global power.

The same treaty did however give certain territorial advantages to France and Spain. Although France had been forced to cede its holdings in Canada, it gained some concessions – including protection of the Roman Catholic population – and retained its fishing rights off Newfoundland together with the two small islands of Saint Pierre and Miquelon, where it could dry fish. In the Caribbean, Guadeloupe and Martinique were also returned – while this played its part in healing French pride, the concessions seemed weak to opponents of the treaty. Pitt made his feelings clear during the debate in the House of Commons, remarking: 'The peace was insecure, because it restored the enemy to her former greatness. The peace was inadequate, because the places gained were no equivalent for the places surrendered.'[25] The reckoning would come sooner than expected.

In common with those that preceded it, the conflict which came to be known as the Seven Years War did not settle the long-standing struggle between Britain and France for global power. Neither did it temper Prussia's territorial ambitions in Europe. On the contrary, in the years ahead the intermeshing of those disparate interests only complicated matters still further. Prussia was confirmed as a major European power, while France had to accept that during the war its military and naval power had been badly dented, if only for the time being. At the same time, the failure of Russia and the Hapsburg Empire to curb Prussian ambitions created problems which would continue into the next century and beyond.

Although Britain had to accept a compromise agreement at the Treaty of Paris, at the time it had scored a spectacular triumph over the French, cementing its control on the high seas and making significant territorial advances (with the attendant financial gains) in North America and India. This paved the way for the later creation of the British Empire and for the Industrial Revolution which in no small part funded it. But one negative aspect of the Seven Years War turned out to be the sheer cost of waging a global conflict. It is one of the historical ironies of the war in North America that Britain was eventually required to attempt to recover its investment by introducing taxation from the American colonists. Within months of the end of the fighting those measures would prove to be so unpopular that the American colonists who had demanded British intervention in the first place would be up in arms against the mother country.

Known to history as the American War of Independence, the conflict between the colonists of North America and their British masters does not form a part of the main narrative of this book, but it has been included in outline as some of its leading personalities, notably Gage, Conway and Sackville (Germain), had served under Cumberland's command during the Jacobite uprising. Within two years of the end of the Seven Years War, the first flames were ignited by the British government with the passing of the Stamp Act of 1765, a direct tax on certain printed materials which was aimed at offsetting the cost of maintaining the British garrison of 10,000 soldiers in the American colonies. Not only was it vastly unpopular, being regarded as an unfair and arbitrary piece of legislation, but many Americans considered it to be a violation of their constitutional rights as English citizens. The move generated considerable opposition, with protests degenerating into violence, and although the act was repealed in March 1766 the fire smouldered, breaking into a greater conflagration in the following decade. During that time the relationship between London and the American colonies worsened, rebels became 'Patriots', mistakes were made by both sides – notably by the British in 1773 when legislation was passed granting the East India Company a monopoly to sell tea in North America – and confrontation became inevitable. War broke out in April 1775 with fighting between Patriot militias and British regular forces at Lexington and Concord, and it rapidly escalated into a full-blown conflict as General George Washington took command of the Continental Army and forced the British out of Boston. As had happened earlier in the century, France saw an opportunity to intervene; following a disastrous defeat for the British at Saratoga in 1777, the French signed an alliance with the United States of America, which had come into being on 4 July the previous year. Spain followed suit in 1779, and that intervention proved to be decisive: weapons and men flowed across the Atlantic and the French navy took command of the seas.

The end came on 17 October 1781 when, following a badly managed and half-hearted campaign, the entire British army in North America surrendered at Yorktown, bringing to an end British involvement in the affairs of the recently created United States of America. 'Oh, God, it is all over!' exclaimed Lord North on hearing the news five weeks later. As the British prime minister he was largely responsible for what had happened; within a year he had resigned, becoming the first holder of his position to be forced out of office as a result of a vote of no confidence in parliament. Fittingly, perhaps, it was left to the veteran Seymour Conway to voice the obvious when he made a memorable speech in the House of Lords on 22 February 1778 declaring the war to be unwinnable and insisting that American independence had to be recognised.[26]

Their obsequies were not unjustified, for by any military standards the loss of the American colonies was a disgrace to the British Army at an operational level. Germain had set the tone when he declared that 'these country clowns cannot whip us', and North had echoed such thinking with a strategy based on an understanding that the American militias, thought to be unruly and badly disciplined, would be unable to withstand the sustained volleys of British infantrymen.[27]

That proved not to be the case, but the loss of the colonies was not decided only at a tactical level. There were instances in the war when the British had the beating of the Patriots – for example, Burgoyne's rout of Washington at Brooklyn early in the conflict. Although later historians such as Macaulay denounced the British Army as 'the laughing stock of all Europe', the land forces in North America were often on a hiding to nothing, being let down by poor leadership in the field and an absence of logistical support, while attempting to cope with the sheer difficulty of waging a war over a large area far away from home.[28] They were also stymied by the Royal Navy's loss of command of the seas, which hindered the arrival of supplies and reinforcements, and by the fact that with the exception of some Hessian regiments, they were fighting without the support of any major European ally. Poor judgement and confusion over the meaning of orders from London – often out of date before they arrived – also played a part in creating confusion and misunderstandings.

Scale was the main problem facing British ministers and commanders on the ground. At the height of the fighting the British forces in North America never numbered more than 56,000 men, yet they had to cover an area which stretched from the Canadian border to Florida; having lost command of coastal waters it was no longer possible to transport men by sea on the north–south axis. Due to the small numbers on both sides, none of the battles were large-scale affairs of the kind fought in Germany during the Seven Years War; most were conducted on the scale of Culloden, where Cumberland had 9000 men and sixteen guns compared to the 42,500 men and 187 guns under Ferdinand of Brunswick at Minden fourteen years later.[29] Put another way, the British Army in North America was over-stretched, and as a result was unable to hold ground once it had been taken in battle. Even after a successful operation such as the taking of Philadelphia by General Sir William Howe in September 1777, it proved impossible to hold the city for any length of time.

Ostensibly the British forces were supported by some 25,000 Loyalists who had refused to join the revolution and most of whom served in the southern states, but they were a mixed blessing. While many had rudimentary training and proved to be stubborn fighters, Loyalist areas had to be protected against Patriot attack and British commanders often had to trim their thinking in order not to offend Loyalist opinion. This necessity made it difficult to live off the land – Loyalists and Patriots often lived side by side – and it meant that care had to be taken in dealing with local communities. It would have been impossible to employ the kind of aggressive tactics used in the West Highlands of Scotland in the aftermath of Culloden. As for the American Patriot army, it was frequently well led by British-trained officers and showed resilience in adversity. Its soldiers also had the advantage of fighting on home territory; for the most part they enjoyed the support of the population, an important factor in sustaining morale. They were also fighting for a cause, and that had a positive effect on their performance in battle.

The war was ended in September 1783 by a second Treaty of Paris. Britain was forced to come to terms with the new dispensation, which saw its holdings in America reduced to Canada and to its remaining islands in the Caribbean. India increasingly became the focus of its colonial ambitions, and as a result defence expenditure was concentrated on the Royal Navy and its requirement for ships and manpower (110,000 sailors and marines). The thinking was straightforward: never again would British policy be trammelled by losing command of the seas. As a result the army was neglected and many of the regiments raised for service in America were disbanded; it was not until 1778 that the position of commander-in-chief was finally filled by Jeffrey Amherst, by then enfeebled by poor health. He held the post for four years when he was succeeded by his contemporary Seymour Conway, but was recalled in 1793. That second tour of duty was not a success: as Pitt told King George III, it was only a stop-gap, for Amherst did not possess 'the activity and energy which the present moment seems to call for'.[30] Amherst died on 3 August 1797 at his home (fittingly called 'Montreal') at Riverhead, Kent and was buried a week later at Sevenoaks. With his death one of the last members of Cumberland's military family departed the scene.

Meanwhile the world had changed once more. Largely as a result of the French revolution of 1789, which had seen the country plunged into anarchy and its royal family executed, Britain was again at war with France.

12

FORTY YEARS ON:
THE END OF AN OLD SONG

In forcing the British government to recognise that they could no longer hold on to the North American colonies, the American Patriots achieved what the Jacobites had failed to do – inflict a decisive defeat on the authority of the British Crown. With the support of the French they had won independence for the newly formed United States of America, and following the second Treaty of Paris of 1783 they were free of British rule. The new nation's first president was George Washington; he was elected to the post on 30 April 1789, thirty-five years after receiving his first military commission from the British in the fighting that would lead to the expulsion of the French from North America.

By then the Jacobite cause had passed into history and many of its leading lights had gone into exile in Europe. Amongst them was Lord George Murray, perhaps the ablest soldier in the Jacobite army, who spent the next few years restlessly on the move. Having been punished by the forfeiture of his estates, his family was turned out of the family home at Tullibardine Castle in Perthshire; to add to his sense of betrayal, Murray was permanently estranged from Prince Charles Edward Stuart, a result of their disagreements over strategy during the campaign. He died in Medemblik in the Netherlands in 1760, aged sixty-six.

Other Jacobite supporters went into the service of the French army, thereby continuing a long tradition. Both Cameron of Lochiel and Lord Ogilvy took this route, becoming in time the commanding officers of, respectively, Le Regiment d'Albanie and Le Regiment d'Ogilvie, both of which were formed largely 'from the debris of units that had fought at Culloden and managed to escape'.[1] Ogilvy is also interesting in that he represented his family's interests while his father, the Earl of Airlie, remained at home. He was not alone in taking that course; so too did other heads of families.

If any family name sums up the mass of social contradictions which encompass the Battle of Culloden, it is Chisholm of Strathglass whose clan chief MacIain had not joined the Jacobite revolt, either because he was too old or, more likely, too canny to commit his people. As a result, during the charge of Clan Chattan some one hundred Chisholms were led into battle by MacIain's youngest son, Roderick Og Chisholm, who was killed during the last desperate Jacobite onslaught. On the opposing side less than 600 yards away were two of Roderick Og's brothers, James and John, who wore the red-coated uniform of the Duke of Cumberland's government army. Both survived the battle. Elsewhere on the field, when the fighting died down, William Boyd, 4th Earl of Kilmarnock and commander of a troop of Prince Charles's Horse Guards, had been surrounded and offered his surrender to a fusilier officer in Campbell's regiment. That officer was his eldest son, James Boyd, who eventually succeeded to the earldom following his father's execution for treason. Like every other internecine war, the Jacobite rebellion had pitted family against family, brother against brother and father against son, proving the adage that in civil war the winners usually gain their victories at dreadful personal cost.

As for the Bonnie Prince, after returning to France in September 1746 he had been upbeat about his position and tried to use his popularity within the country to encourage Louis XV to support a new military expedition aimed at fomenting another Jacobite uprising in Britain. It was not to be: despite the prince's blandishments and his fading personal charm, the French king proved evasive. Not only had he come to view Charles and his father as a lost cause, but senior commanders such as Saxe argued against any further cross-Channel adventuring on the grounds that it would remove vital military assets from his campaigning in Flanders. After peace in Europe had been settled by the Treaty of Aix-la-Chapelle, French impatience and British demands led to Charles's exile to the papal enclave at Avignon at the end of 1748. France had also been able to obfuscate by claiming that any future contact with the Jacobites had to be restricted to the Old Pretender's court in exile in Rome, and that requisite lasted for a further twenty years – James was not to die until New Year's Day 1766.

Even so, the flame was not quite extinguished. In the following decade Charles was constantly on the move trying to drum up support, even travelling to London in disguise in 1750 on a vain mission to encourage a fresh uprising amongst English Jacobites. Nothing came of these meetings, and the last realisable effort to mount a coup came in early 1753 with the so-called Elibank Plot. In common with so many Jacobite initiatives, this was strong on optimism and weak on planning and execution. It was also absurd. Dreamed up by Alexander Murray of Elibank, a member of Charles's inner circle and brother of the James Murray who had served in Wolfe's army, it involved a convoluted plot to kidnap King George II and his family, who would be held by several hundred Jacobites and taken to France prior to the king's abdication. Plans were put in place, but so many people became involved in them that confidentiality was impossible and the details became widely known. Thanks to Alastair Ruadh Macdonnell, chief of Glengarry, a former Jacobite supporter who turned coat, the details of the plot were revealed to the authorities; when Charles sent an emissary to Scotland in the shape of Andrew Cameron, Lochiel's younger brother, he was promptly arrested, tried and executed. Some idea of the quixotic nature of the ill-fated scheme can be seen in Glengarry's nom de guerre – 'Pickle the Spy'.[2]

Despite the setback, Charles continued his efforts to find backing. Towards the end of the Seven Years War there was one more attempt to gain French support when the new foreign minister, Étienne François, Duc de Choiseul, proposed a twin-pronged plan for the summer of 1759 which was designed to redress the setbacks in North America. The first part of the plan involved the French in the attack towards Hanover which was to be thwarted by the defeat at Minden in August 1759, while the second part envisaged a projected invasion of Britain later in the year which would involve support from the Jacobites.

Recently ennobled, Choiseul had already served his country as a soldier in the Low Countries, where he reached the rank of lieutenant-general, and had also served as a diplomat in Rome and Vienna. Crucially, he enjoyed the patronage of the king's mistress and confidante Madame de Pompadour (Jeanne Antoinette Poisson, 1721–64, wife of Charles Guillaume Le Normant d'Étiolles), but he was not without personal merit himself, being highly intelligent, utterly ruthless and remarkably quick witted. He was also a compulsive womaniser and philanderer, who overcame an unexceptional physical appearance with exceptional personal charm which he used to good effect. On a darker note, he was indiscreet and had a reputation for being frivolous and cynical; as one recent commentator put it, 'all in all he was a seductive but slightly disturbing person'.[3]

In short, Choiseul was probably the right man to oversee France's diplomatic affairs at a juncture when the Seven Years War was in serious danger of draining France's exchequer. On the positive side he brought new thinking to the problem and was sufficiently motivated and self-confident to turn ideas into action, but on the negative side he could be a menace in his personal dealings. Although his virtues made him exceptionally sure of himself and therefore an ideal public servant, they also encouraged him to be reckless and frequently vainglorious.

That was the case when he met Charles Edward Stuart in Paris on the evening of 5 February 1759 with a view to resurrecting the invasion plans. It was not an auspicious meeting: not only was the prince hopelessly inebriated – by then a common occurrence – but he was accompanied by Murray of Elibank, whom Choiseul despised. Even so, the meeting did have an agenda, although few notes were taken, and on the surface it should have been to the prince's liking: Choiseul made it clear that there was no problem finding the money and the forces to mount an invasion of England under the command of Prince Charles de Soubise, who was anxious to regain his military reputation following his crushing defeat by Prussian forces at the Battle of Rossbach in November 1757. There was only one stipulation: that the Jacobites would have to join the enterprise by mounting a diversion on the periphery, in Scotland or Ireland or both.

Unsurprisingly, Charles rejected this plan, not because it failed to give him what he wanted but because he was only interested in acting directly to bring about the defeat of England and the destruction of the house of Hanover. Scotland and Ireland held little interest for him; indeed he continued to fulminate that the failure at Derby had been the fault of his Scottish supporters. For his part, Choiseul made it clear that if the prince's counter-proposal were to be accepted, he would need firm guarantees about military support from sufficient English Jacobites to act in support of the French invasion. Of course Charles could not provide any such assurance, and with some inevitability the evening came to an inconclusive end.

However, that did not put an end to Choiseul's scheming. Ultimately he was not particularly interested in helping the Jacobites, while Charles's bibulous behaviour must have repelled him; there was the added frisson that both men were of similar age, but while Choiseul's star was in the ascendant Charles was going in the opposite direction. Even so, the French foreign minister did not lose sight of the possibility of mounting a cross-Channel invasion in 1759, its main impetus being not so much the restitution of the Stuart dynasty but the defeat of Britain and the crushing of the Hanoverian throne. France had effectively lost control of North America, but if the territory could not be recovered on the other side of the Atlantic it might be won in the English Channel by way of a large-scale invasion of Britain. In other words, French possession of North America could be wrested back in the fields of southern England.

The problem was finding the necessary forces at a time when France was becoming increasingly exhausted by the war and was not in a position to produce the men to mount an invasion. Having decided that the prince was a broken reed and that support from the English Jacobites would not be forthcoming, Choiseul turned his attention to mounting a diplomatic offensive across Europe to gain the necessary military and financial support. But he could find no takers. Sweden, Denmark and the Dutch Republic had the necessary land and naval forces, but were alarmed by the thought of the Stuarts being restored to the British throne and could see no advantages in accepting the French proposal. Not even Spain, no friend of Britain, took up the challenge.

Undeterred, Choiseul pushed ahead with his plans. In August an army of 100,000 began mustering at Vannes in Brittany, and with some difficulty a fleet of transport ships (including flat-bottomed barges) from Nantes and Bordeaux began assembling in the nearby gulf of Morbihan. The plan was that the invasion fleet would be protected by twenty-one warships from Brest under the command of the Marquis de Conflans, who would be joined from Toulon by a smaller fleet of twelve led by Admiral Jean-François de la Clue-Sabran. Unfortunately for the latter commander, when the Toulon fleet left port it was intercepted near Gibraltar by fourteen British ships of the line under the command of Admiral Edward Boscawen, who gave chase off the coast of Cadiz. The resultant battle took place in Portuguese waters near Lagos over two days, 18 and 19 August. During that time *Océan* (de la Clue-Sabran's flagship) and *Redoutable* were driven ashore and destroyed, while *Téméraire* and *Modeste* were captured.

It was a decisive victory for Boscawen and effectively ended French hopes of mounting a successful invasion. Even when Conflans put to sea in November with his Brest fleet, having taken advantage of a heavy gale, it was intercepted by twenty-four British ships of the line under the command of Admiral Sir Edward Hawke and decisively defeated on 20 November at Quiberon Bay.

For the French this was a serious blow to their naval pride. Not only had six ships been destroyed with the loss of 2500 lives, but their maritime power had been neutralised. Quiberon Bay sealed the fate of the French garrison in Quebec and made the fall of New France inevitable, thus ensuring that Choiseul's plans for an invasion of England would never come to fruition.

For the Jacobites it was not the end, but it was the beginning of the end. Choiseul's failure to mount an invasion finally sidelined Charles Edward Stuart. Shorn of leadership, the Jacobites quickly degenerated into a meaningless lost cause, long on sentiment and short on realisable action. Charles's last years were pitiful. In July 1760 his long-term companion Clementine Walkinshaw tired of his behaviour and left him, taking with her their daughter Charlotte, and he became increasingly isolated. Already a slave to drink, he became ever more abusive and cantankerous and gradually his old entourage drifted away from him. Attempts at arranging a dynastic marriage came to nothing other than a bizarre proxy marriage in 1772 with Princess Louisa of Stolberg-Gedern (1752–1824), and by the following decade the 'Young Chevalier' was but a memory from the distant past. On 30 January 1788, almost half a century after Culloden, he died of a stroke in Rome, mainly forgotten and mostly unloved.

It was a sad and unbecoming end for a romantic and once attractive young man who could have changed the course of British history. In his prime Charles was energetic, forceful and charismatic. Those who knew him well testified to his charm and his gallantry; those who served with him in the Jacobite army did not doubt his hardihood, physical courage and soldierly qualities. There is little question that he fulfilled many of the criteria needed by the successful military leader in the field. He had a forceful personality, possessed a firm grasp of tactical thinking and, more than anything else, he was able to maintain the impression that he would not ask his soldiers to do anything he was not prepared to do himself. This was not about cultivating popularity but an integral aspect of his belief that his soldiers needed to be inspired. Encouraging men to believe that they can rise above themselves and master their doubts and fears is one of the marks of a forceful and successful battlefield commander. Whatever his other faults Prince Charles had those qualities.

But there was a less attractive side. He could be headstrong and dogmatic to the point of becoming paranoid about those who served him and who could have saved him from himself. As one of his recent biographers has described him, Charles was 'the man to create a crisis not to solve it'. His personality existed at two extremes which seldom if ever met. In time those character traits became more accentuated, and it is fair to say that towards the end of his life Charles was a most unstable and most unlovable character. His hour came in the wind and the rain of an April day in 1746, yet even by then he had flunked the opportunity to achieve something approaching greatness. As a result of such dichotomies it is still difficult to provide an accurate and fair assessment of this man-child who would be king.[4]

Because of that, and because a heroic lost cause will always live on in people's hearts, the prince was captured in aspic; he remained 'Bonnie Prince Charlie', the romantic figure who launched a thousand whisky bottles and shortbread tins. In time, heroic portraits such as Antonio David's study of 1729 became the exemplar of the prince in the springtime of life, while Hugh Douglas Hamilton's grim-faced visage of the same man in middle age, painted in 1785, was an unforgiving memento mori. For good or for ill, both images have helped to cement Prince Charles into historical memory. He remains the courageous leader whose time in Scotland – *Bliadhna*

Thearlaich, 'the year of Prince Charlie' – raised hopes for his supporters that the Stuart dynasty could be restored and that he would come into his own. But the harsh fact is that he died a disappointed man, a paranoid soak who failed to understand that his cause was lost not only because he could not restore his power base in the Scottish Highlands but because his French allies were no longer prepared to invest in him. Choiseul's plan of 1759 was the last and best French chance to invade Britain, and although there were further opportunities in 1779 during the American War of Independence and in 1803–4 during the Napoleonic War, neither plan was realised; nor would either have involved the presence of an 'enemy within', as the Jacobites had been in the middle of the eighteenth century. Seen in that unforgiving light, the attempts to unseat the settled order in Britain could never have succeeded without determined French support, and for all Prince Charles's wishful thinking that failure meant that the Jacobite cause was doomed in 1745 and 1746. Throughout those years, the French flattered to deceive by doing very little to help the Jacobites, while at the same time benefiting from the British government's very real fears of imminent invasion.

As for those who had fought on either side at Culloden and went on to participate in the Seven Years War, many survived the conflict to serve the Hanoverian dynasty as it attempted to curb the rebellion in North America in the 1770s. Cumberland had died in 1765 as an indirect result of the stroke that had incapacitated him five years earlier; curiously, Ligonier, the man whom he had replaced at the beginning of the Jacobite campaign, survived him by five years even though Cumberland was forty-one years his junior. By then Ligonier had also had the satisfaction of being appointed commander-in-chief in 1757 following Cumberland's disastrous campaign in Europe and its humiliating end at

Klosterzeven. That same year he was promoted colonel of the 1st Foot Guards and raised to the Irish peerage as Viscount Ligonier of Enniskillen. The experiment of bringing him out of semi-retirement proved to be a great success. Ligonier was an inspired choice: always a team player (as it would be known in later years), his knowledge of military affairs and his shrewd judgement of character added enormously to his reputation. Justly so, his career ended on a high note at the conclusion of the Seven Years War. Although by then he was in his eighties, his period in office as head of the army had been a case of the right man being unexpectedly present at the right time. He died on 28 April 1770 widely respected and full of honours.

Cumberland's immediate subordinates during the Culloden campaign also prospered. Humphrey Bland came back to Scotland as commander-in-chief after a term as governor of Gibraltar – where he had been sent at his own request – between 1749 and 1751. The Mediterranean could have been considered a backwater, but Bland retained his belief that the army was a civilising influence and a force for good, especially in Gibraltar, a garrison which was gaining in strategic importance. Charged with the responsibility of regularising the status of the racially diverse local civilian population – according to the government a mixture of 'Jews, Moors, Papists of different nations' – Bland considered the possibility of replacing them with northern European Protestants, but he recognised that this carried too many legal risks.[5] Faced by such a heterogeneous mixture, and alarmed that they might evade taxation, Bland turned again to the idea, first mooted in Scotland, of settling the area with retired soldiers and imposing for the short term at least a form of military administration.

For a short time between 1751 and 1753 Bland was replaced in Edinburgh by Lieutenant-General George Churchill, who died early in his tenure forcing Bland to return to Scotland for a second term. In 1755 Bland cemented his ties with Scotland by marrying Elizabeth Dalrymple of Dalmahoy, the twenty-three-year-old niece of Field Marshal John Dalrymple, second Earl of Stair. By then in his late sixties – the exact date of his birth is unknown – Bland ended his career in Edinburgh, which seems to have become his spiritual home, but in 1756 ill health forced him to leave the city and he died in London on 8 May 1763. To the end of his days he retained the gruff, no-nonsense bluntness that had marked his entire military career, telling an unfortunate subordinate officer in Edinburgh who had treated him with scant respect: 'you are quite unacquainted with my character, or you wou'd have been more punctual in several parts of your Duty'.[6]

William Blakeney also gravitated towards the Mediterranean. As reward for his services in defending Stirling Castle in 1747 he became lieutenant-governor of the island of Minorca in the rank of lieutenant-general. It was not the ideal moment to assume command of the island. Minorca had become a British possession in 1713 but the bulk of the Spanish-speaking population was anti-British and resented the presence of the small British garrison. To this Blakeney reacted badly: forced to deal with the population as he found them and not as he would have preferred them to be – northern European and Protestant – he fell back on the notion of the army as an engine of reform and encouraged his soldiers to marry locally. He also tried unsuccessfully to take over the administration of the island's convents and monasteries, because they also ran schools and Blakeney wanted to limit the influence of the Catholic Church. Meanwhile he was not getting any younger. By the time war broke out with France in 1756 he was in his eighties (his exact date of birth is uncertain) and showing his age, but even so he demonstrated his resilience by holding out against the threatened French invasion of the island in the spring of that year. This was the incident that led to the disgrace of Admiral Byng, but Blakeney was allowed to surrender on honourable terms and no blame was ever attached to his name. On the contrary he was knighted, and retired from the army with his reputation intact. After being appointed a Knight of the Bath he retired to his native Ireland, where he was elected member for Kilmallock in the Irish parliament and succeeded his father as Lord Blakeney, living out his life on the family estates in Country Limerick. He died on 20 September 1761 at the age of eighty-nine and was later buried in Westminster Abbey. Right up to his death Blakeney remained a popular figure, especially in Ireland, where a masonic group known as the Friends of St Patrick raised a statue to him in Dublin's Sackville Street on St Patrick's Day 1759.[7] All this was in stark contrast to Byng, whose trial by court martial and subsequent execution remained controversial for many years.

By a quirk of fate, one of the army officers accompanying Byng during the ill-fated Minorca operation and who urged him to withdraw during a council of war was Edward Cornwallis, fresh from his exploits in Nova Scotia. Fate brought these veterans of the Culloden campaign together in the Mediterranean at the outset of the Seven Years War, but all three were treated differently. The strength of Cornwallis's political connections meant that not only was he absolved of any blame for the debacle of Minorca but he was promoted major-general in 1760 and two years later became governor of Gibraltar in the rank of lieutenant-general. He died in January 1776 from a malady which he described as a 'disorder' in his head and was buried in Bury St Edmunds.

By a further coincidence Seymour Conway was also on the island of Minorca during the siege. After Culloden and the mopping-up operations in the West Highlands, in which he worked in an intelligence-gathering role, he remained in the army by accepting command of the 48th Foot while pursuing a career in politics as member for Higham Ferrers in Northamptonshire. While serving with Cumberland at the Battle of Lauffeld he was injured and taken prisoner, but he was returned on parole and used the opportunity to marry Caroline Bruce, Countess of Ailesbury (1721–1803), the widow of Charles Bruce, 3rd Earl of Ailesbury who had died in February 1747. After transferring his command to the 34th Foot Conway moved with them to the Minorca garrison, but was not impressed by the posting, telling his cousin Horace Walpole that 'the country is one entire heap of rock and sand; not a tree for shelter nor a brook for refreshment in the whole island'.[8] In common with Cornwallis, Conway avoided any blame for the loss of Minorca, and after lobbying Cumberland he was transferred to the 13th Dragoons at the end of 1751. On being stationed with his regiment at Sligo in Ireland, Conway seemed content to settle down to the life of a rural gentleman, but in 1755 he returned to politics, becoming member for Antrim in the Irish parliament. Thanks to Cumberland's further intervention he was also appointed chief secretary for Ireland by the new Lord Lieutenant, William Cavendish, Marquess of Hartington and later 4th Duke of Devonshire.

Of all Cumberland's protégés from Culloden, Conway was one of the most adept in both his military and political careers. He was also one of the most attractive, being not only physically good-looking but possessing a lively interest in literature, architecture and arboreal cultivation. He had the added advantage of rarely making enemies amongst his immediate peer group, and throughout his life he displayed a delicate but unstated sense of personal honour. His easy personality allowed him to shine in Irish politics, making himself indispensable to Newcastle when he was First Lord of the Treasury between 1754 and 1756. Despite (together with Cornwallis) being the object of George II's wrath for his role in the disastrous Rochefort expedition of 1757, Conway returned to favour after the accession of George III, when he cleverly allied himself with the rising political star of the Earl of Bute. Once again Conway's good luck held. Following Bute's intervention, he was posted to the army in Germany in April 1761 when he became second-in-command to the Marquess of Granby.

Towards the end of the war Conway quarrelled with Bute over his handling of the peace negotiations with France and as a result fell out of favour with the king, being obliged to resign the colonelcy of the Royal Dragoons in 1764 after voting against the government in parliament. Showing remarkable tenacity, he returned to public life a year later as a member of the administration led by Charles Wentworth-Watson, Marquess of Rockingham, thanks largely to one of Cumberland's last acts of patronage. (Another product of Westminster School and the son of Lord Malton, Rockingham had caused a sensation as a fifteen-year-old during the Jacobite rebellion by raising a regiment of volunteers and marching them to Carlisle to offer their services to Cumberland.) Conway lived until 9 July 1795, when he died at his home at Park Place, Remenham near Henley on Thames.[9] By then he had been promoted field marshal and had enjoyed a variegated political career, with ministerial appointments in the Rockingham and Chatham administrations of, respectively, 1765–6 and 1766–8. He also enjoyed a short period as commander-in-chief during the Rockingham–Shelburne administration, and in his retirement he pursued his literary interests, including an adaptation of Louis de Boissy's play *Les Dehors Trompeurs ou L'Homme u Jour* (The False Appearances or the Man of the Moment), which was performed at the Theatre Royal, Drury Lane. During the American War of

Independence Conway opposed the use of violence, describing it as 'cruel, unnecessary and unnatural', and at the end of the conflict he insisted that American independence should be a pre-condition of any settlement.[10] History has not been kind to Conway's reputation but he proved to be a great survivor – perhaps something of a political innocent, as his quarrel with Bute showed, but a man of principle who made the most of the many opportunities which came his way.

When Conway commanded the 48th Foot at Culloden, one of his officers had been Thomas Gage, a near-contemporary who had enjoyed mixed fortunes in making his career in North America. A conscientious soldier who had caught Wolfe's eye and earned his praise (no easy matter) in Canada, Gage proved to be an ineffective administrator while serving under Amherst towards the end of the Seven Years War. Having been promoted major-general in 1761 and succeeded his superior as commander-in-chief in North America after Amherst's recall, he had the misfortune to be plunged immediately into the fighting against the native Americans which later came to be known as Pontiac's War. Although he did well to energise the peacetime garrison when it was forced into fighting a counter-insurgency campaign against the tribes allied with Pontiac, he was less successful in his dealings with the colonists, emerging as an officer of severely limited talents and being excessively over-cautious during the growing public disorder in New York, Boston and Philadelphia in 1768. In his correspondence with the government towards the end of that decade, Gage failed to comment on the deteriorating situation and rarely ventured outside his headquarters in New York to assess what was happening elsewhere in the country. In 1773 he was on leave in London when the rebellion broke out in Boston; instructed to return to North America with orders to use extreme force and to arrest the ringleaders his response was to ask for more troops. Inevitably perhaps, his passivity reduced official confidence in him and led to his replacement by three younger generals, William Howe (1729–1814), Henry Clinton (1730–95) and John Burgoyne (1722–92). Although Gage was involved in the opening shots of the revolt which became the American War of Independence, he was recalled to England in the summer of 1775. He died thirteen years later, not long after the British defeat at Yorktown which ended the conflict and led to the emergence of the United States of America.

In many respects Gage was unfortunate in the reputation he left to posterity. Unlike other officers who served in the American War of Independence, he recognised that the colonists were not 'the despicable rabble many of them have supposed them to be', but a well-organised and proficient force which demonstrated more 'conduct, attention and perseverance' than they had ever revealed against the French during the Seven Years War.[11]

In the aftermath of the loss of North America, Gage was criticised for his docile behaviour and for his refusal to crush the rebellion if necessary by employing overwhelming force from the very beginning. It was not as if he did not have the necessary experience. At Monongahela he had seen what happened when trained and disciplined infantrymen allowed themselves to be overwhelmed by lightly armed skirmishers; at Culloden he had witnessed the precise opposite when the government army stood firm and used its superior firepower to defeat weaker and less well organised opposition. The argument seems to have been that if Gage had possessed Cumberland's instincts, the rebellion could have been nipped in the bud – full-blooded repression usually achieves the desired result in the short term – but Gage was not the kind of soldier to apply a mailed fist against the colonists. He also realised that it could only be a short-term solution. At the time he told his political masters that 'small numbers [of soldiers] will encourage resistance, and not terrify and will in the end cost more blood and treasure'; in any case he simply did not possess a sufficiently large garrison of suitably trained troops to direct large-scale operations.[12] That much became disastrously clear in April 1775 when he dispatched a small force led by an overweight and unfit commander, Lieutenant-Colonel Francis Smith, to arrest the illegal provincial congress at Concord. As happened at other times during the conflict, the available intelligence was good, but its interpretation left much to be desired and as a result operations were often botched. In any case Gage was not cut out to be an oppressor or bully: as John Shy, his most capable biographer, put it, 'a harsh but fair epitaph might have been "Good soldier but no warrior".'[13]

Ironically, William Haviland, his fellow brigadier-general in the 1758 campaign, continued to serve in the army with considerable distinction, joining Amherst's staff and commanding the western district at Plymouth during the American War of Independence. As a reward for his services in North America he was appointed colonel of the 45th Foot (later The Sherwood Foresters), in which he took a friendly proprietorial interest, not least by offering encouragement and hospitality to its younger officers. He reached the rank of full general before his death in Buckinghamshire on 16 September 1784.

George Townshend, another protégé of Cumberland and North America veteran, lived on until 1807 when he died in Norfolk aged eighty-three, full of honours in respect of a life well led. His support of Bute in 1760 meant that he was able to resume his military career unsullied by his comments on Wolfe's handling of the battle to capture Quebec. Having succeeded to his father's viscountcy in 1764, he was afterwards appointed Lord Lieutenant of Ireland, a post he held until 1772. During that time he retained his reputation as a parodist and his skills as a cartoonist remained intact, a trait which did not endear him to the upper classes, who also disapproved of his habit of carousing late into the night in Dublin Castle.[14] As an administrator he encouraged a policy of direct rule over Ireland, and it can be claimed that his thinking looked forward to the Act of Union of 1801. Although his military career had ended with the conclusion of the Seven Years War, when he served with the British troops sent to Portugal to help forestall a Spanish invasion, he remained a firm supporter of the militia. In 1796 he was created field marshal, living to enjoy the privilege until his death in September 1807.

All told, seven veterans of the Jacobite campaign were promoted to the rank of field marshal, the others being Wade, Ligonier, Howard, Conway, John Campbell and the little-remembered Studholme Hodgson (1707–98), who had served as an aide-de-camp to Cumberland at Culloden and attained the position in 1796, at the great age of eighty-nine. Campbell succeeded his father as 5th Duke of Argyll in 1770, after the 3rd Duke had died childless in 1761 and the title passed to the Mamore side of the family. At Culloden he had emerged with a good account of his abilities, so much so that in 1749 he was given command of the 42nd Highlanders, then serving in Ireland. His subsequent progress was slow but steady – major-general in 1759 and lieutenant-general two years later – and he crowned his military career by being promoted field marshal in 1796, the same year as Townshend and Hodgson. He died on 26 May 1806 having spent his later years at his seat at Inverary, where he involved himself in agricultural improvement. Campbell owed much of his preferment to his name and his Argyll family connections, but as 'Colonel

349

Jack' at Falkirk and Culloden he made good the soldierly promise which had marked his early career in the army. It was also advantageous to his subsequent political career that he had an enticing wife in the celebrated society hostess Elisabeth Gunning, widow of the 6th Duke of Hamilton, whom he married in 1759. Like other members of his family he remained a confirmed Hanoverian throughout his life – as did his kinsman John Campbell, Earl of Loudoun, another Culloden veteran who ended his military career at the conclusion of the Seven Years War serving with Townshend in Portugal. He died, a bachelor, at Loudoun Castle on 27 April 1782 and was succeeded by his cousin John Mure Campbell, who shot himself four years later when he found that it was impossible 'to support the financial burden of the great [Loudoun] estate'.[15]

Perhaps the most able soldier to emerge from Cumberland's army did not fight at Culloden, but even so his career was touched by the fact that he had served in the government forces during the Jacobite campaign. Eyre Coote had been fortunate to escape with his reputation intact after Hawley contrived to lose the day at Falkirk at the beginning of 1746, but he lived to fight another day. By running away from Falkirk Muir he had laid himself open to the charge of cowardice and deserting his post, but fortunately good sense prevailed. Although he did not serve in North America, where many Culloden veterans made their reputations, he was able to pick up his military career in India, first with the 39th Foot and then with the 84th, which formed the backbone of his army during the decisive victory at Wandiwash that laid the foundations for British rule in India. In the aftermath he cemented his career in India by reducing the remaining French positions in the Carnatic before taking himself off to Bengal, where he remained until his return home in 1763. In common with many others in the East India Company's service, Coote enjoyed the rewards of his success, buying an estate near Fordingbridge in Hampshire and purchasing a parliamentary seat in Leicestershire. His life was also enriched by a happy marriage to Susannah Hutchinson, the universally admired daughter of the governor of St Helena, described by a contemporary as 'a living pattern of excellence with engaging and noble merits'.[16]

Clearly a soldier of such merit could not be ignored, and in 1769 the East India Company appointed him commander-in-chief of all their forces in India. It should have been a high point of his career, but with no enemy in sight and with time on his hands he quarrelled with his civilian colleagues, returning to England two years later angry and disappointed. Whatever his abilities as a soldier, Coote was no diplomat; yet he clearly enjoyed the confidence of King George III. On his return he was knighted, promoted colonel in the British Army and given command of his old regiment the 27th Foot, stationed at Fort George outside Inverness. Amongst his many guests was James Boswell, who arrived with Dr Samuel Johnson, and both visitors were entertained on 28 August 1773 to 'a dinner of two complete courses, variety of wines, and the regimental band of musick playing in the square, before the window, after it'.[17] For Coote and his wife – 'a very agreeable woman' according to Boswell (from the evidence of his diary a good judge) – this was a pleasant interlude, but a return to India beckoned in 1778 following the appointment of Warren Hastings to the new post of governor-general. This time Coote's main opponent was Haidar Ali, the mettlesome ruler of Mysore, an excellent soldier who commanded a numerically superior army which he had used to good effect to ravage the Carnatic. It was a tumultuous time. Coote was deficient in transport and cavalry and faced an army which outnumbered him ten to one; Haidar had moreover entered into an alliance with the French, who were now at war again with Britain – this time over America's declaration of independence. On paper it should have been no contest, but Coote rose magnificently to the occasion, showing strategic awareness and tactical acumen. Determined to avoid a pitched battle unless it suited him, Coote marched and counter-marched to keep his opponent guessing. On 1 July 1781 near Cuddalore he won the first of four encounters at the Battle of Porto Novo (Parangipettai), coolly marching his little army across Haidar's front line and taking advantage of the shelter of the sand hills to use his artillery to good effect before launching his main attack against the Mysorean left flank. The move was decisive, and it drove Haidar from the field. Only the lack of numbers and logistical support prevented Coote from exploiting a brilliant victory.

Coote again won the advantage on the three further occasions – at Pollilur, Sholingur and Arnee – when the two armies met again, but none of the engagements was decisive and Haidar's army remained at large in the Carnatic. On the other hand, the very fact that Coote was undefeated in the field meant that Haidar could not make good his territorial claims.

By the end of the year the impasse was still unresolved, but by then Coote was a sick man worn down by his years of campaigning, and he took himself to Calcutta to recuperate during the monsoon season of 1782–3. 'I have one foot in the grave and one on the edge of it,' he said before returning to Madras for what would almost certainly be the last time.[18] He died on 27 April 1783 and was later interred in the parish church near his estate in Hampshire. Because he died childless the baronetcy passed to a nephew of the same name, but the battle-cry 'Coote Bahadur' lived on in the East India Company's forces, which formed the basis of the modern Indian army.

Of all those who served in Cumberland's army, Coote emerged as the most complete battlefield commander. At Quebec Wolfe owed his lasting fame to his death in action, but the triumph on the Plains of Abraham came from the adoption of a plan which was not of his own making; whereas the ensign who failed his first test of battle grew into a general who was praised in the following terms by Fortescue: 'in the matter of tactics on the field he seems to have been one of the greatest masters of his own or any other time.'[19]

With the exceptions of Stringer Lawrence, William Draper and John Caillaud, Eyre Coote was the only officer of the first class from Cumberland's army to forge a successful military career in India. The majority of the others, particularly James Wolfe, Thomas Gage and George Townshend, perhaps the most noted recipients of lessons learned during the Culloden campaign, came to fame in North America during the Seven Years War.

But for Sackville's hesitation at Minden and the consequent belittling of his reputation, he could have emerged as one of the leading military lights of his generation. Instead, his name was tainted by the charge of cowardice. In that respect he might have benefited at Minden from the advice given to soldiers over the years – better to do something than do nothing. As for his immediate subordinate Granby, he was very much a soldier's soldier: good in action, less so in administrative matters, brave to a fault but lacking in judgement. His career in command began and ended in the last three years of the Seven Years War, where he discovered his true metier fighting in the open landscapes of the north German plain. In those surroundings his beloved heavy cavalry and his bold leadership came into their own, but his success in the field led to his eventual undoing. Being a dashing and hugely successful battlefield commander, he was courted by politicians who wanted to bask in his reflected glory. Granby was, however, unequal to the task of dealing with the deadly cut and thrust of the political world in the early years of the reign of King George III, and the monarch never quite trusted him. Although he became commander-in-chief in succession to Ligonier in the summer of 1766, it was not a successful appointment and he soon found himself under fire over the government's treatment of the army and the navy as a result of the inevitable cutbacks introduced at the end of the Seven Years War.

It was not Granby's fault that, to help reduce the National Debt of £133 million (£13 billion today), the size of the army was fixed at 45,000 men – 17,000 in Britain, 10,000 in the colonial empire, 4000 in Gibraltar and Minorca and 12,000 in Ireland, with 1800 specialist artillerymen – but as the new commander-in-chief he had to take most of the blame. In January 1769 this unhappy episode in Granby's career culminated with a vicious attack in the pages of the *Public Advertiser* written by an unknown controversialist under the pseudonym of 'Junius' (generally thought to be a senior clerk in the War Office called Philip Francis), who accused Granby of all manner of peculation including nepotism and the sale of commissions.[20] The real target, though, was the Grafton ministry; such was Granby's personal standing in the country that he would probably have ridden out the storm but for the intervention of William Draper, who unwisely entered the fray on behalf of his old army colleague from the Culloden campaign.

Having served in India under Coote, Draper had crowned his career with command of the operation to seize the Spanish holding of Manila in the Philippines in 1762, a feat that brought him a knighthood and substantial prize money from the East India Company. At the time Draper was very much in the public eye, but his uninvited intervention on behalf of Granby was disastrous.

It seemed to 'Junius' that in trying to excuse his old friend for being merely forgetful in his dealings, he had represented him 'in the character of a drunken landlord, who deals out his promises as liberally as his liquor'.[21] Draper's intervention did not help matters and unintentionally may have made them worse; within a year Granby had resigned his posts as commander-in-chief and Master-General of the Ordnance and was forced to leave public life. In retirement his many debts came back to haunt him and he died intestate on 28 October 1770, a sad end for one of the most energetic and successful soldiers of his generation.

Draper's backing of Granby had caused merriment and contempt in equal measure and he was forced to withdraw his support, but clearly he had learned nothing from the furore. Ten years later, having returned to military service in the rank of lieutenant-general, Draper was appointed lieutenant-governor of Minorca, where his immediate superior was James Murray, a victor of Quebec who had served as its first governor until 1766. Although both men were former comrades and enjoyed an initially cordial relationship, this was put under considerable strain when war broke out with Spain and the island was besieged. Both men had strong personalities and both had enjoyed successful military careers; perhaps it was as a result of that common background that they soon clashed over the direction of the operations to save the island. Things became so fraught that Draper was relieved of his command before the siege came to an end in February 1782, but that was not the end of the matter. When Draper returned to London he brought twenty-nine charges against Murray, who was forced to face trial by court martial at the end of the year. Such a tedious and unnecessary process was criticised by King George III as being unworthy of both men and Murray was acquitted early in 1783. Promoted general that same year, he retired to live near

Battle in Sussex where he died on 18 June 1794. As for Draper, he too retired from public life, in his case to live in Bath where he died on 8 January 1787.

By the end of the eighteenth century most of the officers in Cumberland's army at Culloden had died and only two of any note – John Campbell and George Townshend – survived into the new century. Two others – Ligonier and Granby – had held the prestigious position of commander-in-chief and Master-General of the Ordnance, a dual role which gave them undisputed political and military power over the country's armed forces, while Townshend had held the post of Master-General of the Ordnance alone and Conway and Amherst had been appointed commander-in-chief while being denied the Ordnance. (Between 1759 and 1766 and between 1769 and 1788 the post of commander-in-chief had been vacant.) It all went to show how strongly Cumberland's protégés had influenced the shape and direction of the army in the half-century after Culloden. All of those men and many of their fellows were also members of parliament who combined military careers with their role as parliamentarians, just as many lawyers did during the same period. Many sat for garrison towns and all were expected to support the king, an important consideration when appointments to senior positions could be influenced by royal favour.

Even so, for much of the eighteenth century there was no permanent senior serving soldier in peacetime, either in the rank of captain-general or commander-in-chief. There was a Secretary at War, but this was a political position and did not always carry Cabinet rank. Subordinate to him at the War Office were two senior soldiers: the Adjutant-General was responsible for personnel and discipline; the Quartermaster-General (a post held between 1742 and 1763 by Humphrey Bland) responsible for supply. Outside this hierarchy the most senior soldier was the Master-General of the Ordnance, who presided over the all-powerful Board of Ordnance, was responsible for questions of disbursement and supply, and had command of the Royal Artillery and Royal Engineers. The post was always in the hands of a senior general who normally sat in the Cabinet, and was removed with any change of administration. In short, whoever occupied the position had the ear of the king and his leading politicians. If this were combined with the post of commander-in-chief it gave the holder great power and authority. In that close-knit world in which connections and friendships were important for lubricating promotion, patronage was a crucial ingredient in the military life. For those in receipt of it, patronage was essential for their advancement; for those giving it, patronage was important for developing and supporting their own careers. Throughout the eighteenth century and into the nineteenth, successful senior soldiers from Marlborough to Wellington understood that maxim, using it to good effect to further their own military careers and the careers of those who served them.

Ligonier and Granby achieved the highest ranks in the British Army, but the main thing that they had in common was service under Cumberland, both in Flanders and Germany and in the campaign to put down the Jacobite uprising in 1745–6. This background they shared with several other high achievers who emerged as leading commanders in the war against France. Although they had not recognised it at the time, service with Cumberland touched their lives in ways that were far-reaching and played a significant role in determining the direction of their later careers. The same goes for the other prominent members of Cumberland's Ring such as Conway, Coote, Cornwallis, Sackville and Wolfe, who all emerged as leading soldiers of their generation. They were the forerunners of a group of generals who prospered in the late

Victorian period as a result of the patronage of successful commanders such as Lord Wolseley, Lord Roberts and Lord Kitchener.

These 'rings' were well known and acknowledged as a means of promotion, their members having served in campaigns in which loyalty to the commander was noted and prized – Wolseley, for example, in Ashanti (Africa), Roberts in Afghanistan and Kitchener in India and Sudan. In that later age the existence of the generals' 'rings' introduced a political dimension which worked to the advantage and disadvantage of both the generals and the politicians. Both sides used the press for leverage, both schemed and plotted against one another and rivalries were ever-present as officers did whatever they could to climb promotion's greasy pole. By that time, too, the Victorian generals (all three of the aforementioned became field marshals) were hugely popular, and were celebrated as national heroes with instantly recognised nicknames – 'All Sir Garnet', 'Bobs' and 'K of K'.[22] In Cumberland's reception as the 'conquering hero' after Culloden it is possible to see the beginning of that fashion, and in the promotion and preferment of his favourites can be found the creation of his 'ring' – although in the less fastidious Georgian period Cumberland never achieved a popular nickname outside that of 'Billy', bestowed upon him by his soldiers. Only later, as qualms grew about the severity of the operations following the Battle of Culloden, did the name 'Butcher' stick to him with a vengeance. Culloden was the only battle Cumberland ever won, but ironically it was the springboard for many of the young officers who leapt to fame later in the century after putting an end to the last civil war to be fought on British soil.

For good or ill, Culloden was always associated indelibly with Cumberland's name. It was never awarded as a battle honour to any of the regiments which served in his army, but it remains a significant moment in British history. Not only was it the last formal battle to be fought on British soil, but at a time of a hostile confrontation with France it put paid to the threat of a cross-Channel invasion and ended all hopes of a resurgence of support for the House of Stuart. As a consequence Britain was also freed from the fear that an autocratic Catholic absolute monarchy would return to replace the 'liberty' and 'true religion' of the legitimate Protestantism which underpinned the rule of the House of Hanover.[23] From that point of view it was all very satisfactory.

Culloden is also an important staging post in the eighteenth-century development of the British Army, and its deployment in the creation of Britain's first empire in North America and India during the Seven Years War. On the open expanses of Drummossie Moor, well-trained British infantry battalions reinforced the lessons of Dettingen and Fontenoy by demonstrating the value of disciplined volley fire in defeating a determined and hitherto unbeatable enemy. Later in the same campaign, in the remote mountain areas of the West Highlands of Scotland, the same commanders used their regular infantrymen to 'pacify' the civilian population and restore order to prevent the recrudescence of another Jacobite rebellion. Most of them were young soldiers – English, Irish and Lowland Scots – with their careers still ahead of them. In turn, the use of the army as an instrument of state policy came to represent an acceptable way of fighting frontier wars against the French and their native American auxiliaries along the Ohio, Missouri and St Lawrence rivers, even if the use of such tactics would later be viewed as unacceptable repression. Cumberland's young men had learned their lesson well, and the result was not only the temporary defeat of France but also the consolidation of lucrative British trading interests across the globe.

For the Stuarts and the Jacobites Culloden was the end of the road; for the Hanoverians and their supporters it seemed that a new age of prosperity and eventual world domination was at hand. The foundation of the United States of America and the emergence of Napoleonic France showed that those fond hopes represented a false dawn, but in reality the sunrise had only been postponed. The men who fought at Culloden under Cumberland's command were not only victors over a reviled enemy and their French supporters, but also harbingers of the greatness that seemed to lie ahead for the people of Britain.

Notes

Preface and Acknowledgements

1 Colley, *Britons*, 46–7
2 William Donaldson, *The Jacobite Song*, Aberdeen, 1988, 46

Prologue

1 Rev. Alexander Gordon, 'United Parishes of Daviot and Drumlichy (Synod of Moray, Presbytery of Inverness)', *First Statistical Account*, Part I, Edinburgh, 1769, vol. XIV, 67
2 Murray Pittock, 'Who were the Jacobites? The Pattern of Jacobite support in 1745', in Lynch, ed., *Jacobitism and the '45*, 60–1; Pittock, *Myth of the Jacobite Clans*, 54–87
3 *The Whole Proceedings in the House of Peers upon the Impeachment ... against Simon Lord Lovat for High Treason*, London, 1747, 27
4 Alan J. Guy, 'The Army of the Georges 1714–1783', in David Chandler, ed., *The Oxford Illustrated History of the British Army*, Oxford, 1994, 109–10

1 The heaviest Curse that can befall an unhappy People

1 The curse was 'popish tyranny', John Wiche, *Englishmen urged to Loyalty, by Their Sense and Love of Liberty. a Sermon Preach'd at Salisbury, October 6, 1745*, Salisbury, 1745, 17

2 NA SP 54, State Papers Scotland, II 25, nos 72, 79

3 Guise's later became the 6th Regiment of Foot and following the army reforms of 1881 was designated the 1st Battalion The Royal Warwickshire Regiment.

4 NA SP 54 State Papers Scotland, II 25, no. 66

5 Johnstone, *Memoirs*, 4

6 Narrative of Aeneas MacDonald, *Lyon in Mourning*, I, 201

7 NA SP 54, State Papers Scotland, II 25, no. 79

8 John Home, *History of the Rebellion in Scotland*, London, 1802, III, 5–6

9 Gibson, *Lochiel of the '45*, 26

10 NA SP 54, State Papers Scotland, II 25, no. 79

11 The Royals, or the Royal Regiment of Foot, later became the 1st Regiment of Foot and after 1881 was designated The Royal Scots.

12 NA SP 36/67, State Papers Domestic, George II, no. 41

13 Lee's later became the 55th Foot and in 1881 was designated 2nd Battalion The Border Regiment; Murray's later became the 57th Foot and in 1881 was designated 1st Battalion The Middlesex Regiment; Lascelles' later became the 58th Foot and in 1881 was designated 2nd Battalion The Northamptonshire Regiment.

14 W.A.S. Hewins, *The Whitefoord Papers*, Oxford, 1898, 22

15 NA SP 54, State Papers Scotland, II 25, no. 106

16 U Nott L, Ne C 1708/1, Letter from Brigadier-General William Blakeney to Henry Pelham, 18 October 1745

17 Hewins, *Whitefoord Papers*, 87

18 Edward Burt, *Letters from a Gentleman in the North of Scotland to His Friend in London*, London, 1754, 18

19 John Home, *The Works of John Home, Esq*, London, 1822, vol. III, 62–3

20 John M. Gray, ed., *Memoirs of the Life of Sir John Clerk of Penicuik, Baronet, 1676–1755*, Edinburgh, 1892, 182

21 Robert Chambers, *Traditions of Edinburgh*, Edinburgh, 1868 (rev. edn), 179

22 Hewins, *Whitefoord Papers*, 93

23 Johnstone, *Memoirs*, 21

24 NLS, Acc. 8392, A plan of the Battle of Tranent (Prestonpans) fought Sept[embe]r 21st 1745; manuscript map, c.1745

25 U Nott L, Ne C 1707: Henry Pelham, 'Some Reflexions on General Cope's Behaviour in Scotland', endorsed 'Facts relating to the Army in Scotland before the Battle of Preston Pans', n.d.

26 Alexander Carlyle, *Autobiography: Memorials of the Men and Events of His Time*, Edinburgh, 1860, I, 118

27 NA SP 36/68, State Papers Domestic, George II, Sir John Cope to Marquis of Tweeddale, 22 September 1745, enclosing a list of officers in the various regiments under his command killed, wounded or taken prisoner by the rebels, with an account of the defeat of his forces by the rebels at Prestonpans.

28 Johnstone, *Memoirs*, 25

29 BL, Add. MSS 32729, Newcastle to Cumberland, 4 September 1745

30 Haydon, *Anti-Catholicism*, 135–41

31 Betty Stuart Hart, 'Forfarshire (Ogilvy's) Regiment', in Livingston, Aikman and Hart, *No Quarter Given*, 93–115

32 Roberts, *Jacobite Wars*, 104

33 U Nott L, Ne C 1680, Letter from General T[homas] Wentworth, Hexham, to Henry Pelham, 19 November 1745

34 Barrell's later became the 4th Regiment of Foot and after the army reforms of 1881 was designated The King's Own Royal Regiment (Lancaster).

35 Willson, *Life and Letters of James Wolfe*, 51

36 Brumwell, *Paths of Glory*, 42

2 Like the savage race they roam for prey

1 Ray, *Compleat History*, 132–3

2 Deacon was one of several leading clergymen of the Church of England who had refused to swear allegiance to William and Mary. While he was a Jacobite sympathiser, his primary concern was the creation of an independent non-juring Church of England.

3 John Harland, *Ballads and Songs of Lancashire*, London, 1875, 61; the village of Long Preston is near Settle in North Yorkshire.

4 Corelli Barnett, *Britain and Her Army 1509–1970: A Military, Political and Social Survey*, London, 1970, 170

5   NA SP 36/76, State Papers Domestic, George II, 1 December 1745

6   NA SP 36/68, State Papers Domestic, George II, fol. 153; RA Cumberland Papers, 6/30

7   Duffy, *The '45*, 278

8   Not to be confused with The Royal Scots (or Royals) in the government army. It was raised in December 1743 by Lord John Drummond to fight in the service of King Louis XV of France.

9   BL Add. MS 32705, Richmond to Newcastle, 25 November 1745

10 RA Cumberland Papers, 7/287, Cumberland to Newcastle, 4 December 1745

11 Elcho, *Affairs of Scotland*, 337

12 W. Drummond Norie, *Life and Adventures of Prince Charles Edward Stuart*, 3 vols, London, 1903, II, 205

13 St Clair's was the 1st Battalion of the Royals, later The Royal Scots, while Murray's, numbered 43rd, later became The Black Watch. The fears of refusal to fight were not groundless. In 1743 the Highlanders had mutinied after refusing to serve in the West Indies.

14 Speck, *The Butcher*, 92

15 RA Cumberland Papers 7/324

16 Ibid., 7/325

17 Ibid., 8/32

18 Duffy, *The '45*, 331; Reid, *1745*, 76. The life guard was formed of Austrian and German troopers brought from Flanders. Bland's Dragoons had also served in Flanders and later became the 3rd King's Own Hussars. The Duke of Kingston's Light Horse was raised to fight in the rebellion and was disbanded in 1746.

19 Johnstone, *Memoirs*, 86

20 Duffy, *The '45*, 335. Cobham's Dragoons had been raised in 1715 and later became the 10th Royal Hussars (Prince of Wales's Own). Lord Mark Kerr's Dragoons had also been formed in 1715 and later became the 11th Royal Hussars (Prince Albert's Own). The two regiments amalgamated in 1969 to form the Royal Hussars (Prince of Wales's Own).

21 Ligonier's 'Black Horse' had fought at Dettingen and later became the 7th Dragoon Guards (Princess Royal's). In 1922 it amalgamated with the 4th Royal Irish Dragoon Guards to form the 4th/7th Royal Dragoon Guards and later became part of the Royal Dragoon Guards. Montagu's later became The Bays (2nd Dragoon Guards) and in 1959 amalgamated

with 1st The King's Dragoon Guards to form 1st The Queen's Dragoon Guards.

22 R.S. Ferguson, 'The Retreat of the Highlanders through Westmoreland in 1745', *Transactions of the Cumberland and Westmoreland Archaeological and Antiquarian Society*, 1889, x, 222

23 Matross derives from German *der Matrose* (sailor) and was the lowest artillery rank, the equivalent of gunner's mate. The rank was abolished in 1783. Lieutenant-fireworker was the junior commissioned rank.

24 RA Cumberland Papers 8/138, 161

25 Independent Companies were first raised in the aftermath of the 1715 Jacobite rebellion to act as a police force in the Highlands, in General Wade's words to be 'employed in disarming the Highlanders, preventing depredations, bringing criminals to justice, and hinder rebels and attainted persons from inhabiting that part of the kingdom'. It was from this system of recruitment that the regiment known as The Black Watch was created in 1739.

26 Duffy, *The '45*, 405

27 RA Cumberland Papers 9/81

28 NAS GM, 1st ser., 13, 1743, 386

29 Blakeney's Regiment later became the 27th Foot and after 1881 was designated 1st Battalion The Royal Inniskilling Fusiliers.

30 NA SP 54/27 f. 117, State Papers Scotland, Hawley to Newcastle, 19 January 1746

31 RA Cumberland Papers 10/18

3 The end of a bad business

1 Speck, *The Butcher*, 112

2 U Nott L, Ne C 1712/4, Blakeney to Guest, 28 December 1745

3 RA Cumberland Papers 10/49

4 Duffy, *The '45*, 438–9

5 Andrew Agnew, *The Agnews of Lochnaw: A History of the Hereditary Sheriffs of Galloway*, Edinburgh, 1864, 543

6 BL Add. MS 35354, f. 203, Yorke to Hardwicke

7 RA Cumberland Papers 12/28, Cumberland to Newcastle, 9 March 1746

8   The sloop had started life as HMS *Hazard*, under Captain Thomas Hill RN, but had surrendered at Montrose on 25 November 1745 and was renamed *Le Prince Charles*.

9   RA Cumberland Papers 13/28, Cumberland to Newcastle, 15 April 1746

10 *Lyon in Mourning*, I, 257

11 Prebble, *Culloden*, 56; Reid, *1745*, 129

12 Duffy, *The '45*, appendix 4, 581

13 John William O'Sullivan, *1745 and After*, Edinburgh, 1938, 154

14 Prebble, *Culloden*, 111–13

15 Holmes, *Redcoat*, 196

16 Michael Hughes, *A Plain Narrative or Journal of the Late Rebellion*, London, 1746, 36

17 In time the Culloden infantry regiments would be renumbered and reformed as follows: front line, 1st Foot (Royal Scots), 34th Foot (Border Regiment), 14th Foot (West Yorkshire Regiment), 21st Fusiliers (Royal Scots Fusiliers), 37th Foot (Hampshire Regiment), 4th Foot (King's Own Royal Regiment); second line, 3rd Foot (The Buffs), 36th Foot (Worcestershire Regiment), 20th Foot (Lancashire Fusiliers), 25th Foot (King's Own Scottish Borderers), 59th Foot (East Lancashire Regiment), 8th Foot (King's Liverpool Regiment); third line, 13th Foot (Somerset Light Infantry), 62nd Foot (Wiltshire Regiment), 27th Foot (Royal Inniskilling Fusiliers).

18 BL Add. MS 35354, f. 203, Yorke to Hardwicke, April 1746

19 Duffy, *The '45*, 521

20 Charteris, *Cumberland*, 247

21 Quoted in Prebble, *Culloden*, 92

22 The Irish infantry contribution to the Jacobite army came from three foot regiments in Lord Clare's Irish Brigade – Dillon, Lally and Roth – under the command of Brigadier Walter Stapleton. The term picquet refers to the practice of creating formations from various battalions or regiments.

23 Andrew Henderson, *The Life of William Augustus, Duke of Cumberland*, London, 1766, 256

24 Quoted in Prebble, *Culloden*, 95

25 Reid, *1745*, 170

26 Speck, *The Butcher*, 144; Willson, *Life and Letters of James Wolfe*, 63

27 Wright, *Wolfe*, 50–1

28   NRS GD 1/322/1, 122, Cumberland order book, 24 April 1746
29   Speck, *The Butcher*, 201
30   Wright, *Wolfe*, 185–6
31   Willson, *Life and Letters of James Wolfe*, 280
32   Elcho, *Affairs of Scotland*, 426

4 Bruise those Bad Seeds spread about this country

1   Livingstone et al, eds, *No Quarter Given*, 93–115
2   Ray, *Compleat History*, 337
3   BL Add. MS 32707, f. 13, Cumberland to Newcastle, 22 March 1745
4   Speck, *The Butcher*, 148–55
5   Ibid., 156
6   Elcho, *Affairs of Scotland*, Appendix G
7   Forbes, *Lyon in Mourning*, II, 128
8   Colonel David M. Lam, US Army Medical Corps, 'Medical Evacuation, History and Development – The Future in the Multinational Environment', Paper presented at the RTO HFM Specialists' Meeting on 'The Impact of NATO/Multinational Military Missions on Health Care Management', Kiev, Ukraine, 4–6 September 2000
9   RA Cumberland Papers 15/16, Orders of Major General John Campbell
10 Trevelyan Williams, *Historical Records of the 11th Hussars*, London, 1908, 39
11 Prebble, *Culloden*, 115; Richard Brett Smith, *The 11th Hussars*, London, 1969, 18
12 Roberts, *Jacobite Wars*, 183
13 NA SP 54/32/24E, State Papers Scotland, Ancrum to Cumberland, 25 June 1746
14 Hewins, *Whitefoord Papers*, 70
15 RA Cumberland Papers 15/101, Memorandum by Duncan Forbes of Culloden, 1746
16 Forbes, *Lyon in Mourning*, III, 97
17 *Scots Magazine*, May 1746
18 Hughes, *Plain Narrative*, 51
19 Speck, *The Butcher*, 165
20 Plank, *Rebellion and Savagery*, 75

21 Donald Gregory, *The History of the Western Highlands and Isles of Scotland*, Edinburgh, 1836, 375

22 Ibid., 10

23 Prebble, *Culloden*, 207; Andrew Lang, *History of Scotland*, vol. IV, London, 1907, 520

24 NA SP 54, State Papers Scotland, III 30, no. 20, Newcastle to Cumberland, 17 April 1746

25 C.R. Wilson, ed., *Old Fort William in Bengal*, vol II, Indian Records Series, 224

26 Forbes, *Lyon in Mourning*, I, 94

27 NA SP 54, State Papers Scotland, II 32, nos 4, 9, 53

28 Godfrey Dalrymple-White, 'The Cumberland Society', *Journal of the Society for Army Historical Research*, 6, 1927, 164–74

29 Terry, *Albemarle Papers*, 221

30 RA Cumberland Papers 15/373

31 *Abolition and Proscription of the Highland Dress Bill*, Ch. 39, Sec. 17, 1746

32 *The Records of the Forfeited Estates Commission*, Public Record Office Handbooks no. 12, HMSO 1968

33 NA SP 54/38, State Papers Scotland, Bland to Newcastle, 23 February 1748

34 Duffy, *The '45*, 537

35 NA State Trials, xviii, 350–1

36 The most comprehensive account is Seton and Arnot, *Prisoners of the 45*

37 Walpole to Sir Horace Mann, 1 August 1745, *Walpole Correspondence*, 19, 288

38 Hewins, *Whitefoord Papers*, 79

39 *The Letters of Sir Walter Scott*, ed. H.J.C. Grierson, London 1933, IV, 433

40 Willson, *Life and Letters of James Wolfe*, 65

41 NRS GD 1/322/1, Order Book, 28 January 1746, 192

42 RA Cumberland Papers 14/303

43 Fry, *Wild Scots*, 93

44 The Pragmatic army consisted of the forces of those countries which had signed the Pragmatic Sanction of Prague, the convention that guaranteed the integrity of Queen Maria Theresa's imperial dominions – principally the Hapsburg Empire, Britain, Hanover and the Dutch Republic.

5 Learning the lessons the hard way

1   Colley, *Britons*, 103–5

2   McCann, *Richmond and Newcastle Correspondence*, 236

3   David Daiches, *The Paradox of Scottish Culture: The Eighteenth Century Experience*, London, 1964, 68–97

4   Guy, *Oeconomy and Discipline*, 59

5   Hew Strachan, *The Politics of the British Army*, Oxford, 1997, 198

6   Alan J. Guy, 'The Army of the Georges 1714–1783', in David Chandler, ed., *The Oxford History of the British Army*, Oxford, 1994, 98

7   NA SP 54/37 f. 198, State Papers Scotland, 'Circular Letter to the Four Regiments in the North', 15 December 1747

8   Trevor Royle, *Civil War: The Wars of the Three Kingdoms 1638–1660*, London, 2004, 674–84

9   Terry, *Albemarle Papers*, I, 483

10 Alexander Allardyce, ed., *Scotland and Scotsmen in the Eighteenth Century: from the MSS of John Ramsay, esq., of Ochtertyre*, Edinburgh, 1888, I, 89

11 Terry, *Albemarle Papers*, II, 447

12 Ibid., II, 480–92

13 BL Add. MSss. 32,707, 128, Cumberland to Newcastle, 30 April 1747

14 'Proposals for Civilising the Highlands', Terry, *Albemarle Papers*, I, 480–91

15 Willson, *Life and Letters of James Wolfe*, 220–1

16 BL Add. MSS 32713, 195, Cumberland to Newcastle, October 1747

17 Charteris, *Cumberland and the Seven Years War*, 44

18 R. Harris, ed., 'A Leicester House political diary, 1742–3', *Camden Miscellany*, XXXI, 393

19 Walpole to Montagu, 20 July 1749, *Correspondence*, II, 398

20 RA Cumberland Papers 39/143

21 Guy, *Oeconomy and Discipline*, 129 note

22 *Constitutional Queries*, 7 February 1751

23 Lewis Namier and John Brooke, *The House of Commons 1754–1790*, London, 1964, 551

24 Horace Walpole, *Letters to Sir Horace Mann*, ed. Lord Dover, London, 1833, III, 210

25 Walpole, *George II*, II, 64

26 Basil Williams, *The Whig Supremacy 1714–1760*, Oxford, 1939, 205 note 1

27 *Debates and Proceedings of the British House of Commons During the Third,*

Fourth and Fifth Sessions of the Third Parliament of the Late Majesty George II, vol. I, London, 1746, 328

28 NA WO 65/1, War Office: printed annual army lists, 1754

29 William Coxe, ed., *Memoirs of the Administration of the Right Honourable Henry Pelham, Collected from the Family Papers and Other Authentic Documents*, 2 vols, London, 1829, I, 194–5

30 Fortescue, *British Army*, II, 263

31 A.J.B. Johnston, *Endgame 1758: The Promise, the Glory, and the Despair of Louisbourg's Last Decade*, Cape Breton, 2008, 38–40

32 John Grenier, *The Far Reaches of Empire: War in Nova Scotia, 1710–1760*, Oklahoma, 2008, 144–5

33 Olive Patricia Dickason, *Canada's First Nations: A History of Founding Peoples from Earliest Times*, Toronto, 1992, 160

34 In 2011 a petition was raised to remove the name 'Cornwallis' from all public places and buildings in Nova Scotia to protest at what was called a 'process of genocide'. http://www.danielnpaul.com/index.html

35 K.H. Ledward, ed., *Journals of the Board of Trade and Plantations*, Vol. 9: January 1750– December 1753, London, 1932, 51–64

36 U Nott L, Ne C 1201, copy of letter from Lords of the Board of Trade, Whitehall, London, to Edward Cornwallis, 2 [13] April 1750

37 Ledward, *Journals*, vol. 9, 50–3

6 Over the Mountains and Over the Main

1 Winston S. Churchill, *History of the English Speaking Peoples*, vol. III, London, 1957, 124

2 BL Add. MS 32851, Newcastle to Albemarle, 16 October 1754

3 Kenneth P. Bailey, *The Ohio Company of Virginia and the Westward Movement 1748–1792*, Glendale, California, 1939, 202–3

4 Pargellis, *Military Affairs in North America 1748–1765*, 45–6

5 G.A. Bellamy, *An Apology for the Life of George Anne Bellamy*, vol. I, London 1786, 194

6 Benjamin Franklin, *Autobiography*, New Haven, 1964, 223

7 Franklin Thayer Nichols, 'The Organization of Braddock's Army', *The William and Mary Quarterly*, Omohundro Institute of Early American History and Culture, IV, no. 2, April 1947, 136

8   Leonard W. Labaree, 'Franklin and the Wagon Affair', *Proceedings of the American Philosophical Society*, 101, 1957, 551–8

9   Major Joseph A. Jackson, *March to Disaster: Major General Edward Braddock and the Monongahela Campaign*, A thesis presented to the Faculty of the US Army Command and General Staff College in partial fulfilment of the requirements for the Degree Master of Military Art and Science, Military History, Fort Leavenworth, Kansas, 2008, 59

10   Worthington Chancery Ford, *The Writings of George Washington*, vol. I, New York, 1889,

11   Winthrop Sargent, *The History of an Expedition against Fort Duquesne in 1755; under Major General Edward Braddock*, vol. I, Philadelphia, 1856, 331

12   The 44th had also lost heavily at Prestonpans and would be decimated again in 1842, having been wiped out at Gandamuk during a retreat from Kabul in Afghanistan. It later became The Essex Regiment.

13   *Gentleman's Magazine*, August 1755, 380

14   Later the new regiment was renumbered the 60th, and later still in its existence it became The King's Royal Rifle Corps.

15   David Gates, *The British Light Infantry Arm*, London, 1987, 14

16   *London Magazine*, 1757, 504

17   McLynn, *1759*, 36–43

18   Pargellis, *Military Affairs in North America 1748–1765*, 166–7

19   Pargellis, *Lord Loudoun*, 197–8

20   Anderson, *Crucible of War*, 184

21   Corbett, *England in the Seven Years War*, I, 171–7

7 The World at War: North America

1   Walpole, *Memoirs of the Reign of King George the Second*, I, 158

2   Charles Tristan, *Marquis de Montholon, Mémoires pour servir a l'histoire de France sous Napoleon*, Paris, 1823, VII, 207–28

3   Charteris, *Cumberland and the Seven Years War*, 312

4   BL Add. MS 32834, f. 471, Newcastle to Hardwicke, 8 October 1757

5   Speck, *The Butcher*, 5–6

6   Whitworth, *Cumberland*, 50

7   Parkman, *France and England in North America*, V, 304

8   Willson, *Life and Letters of James Wolfe*, 237

9   *The Report of the General Officers appointed by His Majesty's Warrant of 1st November 1757, to inquire into the Causes of the Failure of the late expedition to the Coast of France*, London, 1758, 28

10 Walpole, *Memoirs of the Reign of King George the Second*, III, 5

11 Willson, *Life and Letters of James Wolfe*, 337

12 Ibid., 339–40

13 Rowena Buell, *The Memoirs of Rufus Putnam*, Boston, 1903, 23

14 *Writings of General John Forbes*, 226

15 Henderson, *Highland Soldier*, 14

16 Stewart of Garth, *Sketches*, I, 235–6

17 Ibid., 256

18 Frederick B. Richards, 'The Black Watch at Ticonderoga', *Proceedings of the New York Historical Association*, vol. X, New York: New York State Historical Association, 1912

19 Anderson, *Crucible of War*, 260

20 *An Impartial account of Lieutenant Colonel Bradstreet's Expedition to Fort Frontenac to which are added a Few Reflections on the Conduct of that Enterprise and the Advantages resulting from its Success, London, by a Volunteer on the Expedition*, London, 1759

21 Paul David Nelson, 'Lee, Charles (1732–1782)', *Oxford Dictionary of National Biography*, Oxford University Press, 2004; online edn, Jan 2008 [http://www.oxforddnb.com/view/article/16276]

22 Ibid.

23 Pitt, *Correspondence*, I, 422

24 *The Papers of Colonel Henry Bouquet*, 6 vols, ed. S K. Stevens, Donald H. Kent and A.L. Leonard, Harrisburg et al, 1951, I, 298

25 Forbes, *Writings*, 125

26 *Bouquet Papers*, II, 535–8

27 Pitt, *Correspondence*, I,

28 Anderson, *Crucible of War*, 284

29 James Clephane, *A Genealogical Deduction of the Family of Rose of Kilravock*, Edinburgh, 1898, 463–4

30 Waugh, *Wolfe*, 101

8 Paths of Glory

1 *Great Lakes Shipping, Trade, and Aquatic Invasive Species: Special Report 29*, Montreal 2008, 20

2 NA, Records of the British Colonial Office, part 3, 53, 665–9

3 Pitt, *Correspondence*, I, 370

4 Willson, *Life and Letters of James Wolfe*, 400

5 'Anecdote of the late Mr Reddish, the Player from Mr Ireland's Life of Mr Henderson', *The Town and Country Magazine*, June 1786, 317

6 Later these became: East Yorkshire Regiment (15th), Oxfordshire and Buckinghamshire Light Infantry (43rd), 2nd Northamptonshire Regiment (58th), Gloucestershire Regiment (28th), Loyal North Lancashire (47th), King's Royal Rifle Corps (60th), Royal Sussex Regiment (35th), 1st Northamptonshire Regiment (48th). Fraser's Highlanders was disbanded in 1763.

7 Willson, *Life and Letters of James Wolfe*, 427

8 Pitt to the Governors of New England, 30 December 1757, in Pitt, *Correspondence*, I, 136–40

9 James Sullivan, ed., *The Papers of William Johnson*, vol II, Albany 1921. The bulk of Johnson's original manuscript papers were destroyed in the New York State Capitol fire of 1911.

10 Louis-Antoine de Bougainville, *Adventures in the Wilderness: The American Journals of Louis Antoine de Bougainville, 1756–17*, ed. Edward Pierce Hamilton, Oklahoma, 1964

11 Amherst to Pitt, 28 February 1759, Pitt, *Correspondence*, II, 44

12 Later the 84th Foot became the 2nd Battalion The York and Lancaster Regiment.

13 Brumwell, *Paths of Glory*, 123; Willson, *Life and Letters of James Wolfe*, 363

14 William H. Whiteley, 'Saunders, Sir Charles', in *Dictionary of Canadian Biography*, vol. 4, University of Toronto/Université Laval, 2003– , http://www.biographi.ca/en/bio/saunders_charles_4E.html

15 Barry Gough, 'Vice-Admiral Sir Charles Saunders, Naval Victor of Quebec 1759', *The Northern Mariner/Le Marin du Nord*, XIX No. 1 (January 2009), 7–25

16 Knox, *Journal*, II, 91–3

17 Francis Parkman, *Montcalm and Wolfe*, New York, 1901, Vol. III, 40

18 Ibid., 317

19 Willson, *Life and Letters of James Wolfe*, 427–9

20 Brumwell, *Redcoats*, 237

21 Wright, *Wolfe*, 517–18

22 Knox, *Journal*, II

23 A.G. Doughty and G.W. Parmelee, eds, *The Siege of Quebec and the Battle of the Plains of Abraham*, Quebec, 1901, vol. V, 11

24 Willson, *Life and Letters of James Wolfe*, 384–5

25 Ibid., 453

26 Ibid., 456

27 *A Journal of the Expedition up the River St Lawrence ... by the Serjeant-Major of General Hopson's Grenadiers*, Boston, 1759, 105

28 Lieutenant Colonel C.V.F. Townshend, *The Military Life of Field Marshal George First Marquess Townshend*, London, 1901, 196

29 Historical Manuscripts Commission, *The Manuscripts of the Marquess Townshend*, Vol. IV, London, 1887, 9–10

30 Knox, *Journal*, II, 29

31 Willson, *Life and Letters of James Wolfe*, 466

32 Wolfe to Pitt, 2 September 1759, Pitt, *Correspondence*, II, 158

33 Doughty and Parmelee, *Siege of Quebec*, V, 65

34 Wright, *Wolfe*, 572

35 Bougainville, *Adventures*, 108

36 Knox, *Journal*, II, 71

9 Winning the West: Canada and the Caribbean

1 Quoted in Brumwell, *Paths of Glory*, 297

2 Stuart Reid, 'Wolfe, James (1727–1759)', *Oxford Dictionary of National Biography*, Oxford University Press, 2004; online edn, Oct 2008 [http://www.oxforddnb.com/view/article/29833]

3 Willson, *Life and Letters of James Wolfe*, 337

4 Walpole, *Memoirs of the Reign of George the Third*, I, 17–18

5 Richard Cannon, *Historical Records of The Fifteenth or Yorkshire East Riding Regiment of Foot*, London, 1858, 39–44

6 J.C. Long, *Lord Jeffery Amherst: A Soldier of the King*, New York, 1933, 133

7   David, *All the King's Men*, 189

8   Shy, *Toward Lexington*, 93

9   NA WO/34/41/113–1117, Amherst Letters from New York, 15 July 1763

10 Knox, *Journal*, II, 248–9

11 Forbes, *Lyon in Mourning*, III, 117

12 Robert Paterson, *Pontius Pilate's Bodyguard: A History of the Royal Regiment of Foot, the Royal Scots (The Royal Regiment)*, 3 vols, Edinburgh, 2000, I, 82–7

13 Lenman, *Jacobite Clans*, 196

14 'Like roaring lions breaking from their chains', *Bulletin of the Fort Ticonderoga Museum*, vol. 16 (1998), 16–19

15 Forbes, *Writings*, 117; Brumwell, 'The Highland Battalions in the Americas', in *Redcoats*, 264–89

16 There is a comprehensive discussion in Colin G. Calloway, *White People, Indians, and Highlanders: Tribal Peoples and Colonial Encounters in Scotland and America*, Oxford, 2008

17 Stewart of Garth, *Sketches*, I, 303

18 Colin G. Calloway, 'Sir William Johnson, Highland Scots, and American Indians', *New York History*, vol. 89, no. 2, Spring 2008

19 Long, *Amherst*, 128

20 John W. Harpster, ed., *Journal of William Trent 1763, from Pen Pictures of Early Western Pennsylvania*, Pittsburgh, 1938, 103–4

21 *Bouquet Papers*, ser. 21634, 161

22 Carl Waldman, *Atlas of the North American Indian*, New York, 1980, 108

23 Elizabeth A. Fenn, 'Biological Warfare in Eighteenth-Century North America: Beyond Jeffery Amherst', *Journal of American History*, Vol. 86, No. 4, March 1999, 1552–80. See also Barbara Alice Man, *The Tainted Gift: The Disease Method of Frontier Expansion*, Santa Barbara, 2009

24 Fortescue, *British Army*, III, 18

10 The World at War: India

1   Penderel Moon, *The British Conquest and Dominion of India*, London, 1989, 44

2   Keay, *Honourable Company*, 274

3   G.J. Bryant, 'Lawrence, Stringer (1697–1775)', *Oxford Dictionary of National Biography*, Oxford University Press, 2004 [http://www.oxforddnb.com/view/article/16187]

4   Keay, *Honourable Company*, 289

5   Biddulph, *Stringer Lawrence*, 29

6   'List of names of French refugees', 1841, *Proceedings of the Huguenot Society*, 26 (1997), 611–34

7   Fortescue, *British Army*, II, 237

8   S.C. Hill, *Three Frenchmen in Bengal or The Commercial Ruin of the French Settlements in 1757*, London, 1903, 4

9   C.R. Wilson, *Old Fort William in Bengal*, India Records Series, London, 1906, 128

10 Lieutenant Colonel E.W.C. Sandes, *The Military Engineer in India*, London, 1932, 42

11 Wilson, *Old Fort William in Bengal*, 258

12 It was published in 1758 under the title *A genuine narrative of the deplorable deaths of the English gentlemen and others, who were suffocated in the Black Hole.*

13 The British were notorious for anglicising Indian names. Siraj-ud-Daula became Surajah Dowlah, or even Sir Roger Dowler.

14 Ernest Protheroe, *The British Navy, Its Making and Its Meaning*, London, 1914, 204–5

15 Sheppard, *Coote*, 41

16 'Bengal Past and Present', *Journal of the Calcutta Historical Society*, Calcutta, 1916, 141

17 S.C. Hill, ed., *Bengal in 1756–1757: A Selection of Public and Private Papers Dealing with the Affairs of the British in Bengal During the Reign of Siraj-ud-daula*, vol. II, India Records Series, London, 1905, 286

18 Ibid., 369

19 Luke Scrafton, *Reflections on the Government of Indostan*, London, 1761, 80

20 Wylly, *Coote*, 40

21 Ibid., 41

22 K.M. Panikkar, *Asia and Western Dominance*, New York, 1953, 100

23 Draper also found time in 1771 to chair the committee which codified the laws of cricket.

24 Major General Sir John Malcolm, *The Life of Robert, Lord Clive Collected from the Family Papers Communicated by the Earl of Powis*, vol. II, London, 1836, 177

25 G.B. Malleson, *Dupleix*, London, 1899, 168–9

26 *British Naval Biography from Howard to Codrington*, London, 1840, 305

27 Sheppard, *Coote*, 71

28 Wylly, *Coote*, 76

29 *London Gazette*, 23 September 1760

30 Mason, *Matter of Honour*, 153

31 Innes Munro, *A narrative of the military operations on the Coromandel coast against the combined forces of the French, Dutch and Hyder Ally Cawn, from the year 1780 to the peace in 1784*, London, 1789, 317

32 Walpole, *Correspondence*, IV, 314

33 Nicholas Rogers, 'Brave Wolfe: The Making of a Hero', in Kathleen Wilson, ed., *A New Imperial History: Culture, Identity and Modernity in Britain and the Empire 1660–1840*, Cambridge, 2004, 240

11 The World at War: Europe

1 Mackesy, *Coward of Minden*, 19

2 The 12th later became The Suffolk Regiment, the 23rd The Royal Welch Fusiliers and the 51st The King's Own Yorkshire Light Infantry.

3 Baron Fitzmaurice, *Life of William, Earl of Shelburne*, 2 vols, London, 1912, I, 238

4 Walpole, *Memoirs of the Reign of George the Second*, III, 107–8

5 Savory, *His Britannic Majesty's Army*, 144

6 Mackesy, *Coward of Minden*, 69–73

7 Benjamin Smyth, *History of the XXth Regiment, 1688–1888*, London, 1889, 37 n.

8 Savory, *His Britannic Majesty's Army*, 180

9 Captain R.T. Higgins, *The Records of The King's Own Borderers or Old Edinburgh Regiment*, London, 1873, 100–1

10 Fortescue, *British Army*, II, 494

11 Ibid., 496

12 *The London Magazine, Or, Gentleman's Monthly Intelligencer*, Vol. 28, 459

13 Fortescue, *British Army*, II, 494

14 'Orders of His Serene Highness Prince Ferdinand of Brunswick Relative to the Troops Under Him at the Famous Battle near Minden, on the 1st of August 1759', in David Hume and Tobias Smollett, *The History of England*, London, 1825, Vol. XIII, 188 note f

15 Ferdinand to George II, 13 August 1759, Savory, *His Britannic Majesty's Army*, Appendix XI, 474

16 The trial was recorded in 'The Proceedings of General Court Martial Held at the Horse Guards ... Upon the Trial of Lord George Sackville', London, 1760; see also Gerald S. Brown, 'The Court Martial of Lord George Sackville: Whipping Boy of the Revolutionary War', *The William and Mary Quarterly*, Third Series, Vol. 9, No. 3 July 1952, 317–37

17 Walpole, *Memoirs of the Reign of George the Second*, II, 365

18 Sedgwick, *Letters from George III to Lord Bute*, 179

19 Richard Cumberland, *Character of the Late Lord Viscount Sackville*, 2 vols, London, 1785, II, 12

20 BL Add. MS 32729, f. 9, Newcastle to Pelham, 14 August 1752

21 National Army Museum, Accession NAM 1963-07-31-1

22 Sedgwick, *Letters of George III to Lord Bute*, 57

23 Historical Manuscripts Commission, Twelfth Report, Appendix, Part X, *The Manuscripts and Correspondence of James First Earl of Charlemont*, 2 vols, London, 1891, I, 10

24 BL Add. MS 329222, f. 452, Bedford to Newcastle, 9 May 1761

25 Francis Thackeray, *The History of the Right Honourable William Pitt, Earl of Chatham*, 2 vols, London, 1827, II, 23

26 Romney Sedgwick, 'Conway, Hon. Henry Seymour', *History of Parliament, House of Commons, 1715–54*, 2 vols, London, 1970

27 Allan Mallinson, *The Making of the British Army: From the English Civil War to the War on Terror*, London, 2009, 119

28 Thomas Babington Macaulay, *The History of England from the Accession of James the Second*, 5 vols, III, 687

29 Peter Young, *Washington's Army*, Botley, 1972, 31

30 Arthur Aspinall, ed., *The Later Correspondence of George III*, 5 vols, 1962–70, II, 298

12 Forty Years On: The End of an Old Song

1   Stephen Wood, *The Auld Alliance, Scotland and France: The Military Connection*, Edinburgh, 1989, 87
2   Glengarry was identified by the historian Andrew Lang in his study *Pickle the Spy*, London, 1897
3   McLynn, *1759*, 63
4   Biographies of Prince Charles are legion and range from serious research to hagiography and romantic sentimentality. The fairest recent account is McLynn's study of 1988.
5   BL Newcastle Papers, Add, MS 32731-888
6   William Taylor, *The Military Roads of Scotland*, Edinburgh 1976, 29
7   The bronze statue was financed by the Friendly Brothers of St Patrick, a masonic fraternity, and was the work of the Dutch sculptor John Van Nost, but its erection divided opinion. Four years later it was pulled down from its pedestal and was so badly damaged that it had to be removed.
8   Walpole, *Correspondence*, 37, 310
9   Conway purchased the house in 1752 and made several improvements, including a bridge over the River Thames designed by Humphrey Gainsborough. In 2011 it became Britain's most expensive house when it was sold to a Russian businessman for £140 million.
10   P.D.G. Thomas, *Tea Party to Independence: The Third Phase of the American Revolution, 1773–1776*, London, 1991, 278
11   Gage to Lord Barrington, 25 June 1775, in Carter, ed., *Gage Correspondence*, II, 655–6
12   Gage to Lord Barrington, 3 October 1774, ibid., I, 406
13   John Shy, 'Thomas Gage', in George Athan Billias, ed., *George Washington's Opponents*, Washington, 1969, 3–38
14   J.H. Jesse, *Lord Selwyn and His Contemporaries, With Memoirs and Notes*, vol. I, London, 1843, 112–13
15   Craufuird C. Loudoun, *History of the House of Loudoun and Associated Families*, Darvel, n.d., 62
16   Sheppard, *Coote*, 98
17   James Boswell, *The Journal of a Tour to the Hebrides*, London, 1785, 113
18   *The Parliamentary Register or History of the Proceedings and Debates of the House of Lords, during the Fifth Session of the Seventeenth Parliament of Great Britain*, London, 1795, 363

19   Fortescue, *British Army*, III, 490

20   Joseph Parkes and Herman Merival, eds, *Memoirs of Sir Philip Francis, with Correspondence and Journals*, 2 vols, London, 1867

21   John Cannon, ed., *The Letters of Junius*, Oxford, 1978, 41

22   For a recent discussion of the ring system in the late Victorian army see Hew Strachan, *The Politics of the British Army*, London, 1997, 92–117

23   T. M. Devine, *The Scottish Nation 1700-2000* London, 1999, 47

Bibliography

Official Papers and Records

National Archives, Kew (NA)

SP 36/65–104, State Papers Domestic George II, 1727–60

SP 36/105, State Papers Domestic, James Carnegy papers, of Jacobite interest

SP 36/163, State Papers Domestic, Jacobite papers, chiefly regarding Cameron of Lochiel

SP 37, State Papers Domestic, George III, 1760–83

SP 54, Secretaries of State: State Papers Scotland, Series II, 1714–83

SP 57/33, State Papers Scotland, 1736–53, Duke of Newcastle, Lord Harrington, Lord Carteret, Marquis of Tweeddale

SP 63/408–409, State Papers Ireland, 1745–6

SP 87, Other War Office and Secretaries of State: State Papers Foreign, Military Expeditions

WO 1/10 War Office In-Letters 1. From Military Commanders: a. Commanders-in-Chief, North America

WO 3/10 Office of the Commander-in-Chief: Out-letters, 1745–6

WO 4/40 War Office: Secretary-at-War, Out-letters, 1745

WO 10/28–34 Artillery muster books and pay list

WO 26/21 War Office: entry books of warrants, regulations and precedents, 1746

WO 34 Amherst Letters

WO 55/408–9 Ordnance Office and War Office: Miscellaneous Entry Books and Papers

British Library (BL)

Add. MSS 17497–17498, 21501–21503, Conway Papers and Correspondence

Add. MSS 35406–35583, Hardwicke Papers

Add. MSS 32708–33072, Keppel Papers

Add. MSS 23827–23829, Mordaunt Papers

Add. MSS 32705–32707, Newcastle Papers

Add. MSS 35354, Yorke Papers and Correspondence

Add. MSS 36796, Bute Papers

Royal Archives, Windsor (RA)

Duke of Cumberland's Papers and Correspondence

Stuart Manuscripts

University of Nottingham Library (U Nott L)

Blakeney Correspondence

Newcastle Papers

National Records of Scotland, Edinburgh (NRS)

GD 1/271 Letter on 1745 Jacobite Rising, 13 September 1745

GD 1/304 Account of Jacobite retreat from Falkirk, 1746 and miscellaneous documents, 1600–1746

GD 1/322 Duke of Cumberland's Order Book

GD 1/330 Jacobite army at Dunblane, 1746

GD 1/578 Duncan Forbes of Culloden, letters

GD 45/2 Dalhousie Muniments, Forbes Correspondence

National Library of Scotland and Advocates Library (NLS)

Forbes, Robert, Rev, Bishop of Ross and Caithness, *The Lyon in Mourning, A collection of speeches, letters, journals etc. relative to the affairs of Prince Charles Edward Stuart*, vols I–III

Historical papers relating to the Jacobite period, 1699–1750, New Spalding Club, 1895–6

Duff, H.R., ed., *Culloden Papers: comprising an extensive and interesting correspondence from the year 1625 to 1748; including numerous letters from the unfortunate Lord Lovat, and other distinguished persons of the time; with occasional state papers ... The whole published from the originals in the possession of Duncan George Forbes of Culloden, Esq. To which is prefixed an introduction containing memoirs of the Right Honourable Duncan Forbes*, London, 1815

Maxwell, James, *Narrative of Charles Prince of Wales' expedition to Scotland 1745*, copy of the MS, written in France after Maxwell's escape from the battle of Culloden, and printed by the Maitland Club in 1841

Newspapers and journals

Caledonian Mercury
Edinburgh Evening Courant
General Advertiser
Gentleman's Magazine
London Evening Post
Scots Magazine

Secondary sources (selected)

Jacobite uprising and Battle of Culloden

Black, Jeremy, *Culloden and the '45*, London, 1990

Duffy, Christopher, *The '45: Prince Charlie and the untold story of the Jacobite Rising*, London, 2003

Elcho, Lord, *A Short Account of the Affairs of Scotland in the Years 1744, 1745, 1746*, Edinburgh, 1907

Fry, Michael, *Wild Scots: Four Hundred Years of Highland History*, London, 2005

Gibson, J.S., *Lochiel of the '45: The Jacobite Chief and the Prince*, Edinburgh, 1994

Johnstone, Chevalier James de, *Memoirs of the Rebellion in 1745 and 1746*, London, 1822

Lenman, Bruce, *The Jacobite Risings in Britain 1689–1746*, London, 1980

——, *The Jacobite Clans of the Great Glen, 1650–1784*, Edinburgh, 1995

Livingstone of Bachuil, Aikman, Christian W.H. and Hart, Betty Stuart, eds, *No Quarter Given: The Muster Roll of Prince Charles Edward Stuart's Army 1745–1746*, Glasgow, 2001

Lynch, Michael, ed., *Jacobitism and the '45*, The Historical Association, London, 1995

McLynn, Frank, *The Jacobite Army in England, 1745*, Edinburgh, 1983

——, *Charles Edward Stewart: A Tragedy in Many Acts*, London, 1988

Oates, Jonathan, *Sweet William or the Butcher? The Duke of Cumberland and the '45*, Barnsley, 2008

Pittock, Murray, *The Myth of the Jacobite Clans: The Jacobite Army in 1745*, Edinburgh, 2009

Prebble, John, *Culloden*, London, 1961

Ray, James, *A Compleat History of the Rebellion, from Its First Rise in 1745, to Its Total Suppression at the Glorious Battle of Culloden, in April 1746*, Bristol, 1752

Reid, Stuart, *Like Hungry Wolves: Culloden Moor 16 April 1746*, London 1994

——, *1745: A Military History of the last Jacobite Rebellion*, Staplehurst, 1996

Roberts, John L., *The Jacobite Wars: Scotland and the Military Campaigns of 1715 and 1745*, Edinburgh, 2002

Seton, Bruce Gordon and Arnot, Jean Gordon, *The Prisoners of the '45, Edinburgh*, Scottish History Society, Edinburgh, 1928

Speck, W.A., *The Butcher: The Duke of Cumberland and the Suppression of the '45*, Oxford, 1995

Stewart of Garth, David, *Sketches of the Character, Manners and present State of the Highlanders of Scotland, with details of the Military Service of the Highland Regiments*, 2 vols, Edinburgh, 1822

Whitworth, Rex, *William Augustus, Duke of Cumberland: A Life*, Barnsley, 1992

Britain

Brumwell, Stephen, *Paths of Glory: The Life and Death of General James Wolfe*, London, 2004

Charteris, Evan, *William Augustus, Duke of Cumberland, His Early Life and Times (1721–1748)*, London, 1913

——, *William Augustus Duke of Cumberland and the Seven Years War*, London, 1925

Colley, Linda, *Captives: Britain, Empire and the World 1600–1850*, London, 2002

——, *Britons: Forging the Nation 1707–1837*, revised edition, London, 2014

Conway, Stephen, *War, State, and Society in Mid-Eighteenth-Century Britain and Ireland*, Oxford, 2006

Corbett, Julian S., *England in the Seven Years War: A Study in Combined Strategy*, London, 2 vols, 1907

David, Saul, *All the King's Men: The British Soldier from the Restoration to Waterloo*, London, 2012

Fortescue, Sir John, *The History of the British Army*, vol. II, London, 1899

Guy, Alan J., *Oeconomy and Discipline: Officership and Administration in the British Army 1714–1763*, Manchester, 1985

Haydon, Colin, *Anti-Catholicism in Eighteenth-century England, c. 1714–80: a Political and Social Study*, Manchester, 1993

Hibbert, Christopher, *Wolfe at Quebec*, London, 1959

Holmes, Richard, *Redcoat: The British Soldier in the Age of Horse and Musket*, London, 2001

Lenman, Bruce, *Britain's Colonial Wars 1688–1783*, Harlow, 2001

McCann, Timothy J., ed., *The Correspondence of the Dukes of Richmond and Newcastle 1724–1750*, Trowbridge, 1984

McLynn, Frank, *1759: The Year Britain became Master of the World*, London, 2004

Middleton, Richard, *The Bells of Victory: The Pitt-Newcastle Ministry and the Conduct of the Seven Years' War*, Cambridge, 1985

Peters, Marie, *Pitt and Popularity: The Patriot Minister and London Opinion during the Seven Years War*, Oxford, 1980

Pitt, William, *Correspondence of William Pitt*, ed. Gertrude Selwyn Kimball, 2 vols, London, 1969

Plank, Geoffrey, *Rebellion and Savagery: The Jacobite Rising of 1745 and the British Empire*, Philadelphia, 2006

Pocock, Tom, *Battle for Empire: The Very First World War 1756–1763*, London, 1998

Sedgewick, Romney, ed., *Letters from George III to Lord Bute*, London, 1939

Terry, Charles S., ed., *The Albemarle Papers; being the correspondence of William Anne, second Earl of Albemarle, commander-in-chief in Scotland, 1746–1747, with an appendix of letters from Andrew Fletcher, Lord Justice-Clerk, to the Duke of Newcastle, 1746–1748*, 2 vols, Aberdeen, 1902

Walpole, Horace, *Correspondence*, 48 vols, Yale Edition, New Haven, 1937–83

——, *Memoirs of the Reign of King George the Second*, 3 vols, Yale Edition, New Haven, 1985

——, *Memoirs of the Reign of King George the Third*, 4 vols, Yale Edition, New Haven, 2000

Waugh, W.T., *James Wolfe: Man and Soldier*, New York, 1928

Willson, Beckles, *The Life and Letters of James Wolfe*, London, 1909

Wright, Robert, *The Life of Major-General James Wolfe*, London, 1864

Europe

Asprey, Robert B., *Frederick the Great: The Magnificent Enigma*, New York, 1986

Duffy, Christopher, *Frederick the Great: A Military Life*, London, 1985

Füssel, Marian, *Der Siebenjahrige Krieg: Ein Weltkrieg im 18. Jahrhundert*, Munich, 2010

Mackesy, Piers, *The Coward of Minden: The Affair of Lord George Sackville*, London, 1979

Riley, James C., *The Seven Years War and the Old Regime in France: The Economic and Financial Toll*, Princeton, 1986

Savory, Lieutenant-General Sir Ronald, *His Britannic Majesty's Army during the Seven Years War*, Oxford, 1966

Szabo, Franz, *The Seven Years War in Europe: 1756–1763*, London, 2007

North America

Amherst, Jeffery, *The Journal of Jeffery Amherst: Recording the Military Career of General Amherst in America from 1758 to 1763*, ed. John Clarence Webster, Chicago, 1931

Anderson, Fred, *A People's Army: Massachusetts Soldiers and Society in the Seven Years' War*, Chapel Hill, 1984

——, *Crucible of War: The Seven Years War and the Fate of Empire in British North America, 1754–1766*, London, 2000

Borneman, Walter R., *The French and Indian War: Deciding the Fate of North America*, New York, 2006

Brumwell, Stephen, *Redcoat: The British Soldier and War in the Americas 1755–1763*, Cambridge, 2002

Calloway, Colin G., *The Scratch of a Pen: 1763 and the Transformation of North America*, New York, 2006

Carter, Clarence, ed., *The Correspondence of General Thomas Gage with the Secretaries of State and with the War Office and the Treasury 1763–1775*, 2 vols, New Haven, 1931

Faragher, John Mack, *A Great and Noble Scheme: The Tragic Story of the Expulsion of the French Acadians from their American Homeland*, New York, 2005

Forbes, John, *Writings of General John Forbes Relating to His Service in North America*, ed. Alfred Proctor James, Menasha, WI, 1938

Fowler, William M., *Empires at War: The French and Indian War and the Struggle for North America, 1754–1763*, New York, 2006

Gipson, Lawrence Henry, *The British Empire Before the American Revolution*, vols 6, 7, 8, New York, 1958–1970

Knox, John, *An Historical Journal of the Campaigns in North America for the Years 1757, 1758, 1759, and 1760, by Captain John Knox*, ed. Arthur G. Doughty, 3 vols, Toronto, 1914–1916

Marshall, P.J., *The Making and Unmaking of Empires: Britain, India, and America, c. 1750–1783*, Oxford, 2005

Marston, Daniel, *The Seven Years' War*, Chicago and London, 2001.

Nester, William R., *The First Global War: Britain, France and the Fate of America 1756–1773*, Westport, Connecticut, 2000

Pargellis, Stanley, ed., *Military Affairs in North America 1748–1765: Selected Documents from the Papers in Windsor Castle*, New Haven, Conn, 1969

——, *Lord Loudon in North America*, New York, 1933

Parkman, Francis, *France and England in North America*, 7 vols, New York, 1865–92

Peckham, Howard H., *The Colonial Wars, 1689–1762*, Chicago, 1964

Plank, Geoffrey, *An Unsettled Conquest: The British Campaign against the Peoples of Acadia*, Philadelphia, 2001

Reid, Stuart, *Wolfe: The Career of General James Wolfe, from Culloden to Quebec*, Staplehurst, 2000

Shy, John W., *Toward Lexington: The Role of the British Army in the Coming of the American Revolution*, Princeton, 1965

Silver, Peter, *Our Savage Neighbors: How Indian War Transformed Early America*, New York, 2008

Ward, Matthew C., *Breaking the Backcountry: The Seven Years' War in Virginia and Pennsylvania, 1754–1765*, Pittsburgh, 2003

India

Biddulph, John, *Stringer Lawrence: Father of the Indian Army*, London, 1901

Keay, John, *Honourable Company: History of the English East India Company*, London, 1991

Lawson, Philip, *The East India Company: A History*, New York, 1993

Mason, Philip, *A Matter of Honour: An Account of the Indian Army, Its Officers and Men*, London, 1974

Shepherd, E.W., *Coote Bahadur: A Life of Lieutenant-General Sir Eyre Coote, KB*, London, 1956

Wylly, H.C., *A Life of Lieutenant General Sir Eyre Coote*, London, 1922

Index

Abercromby, Major-General James, 173, 190, 200–1, 204, 206, 221, 222; attack on Fort Carillon, 191, 195, 197, 198, 199, 200, 202; and Fort Frontenac, 202, 203

Aberdeen, 71–2, 74, 75, 89, 103

d'Aché, Vice-Admiral Comte Ann-Antoine, 294, 295, 299

Act of Union (1707), x, 3, 8, 132

Act of Union (1801), 349

Ailesbury, Caroline Bruce, Countess of, 344

Albemarle, Lieutenant-General William Ann Keppel, 2nd Earl of, 32, 33, 73, 84, 90, 113, 119, 249, 319

Aldercron, Colonel John, 273, 283

American War of Independence, x, 205, 272, 326–30, 331, 340, 345–8, 352

Amherst, Jeffrey: advance on Montreal, 250, 252–3, 258; and Canadian military government, 266, 267, 268, 269–70, 271; career decline, 271–2; Caribbean operations, 263, 266; as commander-in-chief in North America, 272, 330, 346, 348; contempt for native Americans, 222, 255, 256–7,

268, 269–70; dislike of North America, 254–5; invasion of Canada, 221–6, 249, 250, 252–3; and Pitt's American strategy, 190, 191, 195, 208–9, 211, 212–13, 215, 217, 219, 247; victory at Montreal, 253, 254

Ancrum, William Henry Kerr, Earl of, 102–3, 119

Anderson, Robert, 27

Antwerp, 122, 135

Appin, Stewarts of, 3, 19, 57, 58, 85, 119

Argyll, house of, 108, 109, 349–50

artillery, British, xi, 25, 60–1, 82, 128, 313–14; at Culloden, 5, 82, 83, 85, 86, 88, 91, 92; in North America, 163, 167, 196, 199–200, 211–12, 228, 234, 251

Atholl, men of, 3, 35, 70, 75, 84, 92

Austria, viii, 170, 171, 304

the Austrian Succession, War of, viii, 125; Anglo-French conflict in India, 147, 275–8; fighting in Flanders, ix, 6, 9, 12, 16, 32, 42, 43–4, 122–3, 128–9, 135–6; peace of Aix-la-Chapelle (1748), 136, 143, 147, 156, 180, 273, 276, 333; War of Jenkins' Ear, 53, 59, 144

The Step-Daughter [*stops, bends over the* CHILD *and takes the latter's face between her hands*]. My little darling! You're frightened, aren't you? You don't know where we are, do you? [*Pretending to reply to a question of the* CHILD.] What is the stage? It's a place, baby, you know, where people play at being serious, a place where they act comedies. We've got to act a comedy now, dead serious, you know; and you're in it also, little one. [*Embraces her, pressing the little head to her breast, and rocking the* CHILD *for a moment*.] Oh darling, darling, what a horrid comedy you've got to play! What a wretched part they've found for you! A garden . . . a fountain . . . look . . . just suppose, kiddie, it's here. Where, you say? Why, right here in the middle. It's all pretence you know. That's the trouble, my pet: it's all make-belive here. It's better to imagine it though, because if they fix it up for you, it'll only be painted cardboard, painted cardboard for the rockery, the water, the plants . . . Ah, but I think a baby like this one would sooner have a make-believe fountain than a real one, so she could play with it. What a joke it'll be for the others! But for you, alas! not quite such a joke: you who are real, baby dear, and really play by a real fountain that is big and green and beautiful, with ever so many bamboos around it that are reflected in the water, and a whole lot of little ducks swimming about . . . No, Rosetta, no, your mother doesn't bother about you on account of that wretch of a son there. I'm in the devil of a temper, and as for that lad . . . [*Seizes* BOY *by the arm to force him to take one of his hands out of his pockets*.] What have you got there? What are you hiding? [*Pulls his hand out of his pocket, looks into it and catches the glint of a revolver*.] Ah! where did you get this? [*The* BOY, *very pale in the face, looks at her, but does not answer*]. Idiot! If I'd been in your place, instead of killing myself, I'd have shot one of those two, or both of them: father and son.

think there's the stuff for a drama in all this, and not a bad drama either.

The Step-Daughter [*coming forward*]. When you've got a character like me.

The Father [*shutting her up, all excited to learn the decision of the* MANAGER]. You be quiet!

The Manager [*reflecting, heedless of interruption*]. It's new . . . hem . . . yes . . .

The Father. Absolutely new!

The Manager. You've got a nerve though, I must say, to come here and fling it at me like this . . .

The Father. You will understand, sir, born as we are for the stage . . .

The Manager. Are you amateur actors then?

The Father. No. I say born for the stage, because . . .

The Manager. Oh, nonsense. You're an old hand, you know.

The Father. No sir, no. We act that rôle for which we have been cast, that rôle which we are given in life. And in my own case, passion itself, as usually happens, becomes a trifle theatrical when it is exalted.

The Manager. Well, well, that will do. But you see, without an author . . . I could give you the address of an author if you like . . .

The Father. No, no. Look here! You must be the author.

The Manager. I? What are you talking about?

The Father. Yes, you, you! Why not?

The Manager. Because I have never been an author: that's why.

The Father. Then why not turn author now? Everybody does it. You don't want any special qualities. Your task is made much easier by the fact that we are all here alive before you . . .

The Manager. It won't do.

The Father. What? When you see us live our drama . . .

The Manager. Yes, that's all right. But you want someone to write it.

The Father. No, no. Someone to take it down, possibly, while we play it, scene by scene! It will be enough to sketch it out at first, and then try it over.

The Manager. Well . . . I am almost tempted. It's a bit of an idea. One might have a shot at it.

The Father. Of course. You'll see what scenes will come out of it. I can give you one, at once . . .

The Manager. By Jove, it tempts me. I'd like to have a go at it. Let's try it out. Come with me to my office. [*Turning to the* ACTORS.] You are at liberty for a bit, but don't step out of the theatre for long. In a quarter of an hour, twenty minutes, all back here again! [*To the* FATHER.] We'll see what can be done. Who knows if we don't get something really extraordinary out of it?

The Father. There's no doubt about it. They [*Indicating the* CHARACTERS.] had better come with us too, hadn't they?

The Manager. Yes, yes. Come on! come on! [*Moves away and then turning to the* ACTORS.] *Be punctual, please!* [MANAGER *and the* SIX CHARACTERS *cross the stage and go off. The other* ACTORS *remain, looking at one another in astonishment.*]

Leading Man. Is he serious? What the devil does he want to do?

Juvenile Lead. This is rank madness.

Third Actor. Does he expect to knock up a drama in five minutes?

Juvenile Lead. Like the improvisers!

Leading Lady. If he thinks I'm going to take part in a joke like this . . .

Juvenile Lead. I'm out of it anyway.

Fourth Actor. I should like to know who they [*Alludes to* CHARACTERS].

Third Actor. What do you suppose? Madmen rascals!

Juvenile Lead. And he takes them seriously!

L'Ingénue. Vanity! He fancies himself as an aut now.

Leading Man. It's absolutely unheard of. If the st has come to this . . . well I'm . . .

Fifth Actor. It's rather a joke.

Third Actor. Well, we'll see what's going to happ next.

[*Thus talking, the* ACTORS *leave the stage; some goi out by the little door at the back; others retiring to the dressing-rooms.*

The curtain remains up.

The action of the play is suspended for twen minutes].

ACT II

The stage call-bells ring to warn the company that t play it about to begin again.

The STEP-DAUGHTER *comes out of the* MANAGER'S *offi along with the* CHILD *and the* BOY. *As she comes out the office, she cries:—*

Nonsense! nonsense! Do it yourselves! I'm not going mix myself up in this mess. [*Turning to the* CHILD a coming quickly with her on to the stage.*] Come Rosetta, let's run!

[*The* BOY *follows them slowly, remaining a little hind and seeming perplexed.*]

[*The* FATHER *enters from the office, all excited from his work. The* MANAGER *follows him.*]

The Father. Come on, come on dear! Come here for a minute! We've arranged everything. It's all fixed up.

The Manager [*also excited*]. If you please, young lady, there are one or two points to settle still. Will you come along?

The Step-Daughter [*following him towards the office*]. Ouff! what's the good, if you've arranged everything.

[*The* FATHER, MANAGER *and* STEP-DAUGHTER *go back into the office again* (*off*) *for a moment. At the same time, The* SON *followed by The* MOTHER, *comes out.*]

The Son [*looking at the three entering office*]. Oh this is fine, fine! And to think I can't even get away!

[*The* MOTHER *attempts to look at him, but lowers her eyes immediately when* HE *turns away from her.* SHE *then sits down. The* BOY *and The* CHILD *approach her.* SHE *casts a glance again at the* SON, *and speaks with humble tones, trying to draw him into conversation.*]

The Mother. And isn't my punishment the worst of all? [*Then seeing from the* SON'S *manner that he will not bother himself about her.*] My God! Why are you so cruel? Isn't it enough for one person to support all this torment? Must you then insist on others seeing it also?

The Son [*half to himself, meaning the* MOTHER *to hear, however*]. And they want to put it on the stage! If there was at least a reason for it! He thinks he has got at the meaning of it all. Just as if each one of us in every circumstance of life couldn't find his own explanation of it! [*Pauses.*] He complains he was discovered in a place where he ought not to have been seen, in a moment of his life which ought to have remained hidden and kept out of the reach of that convention which he has to maintain for other people. And what about my case?

Haven't I had to reveal what no son ought ever to reveal:
how father and mother live and are man and wife for
themselves quite apart from that idea of father and
mother which we give them? When this idea is revealed,
our life is then linked at one point only to that man and
that woman; and as such it should shame them, shouldn't
it?

[*The* Mother *hides her face in her hands. From the
dressing-rooms and the little door at the back of
the stage the* Actors *and* Stage Manager *return,
followed by the* Property Man, *and the* Prompter.
At the same moment, The Manager *comes out of
his office, accompanied by the* Father *and the* Step-
Daughter.]

The Manager. Come on, come on, ladies and gentlemen! Heh! you there, machinist!

Machinist. Yes sir?

The Manager. Fix up the white parlor with the floral
decorations. Two wings and a drop with a door will do.
Hurry up!

[*The* Machinist *runs off at once to prepare the scene,
and arranges it while The* Manager *talks with the*
Stage Manager, *the* Property Man, *and the*
Prompter *on matters of detail.*]

The Manager [*to* Property Man]. Just have a look,
and see if there isn't a sofa or divan in the wardrobe . . .

Property Man. There's the green one.

The Step-Daughter. No no! Green won't do. It was
yellow, ornamented with flowers—very large! and most
comfortable!

Property Man. There isn't one like that.

The Manager. It doesn't matter. Use the one we've
got.

The Step-Daughter. Doesn't matter? It's most important!

The Manager. We're only trying it now. Please don't

interfere. [*To* PROPERTY MAN.] See if we've got a shop window—long and narrowish.

The Step-Daughter. And the little table! The little mahogany table for the pale blue envelope!

Property Man [*to* MANAGER]. There's that little gilt one.

The Manager. That'll do fine.

The Father. A mirror.

The Step-Daughter. And the screen! We must have a screen. Otherwise how can I manage?

Property Man. That's all right, Miss. We've got any amount of them.

The Manager [*to the* STEP-DAUGHTER]. We want some clothes pegs too, don't we?

The Step-Daughter. Yes, several, several!

The Manager. See how many we've got and bring them all.

Property Man. All right!

[*The* PROPERTY MAN *hurries off to obey his orders. While he is putting the things in their places, the* MANAGER *talks to the* PROMPTER *and then with the* CHARACTERS *and the* ACTORS.]

The Manager [*to* PROMPTER]. Take your seat. Look here: this is the outline of the scenes, act by act. [*Hands him some sheets of paper.*] And now I'm going to ask you to do something out of the ordinary.

Prompter. Take it down in shorthand?

The Manager [*pleasantly surprised*]. Exactly! Can you do shorthand?

Prompter. Yes, a little.

The Manager. Good! [*Turning to a* STAGE HAND.] Go and get some paper from my office, plenty, as much as you can find.

[*The* STAGE HAND *goes off, and soon returns with a handful of paper which he gives to the* PROMPTER.]

The Manager [*to* PROMPTER]. You follow the scenes

as we play them, and try and get the points down, at any rate the most important ones. [*Then addressing the* AC-TORS.] Clear the stage, ladies and gentlemen! Come over here [*Pointing to the left.*] and listen attentively.

Leading Lady. But, excuse me, we . . .

The Manager [*guessing her thought*]. Don't worry! You won't have to improvise.

Leading Man. What have we to do then?

The Manager. Nothing. For the moment you just watch and listen. Everybody will get his part written out afterwards. At present we're going to try the thing as best we can. They're going to act now.

The Father [*as if fallen from the clouds into the confusion of the stage*]. We? What do you mean, if you please, by a rehearsal?

The Manager. A rehearsal for them. [*Points to the* ACTORS.]

The Father. But since we are the characters . . .

The Manager. All right: "characters" then, if you insist on calling yourselves such. But here, my dear sir, the characters don't act. Here the actors do the acting. The characters are there, in the "book" [*Pointing towards* PROMPTER's *box.*]—when there is a "book"!

The Father. I won't contradict you; but excuse me, the actors aren't the characters. They want to be, they pretend to be, don't they? Now if these gentlemen here are fortunate enough to have us alive before them . . .

The Manager. Oh this is grand! You want to come before the public yourselves then?

The Father. As we are . . .

The Manager. I can assure you it would be a magnificent spectacle!

Leading Man. What's the use of us here anyway then?

The Manager. You're not going to pretend that you

can act? It makes me laugh! [*The* ACTORS *laugh.*] There,
you see, they are laughing at the notion. But, by the way,
I must cast the parts. That won't be difficult. They cast
themselves. [*To the* SECOND LADY LEAD.] You play the
Mother. [*To the* FATHER.] We must find her a name.

The Father. Amalia, sir.

The Manager. But that is the real name of your wife.
We don't want to call her by her real name.

The Father. Why ever not, if it is her name? . . .
Still, perhaps, if that lady must . . . [*Makes a slight motion of the hand to indicate the* SECOND LADY LEAD.] I
see this woman here [*Means the* MOTHER.] as Amalia. But
do as you like. [*Gets more and more confused.*] I don't
know what to say to you. Already, I begin to hear my
own words ring false, as if they had another sound . . .

The Manager. Don't you worry about it. It'll be our
job to find the right tones. And as for her name, if you
want her Amalia, Amalia it shall be; and if you don't
like it, we'll find another! For the moment though, we'll
call the characters in this way: [*To* JUVENILE LEAD.] You
are the Son. [*To the* LEADING LADY.] You naturally are
the Step-Daughter . . .

The Step-Daughter [*excitedly*]. What? what? I, that
woman there? [*Bursts out laughing.*]

The Manager [*angry*]. What is there to laugh at?

Leading Lady [*indignant*]. Nobody has ever dared to
laugh at me. I insist on being treated with respect; otherwise I go away.

The Step-Daughter. No, no, excuse me . . . I am not
laughing at you . . .

The Manager [*to* STEP-DAUGHTER]. You ought to feel
honored to be played by . . .

Leading Lady [*at once, contemptuously*]. "That
woman there" . . .

The Step-Daughter. But I wasn't speaking of you,

you know. I was speaking of myself—whom I can't see at
all in you! That is all. I don't know . . . but . . . you
. . . aren't in the least like me . . .

The Father. True. Here's the point. Look here, sir,
our temperaments, our souls . . .

The Manager. Temperament, soul, be hanged! Do
you suppose the spirit of the piece is in you? Nothing of
the kind!

The Father. What, haven't we our own temperaments, our own souls?

The Manager. Not at all. Your soul or whatever you
like to call it takes shape here. The actors give body and
form to it, voice and gesture. And my actors—I may tell
you—have given expression to much more lofty material
than this little drama of yours, which may or may not
hold up on the stage. But if it does, the merit of it, believe
me, will be due to my actors.

The Father. I don't dare contradict you, sir; but, believe me, it is a terrible suffering for us who are as we are,
with these bodies of ours, these features to see . . .

The Manager [*cutting him short and out of patience*].
Good heavens! The make-up will remedy all that, man,
the make-up . . .

The Father. Maybe. But the voice, the gestures . . .

The Manager. Now, look here! On the stage, you
as yourself, cannot exist. The actor here acts you, and
that's an end to it!

The Father. I understand. And now I think I see why
our author who conceived us as we are, all alive, didn't
want to put us on the stage after all. I haven't the least
desire to offend your actors. Far from it! But when I
think that I am to be acted by . . . I don't know by
whom . . .

Leading Man [*on his dignity*]. By me, if you've no
objection!

The Father [*humbly, mellifiously*]. Honored, I assure you, sir. [*Bows.*] Still, I must say that try as this gentleman may, with all his good will and wonderful art, to absorb me into himself . . .

Leading Man. Oh chuck it! "Wonderful art!" Withdraw that, please!

The Father. The performance he will give, even doing his best with make-up to look like me . . .

Leading Man. It will certainly be a bit difficult! [*The* ACTORS *laugh.*]

The Father. Exactly! It will be difficult to act me as I really am. The effect will be rather—apart from the make-up—according as to how he supposes I am, as he senses me—if he does sense me—and not as I inside of myself feel myself to be. It seems to me then that account should be taken of this by everyone whose duty it may become to criticize us . . .

The Manager. Heavens! The man's starting to think about the critics now! Let them say what they like. It's up to us to put on the play if we can. [*Looking around.*] Come on! come on! Is the stage set? [*To the* ACTORS *and* CHARACTERS.] Stand back—stand back! Let me see, and don't let's lose any more time! [*To the* STEP-DAUGHTER.] Is it all right as it is now?

The Step-Daughter. Well, to tell the truth, I don't recognize the scene.

The Manager. My dear lady, you can't possibly suppose that we can construct that shop of Madame Pace piece by piece here? [*To the* FATHER.] You said a white room with flowered wall paper, didn't you?

The Father. Yes.

The Manager. Well then. We've got the furniture right more or less. Bring that little table a bit further forward. [*The* STAGE HANDS *obey the order. To* PROPERTY MAN.] You go and find an envelope, if possible, a pale blue one; and give it to that gentleman. [*Indicates* FATHER.]

Property Man.   An ordinary envelope?

Manager and Father.   Yes, yes, an ordinary envelope.

Property Man.   At once, sir. [*Exit.*]

The Manager.   Ready, everyone! First scene—the Young Lady. [*The* LEADING LADY *comes forward.*] No, no, you must wait. I meant her [*Indicating the* STEP-DAUGH-TER.] You just watch—

The Step-Daughter [*adding at once*]. How I shall play it, how I shall live it! . . .

Leading Lady [*offended*].   I shall live it also, you may be sure, as soon as I begin!

The Manager [*with his hands to his head*].   Ladies and gentlemen, if you please! No more useless discussions! Scene I: the young lady with Madame Pace: Oh! [*Looks around as if lost.*] And this Madame Pace, where is she?

The Father.   She isn't with us, sir.

The Manager.   Then what the devil's to be done?

The Father.   But she is alive too.

The Manager.   Yes, but where is she?

The Father.   One minute. Let me speak! [*Turning to the* ACTRESSES.] If these ladies would be so good as to give me their hats for a moment . . .

The Actresses [*half surprised, half laughing, in chorus*].
What?

Why?

Our hats?

What does he say?

The Manager.   What are you going to do with the ladies' hats? [*The* ACTORS *laugh.*]

The Father.   Oh nothing. I just want to put them on these pegs for a moment. And one of the ladies will be so kind as to take off her mantle . . .

The Actors.   Oh, what d'you think of that?

Only the mantle?

He must be mad.

Some Actresses.   But why?

Mantles as well?

The Father. To hang them up here for a moment. Please be so kind, will you?

The Actresses [*taking off their hats, one or two also their cloaks, and going to hang them on the racks*]. After all, why not?

There you are!

This is really funny.

We've got to put them on show.

The Father. Exactly; just like that, on show.

The Manager. May we know why?

The Father. I'll tell you. Who knows if, by arranging the stage for her, she does not come here herself, attracted by the very articles of her trade? [*Inviting the* ACTORS *to look towards the exit at back of stage.*] Look! Look!

[*The door at the back of stage opens and* MADAME PACE *enters and takes a few steps forward. She is a fat, oldish woman with puffy oxygenated hair. She is rouged and powdered, dressed with a comical elegance in black silk. Round her waist is a long silver chain from which hangs a pair of scissors. The* STEP-DAUGHTER *runs over to her at once amid the stupor of the actors.*]

The Step-Daughter [*turning towards her*]. There she is! There she is!

The Father [*radiant*]. It's she! I said so, didn't I? There she is!

The Manager [*conquering his surprise, and then becoming indignant*]. What sort of a trick is this?

Leading Man [*almost at the same time*]. What's going to happen next?

Juvenile Lead. Where does *she* come from?

L'Ingénue. They've been holding her in reserve, I guess.

Leading Lady. A vulgar trick!

The Father [*dominating the protests*]. Excuse me, all of you! Why are you so anxious to destroy in the name of a vulgar, commonplace sense of truth, this reality which comes to birth attracted and formed by the magic of the stage itself, which has indeed more right to live here than you, since it is much truer than you—if you don't mind my saying so? Which is the actress among you who is to play Madame Pace? Well, here is Madame Pace herself. And you will allow, I fancy, that the actress who acts her will be less true than this woman here, who is herself in person. You see my daughter recognized her and went over to her at once. Now you're going to witness the scene!

[*But the scene between the* STEP-DAUGHTER *and* MA-DAME PACE *has already begun despite the protest of the actors and the reply of* The FATHER. *It has begun quietly, naturally, in a manner impossible for the stage. So when the actors, called to attention by The* FATHER, *turn round and see* MADAME PACE, *who has placed one hand under the* STEP-DAUGHTER's *chin to raise her head, they observe her at first with great attention, but hearing her speak in an unintelligible manner their interest begins to wane.*]

The Manager. Well? well?

Leading Man. What does she say?

Leading Lady. One can't hear a word.

Juvenile Lead. Louder! Louder please!

The Step-Daughter [*leaving* MADAME PACE, *who smiles a Sphinx-like smile, and advancing towards the actors*]. Louder? Louder? What are you talking about? These aren't matters which can be shouted at the top of one's voice. If I have spoken them out loud, it was to shame him and have my revenge. [*Indicates* FATHER.] But for Madame it's quite a different matter.

The Manager. Indeed? indeed? But here, you know, people have got to make themselves heard, my dear. Even we who are on the stage can't hear you. What will it be when the public's in the theatre? And anyway, you can very well speak up now among yourselves, since we shan't be present to listen to you as we are now. You've got to pretend to be alone in a room at the back of a shop where no one can hear you.

[*The* STEP-DAUGHTER *coquettishly and with a touch of malice makes a sign of disagreement two or three times with her finger.*]

The Manager. What do you mean by no?

The Step-Daughter [*sotto voce, mysteriously*]. There's someone who will hear us if she [*Indicating* MADAME PACE.] speaks out loud.

The Manager [*in consternation*]. What? Have you got someone else to spring on us now? [*The* ACTORS *burst out laughing.*]

The Father. No, no sir. She is alluding to me. I've got to be here—there behind that door, in waiting; and Madame Pace knows it. In fact, if you will allow me, I'll go there at once, so I can be quite ready. [*Moves away.*]

The Manager [*stopping him*]. No! Wait! wait! We must observe the conventions of the theatre. Before you are ready . . .

The Step-Daughter [*interrupting him*]. No, get on with it at once! I'm just dying, I tell you, to act this scene. If he's ready, I'm more than ready.

The Manager [*shouting*]. But, my dear young lady, first of all, we must have the scene between you and this lady . . . [*Indicates* MADAME PACE.] Do you understand? . . .

The Step-Daughter. Good Heavens! She's been telling me what you know already: that mamma's work is badly done again, that the material's ruined; and that if I want her to continue to help us in our misery I must be patient . . .

Madame Pace [*coming forward with an air of great*

importance].   Yes indeed, sir, I no wanta take advantage
of her, I no wanta be hard . . .
   [*Note.* MADAME PACE *is supposed to talk in a jargon
   half Italian, half English.*]
   The Manager [*alarmed*].   What? What? She talks like
that? [*The* ACTORS *burst out laughing again.*]
   The Step-Daughter [*also laughing*].   Yes yes, that's the
way she talks, half English, half Italian! Most comical
it is!
   Madame Pace.   Itta seem not verra polite gentlemen
laugha atta me eef I trya best speaka English.
   The Manager.   Diamine! Of course! Of course! Let
her talk like that! Just what we want. Talk just like that,
Madame, if you please! The effect will be certain. Exactly
what was wanted to put a little comic relief into the
crudity of the situation. Of course she talks like that!
Magnificent!
   The Step-Daughter.   Magnificent? Certainly! When
certain suggestions are made to one in language of that
kind, the effect is certain, since it seems almost a joke.
One feels inclined to laugh when one hears her talk about
an "old signore" "who wanta talka nicely with you."
Nice old signore, eh, Madame?
   Madame Pace.   Not so old my dear, not so old! And
even if you no lika him, he won't make any scandal!
   The Mother [*jumping up amid the amazement and
consternation of the actors who had not been noticing
her.* THEY *move to restrain her*].   You old devil! You
murderess!
   The Step-Daughter [*running over to calm her*
MOTHER].   Calm yourself, Mother, calm yourself! Please
don't . . .
   The Father [*going to her also at the same time*].   Calm
yourself! Don't get excited! Sit down now!
   The Mother.   Well then, take that woman away out
of my sight!

The Step-Daughter [*to* MANAGER]. It is impossible for my mother to remain here.

The Father [*to* MANAGER]. They can't be here together. And for this reason, you see: that woman there was not with us when we came . . . If they are on together, the whole thing is given away inevitably, as you see.

The Manager. It doesn't matter. This is only a first rough sketch—just to get an idea of the various points of the scene, even confusedly . . . [*Turning to the* MOTHER *and leading her to her chair.*] Come along, my dear lady, sit down now, and let's get on with the scene . . .

[*Meanwhile, the* STEP-DAUGHTER, *coming forward again, turns to* MADAME PACE.]

The Step-Daughter. Come on, Madame, come on!

Madame Pace [*offended*]. No, no, *grazie.* I not do anything witha your mother present.

The Step-Daughter. Nonsense! Introduce this "old signore" who wants to talk nicely to me. [*Addressing the* COMPANY *imperiously.*] We've got to do this scene one way or another, haven't we? Come on! [*To* MADAME PACE.] You can go!

Madame Pace. Ah yes! I go'way! I go'way! Certainly! [*Exits furious.*]

The Step-Daughter [*to the* FATHER]. Now you make your entry. No, you needn't go over here. Come here. Let's suppose you've already come in. Like that, yes! I'm here with bowed head, modest like. Come on! Out with your voice! Say "Good morning, Miss" in that peculiar tone, that special tone . . .

The Manager. Excuse me, but are you the Manager, or am I? [*To the* FATHER, *who looks undecided and perplexed.*] Get on with it, man! Go down there to the back of the stage. You needn't go off. Then come right forward here.

[*The* FATHER *does as he is told, looking troubled and perplexed at first. But as soon as he begins to move, the reality of the action affects him, and he begins to smile and to be more natural. The* ACTORS *watch intently.*]

The Manager [*sotto voce, quickly to the* PROMPTER *in his box*]. Ready! ready? Get ready to write now.

The Father [*coming forward and speaking in a different tone*]. Good afternoon, Miss!

The Step-Daughter [*head bowed down slightly, with restrained disgust*]. Good afternoon!

The Father [*looks under her hat which partly covers her face. Perceiving she is very young, he makes an exclamation, partly of surprise, partly of fear lest he compromise himself in a risky adventure*]. Ah . . . but . . . ah . . . I say . . . this is not the first time that you have come here, is it?

The Step-Daughter [*modestly*]. No sir.

The Father. You've been here before, eh? [*Then seeing her nod agreement.*] More than once? [*Waits for her to answer, looks under her hat, smiles, and then says.*] Well then, there's no need to be so shy, is there? May I take off your hat?

The Step-Daughter [*anticipating him and with veiled disgust*]. No sir . . . I'll do it myself. [*Takes it off quickly.*]

[*The* MOTHER, *who watches the progress of the scene with The* SON *and the other two children who cling to her, is on thorns; and follows with varying expressions of sorrow, indignation, anxiety, and horror the words and actions of the other two. From time to time* SHE *hides her face in her hands and sobs.*]

The Mother. Oh, my God, my God!

The Father [*playing his part with a touch of gallantry*]. Give it to me! I'll put it down. [*Takes hat from her hands.*] But a dear little head like yours ought to have a smarter hat. Come and help me choose one from the stock, won't you?

L'Ingénue [*interrupting*]. I say . . . those are our hats you know.

The Manager [*furious*]. Silence! silence! Don't try and be funny, if you please . . . We're playing the scene now I'd have you notice. [*To the* STEP-DAUGHTER.] Begin again, please!

The Step-Daughter [*continuing*]. No thank you, sir.

The Father. Oh, come now. Don't talk like that. You must take it. I shall be upset if you don't. There are some lovely little hats here; and then—Madame will be pleased. She expects it, anyway, you know.

The Step-Daughter. No, no! I couldn't wear it!

The Father. Oh, you're thinking about what they'd say at home if they saw you come in with a new hat? My dear girl, there's always a way round these little matters, you know.

The Step-Daughter [*all keyed up*]. No, it's not that. I couldn't wear it because I am . . . as you see . . . you might have noticed . . . [*Showing her black dress.*]

The Father. . . . In mourning! Of course: I beg your pardon: I'm frightfully sorry . . .

The Step-Daughter [*forcing herself to conquer her indignation and nausea*]. Stop! Stop! It's I who must thank you. There's no need for you to feel mortified or specially sorry. Don't think any more of what I've said. [*Tries to smile.*] I must forget that I am dressed so . . .

The Manager [*interrupting and turning to the* PROMPTER]. Stop a minute! Stop! Don't write that down. Cut out that last bit. [*Then to the* FATHER *and* STEP-DAUGHTER.] Fine! it's going fine! [*To the* FATHER *only.*] And now you can go on as we arranged. [*To the* ACTORS.] Pretty good that scene, where he offers her the hat, eh?

The Step-Daughter. The best's coming now. Why can't we go on?

The Manager. Have a little patience! [*To the* Actors.] Of course, it must be treated rather lightly.

Leading Man. Still, with a bit of go in it!

Leading Lady. Of course! It's easy enough! [*To*
Leading Man.] Shall you and I try it now?

Leading Man. Why, yes! I'll prepare my entrance.
[*Exit in order to make his entrance.*]

The Manager [*to* Leading Lady]. See here! The scene
between you and Madame Pace is finished. I'll have it
written out properly after. You remain here . . . oh,
where are you going?

Leading Lady. One minute. I want to put my hat on
again. [*Goes over to hat-rack and puts her hat on her
head.*]

The Manager. Good! You stay here with your head
bowed down a bit.

The Step-Daughter. But she isn't dressed in black.

Leading Lady. But I shall be, and much more effectively than you.

The Manager [*to* Step-Daughter]. Be quiet please,
and watch! You'll be able to learn something. [*Clapping
his hands.*] Come on! come on! Entrance, please!

[*The door at rear of stage opens, and the* Leading Man
*enters with the lively manner of an old gallant. The
rendering of the scene by the* Actors *from the very
first words is seen to be quite a different thing,
though it has not in any way the air of a parody.
Naturally, the* Step-Daughter *and the* Father, *not
being able to recognize themselves in the* Leading
Lady *and the* Leading Man, *who deliver their words
in different tones and with a different psychology,
express, sometimes with smiles, sometimes with gestures, the impression they receive.*]

Leading Man. Good afternoon, Miss . . .

The Father [*at once unable to contain himself*]. No!
no!

[*The* STEP-DAUGHTER *noticing the way the* LEADING MAN *enters, bursts out laughing.*]

The Manager [*furious*]. Silence! And you please just stop that laughing. If we go on like this, we shall never finish.

The Step-Daughter. Forgive me, sir, but it's natural enough. This lady [*Indicating* LEADING LADY.] stands there still; but if she is supposed to be me, I can assure you that if I heard anyone say "Good afternoon" in that manner and in that tone, I should burst out laughing as I did.

The Father. Yes, yes, the manner, the tone . . .

The Manager. Nonsense! Rubbish! Stand aside and let me see the action.

Leading Man. If I've got to represent an old fellow who's coming into a house of an equivocal character . . .

The Manager. Don't listen to them, for Heaven's sake! Do it again! It goes fine. [*Waiting for the* ACTORS *to begin again.*] Well?

Leading Man. Good afternoon, Miss.

Leading Lady. Good afternoon.

Leading Man [*imitating the gesture of the* FATHER *when he looked under the hat, and then expressing quite clearly first satisfactin and then fear*]. Ah, but . . . I say . . . this is not the first time that you have come here, is it?

The Manager. Good, but not quite so heavily. Like this. [*Acts himself.*] "This isn't the first time that you have come here" . . . [*To* LEADING LADY.] And you say: "No, sir."

Leading Lady. No, sir.

Leading Man. You've been here before, more than once.

The Manager. No, no, stop! Let her nod "yes" first. "You've been here before, eh?" [*The* LEADING LADY lifts *up her head slightly and closes her eyes as though in disgust. Then* She *inclines her head twice.*]

The Step-Daughter [*unable to contain herself*]. Oh my God! [*Puts a hand to her mouth to prevent herself from laughing.*]

The Manager [*turning round*]. What's the matter?

The Step-Daughter. Nothing, nothing!

The Manager [*to* Leading Man]. Go on!

Leading Man. You've been here before, eh? Well then, there's no need to be so shy, is there? May I take off your hat?

[*The* Leading Man *says this last speech in such a tone and with such gestures that the* Step-Daughter, *though she has her hand to her mouth, cannot keep from laughing.*]

Leading Lady [*indignant*]. I'm not going to stop here to be made a fool of by that woman there.

Leading Man. Neither am I! I'm through with it!

The Manager [*shouting to* Step-Daughter]. Silence! for once and all, I tell you!

The Step-Daughter. Forgive me! forgive me!

The Manager. You haven't any manners: that's what it is! You go too far.

The Father [*endeavouring to intervene*]. Yes, it's true, but excuse her . . .

The Manager. Excuse what? It's absolutely disgusting.

The Father. Yes, sir, but believe me, it has such a strange effect when . . .

The Manager. Strange? Why strange? Where is it strange?

The Father. No, sir; I admire your actors—this gentleman here, this lady; but they are certainly not us!

The Manager. I should hope not. Evidently they cannot be you, if they are actors.

The Father. Just so: actors! Both of them act our parts exceedingly well. But, believe me, it produces quite a different effect on us. They want to be us, but they aren't, all the same.

The Manager. What is it then anyway?

The Father. Something that is . . . that is theirs—and no longer ours . . .

The Manager. But naturally, inevitably. I've told you so already.

The Father. Yes, I understand . . . I understand . . .

The Manager. Well then, let's have no more of it! [*Turning to the* ACTORS.] We'll have the rehearsals by ourselves, afterwards, in the ordinary way. I never could stand rehearsing with the author present. He's never satisfied! [*Turning to* FATHER *and* STEP-DAUGHTER.] Come on! Let's get on with it again; and try and see if you can't keep from laughing.

The Step-Daughter. Oh, I shan't laugh any more. There's a nice little bit coming for me now: you'll see.

The Manager. Well then: when she says "Don't think any more of what I've said. I must forget, etc.," you [*Addressing the* FATHER.] come in sharp with "I understand, I understand"; and then you ask her . . .

The Step-Daughter [*interrupting*]. What?

The Manager. Why she is in mourning.

The Step-Daughter. Not at all! See here: when I told him that it was useless for me to be thinking about my wearing mourning, do you know how he answered me? "Ah well," he said, "then let's take off this little frock."

The Manager. Great! Just what we want, to make a riot in the theatre!

The Step-Daughter. But it's the truth!

The Manager. What does that matter? Acting is our business here. Truth up to a certain point, but no further.

The Step-Daughter. What do you want to do then?

The Manager. You'll see, you'll see! Leave it to me.

The Step-Daughter. No sir! What you want to do is to piece together a little romantic sentimental scene out of my disgust, out of all the reasons, each more cruel and viler than the other, why I am what I am. He is to ask me why I'm in mourning; and I'm to answer with tears in my eyes, that it is just two months since papa died. No sir, no! He's got to say to me; as he did say: "Well, let's take off this little dress at once." And I; with my two months' mourning in my heart, went there behind that screen, and with these fingers tingling with shame . . .

The Manager [*running his hands through his hair*]. For Heaven's sake! What are you saying?

The Step-Daughter [*crying out excitedly*]. The truth! The truth!

The Manager. It may be. I don't deny it, and I can understand all your horror; but you must surely see that you can't have this kind of thing on the stage. It won't go.

The Step-Daughter. Not possible, eh? Very well! I'm much obliged to you—but I'm off!

The Manager. Now be reasonable! Don't lose your temper!

The Step-Daughter. I won't stop here! I won't! I can see you've fixed it all up with him in your office. All this talk about what is possible for the stage . . . I understand! He wants to get at his complicated "cerebral drama," to have his famous remorses and torments acted; but I want to act my part, *my part!*

The Manager [*annoyed, shaking his shoulders*]. Ah! Just *your* part! But, if you will pardon me, there are other parts than yours: His [*Indicating the* FATHER.] and hers! [*Indicating the* MOTHER.] On the stage you can't have a character becoming too prominent and overshadowing all the others. The thing is to pack them all into a neat little framework and then act what is actable. I am aware of the fact that everyone has his own interior life which he wants very much to put forward. But the difficulty lies in this fact: to set out just so much as is neces-

sary for the stage, taking the other characters into consideration, and at the same time hint at the unrevealed
interior life of each. I am willing to admit, my dear young
lady, that from your point of view it would be a fine
idea if each character could tell the public all his troubles
in a nice monologue or a regular one hour lecture.
[*Good humoredly.*] You must restrain yourself, my dear,
and in your own interest, too; because this fury of yours,
this exaggerated disgust you show, may make a bad
impression, you know. After you have confessed to me
that there were others before him at Madame Pace's and
more than once . . .

The Step-Daughter [*bowing her head, impressed*].
It's true. But remember those others mean him for me all
the same.

The Manager [*not understanding*]. What? The others?
What do you mean?

The Step-Daughter. For one who has gone wrong,
sir, he who was responsible for the first fault is responsible for all that follow. He is responsible for my faults,
was, even before I was born. Look at him, and see if it
isn't true!

The Manager. Well, well! And does the weight of so
much responsibility seem nothing to you? Give him a
chance to act it, to get it over!

The Step-Daughter. How? How can he act all his
"noble remorses," all his "moral torments," if you want
to spare him the horror of being discovered one day—
after he had asked her what he did ask her—in the arms
of her, that already fallen woman, that child, sir, that
child he used to watch come out of school? [SHE *is moved.*]

[*The* MOTHER *at this point is overcome with emotion,
and breaks out into a fit of crying.* ALL *are touched.
A long pause.*]

The Step-Daughter [*as soon as the* MOTHER *becomes
a little quieter, adds resolutely and gravely*]. At present,

we are unknown to the public. Tomorrow, you will act us as you wish, treating us in your own manner. But do you really want to see drama, do you want to see it flash out as it really did?

The Manager. Of course! That's just what I do want, so I can use as much of it as is possible.

The Step-Daughter. Well then, ask that Mother there to leave us.

The Mother [*changing her low plaint into a sharp cry*]. No! No! Don't permit it, sir, don't permit it!

The Manager. But it's only to try it.

The Mother. I can't bear it. I can't.

The Manager. But since it has happened already . . . I don't understand!

The Mother. It's taking place now. It happens all the time. My torment isn't a pretended one. I live and feel every minute of my torture. Those two children there—have you heard them speak? They can't speak any more. They cling to me to keep up my torment actual and vivid for me. But for themselves, they do not exist, they aren't any more. And she [*Indicating the* STEP-DAUGHTER.] has run away, she has left me, and is lost. If I now see her here before me, it is only to renew for me the tortures I have suffered for her too.

The Father. The eternal moment! She [*Indicating the* STEP-DAUGHTER.] is here to catch me, fix me, and hold me eternally in the stocks for that one fleeting and shameful moment of my life. She can't give it up! And you sir, cannot either fairly spare me it.

The Manager. I never said I didn't want to act it. It will form, as a matter of fact, the nucleus of the whole first act right up to her surprise. [*Indicates the* MOTHER.]

The Father. Just so! This is my punishment: the passion in all of us that must culminate in her final cry.

The Step-Daughter. I can hear it still in my ears. It's driven me mad, that cry!—You can put me on as you like; it doesn't matter. Fully dressed, if you like—provided I have at least the arm bare; because, standing like this [*She goes close to the* FATHER *and leans her head on his breast.*] with my head so, and my arms round his neck, I saw a vein pulsing in my arm here; and then, as if that live vein had awakened disgust in me, I closed my eyes like this, and let my head sink on his breast. [*Turning to the* MOTHER.] Cry out mother! Cry out! [*Buries head in* FATHER's *breast, and with her shoulders raised as if to prevent her hearing the cry, adds in tones of intense emotion.*] Cry out as you did then!

The Mother [*coming forward to separate them*]. No! My daughter, my daughter! [*And after having pulled her away from him.*] You brute! you brute! She is my daughter! Don't you see she's my daughter?

The Manager [*walking backwards towards footlights*]. Fine! fine! Damned good! And then, of course—curtain!

The Father [*going towards him excitedly*]. Yes, of course, because that's the way it really happened.

The Manager [*convinced and pleased*]. Oh, yes, no doubt about it. Curtain here, curtain!

[*At the reiterated cry of The* MANAGER, *The* MACHINIST *lets the curtain down, leaving The* MANAGER *and The* FATHER *in front of it before the footlights.*]

The Manager. The darned idiot! I said "curtain" to show the act should end there, and he goes and lets it down in earnest. [*To the* FATHER, *while he pulls the curtain back to go on to the stage again.*] Yes, yes, it's all right. Effect certain! That's the right ending. I'll guarantee the first act at any rate.

ACT III

When the curtain goes up again, it is seen that the stage hands have shifted the bit of scenery used in the last part, and have rigged up instead at the back of the stage a drop,

with some trees, and one or two wings. A portion of a
fountain basin is visible. The MOTHER *is sitting on the*
right with the two children by her side. The SON *is on*
the same side, but away from the others. He seems bored,
angry, and full of shame. The FATHER *and the* STEP-
DAUGHTER *are also seated towards the right front. On*
the other side (left) are the ACTORS, *much in the positions*
they occupied before the curtain was lowered. Only the
MANAGER *is standing up in the middle of the stage, with*
his hand closed over his mouth in the act of meditating.

   The Manager [shaking his shoulders after a brief
pause]. Ah yes: the second act! Leave it to me, leave it
all to me as we arranged, and you'll see! It'll go fine!

   The Step-Daughter. Our entry into his house [*Indicates* FATHER.] in spite of him . . . [*Indicates the* SON.]

   The Manager [out of patience]. Leave it to me, I tell
you!

   The Step-Daughter. Do let it be clear, at any rate,
that it is in spite of my wishes.

   The Mother [from her corner, shaking her head]. For
all the good that's come of it . . .

   The Step-Daughter [turning towards her quickly].
It doesn't matter. The more harm done us, the more remorse for him.

   The Manager [impatiently]. I understand! Good
Heavens! I understand! I'm taking it into account.

   The Mother [supplicatingly]. I beg you, sir, to let it
appear quite plain that for conscience' sake I did try in
every way . . .

   *The Step-Daughter [interrupting indignantly and con-
tinuing for the* MOTHER]. . . . to pacify me, to dissuade
me from spiting him. [*To* MANAGER.] Do as she wants:
satisfy her, because it is true! I enjoy it immensely. Anyhow, as you can see, the meeker she is, the more she tries

to get at his heart, the more distant and aloof does he become.

The Manager. Are we going to begin this second act or not?

The Step-Daughter. I'm not going to talk any more now. But I must tell you this: you can't have the whole action take place in the garden, as you suggest. It isn't possible!

The Manager. Why not?

The Step-Daughter. Because he [*Indicates the* Son *again.*] is always shut up alone in his room. And then there's all the part of that poor dazed-looking boy there which takes place indoors.

The Manager. Maybe! On the other hand, you will understand—we can't change scenes three or four times in one act.

The Leading Man. They used to once.

The Manager. Yes, when the public was up to the level of that child there.

The Leading Lady. It makes the illusion easier.

The Father [*irritated*]. The illusion! For Heaven's sake, don't say illusion. Please don't use that word, which is particularly painful for us.

The Manager [*astounded*]. And why, if you please?

The Father. It's painful, cruel, really cruel; and you ought to understand that.

The Manager. But why? What ought we to say then? The illusion, I tell you, sir, which we've got to create for the audience . . .

The Leading Man. With our acting.

The Manager. The illusion of a reality.

The Father. I understand; but you, perhaps, do not understand us. Forgive me! You see . . . here for you and your actors, the thing is only—and rightly so . . . a kind of game . . .

The Leading Lady [*interrupting indignantly*]. A game! We're not children here, if you please! We are serious actors.

The Father. I don't deny it. What I mean is the game, or play, of your art, which has to give, as the gentleman says, a perfect illusion of reality.

The Manager. Precisely—!

The Father. Now, if you consider the fact that we [*Indicates himself and the other five* CHARACTERS.], as we are, have no other reality outside of this illusion . . .

The Manager [*astonished, looking at his* ACTORS, *who are also amazed*]. And what does that mean?

The Father [*after watching them for a moment with a wan smile*]. As I say, sir, that which is a game of art for you is our sole reality. [*Brief pause. He goes a step or two nearer the* MANAGER *and adds.*] But not only for us, you know, by the way. Just you think it over well. [*Looks him in the eyes.*] Can you tell me who you are?

The Manager [*perplexed, half smiling*]. What? Who am I? I am myself.

The Father. And if I were to tell you that that isn't true, because you and I . . . ?

The Manager. I should say you were mad—! [*The* ACTORS *laugh.*]

The Father. You're quite right to laugh: because we are all making believe here. [*To* MANAGER.] And you can therefore object that it's only for a joke that that gentleman there [*Indicates the* LEADING MAN.], who naturally is himself, has to be me, who am on the contrary myself—this thing you see here. You see I've caught you in a trap! [*The* ACTORS *laugh.*]

The Manager [*annoyed*]. But we've had all this over once before. Do you want to begin again?

The Father. No, no! That wasn't my meaning! In fact, I should like to request you to abandon this game of art [*Looking at the* LEADING LADY *as if anticipating her.*]

which you are accustomed to play here with your actors, and to ask you seriously once again: who are you?

The Manager [*astonished and irritated, turning to his* ACTORS]. If this fellow here hasn't got a nerve! A man who calls himself a character comes and asks me who I am!

The Father [*with dignity, but not offended*]. A character, sir, may always ask a man who he is. Because a character has really a life of his own, marked with his especial characteristics; for which reason he is always "somebody." But a man—I'm not speaking of you now—may very well be "nobody."

The Manager. Yes, but you are asking these questions of me, the boss, the manager! Do you understand?

The Father. But only in order to know if you, as you really are now, see yourself as you once were with all the illusions that were yours then, with all the things both inside and outside of you as they seemed to you—as they were then indeed for you. Well, sir, if you think of all those illusions that mean nothing to you now, of all those things which don't even *seem* to you to exist any more, while once they *were* for you, don't you feel that—I won't say these boards—but the very earth under your feet is sinking away from you when you reflect that in the same way this *you* as you feel it today—all this present reality of yours—is fated to seem a mere illusion to you tomorrow?

The Manager [*without having understood much, but astonished by the specious argument*]. Well, well! And where does all this take us anyway?

The Father. Oh, nowhere! It's only to show you that if we [*Indicating the* CHARACTERS.] have no other reality beyond the illusion, you too must not count overmuch on your reality as you feel it today, since, like that of yesterday, it may prove an illusion for you tomorrow.

The Manager [*determining to make fun of him*]. Ah,

excellent! Then you'll be saying next that you, with this comedy of yours that you brought here to act, are truer and more real than I am.

The Father [*with the greatest seriousness*]. But of course; without doubt!

The Manager. Ah, really?

The Father. Why, I thought you'd understand that from the beginning.

The Manager. More real than I?

The Father. If your reality can change from one day to another . . .

The Manager. But everyone knows it can change. It is always changing, the same as anyone else's.

The Father [*with a cry*]. No, sir, not ours! Look here! That is the very difference! Our reality doesn't change: it can't change! It can't be other than what it is, because it is already fixed for ever. It's terrible. Ours is an immutable reality which should make you shudder when you approach us if you are really conscious of the fact that your reality is a mere transitory and fleeting illusion, taking this form today and that tomorrow, according to the conditions, according to your will, your sentiments, which in turn are controlled by an intellect that shows them to you today in one manner and tomorrow . . . who knows how? . . . Illusions of reality represented in this fatuous comedy of life that never ends, nor can ever end! Because if tomorrow it were to end . . . then why, all would be finished.

The Manager. Oh for God's sake, will you *at least* finish with this philosophizing and let us try and shape this comedy which you yourself have brought me here? You argue and philosophize a bit too much, my dear sir. You know you seem to me almost, almost . . . [*Stops and looks him over from head to foot.*] Ah, by the way, I think you introduced yourself to me as a—what shall . . . we say—a "character," created by an author who did not afterward care to make a drama of his own creations.

The Father. It is the simple truth, sir.

The Manager. Nonsense! Cut that out, please! None of us believes it, because it isn't a thing, as you must recognize yourself, which one can believe seriously. If you want to know, it seems to me you are trying to imitate the manner of a certain author whom I heartily detest—I warn you—although I have unfortunately bound myself to put on one of his works. As a matter of fact, I was just starting to rehearse it, when you arrived. [*Turning to the* Actors.] And this is what we've gained—out of the frying-pan into the fire!

The Father. I don't know to what author you may be alluding, but believe me I feel what I think; and I seem to be philosophizing only for those who do not think what they feel, because they blind themselves with their own sentiment. I know that for many people this self-blinding seems much more "human"; but the contrary is really true. For man never reasons so much and becomes so introspective as when he suffers; since he is anxious to get at the cause of his sufferings, to learn who has produced them, and whether it is just or unjust that he should have to bear them. On the other hand, when he is happy, he takes his happiness as it comes and doesn't analyze it, just as if happiness were his right. The animals suffer without reasoning about their sufferings. But take the case of a man who suffers and begins to reason about it. Oh no! it can't be allowed! Let him suffer like an animal, and then—ah yet, he is "human"!

The Manager. Look here! Look here! You're off again, philosophizing worse than ever.

The Father. Because I suffer, sir! I'm not philosophizing: I'm crying aloud the reason of my sufferings.

The Manager [*makes brusque movement as he is taken with a new idea*]. I should like to know if anyone has ever heard of a character who gets right out of his part and perorates and speechifies as you do. Have you ever heard of a case? I haven't.

The Father. You have never met such a case, sir, because authors, as a rule, hide the labour of their creations. When the characters are really alive before their author, the latter does nothing but follow them in their action, in their words, in the situations which they suggest to him; and he has to will them the way they will themselves—for there's trouble if he doesn't. When a character is born, he acquires at once such an independence, even of his own author, that he can be imagined by everybody even in many other situations where the author never dreamed of placing him; and so he acquires for himself a meaning which the author never thought of giving him.

The Manager. Yes, yes, I know this.

The Father. What is there then to marvel at in us? Imagine such a misfortune for characters as I have described to you: to be born of an author's fantasy, and be denied life by him; and then answer me if these characters left alive, and yet without life, weren't right in doing what they did do and are doing now, after they have attempted everything in their power to persuade him to give them their stage life. We've all tried him in turn, I, she [*Indicating the* STEP-DAUGHTER.] and she. [*Indicating the* MOTHER.]

The Step-Daughter. It's true. I too have sought to tempt him, many, many times, when he has been sitting at his writing table, feeling a bit melancholy, at the twilight hour. He would sit in his armchair too lazy to switch on the light, and all the shadows that crept into his room were full of our presence coming to tempt him. [*As if she saw herself still there by the writing table, and was annoyed by the presence of the* ACTORS.] Oh, if you would only go away, go away and leave us alone—mother here with that son of hers—I with that Child—that Boy there always alone—and then I with him [*Just hints at the* FATHER.]—and then I alone, alone . . . in those shadows! [*Makes a sudden movement as if in the vision she has of herself illuminating those shadows she wanted to seize hold of herself.*] Ah! my life! my life! Oh, what scenes we proposed to him—and I tempted him more than any of the others!

The Father. Maybe. But perhaps it was your fault that he refused to give us life: because you were too insistent, too troublesome.

The Step-Daughter... Nonsense! Didn't he make me so himself? [*Goes close to the* MANAGER *to tell him as if in confidence.*] In my opinion he abandoned us in a fit of depression, of disgust for the ordinary theatre as the public knows it and likes it.

The Son. Exactly what it was, sir; exactly that!

The Father. Not at all! Don't believe it for a minute. Listen to me! You'll be doing quite right to modify, as you suggest, the excesses both of this girl here, who wants to do too much, and of this young man, who won't do anything at all.

The Son. No, nothing!

The Manager. You too get over the mark occasionally, my dear sir, if I may say so.

The Father. I? When? Where?

The Manager. Always! Continuously! Then there's this insistence of yours in trying to make us believe you are a character. And then too, you must really argue and philosophize less, you know, much less.

The Father. Well, if you want to take away from me the possibility of representing the torment of my spirit which never gives me peace, you will be suppressing me: that's all. Every true man, sir, who is a little above the level of the beasts and plants does not live for the sake of living, without knowing how to live; but he lives so as to give a meaning and a value of his own to life. For me this is *everything*. I cannot give up this, just to represent a mere fact as she [*Indicating the* STEP-DAUGHTER.] wants. It's all very well for her, since her "vendetta" lies in the "fact." I'm not going to do it. It destroys my *raison d'être*.

The Manager. Your *raison d'être!* Oh, we're going ahead fine! First she starts off, and then you jump in. At this rate, we'll never finish.

The Father. Now, don't be offended! Have it your own way—provided, however, that within the limits of the parts you assign us each one's sacrifice isn't too great.

The Manager. You've got to understand that you can't go on arguing at your own pleasure. Drama is action, sir, action and not confounded philosophy.

The Father. All right. I'll do just as much arguing and philosophizing as everybody does when he is considering his own torments.

The Manager. If the drama permits! But for Heaven's sake, man, let's get along and come to the scene.

The Step-Daughter. It seems to me we've got too much action with our coming into his house. [*Indicating* FATHER.] You said, before, you couldn't change the scene every five minutes.

The Manager. Of course not. What we've got to do is to combine and group up all the facts in one simultaneous, close-knit, action. We can't have it as you want, with your little brother wandering like a ghost from room to room, hiding behind doors and meditating a project which—what did you say it did to him?

The Step-Daughter. Consumes him, sir, wastes him away!

The Manager. Well, it may be. And then at the same time, you want the little girl there to be playing in the garden . . . one in the house, and the other in the garden: isn't that it?

The Step-Daughter. Yes, in the sun, in the sun! That is my only pleasure: to see her happy and careless in the garden after the misery and squalor of the horrible room where we all four slept together. And I had to sleep with her—I, do you understand?—with my vile contaminated body next to hers; with her folding me fast in her loving little arms. In the garden, whenever she spied me, she would run to take me by the hand. She didn't care for the big flowers, only the little ones; and she loved to show me them and pet me.

The Manager. Well then, we'll have it in the garden. Everything shall happen in the garden; and we'll group the other scenes there. [*Calls a* STAGE HAND.] Here, a back-cloth with trees and something to do as a fountain basin. [*Turning round to look at the back of the stage.*] Ah, you've fixed it up. Good! [*To* STEP-DAUGHTER.] This is just to give an idea, of course. The Boy, instead of hiding behind the doors, will wander about here in the garden, hiding behind the trees. But it's going to be rather difficult to find a child to do that scene with you where she shows you the flowers. [*Turning to the* BOY.] Come forward a little, will you please? Let's try it now! Come along! come along! [*Then seeing him come shyly forward, full of fear and looking lost.*] It's a nice business, this lad here. What's the matter with him? We'll have to give him a word or two to say. [*Goes close to him, puts a hand on his shoulders, and leads him behind one of the trees.*] Come on! come on! Let me see you a little! Hide here . . . yes, like that. Try and show your head just a little as if you were looking for someone . . . [*Goes back to observe the effect, when the* BOY *at once goes through the action.*] Excellent! fine! [*Turning to* STEP-DAUGHTER.] Suppose the little girl there were to surprise him as he looks round, and run over to him, so we could give him a word or two to say?

The Step-Daughter. It's useless to hope he will speak, as long as that fellow there is here . . . [*Indicates the* SON.] You must send him away first.

The Son [*jumping up*]. Delighted! Delighted! I don't ask for anything better. [*Begins to move away.*]

The Manager [*at once stopping him*]. No! No! Where are you going? Wait a bit!

[*The* MOTHER *gets up alarmed and terrified at the thought that he is really about to go away. Instinctively she lifts her arms to prevent him, without, however, leaving her seat.*]

The Son [*to* MANAGER *who stops him*]. I've got nothing to do with this affair. Let me go please! Let me go!

The Manager. What do you mean by saying you've got nothing to do with this?

The Step-Daughter [*calmly, with irony*]. Don't bother to stop him: he won't go away.

The Father. He has to act the terrible scene in the garden with his mother.

The Son [*suddenly resolute and with dignity*]. I shall act nothing at all. I've said so from the very beginning. [*To the* MANAGER.] Let me go!

The Step-Daughter [*going over to the* MANAGER]. Allow me? [*Puts down the* MANAGER'S *arm which is restraining the* SON.] Well, go away then, if you want to! [*The* SON *looks at her with contempt and hatred. She laughs and says.*] You see, he can't, he can't go away! He is obliged to stay here, indissolubly bound to the chain. If I, who fly off when that happens which has to happen, because I can't bear him—if I am still here and support that face and expression of his, you can well imagine that he is unable to move. He has to remain here, has to stop with that nice father of his, and that mother whose only son he is. [*Turning to the* MOTHER.] Come on, mother, come along! [*Turning to* MANAGER *to indicate her.*] You see, she was getting up to keep him back. [*To the* MOTHER, *beckoning her with her hand.*] Come on! come on! [*Then to* MANAGER.] You can imagine how little she wants to show these actors of yours what she really feels; but so eager is she to get near him that . . . There, you see? She is willing to act her part. [*And in fact, the* MOTHER *approaches him; and as soon as the* STEP-DAUGHTER *has finished speaking, opens her arms to signify that she consents.*]

The Son [*suddenly*]. No! no! If I can't go away, then I'll stop here; but I repeat: I act nothing!

The Father [*to* MANAGER *excitedly*]. You can force him, sir.

The Son. Nobody can force me.

The Father. I can.

The Step-Daughter. Wait a minute, wait . . . First of all, the baby has to go to the fountain . . . [*Runs to take the* CHILD *and leads her to the fountain.*]

The Manager. Yes, yes of course; that's it. Both at the same time.

[*The second* LADY LEAD *and the* JUVENILE LEAD *at this point separate themselves from the group of* ACTORS. *One watches the* MOTHER *attentively; the other moves about studying the movements and manner of the* SON *whom he will have to act.*]

The Son [*to* MANAGER]. What do you mean by both at the same time? It isn't right. There was no scene between me and her. [*Indicates the* MOTHER.] Ask her how it was!

The Mother. Yes, it's true. I had come into his room . . .

The Son. Into my room, do you understand? Nothing to do with the garden.

The Manager. It doesn't matter. Haven't I told you we've got to group the action?

The Son [*observing the* JUVENILE LEAD *studying him*]. What do you want?

The Juvenile Lead. Nothing! I was just looking at you.

The Son [*turning towards the second* LADY LEAD]. Ah! she's at it too: to re-act her part! [*Indicating the* MOTHER.]

The Manager. Exactly! And it seems to me that you ought to be grateful to them for their interest.

The Son. Yes, but haven't you yet perceived that it isn't possible to live in front of a mirror which not only freezes us with the image of ourselves, but throws our likeness back at us with a horrible grimace?

The Father. That is true, absolutely true. You must see that.

The Manager [*to second* LADY LEAD *and* JUVENILE LEAD]. He's right! Move away from them!

The Son. Do as you like. I'm out of this!

The Manager. Be quiet, you, will you? And let me hear your mother! [*To* MOTHER.] You were saying you had entered . . .

The Mother. Yes, into his room, because I couldn't stand it any longer. I went to empty my heart to him of all the anguish that tortures me . . . But as soon as he saw me come in . . .

The Son. Nothing happened! There was no scene. I went away, that's all! I don't care for scenes!

The Mother. It's true, true. That's how it was.

The Manager. Well now, we've got to do this bit between you and him. It's indispensable.

The Mother. I'm ready . . . when you are ready. If you could only find a chance for me to tell him what I feel here in my heart.

The Father [*going to* SON *in a great rage*]. You'll do this for your mother, for your mother, do you understand?

The Son [*quite determined*]. I do nothing!

The Father [*taking hold of him and shaking him*].

For God's sake, do as I tell you! Don't you hear your mother asking you for a favor? Haven't you even got the guts to be a son?

The Son [*taking hold of the* FATHER]. No! No! And for God's sake stop it, or else . . . [*General agitation. The* MOTHER, *frightened, tries to separate them.*]

The Mother [*pleading*]. Please! please!

The Father [*not leaving hold of the* SON]. You've got to obey, do you hear?

The Son [*almost crying from rage*]. What does it mean, this madness you've got? [*They separate.*] Have you no decency, that you insist on showing everyone our shame? I won't do it! I won't! And I stand for the will of our author in this. He didn't want to put us on the stage, after all!

The Manager. Man alive! You came here . . .

The Son [*indicating* FATHER]. *He* did! I didn't!

The Manager. Arent't you here now?

The Son. It was his wish, and he dragged us along with him. He's told you not only the things that did happen, but also things that have never happened at all.

The Manager. Well, tell me then what did happen. You went out of your room without saying a word?

The Son. Without a word, so as to avoid a scene!

The Manager. And then what did you do?

The Son. Nothing . . . walking in the garden . . . [*Hesitates for a moment with expression of gloom.*]

The Manager [*coming closer to him, interested by his extraordinary reserve*]. Well, well . . . walking in the garden . . .

The Son [*exasperated*]. Why on earth do you insist? It's horrible! [*The* MOTHER *trembles, sobs, and looks towards the fountain.*]

The Manager [*slowly observing the glance and turning towards the* SON *with increasing apprehension*]. The baby?

The Son. There in the fountain . . .

The Father [*pointing with tender pity to the* MOTHER]. She was following him at the moment . . .

The Manager [*to the* SON *anxiously*]. And then you . . .

The Son. I ran over to her; I was jumping in to drag her out when I saw something that froze my blood . . . the boy standing stock still, with eyes like a madman's, watching his little drowned sister, in the fountain! [*The* STEP-DAUGHTER *bends over the fountain to hide the* CHILD. *She sobs.*] Then . . . [*A revolver shot rings out behind the trees where the* BOY *is hidden.*]

The Mother [*with a cry of terror runs over in that direction together with several of the* ACTORS *amid general confusion*]. My son! My son! [*Then amid the cries and exclamations one hears her voice.*] Help! Help!

The Manager [*pushing the* ACTORS *aside while* THEY *lift up the* BOY *and carry him off.*] Is he really wounded?

Some Actors. He's dead! dead!

Other Actors. No, no, it's only make believe, it's only pretence!

The Father [*with a terrible cry*]. Pretence? Reality, sir, reality!

The Manager. Pretence? Reality? To hell with it all! Never in my life has such a thing happened to me. I've lost a whole day over these people, a whole day!

Curtain.

EACH IN HIS OWN WAY

(*Ciascuno a suo modo*)

A COMEDY IN TWO OR THREE ACTS WITH CHORAL INTERLUDES

English version by

ARTHUR LIVINGSTON

CHARACTERS OF THE COMEDY ON THE STAGE

DELIA MORELLO (*referred to in the interludes as "the leading lady"*)

MICHELE ROCCA

DONNA LIVIA PALEGARI (*an old lady*)

HER GUESTS (*men and women of her own age who feel quite at home in her house*)

DORO PALEGARI (*her son*)

DIEGO CINCI (*a young friend of Palegari*)

FILIPPO (*a butler of long service in the Palegari household*)

FRANCESCO SAVIO (*who starts the quarrel*)

PRESTINO (*one of several other friends of Savio*)

FENCING MASTER

BUTLER (*in Francesco Savio's house*)

"REAL" PEOPLE, APPEARING IN THE THEATRE LOBBY

DELIA MORENO (*whose connection with the play everybody understands*)

BARON NUTI

STAGE MANAGER

LEADING LADY (*who is the same as Delia Morello in the play*)

OWNER OF THE THEATRE

BUSINESS MANAGER

USHERS

POLICEMEN

FIVE DRAMATIC CRITICS

OLD AUTHOR (*who never had a play accepted*)

YOUNG AUTHOR

LITERARY MAN (*who would write if the public were not beneath his contempt*)

GOOD-NATURED SPECTATOR

BAD-HUMORED SPECTATOR

A MAN WHO UNDERSTANDS

A MAN WHO NEVER UNDERSTANDS

ONE OR TWO SUPPORTERS OF PIRANDELLO

AN ARMY OF ANTAGONISTS

SPECTATOR FROM THE SOCIAL SET

LADIES AND GENTLEMEN (*from the audience*)

277

The public is requested to remain seated at the end of the first and second acts, for the curtain will at once rise again for the choral interludes. The number of acts in the comedy cannot be made more specific in view of unpleasant incidents that will arise during the course of the performance.

ACT I

The ancient palace of Donna Livia Palegari. *It is tea time, and the guests are about to leave. Through the back drop, which presents three arches and two columns, a sumptuous drawing-room brightly lighted and with an animated company—ladies and gentlemen—can be seen. The front of the stage, less brightly lighted, is a smaller parlor ornately decorated in damask, and with ancient paintings (of religious subjects for the most part) on the walls. As we look at the stage we should get the impression of being in a shrine in a church, of which the drawing-room beyond the columns might be the nave—the sacred chapel of a very worldly church! The parlor in the foreground is unfurnished save for one or two benches or wooden stools for the convenience of people desirous of studying the paintings on the walls. There are no doors. The guests will come into this retreat two or three at a time to exchange confidences in private; and in fact as the curtain rises, we meet there: an* Old Friend *of* Donna Livia *and a* Young Man *(one of the guests), engaged in conversation.*

Young Man. Well, what's your idea of it?

Old Man [*with a sigh*]. My idea of it? [*Pause.*] I really couldn't explain. [*Pause.*] What are other people saying?

Young Man. Oh, some one thing, some another.

Old Man. Of course, each his own private opinion!

Young Man. But none of them, when you come down to it, seem to be sure of themselves. They are all like you.

Before they'll tell you what they think, they want to know what others are saying.

Old Man. Oh, as for me, I am absolutely sure. But . . . it's common sense, isn't it? I'm not anxious to make a fool of myself. Before I say anything definite I ought to know whether other people may not have some information which I have not yet had and which might in part modify my judgment.

Young Man. But what do you think, so far as you know?

Old Man. Oh, my dear boy, we never know everything!

Young Man. Well, in that case, what are opinions worth?

Old Man. Dear me, opinions? My opinion is a view that I hold until—well—until I find out something that changes it.

Young Man. Not at all, if I may press the point. The moment you say that we never know everything, you take it for granted that facts exist which would change your mind.

Old Man [*looking at him thoughtfully and smiling*]. Are you trying to corner me? You're trying to make me say that I have no opinion?

Young Man. How can you? From your point of view I shouldn't think anyone could have an opinion.

Old Man. Well, refusing to have an opinion is a way of having one, isn't it?

Young Man. Yes, but in a purely negative way.

Old Man. A negative way is better than no way at all though, my boy. [*He takes the young man by the arm and starts back with him toward the drawing-room, where some girls can be seen serving tea and cookies to the guests. A pause. Two* YOUNG LADIES *steal cautiously into the parlor.*]

First Young Lady [*eagerly*].   So you know all about it then? Oh, you darling! Tell me! Tell me!

Second Young Lady.   But remember, it's only an impression I have.

First Young Lady.   When *you* have an impression it's sure to be worth hearing. Was he pale? And you said he was sad!

Second Young Lady.   He seemed that way to me.

First Young Lady.   I should never have let him go away! Oh, and I felt that way at the time—here, in my heart. I went as far as the door with him, his hand in mine. He was a step outside, and still I held his hand. We had kissed each other good-bye. We had separated—but our hands—no, no—they just refused to let go! But tell me, won't you? He made no reference—?

Second Young Lady.   Reference to what?

First Young Lady.   No—I mean—well—I mean whether—well, you know—speaking in a general way as one often does—

Second Young Lady.   No, he said nothing in particular. He was listening to what the others were saying.

First Young Lady.   Ah yes. Because he—*he* knows. He knows what harm we do through this silly habit of talking we all have. Whereas, so long as we have the slightest doubt, we ought to keep our lips shut, tight. But we talk—we talk—and we don't know what we are talking about, ourselves! But you said he was pale—and sad! You don't remember what the others were saying, do you?

Second Young Lady.   No, I really don't. However, I shouldn't like to have you disappointed, my dear. You know how it is—we are so easily mistaken. It may have been indifference, but it seemed to me that he was pale; and when he smiled it was such a sad smile. Wait. I do remember! When somebody said—

First Young Lady.   What did somebody say?

Second Young Lady. What was it now? Wait—somebody said: "Women are like dreams—they are never the way you would like to have them."

First Young Lady. He didn't say that, did he? You are sure?

Second Young Lady. No, it wasn't he.

First Young Lady. Oh my, my, my! Anyhow, I don't know whether I am making a mistake or not. I've always been proud of acting in my own way under all circumstances. I'm a very good-natured person; but I can be spiteful on occasion. And if I ever am—well—it'll go hard with him!

Second Young Lady. I hope you will never be any different from what you are, dear.

First Young Lady. But what am I, really? I'm sure I don't know. I assure you I don't know—even myself! All this way and that, fickle, changing, my feet off the ground! First I'm here and then I'm there. I laugh. I go off into a corner to have a good cry all by myself. Oh, how terrible it is! Sometimes I just have to hide my face to keep from seeing myself. I am so ashamed at realizing how different, how incoherent, how unreliable I am from time to time.

[*At this moment other guests come into the room; two* YOUNG MEN (*dressed in the height of fashion*) *much bored with the party; and, with them,* DIEGO CINCI.]

First Young Man. Hope we're not intruding?

Second Young Lady. Not in the least. Please, do come in!

Second Young Man. So here's the chapel! The confessional, you might almost call it, eh?

Diego. Yes. There's only one thing lacking. Donna Livia ought to have a father confessor here for the convenience of her guests!

First Young Man. And why a priest, pray? We have our own consciences.

Diego. Yes, but what do you do with your conscience?

First Young Man. My conscience?

Second Young Man [*solemnly*]. "Mea mihi conscientia pluris est quam hominum sermo."

Second Young Lady. Why, that was Latin, wasn't it?

Second Young Man. Exactly, Signorina. A quotation from Cicero. I remember it from my school days.

First Young Lady. And what does it mean?

Second Young Man [*solemnly*]. "I care more for what my conscience says than for what the world says!"

First Young Man. We have a popular saying something like that. "With conscience clear, never fear!"

Diego. If we were the only ones—

Second Young Man [*not understanding*]. What do you mean? If we were the only ones—?

Diego. I mean that then the approval of our own consciences would be sufficient. But in that case it would hardly be a question of conscience any longer. Unfortunately, my friends, I'm here, and you're here! Unfortunately!

First Young Lady. Unfortunately, he says!

Second Young Lady. And not very nice of him either!

Diego. Why, I mean—we've always got to consider other people, my dear young lady.

Second Young Man. Not at all, not at all. When my own conscience approves—

Diego. But don't you see that that blessed conscience of yours is nothing but other people inside you?

First Young Man. Your usual philosophical clap-trap!

Diego. But it's not so hard to understand. [*To the* SECOND YOUNG MAN.] When you say that you are satisfied with the approval of your own conscience, what do you mean? You mean that other people may think of you and judge you as they choose—even unjustly, let us say; but that you, meantime, will hold your own head high in the assurance that you have done no wrong. Isn't that what you mean?

Second Young Man. Yes, I guess so.

Diego. Well, then, how do you acquire that assurance except from other people? Who can assure you you have done no wrong?

Second Young Man. I do myself. It's my conscience. What else?

Diego. All you're saying is that other people in your place, meeting, in other words, circumstances similar to yours, would have done as you have done. That's all you are saying, isn't it? Or indeed, you mean that above and beyond definite concrete situations in life, certain abstractions, certain general principles, exist on which we can all agree—and why not?—since agreement, in the case of principles merely, costs so little! But notice now: if you shut yourself up disdainfully in your ivory tower and insist that you have your own conscience and are satisfied with its approval, it is because you know that everybody is criticizing you, condemning you, or laughing at you—otherwise you would never think of saying such a thing. The fact is that the general principles in question ever remain abstractions. No one is able to recognize them as you do in the situation in which you find yourself, nor are people able to see themselves acting just as you acted in doing what you did. So then you say that the approval of your own conscience is sufficient— but sufficient for what, if you please? Does it enable you to enjoy standing all by yourself against the world? Not at all, not at all! As a matter of fact, you are afraid of being at outs with everybody. So what do you do? You imagine that there are any number of heads all made like your own, heads in fact that are duplicates, replicas, of your head. And you think you can shake those heads to say 'yes' or 'no,' 'no' or 'yes,' just as you please; and that

comforts you and makes you sure of yourself. Oh, interesting game, I grant you! But what else does that conscience
of yours amount to?

Second Young Man. But what do *you* do, may I ask?

Diego. Oh, I play the game the same as you. I have
my conscience too, I should say so!

First Young Lady. Oh, how interesting! But, I'm
sure it's getting late! I think I must be going!

Second Young Lady. Yes, yes, everybody seems to be
going. [*Turning to* DIEGO *and pretending that she is
much offended.*] How entertaining you have been!

First Young Man. Hadn't we better be going too?
[THEY *step back into the drawing-room to pay their
respects to the hostess and to take their leave. The company in the parlor, meantime, has thinned out percepti-
bly. The last guests are bowing to* DONNA LIVIA, *who
finally steps forward into the parlor, great anxiety written
on her face. She is leading* DIEGO CINCI *by the hand. The*
OLD MAN *whom we saw at the rising of the curtain and
a* SECOND OLD MAN *follow after her.*]

Donna Livia [*to* DIEGO]. Oh no, Diego, please don't
go! Please don't go! You are the best friend my son has
in the world, and I am quite beside myself. Tell me, is
it true? Is it true—what these dear old friends of mine
have been saying?

First Old Man. I was careful to point out, Donna
Livia, that we had no real information to go on.

Diego. You are talking about Doro? What's happened to him?

Donna Livia [*in surprise*]. What? Haven't you heard?

Diego. I haven't heard anything. Nothing serious, I
trust. If it had been, I am sure I should have heard.

Second Old Man [*half closing his eyes to soften the
shock of what he is about to reveal*]. We were referring

to the trouble last night! A bit of a scandal, you know . . .

Donna Livia. . . . at the Avanzi's! Doro stood up for that—that—what's her name?—that woman!

Diego. Scandal! What woman?

First Old Man [as above]. Why, that Morello person. Who else?

Diego. Oh, you are talking about Delia Morello!

Donna Livia. So you know her then?

Diego. Know her? Who doesn't know her, Signora?

Donna Livia. So Doro knows her too? It is true then! He knows her!

Diego. Why, I suppose so. Why shouldn't he? And what was the trouble about?

Donna Livia [turning to the First Old Man*].* And you said he didn't!

Diego. He knows her the way everybody knows her, Signora. But what happened?

First Old Man. But remember, remember! I was careful to say just what I said: that he stood up for the woman, *perhaps without ever having spoken to her in his life!*

Second Old Man. Yes, that's the way he knew her. Just her general reputation!

Donna Livia. And yet he stood up for her, even to the point of coming to blows?

Diego. Blows? With whom?

Second Old Man. With Francesco Savio.

Donna Livia. Why, it's incredible! The idea of starting a fight—a fight—in a respectable house, of respectable people! And for a woman of that breed!

Diego. Why, perhaps in the course of an argument . . .

First Old Man. . . . Just so . . . in the heat of an argument . . .

Second Old Man. . . . as so often happens . . .

Donna Livia. Please, gentlemen, don't try to spare my feelings. [*To* DIEGO.] *You* tell me, Diego, *you* tell me! *You* know all about Doro.

Diego. But why so wrought up, my dear Signora?

Donna Livia [*putting her foot down*]. No! You pretend to be a real friend of my son. In that case it is your duty to tell me frankly all you know about the matter.

Diego. But I know nothing whatever about the matter. Surely it can't be of much importance. Why so excited over a mere word or two?

First Old Man. Ah, as for that—now you're going a step too far! I don't follow you! . . .

Second Old Man. You can't deny that the affair made a very great impression on everybody present.

Diego. But what affair, for heaven's sake?

Donna Livia. Why, he stood up for the woman! Why, he actually came to her defense! Does that seem to you a matter of no consequence?

Diego. But, my dear Signora, the whole town has been talking about Delia Morello for three weeks past. She is the topic of conversation in the cafés, in the clubs, on the sidewalks, wherever you go. She is in the headlines of the papers. You must have read about her yourself.

Donna Livia. Yes, a man committed suicide on her account.

First Old Man. A young painter he was, named Salvi.

Diego. Giorgio Salvi, yes!

Second Old Man. A youth of great promise, it seems.

Diego. And it seems that there was someone before him.

Donna Livia. What! Another man?

First Old Man. Yes, it was mentioned in one of the papers . . .

Second Old Man. . . . that *he* committed suicide too.

Diego. Yes, he was a Russian. That, however, happened some years ago at Capri.

Donna Livia [*shuddering and hiding her face in her
hands*]. Oh dear! Oh dear! Oh dear!

Diego. But for heaven's sake, you're not afraid that
Doro is going to be the third, are you? I must say,
Signora, that we all have a right to deplore the tragedy
that has robbed us of an artist like Giorgio Salvi; but
after all, when we know the situation as it actually was,
it is quite possible—possible, notice—to say something
in defense of the woman.

Donna Livia. So you defend her too?

Diego. Yes, I too, to that extent! Why not?

Second Old Man. Challenging the indignation of all
decent people in town, I suppose!

Diego. Perhaps! I was simply observing that something may be said for the woman.

Donna Livia. But my own son, my Doro! I always
thought he kept the best of company.

First Old Man. He was a good boy . . .

Second Old Man. . . . always knew how to behave
himself.

Diego. But it was an argument, wasn't it? Well, in
an argument he may have said more than he really meant.
He may have exaggerated.

Donna Livia. No! No! Don't you try to spare my
feelings! Don't you conceal anything from me! Delia
Morello—she's an actress, isn't she?

Diego. I should call her a lunatic, Signora.

First Old Man. She has been on the stage.

Diego. But she couldn't hold her job anywhere. No
manager dares take the risk of hiring her any more. Delia
Morello can't be her real name. That must be just the
way she is known on the stage. No one knows who she
really is, nor where she comes from.

Donna Livia. Is she a good-looking woman?

Diego. They call her beautiful.

Donna Livia. Oh, they're all beautiful—those actresses! I suppose Doro met her in some theatre.

Diego. I believe he did. But at the most it couldn't have been more than an introduction, a visit to her dressing-room, back-stage, perhaps. And that is not such a terrible thing as many good people imagine, Signora. Please don't worry!

Donna Livia. But here two men have gone and killed themselves on her account!

Diego. I would not have killed myself for her!

Donna Livia. But she made those two fellows lose their heads.

Diego. I wouldn't have lost mine!

Donna Livia. But I'm not worried on your account— I am thinking of Doro!

Diego. Never fear, Signora! And one more thing: if that unhappy woman has done wrong to other people, she has always done the greatest wrong to herself. She's one of those women who are made haphazard, so to speak, who seem unable to get hold of themselves— wanderers astray on the face of the earth, never knowing where they're going nor where they will end. And yet sometimes, you know, she seems to be just a poor little child afraid of the world and appealing to you for help.

Donna Livia [*much impressed, and seizing him by both elbows*]. Diego, look me in the eye: you got that from Doro!

Diego. No, Signora!

Donna Livia [*insisting*]. Tell me the truth, Diego. Doro is in love with that woman!

Diego. I am sure he isn't.

Donna Livia [*still insisting*]. He is! He is! He is in love with her. What you have just said only a man in love with her could say!

Diego. But they're my words, not Doro's!

Donna Livia. That isn't so. Doro talked that way about her to you. And no one can convince me that he didn't!

Diego [*shrinking before her persistence*]. Oh! Oh! [*Then with a sudden eloquence, his voice becoming clear and light, caressing, inviting.*] Signora, can't you imagine —imagine—a carriage—driving along a country road— through the open fields—on a bright afternoon in summer time?

Dona Livia [*dumbfounded*]. A carriage—on a country road! What's that got to do with it?

Diego [*angrily and deeply moved*]. Signora, can you imagine the condition I was in when I sat up all night watching at the bedside of my mother, dying? I sat there —and do you know what I was doing? I was staring at a fly, a fly that had fallen into a glass of water on the lamp-stand and was swimming about, his wings flat on the surface of the water—And I sat there watching him. I didn't even notice when my poor mother died! I was all taken up in admiring the confidence that poor fly seemed to have in the strength of his two hind legs. They were longer than the others. They were made for him to get his start with. He kept swimming about desperately, always confident that those two hind legs would finally lift him above the liquid surface were he was caught. But whenever he tried to jump, he would find that something was sticking to the ends of them. So every time he failed, he would rub them together furiously, to clean them—and then he would try again! I sat there watching him for more than half an hour; and then I saw him die —and I did not see my poor mother die! Now then, do you understand? Let me alone!

Donna Livia [*dumbfounded, bewildered, stands there looking first at one and then at the other of the two* OLD

Men *who are as much at sea as she is*]. I beg your pardon—I don't see the connection!

Diego. Does it seem to you so absurd? Well, tomorrow now, I assure you, you will laugh . . . you will laugh at all these fancied terrors you are feeling for your son when you think of that carriage on the country road which I have just trundled along before your mind's eye the better to confuse you. But please realize that I can never laugh as I think of that poor fly that came before my eyes while I was sitting there watching at my mother's bedside. [*A pause.* Donna Livia *and the two* Old Men *stand looking at each other after this abrupt diversion, more than ever confused, unable in spite of all their efforts to make this carriage on the country road and this fly in the glass of water fit into the subject which they had just been discussing.* Diego Cinci *is all absorbed in memories of his mother's death; so that when* Doro Palegari *enters, at just this moment,* Doro *will find* Cinci *in a very unusual frame of mind.*]

Doro [*looking first at one and then at the other of the company in surprise*]. Why, what's the matter?

Donna Livia [*coming to herself*]. Oh, it's you! Doro, my boy, what have you been doing? What have you been doing? These gentlemen have been telling me—

Doro [*snapping angrily*]. About the "scandal," I suppose? Saying that I am in love, head over heels in love, with Delia Morello, eh? I suppose so! All my friends wink at me as I pass them on the street. "Eh, how's Delia, old boy?" Heavens above! What's got into you? Have you all lost your minds?

Donna Livia. But if you—

Doro. If I, what? I can't understand it, upon my word! And a scandal made of it, within twenty-four hours!

Donna Livia. But you came to the defense of that—

Doro. I came to nobody's defense.

Donna Livia. At the Avanzi's last evening!

Doro. At the Avanzi's last evening I heard Francesca Savio express, in regard to the tragic suicide of Giorgio Salvi—about whom, by the way, everybody is having his say—an opinion which did not seem to me a fair one. So I contested it! That's all there is to it!

Donna Livia. But you said certain things. . . .

Doro. Oh, I may have talked a lot of nonsense. All I said I really can't remember. In an argument one word follows on another. I may have exaggerated! But hasn't a fellow a right to his opinion on topics of the day? It seems to me we can interpret certain episodes in one fashion or another as we see fit. Today it is this way, tomorrow it's another. For example, if I happen to see Francesco Savio tomorrow, I shall be quite ready to admit that he was right and that I was wrong.

First Old Man. Oh, in that case, very well.

Donna Livia. Do so, please, Doro! Please do so! By all means!

Second Old Man. . . . to put an end to all this gossip, you understand.

Doro. Oh, not for that reason. I don't care a hang about the gossip! I would be doing it only to get rid of the mortification I feel myself!

First Old Man. Quite so. Yes, quite so . . .

Second Old Man. . . . at seeing yourself so misunderstood!

Doro. Not at all, not at all! The mortification I feel at having let myself go so far—an anger justified perhaps by the spectacle of Francesco Savio sitting there, stupidly arguing, with his facts all wrong; though he after all— well yes—he was right, substantially! So now, when I've cooled off a bit, I'm ready—yes, I'm quite ready—to apologize. And I will do so. I will apologize in the presence of everybody, to put an end to this absurd dispute. My, what a row over nothing! I'm disgusted.

Donna Livia. Well, I'm much relieved, Doro, much relieved! And I'm glad to hear you admit right here in the presence of a friend of yours that nothing can be said in defense of such a woman.

Doro. Why, was he trying to defend her too?

First Old Man. Yes, he was—that is to say, after a fashion . . .

Second Old Man. Not in earnest, you understand! Just to soothe your mother's feelings.

Donna Livia. Yes, and I must say he wasn't succeeding very well. But now what you have said is a great relief to me. And thank you, thank you ever so much, my boy.

Doro [*angry, irritated at the implication of his mother's gratitude*]. But—you're really serious? You—why, mother, you make me angrier than ever! I'm getting mad, clear through!

Donna Livia. Angry—because I am thanking you?

Doro. Well, I must say? Why do you thank me, in fact? Why are you so much relieved now! I see, you thought that . . . I swear, mother, I'll be flying off the handle!

Donna Livia. No, no, don't be angry! Let's say no more about it!

Doro [*turning to* Diego]. So you think something can be said for Delia Morello?

Diego. Oh, let's drop the subject—now that your mother is quite herself again.

Doro. No, I insist on knowing. I insist on knowing.

Diego. So you want to start the argument over again with me?

Donna Livia. Please don't, Doro.

Doro [*to his mother*]. No, it was just a matter of curiosity. [*To* Diego.] I wanted to see whether you were making the same points that I brought up last evening in my quarrel with Francesco Savio.

Diego. And suppose I were. You don't mean to say you would be on the other side now?

Doro. Do you think I'm a whirligig? Last evening I took this position: I said: "You can't claim that Delia Morello intended to encompass the ruin of Giorgio Salvi because of the simple fact that the night before she was to be married to him she went off on a lark with another man; since the real ruin of Salvi would have been for him to marry her!"

Diego. Exactly! Just my view of it. And the Morello woman knew this too; and, precisely because she knew it, she was determined to prevent it.

Doro. Nothing of the kind! Savio was right in holding that she went off with that other fellow, Michele Rocca, to push her vengeance on Giorgio Salvi to the limit—because there is no escaping the fact that in all this affair she acted at all times and under all circumstances with the most refined treachery toward him. There!

Diego. So that's your view of it? Well, keep to that opinion. And much good may it do you! At any rate, let's drop the subject now!

First Old Man. Wisely said! And now we must be going, Donna Livia. [*He kisses her hand.*]

Second Old Man. . . . delighted that everything has been cleared up now! [*He also kisses her hand. Then turning to the others.*] Good afternoon, Doro, and you too, Cinci.

Diego. Good afternoon! Good afternoon!

Donna Livia [*turning to the first of the two friends and starting back with them to the drawing-room, from which* THEY *will depart through an exit to the right*]. So then, when you get to Christina's—just tell her that I'll be calling, and ask her to be ready. [DONNA LIVIA *withdraws. For a moment* DORO *and* DIEGO *stand there without speaking. The empty drawing-room brightly lighted in the background behind them should give an interesting effect.*]

Diego [*spreading the fingers of his two hands fan-shaped, then crossing one hand over the other so as to form a network of his fingers, finally stepping up to* DORO *to attract the latter's attention*]. This is the way it is—look!—this way—exactly!

Doro. What?

Diego. That conscience we were talking about in here just before you came. A net, an elastic net! You slacken it up a little like this and good-bye!—the madness we each have in us runs amuck!

Doro [*after a brief silence, worried, suspicious*]. You mean that for me?

Diego [*almost talking to himself*]. Before your mind the images, the memories, piled up during the years, begin to crowd—fragments of the life which you have lived perhaps, but which never gains the forefront of your consciousness because you have never been willing or able to view it in the clear light of reason . . . questionable things you may have done; lies of which you would be ashamed; thoughts that are mean, petty, unworthy of you; crimes you have thought out and planned in their minutest particulars; desires unconfessed and unconfessable—and it all, all, all comes up in your mind and throws you off your balance, till you don't know where you're at, leaving you disconcerted, bewildered, terrified!

Doro [*as above*]. What are you talking about, man?

Diego [*gazing fixedly into space*]. And I hadn't slept for nine nights in succession. . . . [*He turns vehemently upon* DORO.] Try it for yourself! Nine successive nights without a wink of sleep! The white mug on the table beside your bed has a single blue line around it—and that infernal bell! Ding! Ding! Ding! Ding! Eight . . . nine! I used to count them! Ten . . . eleven! The clock

striking, you see! Twelve! Not to mention the quarters
and the halves . . . ! There's no human affection strong
enough to hold its own when you've neglected those
primal needs of the body which must—must, I tell you!
—be satisfied! There I was, outraged at the cruel fate
which had fallen upon the ghastly, unconscious, unrecog-
nizable body of my poor mother—nothing but body left
of her, poor thing—well, do you know what I thought? I
kept thinking: "God! I wish she'd stop that gasping!"

Doro. But my dear Diego! Your mother . . . why
. . she's been dead at least two years, hasn't she?

Diego. Yes! And you have no idea how surprised I
was when the gasping did stop for a moment. The room
fell into a terrible silence, and I turned—I don't know
why—and I looked into the mirror on the dressing-table.
I was bending over the bed to see whether perchance she
might have died. But the mirror was so placed that I
couldn't help seeing—seeing what the expression on my
face was like, the expression, that is, which I was wearing
as I bent over to look at her . . . a sort of joyous terror,
a sort of terrible joy, the joy that would welcome my
liberation. . . . But she gave another gasp, and that
gasp gave me such a shudder of loathing for the thought
I had been thinking that I buried my face in my two
hands as though I had committed a crime. And I began
to weep—to weep like the child I once had been—for my
poor mamma, whose pity . . . yes! yes! it was her pity
I wanted, pity for the fatigue I felt, the fatigue I felt for
having been there nine sleepless nights in succession! You
see . . . yes . . . at that instant I had ceased to hope
that she would die. Poor, poor mamma! How many
nights' sleep had she lost when I was a little child—and
sick?

Doro. Would you mind explaining why you talk
about your mother this way, all of a sudden?

Diego. I don't know, I'm sure. Won't you tell me why you got angry when your mother thanked you for having put her mind at ease?

Doro. Why, it was because she actually suspected for a moment, herself—

Diego. Oh, get out! You can't make me swallow that.

Doro [*shrugging his shoulders*]. I don't know what you're driving at.

Diego. If such a suspicion on her part had not been well founded, you would have laughed instead of getting angry.

Doro. What do you mean? You don't seriously think . . . ?

Diego. I? You are the one who is thinking it?

Doro. But now I'm taking Savio's view of the matter.

Diego. So you see. . . . First here and then there! You are even angry at yourself—for your exaggerations, as you called them!

Doro. That is because I now see . . .

Diego. No! No! Be frank with yourself! Read your own thoughts, accurately!

Doro. But what thoughts shall I read, man alive?

Diego. You're now agreeing with Francesco Savio! But do you know why? It's to hide a feeling which you've had inside you without your knowing that it was there.

Doro. Nothing of the kind! You make me laugh!

Diego. It's true! It's true!

Doro. You make me laugh, I say!

Diego. In the excitement of the argument last evening that feeling suddenly came to the top in your mind. It caught you off your guard . . . and you said things you didn't realize you were saying. . . . Of course you didn't! Of course you didn't! And you imagine you never even thought those things! And yet you did think them . . . you did think them! . . .

Doro. What do you mean? When?

Diego. Secretly . . . unknown even to yourself! Oh, my dear Doro, just as we sometimes have illegitimate children, so we sometimes have illegitimate thoughts!

Doro. Speak for yourself, eh!

Diego. Yes, I'll speak also for myself! . . . We all yearn to marry, and for our whole life long, some one particular soul . . . the soul which seems most convenient, most useful, to us . . . the soul which brings us in dowry the faculties and qualities most likely to help us attain the goals to which we aspire. But later on, outside the honest, conjugal household of our consciousness, we have . . . well . . . one affair after another, numberless little sins with all those other souls which we have rejected and buried in the depths of our being, and from which actions and thoughts are born—actions and thoughts which we refuse to recognize, but which, when we are forced to it, we adopt or legitimize . . . with appropriate adaptations, reserves, and cautions. Now, in this case, one of your own poor, fatherless thoughts has come home to you. You deny paternity . . . but look it over carefully! It's yours! It's yours! You were really in love with Delia Morello . . . head-over-heels in love, as you said!

Doro. Hah! Hah! Hah! Hah! Hah! Hah! Hah! You make me laugh! You make me laugh!

[*At this point the butler,* FILIPPO, *enters the room.*]

Filippo. Signor Francesco Savio, sir.

Doro. Oh, here he is now! [*To* FILIPPO.] Show him in!

Diego. And I will leave you alone with him!

Doro. No! Wait! I want you to see how much in love I am with Delia Morello! [FRANCESCO SAVIO *appears in the drawing-room.*]

Doro. Come in here, Francesco, won't you?

Francesco. Why, my dear Doro! And how are you, Cinci?

Diego.   Glad to see you, Savio!

Francesco [*addressing* DORO].   I came to tell you how sorry I was about our little squabble last evening.

Doro.   I was just on the point of going to look you up to tell you how sorry I was.

Francesco [*taking his hand warmly*].   That's good news, Doro, my boy! You have taken a great weight off my mind!

Diego.   I should like to have a picture of you two fellows, upon my word!

Francesco [*to* DIEGO].   You know, Diego, we two have been friends all our lives . . . and we were on the point of breaking over nothing!

Doro.   Oh, it wasn't quite so bad as that, was it!

Francesco.   Why, it was on my mind all last evening! I can't understand how I could have helped recognizing the generosity which prompted you . . .

Diego [*breaking in*].   Exactly! The *generosity* which prompted him to defend Delia Morello!

Francesco.   Yes! And so that everybody could hear too! And it took some courage . . . with all those people yelping against her!

Doro [*puzzled*].   But . . . do you mean to say . . . ?

Diego [*to* FRANCESCO].   And you more rabid than any of the rest!

Francesco [*warmly*].   Yes. Because I had not given enough weight to certain considerations, one more sound and convincing than the other, which Doro, here, brought forward!

Doro [*with rising anger*].   Ah! So *that's* it! So you now . . . so you now! . . .

Diego [*breaking in*].   Exactly! So you now are standing up for the woman, are you not?

Francesco.   But Doro stood out against the whole crowd! He held his ground in the face of all those fools, and they couldn't find a thing to answer him with!

Doro [*to* FRANCESCO, *at the height of his irritation*]. Listen! You know what you are? . . . You're an ordinary circus clown!

Francesco. What do you mean? I came here to see you to admit that you were right! . . .

Doro. Yes! And that is why I say: you are just an ordinary circus clown!

Diego. You see, just as you now have come to the point of agreeing with him, he had already come to the point of agreeing with you!

Francesco. Agreeing with me?

Diego. Yes, with you . . . with you because of the things you said *against* Delia Morello! . . .

Doro. . . . and now you have the impudence to come and tell me that I was right!

Francesco. But—simply because I have thought over all you said!

Diego. Exactly! Don't you see? Just as *he* has thought over what *you* said! . . .

Francesco. And now he says *I* was right . . .

Diego. Just as you say *he* was right!

Doro. Yes! You say that now . . . after you made a fool of me last night . . . in the presence of everybody! Set them all talking about me . . . and nearly drove my poor mother out of her mind! . . .

Francesco. I? . . .

Doro. Yes! You! You! You just drew me on . . . getting me into an argument . . . trying to compromise me . . . making me say things that I would otherwise never have dreamed of saying! [*He steps up to* FRANCESCO *and faces him angrily.*] Just take a suggestion from me! You be very careful not to go around saying to anybody that I was right! . . .

Diego [*pressing his point*]. Because you see, you recognize the generosity which prompted him! . . .

Francesco. But I do . . . I do! . . .

Doro. You're just an ordinary circus clown!

Diego. You see . . . if you go around saying that he was right that will show that you, too, know the truth now . . . the truth, that is, that *he is in love* with Delia Morello . . . and that he came to her defense *on that account!*

Francesco. That is the third time you've called me a clown, notice!

Doro. But it won't be the last! I'll say you're a clown one hundred times . . . today . . . tomorrow . . . always!

Francesco. Please remember that I am in your house!

Doro. In my house I say that you're a clown . . . but even when I'm not in my own house I'll say you're a clown! You're a clown! A clown! A clown!

Francesco. Very well! Very well! In that case . . . good afternoon! And we'll see each other later, eh? . . . [*He starts to leave the room.*]

Diego [*in an effort to detain him*]. One moment . . . one moment! Let's not go too fast!

Doro [*restraining him*]. No, let him go!

Diego. Are you crazy, man? This will compromise you for good!

Doro. I don't care a damn!

Diego [*breaking away from him*]. But you're crazy, I say! Let me go! [*He dashes out of the room in an effort to overtake* FRANCESCO SAVIO.]

Doro [*calling after him*]. Mind your own business, Diego! [DIEGO, *however, does not stop.*]

Doro [*begins walking up and down the room, muttering furiously to himself*]. Huh! That's a good one! And he has the impudence to come and tell me that I was right! . . . The clown! After making it look to everybody as though . . . [*At this point the* BUTLER *hurries in in some alarm with a visiting card in his hand.*]

Filippo. May I come in, sir?

Doro... Well, what's the matter?

Filippo. A lady calling, sir.

Doro. A lady?

Filippo. Here's her card. [*He holds out a visiting card.*]

Doro [*in great agitation after reading the name on the card*]. Where . . . where is she?

Filippo. She is in the hall, sir, waiting.

Doro [*he looks around him in perplexity. Finally, and with a great effort to conceal his anxiety and confusion*]. Has mamma gone out?

Filippo. Yes, sir, she left a moment ago!

Doro. Show the lady in! Show her in here! [FILIPPO *withdraws.* DORO *advances toward the drawing-room to receive the visitor. He is standing under the central arch between the two columns when* FILIPPO *reappears, introducing* DELIA MORELLO. SHE *is soberly but elegantly costumed, and wears a thick veil.* FILIPPO *withdraws, bowing.*]

Doro. You? Delia? Here?

Delia. I came to thank you. Oh, can I ever tell you how grateful I am, my good, kind, friend!

Doro. Please, please, don't say that!

Delia. Yes! I must say just that! [DORO *has extended his hand.* DELIA *bends over as though to kiss it.*] I must thank you! Thank you, indeed!

Doro. But no . . . no . . . please! . . . I, rather, should warn you that . . .

Delia. Thank you for the kindness . . . the great kindness you did me!

Doro. But what kindness? I simply said . . .

Delia. No! Oh, I see! . . . You thought I was thanking you for having stood up for me? Not at all! What do I care whether people accuse me or defend me? I am my own judge, and my own tormentor! My gratitude, rather, is for what you thought and felt inside yourself

. . . and not because you took the trouble to express it
in the presence of other people.

Doro [*in great bewilderment*]. I thought . . . yes
. . . what . . . knowing the facts as I did . . . it seemed
to me . . . what it seemed to me was just to think.

Delia. Just or unjust . . . what do I care? The fact
is that what you said of me suddenly made me see myself
. . . you understand . . . see myself—the moment I
heard it!

Doro [*in growing bewilderment, but striving to appear
indifferent*]. Ah, so then . . . so then . . . I guessed
right?

Delia. As right as though you had lived my life to the
bottom . . . but understanding me in a way I never
understood myself! Never! Never! And a great shudder
went over me! . . . I cried . . . Yes! Yes! . . . "That's
just the way I am! That's just the way I am!" . . . And
you can't imagine with what joy and with what anguish
I recognized myself, saw myself . . . in all the things
you found to say of me!

Doro. I am happy . . . happy . . . most happy . . .
happy because it all seemed to me so clear at the time,
when in fact I did discover those things—without re-
flection . . . you understand . . . as though by an inspiration coming to me directly from you. Later on, I
confess, I did not feel the same way.

Delia. Ah! Later on—you changed?

Doro. Yes. But if now you tell me that you recognize
yourself in what I said of you . . . if you tell me that I
was right . . .

Delia. I have been living all day on that inspiration
of yours—inspiration you may well call it. What I don't
understand is how you could see through me so easily,
and so clearly—you who scarcely know me, after all.
Whereas I . . . well . . . it's terrible . . . I struggle
and struggle, suffering all the while—I don't know—as

though—as though I were not quite myself, as though I were constantly groping around to find myself . . . to understand the woman that I really am, to ask her what she really wants, why she is suffering so, and what I ought to do to tame her, pacify her, give her a little peace . . .

Doro. That's it . . . a little peace, a little quiet! That's what you need!

Delia. I have him constantly before my eyes . . . just as I saw him there at my feet . . . pale . . . lifeless . . . a dead thing! It all came over me in a flash! I felt myself—I don't know—dying—and I bent over to look at him . . . trying to grasp from the abyss of that instant the eternity of the sudden death I could see before my eyes, there, in his face, a face which in a second had lost consciousness of everything . . . Ah, I knew . . . I alone knew . . . the life there had been in that poor body which had destroyed itself for me, for me who am nothing . . . nothing. Ah! I was quite mad! Imagine the state I must be in at present!

Doro. But quiet, now! Please, be calm!

Delia. Oh, I am calm enough . . . But see . . . when I try to be calm . . . well . . . it's this way . . . I'm stunned, stunned, that's it! All feeling seems to leave me! Just that . . . just that! I pinch myself, but I don't feel it! My hands . . . I look at them, and they don't seem to be mine! And then all the things I have to do—I don't know why I have to do them—I open my handbag and take out my mirror and I am horror-stricken at the pallor and at the coldness that has come over me! Well . . . you can't imagine the impression I get, there, in the circle of that mirror, of my painted lips and my painted eyes! . . .

Doro. That's because you don't see yourself as others see you.

Delia. So you say that, too? Must I actually hate—

hate as my enemies—all the people I have anything to do
with—that they may help me to understand myself?

Doro. Why no . . . why should you?

Delia. Why, I see them walk in front of me and they
seem—well—to be dazzled by my eyes, by my lips, by my
beauty, in short; but no one cares for me . . . no one
cares for what most concerns me.

Doro. Your real self, that is! . . .

Delia. So then I punish them in the things they really
desire. Those desires disgust me, but first I do my best to
fan them, make them worse in order to get my revenge
. . . and that revenge I get by giving myself away, suddenly, capriciously, to the person whom they would have
least expected to win me! [Doro *nods with a suggestion of
reproach.*] I do that, I suppose, to show them my contempt for the things they most highly prize in me. [*Again*
Doro *nods.*] Have I harmed myself? Always . . . always!
But better worthless men like that . . . worthless men
who have no pretensions, and who know how little they
amount to . . . people who bore you, perhaps, but who
do not disappoint you . . . and who may even have their
good points, too—certain fresh and honest qualities which
are the more delightful because you least expect to find
them, just there.

Doro [*surprised*]. Well, that was almost exactly what
I said! Almost exactly!

Delia [*with great emotion*]. Yes! Yes!

Doro. That was the way I explained certain incomprehensible acts of yours! . . .

Delia. Incomprehensible? Yes . . . caprices . . . im-
pulses of the moment . . . leaps into space with my eyes
closed! . . . [*She stands there for a moment, gazing
vacantly into void, as though fascinated by some distant
vision.*] Just imagine . . . [*And then she continues as
though speaking to herself.*] somersaults you might
call them . . . yes . . . somersaults . . . [*falling into*

her abstraction again]. There was a little girl, and the gypsies taught her to turn somersaults . . . handsprings . . . wheeling hand over hand on a green lawn near my house in the country when I was a child! . . . [*Still in her abstraction.*] Was I ever a child? [*A memory of the way her mother used to call her comes into her mind and she shouts:*] "Lilly dear! Lilly dear! Lilli! Lilli!" Hahah! Hahah! She was afraid of those gypsies, poor, dear mamma! She was afraid they would suddenly break camp and carry me off. [*Comes to herself again.*] The gypsies never carried me off. I learned to turn handsprings and somersaults all by myself after I had come away from the country here to town . . . here, where everything is false, fictitious . . . falser and more fictitious every day. And we can't shake it off; because when we try to get back to simplicity again . . . make ourselves true and honest again, our very honesty and our very simplicity seem false and counterfeit! It all seems that way because it is . . . because it is false and counterfeit! Haha! Truth? What is truth? . . . Nothing is true! I should like to see with my eyes, or hear with my ears, or feel with my fingers, one thing . . . just one thing . . . that is true . . . really true . . . in me!

Doro.   There is one thing in you that I imagine is true . . . the goodness and kindness that you have at bottom—a goodness and a kindness hidden from other people, and perhaps even from yourself—a goodness, at any rate, that I tried, in the quarrel yesterday, to make other people see.

Delia.   Yes! Yes! And I'm very grateful! Yes! Goodness . . . you call me "good"—but a goodness so complicated, so complex that when you tried to make people understand it, when you tried to make it look simple and clear, they grew angry at you and laughed at you. . . . But you have explained it, even to me. . . . Yes, people dislike me, just as you say. I was kept at a distance

by everybody—there, at Capri. I'm sure that some of
them thought I was a spy! But what a discovery I made
there, Doro. . . . Love for humanity! Do you know
what it means to love humanity? It means just this: when
you say you are in love with humanity, you are satisfied
with yourself! When a person is satisfied with himself
. . . happy with himself . . . he loves humanity! Full
of just such love, and happy . . . oh, so happy *he* must
have been when *he* came to Capri, after the last exhibi-
tion of his paintings at Naples!

Doro.   Giorgio Salvi, you mean?

Delia.   He had been working on some Neapolitan
studies, as he called them, and he found me when he was
in just that state of mind.

Doro.   There you are! Just as I said! All taken up
with his own art . . . and as for feelings! . . . no feelings for anything except for his art!

Delia.   Color . . . ah, color . . . everything was
color with him! Feeling with him was nothing but color!

Doro.   So he asked you to sit for a portrait? . . .

Delia.   In the beginning . . . yes! But later on . . .
he had a way of his own in asking for anything he wanted
—so funny—petulant, almost impudent—he was like a
spoiled child! So I became his model! . . . It was very,
very true what you said: nothing is more irritating than
to be held aloof, excluded from a joy which . . .

Doro.   . . . which is living, present, before us, around
us, and the reason for which we can neither discover nor
define! . . .

Delia.   Exactly! It was a joy . . . well, a pure joy,
but only for his *eyes* . . . and it proved to me that, after
all, at bottom he saw in me . . . he prized in me . . .
only my body! My body was the only thing he wanted
from me! Oh, don't misunderstand me! Not as other
men wanted me—out of a low desire—oh no!

Doro. But that, in the long run, could only have irritated you the more.

Delia. Precisely! Because if I was disgusted, nauseated, when other men failed to help me in my own spiritual uncertainties and troubles, my disgust at a man who also wanted my body and nothing else—but only to get from me a purely . . . a purely . . .

Doro. . . . ideal joy . . .

Delia. . . . and a joy exclusively his own . . .

Doro. . . . must have been all the stronger precisely because every tangible motive for anger was lacking . . .

Delia. . . . and it was impossible for me to have the satisfaction of that vengeance which at least I was able to inflict upon other men by suddenly giving myself to someone else! Oh, for a woman I assure you, an angel is always more irritating than a beast!

Doro [*triumphantly*]. Well! Well! Well! I used those very words! Absolutely! Those very words!

Delia. Yes, but you forget—I am only repeating them, after you, just as they were reported to me. You see, they suddenly made so many things clear to me!

Doro. Why, yes . . . revealing a real reason . . .

Delia. . . . for what I did! Yes . . . yes . . . it's true: to get my revenge on him, I tried to bring my body gradually to life before him so that it should no longer exist merely for the delight of his eyes . . .

Doro. . . . and later, when you saw that he had become your slave as so many others had been, then, to taste your vengeance to the full, you forbade him any other joy than the one with which, up to that time, he had been content . . .

Delia. Since that was all he had ever asked for . . . since that was the only one truly worthy of him! . . .

Doro. That's enough! I understand! I understand! In that way your vengeance was complete! You never

wanted him to marry you, did you? In fact, you were determined that he shouldn't?

DELIA. Yes! Yes! For a long time I struggled . . . I
did my best to dissuade him . . . But in the end, driven
to a fury, beside himself . . . exasperated beyond endur-
ance by my obstinate refusals, he threatened to do something rash . . . It was then that I decided to go away
. . . disappear forever!

Doro. And then it was that you imposed upon him
conditions which you knew would be terribly hard for
him! . . . You imposed them deliberately upon him! . . .

Delia. Deliberately . . . yes . . . on purpose!

Doro. The condition that he would introduce you
formally, as his fiancée, to his mother and to his sister! . . .

Delia. Yes . . . yes . . . because they were proud
and haughty women, of the most inaccessible aristocracy
—not my kind at all—and he was proud of their pride
and jealous of their high position. Yes, I did it deliberately, so that he would say no! Oh, how he used to talk of
his little sister! . . .

Doro. Exactly! Just as I contended, then! Tell me
the truth now . . . when Rocca, his sister's fiancé . . .

Delia [*horror-stricken*]. Oh, no, no! Don't speak of
him . . . don't speak of him, please!

Doro. But here we would have the real proof of the
position I maintained! You must tell me! You must tell
me that what I said is true!

Delia. Yes, I did go away with him! I did spend a
night with him . . . because I was desperate . . . desperate . . . unable to see any other means of escape!

Doro. Exactly! Exactly!

Delia. And under such circumstances that Giorgio
would be sure to find us together—yes—find me with
Rocca and thus refuse to go on with our marriage . . .
which would have been the ruin of him—utter unhappi-

ness—and the ruin of me also. I would have been wretched, too.

Doro [*triumphantly*]. Exactly! Absolutely what I said! So I defended you—and that fool there saying I was wrong—saying that your refusals of Giorgio . . . all your struggles, all your threats . . . your attempt to run away . . . were just part of a cheap game you were playing to lead him on.

Delia [*alarmed*]. He said that? . . .

Doro. Yes! Treachery premeditated . . . carefully thought out . . . aiming to reduce Salvi to utter despair, after you had made him fall in love with you, after you had led him on!

Delia [*alarmed*]. I . . . led him on . . . I?

Doro. Exactly! And the more desperate he got, the more you held out in order to gain many many things which he would never have granted you otherwise.

Delia [*more and more alarmed and gradually losing her confidence again*]. What things?

Doro. Well, first of all, an introduction to his mother and to his sister, and to the latter's fiancé, social recognition from the three of them!

Delia. Ah! And he didn't see that I hoped to find in Giorgio's refusal to give me those introductions a pretext for breaking off my engagement to him?

Doro. No . . . no! He claimed you had another scheme in that!

Delia [*in utter desperation*]. What scheme?

Doro. He said you wanted to parade your victory in public, before all society, by being seen in the presence of that little sister of his . . . you a model of the studios . . . you an actress . . . you, an adventuress! . . .

Delia [*stabbed to the heart*]. Oh, that is what he said? [*She stands there looking blankly into space, overwhelmed.*]

Doro. That is exactly what he said! And furthermore,

he said that when the introduction you had insisted upon was postponed from day to day, you discovered that the postponement was due to the flat refusal of Rocca, the sister's fiancé, to meet you!

Delia. And so to show my power over Rocca . . . to humiliate him . . . to get even with him! . . . That's the idea, isn't it?

Doro. Yes . . . you sank your claws into Rocca, twisting him around your finger like a blade of grass, quite forgetting Salvi, meantime—just for the pleasure of showing that sister of his and her mother, what the pride and respectability of the pillars of public morals amounted to! [*For a time* DELIA *stands in silence her eyes fixed apparently upon something in distant space. Finally* SHE *covers her face with both her hands and remains in that attitude for some seconds.* DORO *considers her, in perplexity and surprise. Then he asks:*] What's the matter? [DELIA *still keeps her hands to her face, but finally* SHE *lowers them and is again seen staring with the same blank expression into space. Then, opening her two arms in a gesture of discouragement.*]

Delia. And who knows! Who knows! Who knows that those weren't the reasons?

Doro [*startled*]. Weren't the reasons? . . . What do you mean? If they were . . . [*At this moment* DONNA LIVIA *appears in the brightly lighted drawing-room and comes forward on the stage in great agitation, calling, before* SHE *reaches the parlor:*]

Donna Livia. Doro! Doro!

Doro [*leaping to his feet in alarm at the sound of his mother's voice*]. My mother is coming!

Donna Livia [*rushing into the room*]. Doro! Is this true? I've been told that the trouble last evening is to result in a duel!

Doro. Duel? Who ever said such a thing?

Donna Livia [*noticing* DELIA *and turning disdainfully*

upon her].   Ah! Indeed! So I find this woman in my own house!

Doro [*firmly, and stressing the important words*].   Yes, in your house! In *your* house, mamma! You call it *your* house!

Delia.   Oh, but I'm going away . . . I'm going away! But don't be alarmed, Signora! There will be no duel . . . there will be no duel! I assure you, Signora! Don't worry on that account! I will prevent it . . . I will find a way to prevent it! . . . [*With a sob, she starts rapidly for the other room.*]

Doro [*following after her and calling*].   Signora, don't you dare! Please, Signora, don't try to interfere! [DELIA *goes out.*]

Donna Livia [*trying to stop* DORO *and almost in a scream*].   So it's true then?

Doro [*turning and answering vehemently*].   True? What is true? That I'm going to fight a duel? Perhaps! And why? For something that no one understands . . . neither he, nor I, nor the woman herself . . . ah . . . nor the woman herself! . . .

Curtain.

The curtain falls, but almost immediately rises again, uncovering a section of the theatre lobby opening on the orchestra. SPECTATORS, *one by one, are seen coming out of the main hall of the theatre, at the end of the first act. It may be taken for granted that other spectators are similarly entering the corridors that lie invisible to right and left. In fact, newcomers keep appearing from other parts of the lobby from time to time.*

This scene in the lobby—SPECTATORS *coming out of a theatre*—*will show what was first presented on the stage as life itself to be a fiction of art; and the substance of the comedy will accordingly be pushed back, as it were, into a secondary plane of actuality or reality. But later on, toward the end of this interlude, the scene in the lobby will, in its turn, be expelled from the foreground, when it transpires that the comedy which has been witnessed on the stage is a "comedy with a key"—a comedy, that is, based upon an episode in real life, an episode, moreover, with which the newspapers have been recently dealing as a feature: the famous triangular situation between a certain MORENO WOMAN (whom everybody recognizes in the DELIA MORELLO of the comedy): a certain BARON NUTI, and the sculptor, GIACOMO LA VELA (who has committed suicide). The MORENO WOMAN and BARON NUTI are present in the theatre among the spectators. Their appearance, therefore, suddenly and violently establishes a plane of reality still closer to real life, leaving the spec-tators who are discussing the fictitious reality of the staged play on a plane midway between. In the interlude at the end of the second act these three planes of reality will come into conflict with one another, as the partici-pants in the drama of real life attack the participants in the comedy, the SPECTATORS, meantime, trying to inter-fere. Under such circumstances it need not be observed, a comedy cannot go on.*

In the production of this first interlude the greatest naturalness, volubility, and vivacity are necessary. The presupposition is that at the end of every act of these unintelligible, implausible, paradoxical—and what not —comedies of PIRANDELLO, arguments and conflicts are bound to occur. The DEFENDERS OF PIRANDELLO should show toward his uncompromising antagonists a smiling humility of countenance which has the effect of exasper-ating hostilities rather than the contrary.

Various groups of people form in the lobby. Individ-uals may be seen going from one group to the other in quest of light. Comic effects should be derived from their changes of opinion according to the group they hit upon.

*A few placid individuals are smoking unconcernedly,
and the way they smoke will show their boredom, if they
are bored, or their doubts, if they are in doubt; because
smoking, like all vices that become habitual, has this sad
shortcoming: that it eventually fails to satisfy, by itself,
but takes its flavor from the moment in which it is indulged and from the state of mind in which it is indulged.
It follows that even people who dislike* PIRANDELLO's
*plays may console themselves with a good cigar, if they
choose, on occasion.*

*Conspicuous in the crowd in the lobby, the uniforms
of two* POLICEMEN *(carabinieri) may be seen. An* USHER
or two and a TICKET TAKER; *two or three* MAIDS *dressed
in black with white aprons. A* NEWSBOY *intrudes from the
street, calling his headlines. In the groups, arguing and
gesticulating here and there, a few women may be observed. Some of them also are smoking (but not with the
author's approval); others may be seen going in and out
of the doors to the boxes, where they are visiting friends.*

The FIVE DRAMATIC CRITICS *are naturally much in evidence.* THEY *keep away from each other at first, and if
anyone questions them they maintain a stolid silence
(they have to, you see, to live up to a reputation for
"reserve" and "balance"). Gradually, however, they drift
together to get a line on each other's "dope." Individuals
who recognize them edge up as close as possible (without
impoliteness) to hear what these celebrities are saying.
The interest these people manifest gradually attracts a
crowd, whereupon the* CRITICS *either crawl into their
shells or walk away. It is quite possible that here in the
lobby some of the* CRITICS *will say very sharp things about
the comedy and its author; though they will have only
praise for both in the articles they write for their papers
the next day. A profession is one thing, while the man
who professes it is quite another: a critic may have plenty
of reasons for sacrificing as a writer his sincerity as a man*

—granted, of course, that such sacrifice be possible, granted, I mean to say, that he have some sincerity to sacrifice. So with the spectators. Many of those who here appear as bitter critics of the play clapped it uproariously in the theatre at the end of the first act.

It is hardly worth while writing out the dialogue of this choral interlude. People say much the same things and express much the same judgments about all plays and all authors—which, and who, are "good," "bad," "well constructed," "badly constructed," "obscure," "absurd," "improbable," "paradoxical," "cerebral—all from the brain," and so on. Nevertheless, we must here note down such exchanges as are indispensable between the actors who are actors for the moment in this interlude; though the stage manager is intentionally left a free hand to introduce anything he can devise to keep the lobby in a state of lively and confused animation.

At first: monosyllables, exclamations, grunts, brief questions and answers, from phlegmatic SPECTATORS *who make for the lobby at the earliest possible moment (those really interested in the play are still inside witnessing or fomenting the uproar following on the first act).*

Two People [*coming out in a hurry*].   I'll just go upstairs and look for him.

Number eight, second row, balcony. But be sure you find him, eh?

Don't worry, I'll get him all right. [*The* SECOND *starts away to the left.*]

A Man [*meeting him*].   Hello! So you managed to get in?

The Second of the First Two.   As you see. However, I'll be back in a moment. I'm just going upstairs. [*Other* SPECTATORS *come on from the left where a great deal of talking can be heard.* OTHERS *are appearing through the main and side entrances.*]

Somebody [*anybody*].   Good house tonight!
Another.   Full up!
A Third.   See them anywhere?
A Fourth.   I don't think they got past the box-office;
but they were beauts!

[*In the general confusion exchanges of greetings:
"Good evening!" "Good evening!"—Smatterings of light
talk; one word comments on the play: "Some show!"
"Bunk!" etc., etc. A few introductions. A* NEWSBOY *enters
from the street calling his papers. A* MAN *buys one. An
eruption from the theatre—a number of* SPECTATORS *favorable to the author. Enthusiastic, eager, eyes gleaming,*
THEY *crowd together in a group and begin exchanging
first impressions. Later* THEY *scatter in various directions,
approaching this or that hostile circle, defending their
author and his comedy now good-humoredly, now bad-
humoredly, now with irony. Their* ADVERSARIES *have also
been organizing, meantime.*]

Friends of Pirandello.
  Here we are! Here! This way!
  I'll be right there!
  All together now, if there's trouble!
  A great success, it seems to me!
  Splendid! Splendid!
  Seems to have gotten away with it!
  That last scene with the woman . . . !
  Real acting, I say!
  Those fellows both changed their minds!
  The whole act's a ripper!
Opponents.
  His usual line of nonsense!
  What does he think we are, fools?
  Pirandello's in the same old rut!
  You can't make head or tail to the thing!

What's it all mean?

That bird's getting away with murder!

Two dollars, to listen to that stuff!

[*One of the* ADVERSARIES, *calling to the group of* PIRANDELLO'S FRIENDS.] But you fellows, you understand it all, eh?

Another of the Adversaries. Of course they do. They're a bunch of wise ones, all right!

One of Pirandello's Friends [*approaching*]. You said that for my benefit?

The First of the Two Adversaries. No, I didn't mean you—I meant him. [*And he points to another man.*]

The Latter [*advancing*]. You meant that for me?

Adversary. Yes, I meant it for you! I meant it for you! You wouldn't understand "Punch and Judy" if you had it explained to you!

The Man in Question. Yes, but *you* understand, don't you! At least, you understand enough to say it's bunk, don't you?

Voices from Neighboring Groups.

But what is there to understand, anyhow?

Didn't you hear . . . ?

Nobody knows what it's all about!

First it's this, and then it's something else!

First they said one thing, but now they say the opposite!

It's a joke on the audience!

What are those people staring at?

That poor mother dying, eh? . . .

. . . And that carriage on the country road! . . .

And it never gets anywhere! Some flivver!

A Man [*going from one group to another*]. So it's a joke on the audience! A joke on the audience! What's it all mean? No one knows what it means! No one can make head or tail to it!

Another Group [*coming into the foreground*].

But it certainly makes you think, eh?

But why is he always harping on this illusion and reality string?

That's not my view of it!

It's just a way of saying things!

Hasn't he expressed it?

Well, expression is art, and art is expression!

But damned if I can see what he's expressed!

But I saw you clapping . . . yes, you did . . . yes, you did . . . I saw you . . . I saw you! . . .

But a single conception may present different phases, according as you look at it, providing it be a whole conception of life.

Conception be damned! Can you tell me what the conception in this first act is?

Yes, but supposing it didn't pretend to have any meaning! . . .

The Same Man [*going to another group*]. Yes! Exactly! I see! It isn't supposed to have any meaning! Clever, eh? Clever!

A Third Group [*gathering around the critics*]. Nonsense! Just plain damn nonsense! But you critics—you understand the dra-ama! Pray enlighten us. What's it all mean?

First Critic. The construction . . . not bad . . . not bad. Of course one or two places could be left out . . .

One of the Spectators. What was the point in all that high-brow stuff about conscience?

A Second Critic. But gentlemen, gentlemen, you have seen only the first act! . . .

Third Critic. But, honest now . . . is it permissible, I ask you, to play with character that way? There ought to be a law against it . . . and an act without either head or tail? Here we have a drama based, almost casually, you might say, on a discussion that is not even held on the stage! . . .

Fourth Critic.   But the discussion is about the play itself. It is the play itself!

Second Critic.   And the play gets going at last when the woman comes on!

Third Critic.   But why not give us the play then, and have done with it?

A Friend of Pirandello.   But that woman is well conceived!

One of the Adversaries.   It isn't so much the character, though. It's the girl who takes the part. [*He will name the actress doing* DELIA MORELLO.]

The Man [*leaving this group and going back to the first one*]. The drama gets going finally, when the woman comes on! She is well conceived, there's no denying that! Everybody is saying so!

A Man in the First Group [*answering angrily*]. Oh, give us a rest! This play is just one jumble of words!

Another Man [*vehemently*]. He took the plot out of the newspapers! Sheer impudence!

Third [*just as vehemently*]. One trick after another! Just word play! All on the surface!

The Man [*going from the first to the second group*]. Yes, he got the plot from the newspapers! There's no denying it! Everybody says so!

Fourth Critic [*speaking to the third*]. But what characters, in the name of heaven! Where do you find people like that in life?

Third Critic.   That's a great idea! People can talk, can't they, and the moment they talk . . . !

Fourth Critic.   Talk? Exactly! Talk! And you can do what you want when you're playing with words!

Fifth Critic.   But I ask you now, if the theatre is art! . . .

One of the Adversaries.   Art . . . exactly . . . poetry . . . poetry!

Fifth Critic.   But why not controversy? Admirable,

that, I grant you. Conflict . . . the shock of opposite opinions . . . just that!

One of the Friends of Pirandello. But you people are making the controversy, it seems to me. I didn't notice so much of it on the stage!

One of the Adversaries. Yes . . . here we have a great author, haven't we? At least you say so!

The Old Author [*who never had a play produced*]. So far as I am concerned, if you like this play, you're welcome! What I think—you know already!

Voices. No! Tell us! Tell us! What do you think? Let's have it!

Old Author. Oh, little tricks of the mind . . . intellectual altogether, gentlemen . . . little problems . . . what shall I say—little problems of philosophy, as philosophy is studied by men who are not philosophers! . . .

Fourth Critic. I don't agree! I don't agree!

Old Author [*raising his voice*]. But no great travail of the spirit, as we say! Nothing really straightforward and convincing.

Fourth Critic. Yes, we all know what you call straightforward and convincing! . . .

A Literary Man [*who never writes*]. If you ask me, the most objectionable thing about the play is . . . well . . . it's the disagreeableness of the situation itself!

Second Critic. Why, no! This time it seems to me we have an atmosphere much more wholesome than usual.

Literary Man. But no real artistic urge! Why anybody could write like that!

Fourth Critic. For my part, not having seen the whole play as yet, I shouldn't risk a final judgment; but I think there is going to be something to it. It's as though you were looking into a looking-glass that had gone crazy somehow and . . .

[*On the left at this moment a violent clamor is heard.*

Screams. Shouts.] "Lunatic! Fraud! Fraud! Lunatic! Call the ambulance!" [PEOPLE *all look in that direction.*] What's going on in there?

The Bad-Humored Spectator. Can't a fellow ever come to see a play of this fellow Pirandello without getting mixed up in a scrap?

Good-Humored Spectator. Let's hope there'll be no heads broken.

One of the Friends of Pirandello. If you want to sleep, why don't you stick to the other plays? With them you can just lean back in your seat and take what is sent you across the footlights. But with a comedy of Pirandello's you have to be on your pins. You sit up straight and dig your finger nails into the arms of your chair as though you were going to be knocked down by what the author has to say! You hear a word . . . any word at all . . . "chair" for instance! Now with most people that would mean "chair," but with Pirandello you say "A chair? . . . No sir! He isn't going to get away with that! I'm going to find out what's under the chair!"

One of the Adversaries. Yes, yes! That's right! Pirandello gives you everything except a little sentiment! But not a bit of sentiment!

Other Adversaries. That's it! That's it! Not a bit of sentiment . . . and you've got to have sentiment!

One of Pirandello's Friends. If you want sentiment go and find it under the chair that fellow is talking about.

The Adversaries. But let us have done with these spasms, this nihilism . . . this delight he takes in denying everything! We're tired of tearing down. Let us begin to build up!

First of Pirandello's Friends [*vehemently*]. Who is tearing anything down? You people are the Bolshevists!

One of the Adversaries [*storming back at him*]. We, tearing down? We never denied that reality exists!

First of Pirandello's Friends. But who denies your reality, if you never succeeded in creating one?

A Second Friend. You deny the truth as other people see it, you claim that there is only one way of looking at things.

First Friend. The way you look at them yourself, to-day!

Second Friend. Forgetting how you looked at them yesterday!

First Friend. Because you . . . you people get your reality from others—it's a convention . . . a mere convention . . . an empty word . . . any word at all: mountain, tree, stream. You think that reality is something fixed, something definite, and you feel as though you were being cheated if someone comes along and shows you that it was all an illusion on your part. Idiots! This comedy tells you that everyone must build a foundation for himself under his own feet, bit by bit, step by step, if he is to advance. You must kick aside a reality that does not belong to you, for the simple reason that you have not made it for yourselves, but are using it as parasites—yes, gentlemen, as parasites—mourning that old-fashioned sentimentality of yours that we've driven from the stage at last, thank God!

Baron Nuti [*pale, disheveled, in a rage, comes in from the left accompanied by two other* SPECTATORS *who are trying to restrain him*]. And something else, it seems to me, this comedy teaches, my dear sir! It teaches you to malign the dead and to slander the living!

One of the Men with Him [*seizing him by an arm and trying to drag him away*]. But please . . . no . . . please . . . come away . . . come away!

The Other Man with Him [*talking at the same time*]. Yes . . . hush . . . hush! Come . . . come . . . please come! Come!

Baron Nuti [*as he is being dragged off to the left, turns and shouts back*]. To malign the dead and to slander the living!

Voices [*amid general surprise*].

What's the matter? Who's that man?

Who's that man?

What a face!

Has he gone crazy?

What's the matter?

Who is he?

Spectator from the Social Set. It's Baron Nuti.

Voices.

Baron Nuti? Who is Baron Nuti?

Why did he say what he said?

Spectator from the Social Set. But don't you people understand that there is a key to this comedy?

One of the Critics. A key? What do you mean . . . a key?

Spectator from the Social Set. Why yes! This comedy is based on the Moreno affair! Almost word for word! The author has taken it from real life!

Voices.

The Moreno case?

The Moreno woman?

Who is she?

Who is she?

Why, she's that actress that was in Germany for so long!

She's well known in Turin!

Ah, yes, she was mixed up in the suicide of that sculptor named La Vela some months ago!

What do you think of that?

And Pirandello . . . is Pirandello getting so low that he makes comedies on society gossip?

Looks that way . . . looks that way!

And it's not the first time, you know!

But there's nothing wrong in making comedy out of the day's gossip, is there?

No, unless, as that man just said, you use your comedy to malign the dead and slander the living.

But Nuti . . . who is Nuti?

Spectator from the Social Set. He is the other fellow in the triangle! La Vela killed himself on Nuti's account! Nuti was to marry La Vela's sister!

One of the Critics. And he spent the night with the Moreno woman—the night before her marriage to La Vela?

Voices from the Hostile Group. The same situation to a T! It's a crime . . . a downright crime!

Other Voices from the Same Group. And the actors in the real drama have been here in the theatre?

A Third [*calling attention to* NUTI *off the stage, to the left*]. There he is . . . there he is!

Spectator from the Social Set. The Moreno woman has a seat in a box upstairs. She recognized herself immediately in the comedy. They'd better watch out for her! She's a terror when she gets started! She bit her handkerchief to shreds during the first act! She'll be making a noise, you'll see! She'll turn the place upside down!

Voices.

Serve them right if she did!

The idea of putting a woman in a pillory like that!

Her own case right before her eyes on the stage, and that Nuti fellow, too!

He had murder in his eye!

There's going to be trouble here . . . there's going to be trouble!

[*A bell rings, announcing the beginning of the second act.*]

There's the bell . . . there's the bell!

The curtain's going up!

Let's hurry! We mustn't miss anything!

[*There is a general movement toward the entrances to
the theatre proper. Exclamations, comments, murmur-
ings continue as the news spreads. Three individuals
from the group favorable to* PIRANDELLO *bring up the
rear, so that they are present on the stage—that is to say,
in the theatre lobby, now virtually cleared of people—
when the* MORENO WOMAN *appears from the left. She has
come tearing down from her box upstairs despite the efforts of* THREE MALE FRIENDS *who are trying to get her
out of the theatre to prevent trouble. The* TICKET TAKERS
*at the theatre doors are at first caught by surprise; but
then they do their best to quiet the disturbance so that
th' play inside will not be interrupted. The three partisans of* PIRANDELLO *stand aside listening in amazement
and consternation.*]

Signora Moreno. No . . . no! I will! I will! Let me
alone . . . let me alone!

One of Her Friends. But it's madness . . . it's sheer
madness! What can you do about it?

Signora Moreno. I am going behind the scenes!

A Second of Her Friends. What can you do in there?
Have you lost your mind?

Signora Moreno. Let me alone! Let me alone!

The Third of Her Friends. Now I'll just take you to
my car.

Other Two [*in chorus*]. Yes, yes, let's all go home!
Please, now, come along with us!

Signora Moreno. I won't! I won't! Let go of me! Let
go of me! It's a disgrace! It's an insult! And they won't
get away with it scot free!

The First Friend. But what's the idea? What's the
idea? . . . On the stage . . . in front of everybody there?

Signora Moreno. Let go of me, I tell you! Let go of
me! Yes, there on the stage, in front of everybody!

Second Friend. Ah, no, not a bit of it! Not a bit of it! We won't let you make a show of yourself like that!

Signora Moreno. Let go of me, won't you? I'm going in there behind the scenes. . . .

Third Friend. But the actors are out on the stage again!

First Friend. The second act has begun!

Signora Moreno [*suddenly growing calmer*]. Ah, they have begun again? I must hear what they have to say! I'm going back! [*She starts off toward the left again.*]

Her Friends [*all together*]. No! No! Please, let's go away! Do as we say! Please! Please! Let's go home!

Signora Moreno [*virtually dragging them after her*]. No! I'm going back in again! I want to see the rest of it! I will! I will!

One of the Friends [*as they withdraw to the left*]. But why torment yourself any further?

One of the Ticket Takers [*addressing the three partisans of* PIRANDELLO]. What's the matter with those people? Gone nutty? . . .

The First of the Partisans [*to the other two*]. Did you understand? Did you understand?

The Second. It's the Moreno woman!

The Third. But say, is Pirandello in the theatre?

The First. He may be. I think I'll just step inside and advise him to run, while the running is good. This evening there's going to be a rumpus, and no mistake.

Curtain.

ACT II

The house of FRANCESCO SAVIO *the morning after.*
A sort of lounge opening on a wide veranda, where SAVIO *habitually practices fencing. On the veranda, ac-*

cordingly, as we view it through the large windows which occupy almost all the rear wall of the room, there are one or two stools, a long bench for spectators, fencing masks and gloves, chest protectors, sabres, rapiers. A green cloth curtain hangs on the inside of the window and may be run back and forth on rings so as to cut off the view of the veranda and give a little privacy to the room. A similar curtain, stretched between the posts on the veranda, is already drawn, cutting off the veranda from the garden which is supposed to lie beyond, and of which a glimpse will be had at certain moments as some of the characters draw the curtain aside to go down the steps into the garden.

The room is furnished with green wicker furniture— two chairs, a table, a stand, two divans. There must be a door to the right, in addition to one opening upon the veranda, and a small window to the left.

As the curtain rises, FRANCESCO SAVIO *and the* FENCING MASTER, *with masks, protectors, and gloves on, are fencing on the veranda.* PRESTINO *and two other* FRIENDS *stand looking on.*

The Fencing Master. Eh-eh-eh! Look out! Look out! [*He lunges and* FRANCESCO *parries.*] Good! No . . . let's try that again! Eh-eh-eh-eh! [*They cross their rapiers, the fencing master lunges, and* FRANCESCO *parries as before.*] Well done! Well done! Now look out . . . look out! In position! Now attack . . . now attack! That feint is no good! That feint is no good! It leaves you open over here! This way . . . see? There you are! All right! Alt! [*THEY lower their rapiers. The practice bout is over.*] Keep at it that way and you'll come through all right! [*THEY take off their masks.*]

Francesco. Yes! I'm sure I will! But I think I have had enough! Thanks, maestro! [*He shakes hands with the fencing master.*]

Prestino. Yes, better not keep it up too long!

Fencing Master [*taking off his glove and then the protector*]. But I'll tell you one thing . . . you're not going to find Palegari easy! He's a tough customer when he attacks!

One of the Two Friends. And he parries splendidly! Don't give him a chance at you!

The Second. He's as quick as a flash!

Francesco. Yes, I knew that. [*Taking off his glove and protector.*]

The First of His Friends. You keep your eye peeled to the right!

Fencing Master. The main point is to keep your iron on his.

Francesco. I understand . . . I understand!

The Second Friend. The straight lunge works best against Doro.

First Friend. Not a bit of it! You just meet his rush . . . just meet his rush! You take it from me . . . let him alone and he'll beat himself! Keep a stiff arm and he'll spit himself on your weapon!

Fencing Master. Meantime, I must congratulate you . . . you have an air-tight defense!

Prestino. Follow my advice and don't do any attacking! Keep him coming on and you'll get a chance at him sooner or later! Meantime I propose a round of drinks to your good luck! [*He comes forward into the room with the others.*]

Francesco. Yes, yes, right you are! [*He pushes a button in the wall; then turning to the* FENCING MASTER]: And you, maestro, what'll you have?

The Fencing Master. Nothing for me—I never drink in the forenoon.

Francesco. I have some first rate beer.

Prestino. That's the talk! A mug of beer!

First of the Two Friends. Same here! [*The* BUTLER *appears from the door to the right.*]

Francesco. Bring in four or five bottles of beer right away. [*The* BUTLER *goes out, returning almost immediately, however, with bottles and glasses on a tray. He pours the beer, passes it around and withdraws again.*]

First Friend. This will be the craziest duel on record. Your name will go down in history, Francesco.

Second Friend. It certainly will. I doubt whether two men ever cut themselves up before, each for the privilege of saying that the other one was right.

Prestino. But it's all very natural, however.

First Friend. Natural? What is there natural about it?

Prestino. Why, here the two of them were on opposite sides of the same question. They both changed their minds at the same time, each coming around to the view of the other. Naturally, they collided in the process.

Fencing Master. Of course, if while the one who was first attacking has now passed to the defense and fights just as fiercely as before, each of them, meantime, using the arguments of the other . . .

First Friend. Are you sure of that?

Francesco. I assure you I went to his house with the most sincere and cordial intentions.

First Friend. And not because you felt—

Francesco. No, there is no question of pride at all!

First Friend. That isn't what I was going to say. It's not because you felt you had gone a bit too far in publicly assailing the Morello woman so bitterly?

Francesco. Not at all . . . not at all! Why . . . I . . .

First Friend. Wait! Let me finish. I was going to say: without taking account of a fact that was perfectly obvious to everybody that evening?

Second Friend. That he was defending the woman because he was in love with her?

Francesco. Not at all . . . not at all! It was because I had not been thinking of any of those things that all the trouble has arisen. We must look like two blamed fools! This is what I get for letting myself go, for being quite spontaneous and frank for once in my life! What a nuisance! I had planned on a quiet little visit to my sister and her husband in the country day after tomorrow.

Prestino. Nevertheless, you had had a rather heated argument the evening before.

Francesco. But—as I tell you again—without thinking of anything but the merits of the case, and without dreaming that he had any secret passion for the woman!

Second Friend. But are you sure he has?

First Friend. Certainly he has!

Prestino. He must have . . . certainly!

Francesco. If I had even remotely suspected such a thing I would not have gone to his house to admit that he was right, certain as I could be that that would make him furious!

The Second Friend [*violently*]. I wanted to say this . . . [*He breaks off short and* THEY *all turn to look at him in surprise.*]

First Friend [*after waiting a second*]. You wanted to say what?

Second Friend. I wanted to say . . . oh, I have forgotten what. [*At this moment* DIEGO CINCI *appears in the doorway to the right.*]

Diego. Am I intruding?

Francesco [*in surprise*]. Oh, Diego, you here?

Prestino. Has someone sent you?

Diego [*shrugging his shoulders*]. Why should anyone have sent me? Good day, maestro!

Fencing Master. Good day, Cinci! But I must be going. [*Shakes hands with* Savio *warmly.*] See you tomorrow, Savio . . . and don't stay awake, worrying!

Francesco. Never was cooler in my life, don't fear! Thank you, maestro!

Fencing Master [*bowing to the others*]. Gentlemen, I am sorry I can't stay in your good company, but I have an important engagement. [*The* Others *bow to him.*]

Francesco. Look, maestro, if you prefer, you can go out this way. [*He points toward the veranda.*] Just draw the curtain aside and you'll see the stairs. The garden opens on the street.

Fencing Master. Ah, that's a good idea. I'll do that. Once more . . . good morning! [*He withdraws.*]

First Friend [*to* Diego]. We were expecting you to be one of Doro Palegari's seconds.

Diego [*shaking his finger in silent negation*]. No, I couldn't, you see, I was caught between two fires last evening. Good friends of them both! . . . I had to keep out of it.

The Second Friend. But why have you come here now, then?

Diego. To say that I am delighted that there is going to be a duel! Delighted! Delighted! [*The* Others *laugh.*] And I hope that both get hurt! Not mortally, of course . . . not mortally! A little blood-letting would do them both good! A cut, besides, is something you can see and be sure about! A cut two . . . three . . . five inches long! [*He takes* Francesco *by the forearm and looks under the sleeve of his coat.*] Let me look at your wrist! All sound! Well, tomorrow morning you're going to have a cut from here to here. It will be something you can look at!

Francesco. A fine consolation! [*The* Others *laugh again.*]

Diego [*speaking up quickly*]. But Doro will get his too, let us hope! Doro, too! Let's be quite impartial! I

have a surprise for you! You know who came to Palegari's shortly after you went away and I followed you?

Prestino. Delia Morello!

The Second Friend. I suppose she went to thank him
for standing up for her!

Diego. Yes, except that when she found out just why
you accused her . . . well . . . you know what she did?

Francesco. What did she do?

Diego. She admitted that you were right!

Francesco, Prestino, and the First Friend [*all together*].
She did? Really? That's a great idea! And Doro . . .
how about him?

Diego. You can imagine how he took it!

Second Friend. He can't have the least idea now why
he is going to fight.

Francesco. No, he knows the reason for that! He's
going to fight because he insulted me in your presence
while I, as I was saying here to my two friends and as
you know yourself, had simply gone to him to admit that
he was right!

Diego. Now . . .

Francesco. Now what?

Diego. Now that you know that Delia Morello says
that you were right . . .

Francesco. Oh, well, if she herself—

Diego. No, my dear boy, no; Hold your ground . . .
hold your ground . . . because now Delia Morello is in
greater need of a defender than ever, and the job falls to
you! You were the first to accuse her!

Prestino. Let's get this straight! Francesco must defend her against herself, now that she's accused herself
before the man who at first tried to defend her!

Diego. Exactly! Exactly! And my admiration for her
has increased one hundredfold since I found that out!
[*Turns suddenly on* FRANCESCO.] You—who are you?
[*Then turning to* PRESTINO.] Who are you? Who am I?

Who are we all? Your name is Francesco Savio; mine is
Diego Cinci; yours is Prestino. We have of each other re-
ciprocally, and each has of himself, knowledge of some
small, insignificant certainty of today, which is not the
certainty it was yesterday and will not be the certainty
of tomorrow. Francesco, you are living on your income
and you are bored!

Francesco. No . . . who told you that?

Diego. You are not bored? Lucky man! I have worn
my soul out digging, digging tunnels—to China! [*To*
Prestino.] What do you do?

Prestino. Nothing!

Diego. A fine profession! But even people who work,
my dear friends—decent, respectable people like me—we
are all, all alike! This life that is in us and around us—
well examine it as closely as you wish. It is such a continuous, changing thing that if our deepest affections
cannot endure against it, imagine what the case with the
ideas, the opinions, the judgments which we succeed in
forming for ourselves, must be! All our ideas, in short,
change in the restless turmoil we call life. We think we
catch a glimpse of a situation! But let us just discover
something contrary to what we thought! So-and-so was a
white man, eh? Well, at once he's a black man! Our impressions of things change from hour to hour! A word
is often sufficient or even just the manner in which it is
said—to change our minds completely! And then besides,
quite without our knowledge, images of hundreds and
hundreds of things are flitting through our minds, suddenly causing our tempers to vary in the strangest way!
Here along a road darkening with the approach of evening we are walking, sad, gloomy, despondent. We raise
our eyes and we see a cottage still blazing under the setting sun. . . . Or we see a red geranium burning in a
stray burst of sunlight. . . . And we change . . . we

change . . . we brighten! A wave of tenderness sweeps over us!

Prestino.   And where does all that get us?

Diego.   Nowhere! Where are we trying to get, for that matter? I was telling you how things are . . . everything vague, indefinite, changing, insubstantial! Finally, to get hold of something solid, to feel the firm ground under your feet, you drop back into the weariness and affliction of your little certainty of today! . . . of that little which you succeed in knowing about yourself . . . your name, let us say . . . how much money you have in your pocket . . . the number of the house on the street where you live . . . your habits . . . your feelings . . . all these things which are customary, established, fixed, in your existence . . . that poor body of yours, for example, which still moves and can follow the flux of life, until its movements, which grow less and less vigorous every-day and less and less supple the older you get, finally cease altogether and—good night!

Francesco.   But you were talking of Delia Morello!

Diego.   Ah, yes! I was trying to make you understand my great admiration for her; or rather I was trying to make you feel what a joy it is, what a wonderful—though terrible—joy it is, when, caught by the tide of life in one of its moments of tempest, we are able actually to witness the collapse of all those fictitious forms around which our stupid daily life has solidified; and under the dikes, beyond the seawalls, which we had thrown up to isolate, to create, a definite consciousness for ourselves at all hazards, to build a personality of some kind, we are able to see that bit of tide—which was not wholly unknown to us and which seemed something tangible to us because we had carefully harnessed it to serve our feelings, draining it off into the duties which we had assumed, into the habits which we had created—suddenly break forth in a magnificent, overwhelming flood and turns everything topsy-turvy! Ah, at last!—A whirlwind! A volcanic eruption! An earthquake! A cataclysm!

Everybody [*in chorus*]. You like that, eh? No, thank you! None of those things for me! The Lord deliver us!

Diego. But, my dear friends, after we have witnessed the farce of our own absurd changes of opinion, we have before us the tragedy of a bewildered spirit, gone astray and unable to find its way again. And it's not only Delia Morello! Wait, Francesco, you'll see! Soon you'll have them both on your hands! Both here and the other fellow!

Francesco. The other fellow? What other fellow? Michele Rocca?

Diego. Yes, Michele Rocca, himself!

First Friend. He came in last evening from Naples.

Second Friend. Ah, I have it! That was what I was trying to tell you fellows some time ago. I learned that he was looking for Palegari . . . to slap his face!

Prestino. Yes, but we knew all that! [*To* Francesco.] I told you so, didn't I?

Francesco [*to* Diego]. But why should he come here to see me just now?

Diego. Because he insists on fighting a duel with Doro Palegari before you do! But now it would seem that he ought to have the duel with you!

Francesco. What do you mean . . . with me?

The Others [*all together*]. Why with Francesco? Why with Savio?

Diego. With you, of course! You have changed your mind, haven't you, honestly, sincerely? And thereby you assume responsibility for everything said by Palegari against him . . . at the Avanzi's the other night! What could be clearer? You have inverted your respective positions! It is obvious then! Rocca ought to make his fight with you!

Francesco. Not so fast, not so fast! What in the deuce are you talking about?

Diego. Excuse me . . . you are fighting this duel with Doro simply because he insulted you, are you not? Well, why did Doro insult you?

Francesco [*in some irritation*]. Why, of course, of course . . . because I . . .

Diego [*speaking up quickly and carrying on the thought*]. . . . because you, *loyally, sincerely* . . .

The Two Friends [*without letting him finish*]. Yes, yes, he's right! Diego is right!

Diego. So the rôles have been inverted! You are left to defend Delia Morello, putting all the blame on Michele Rocca!

Prestino [*shocked*]. Oh, let's quit joking!

Diego. Joking? [*To* FRANCESCO.] Oh, if you ask me . . . you can boast this time of being right!

Francesco. So you want me to have a duel with Michele Rocca, too?

Diego. Ah, I couldn't say that! A duel with a man in his frame of mind would be a very serious matter! The poor fellow is desperate!

The First Friend. I should say so! With Salvi's corpse lying between him and the girl he was going to marry.

Second Friend. The marriage broken off! . . .

Diego. And Delia Morello making a fool of him!

Francesco [*with a rising irritation*]. What do you mean . . . a fool of him? You are saying she made a fool of him, now!

Diego. That she did use him for her own purposes, no one can deny!

Francesco. Treacherously, therefore, as I claimed at first!

Diego [*trying to stop him with a reproof*]. Ah-ah-ah-ah, ah-ah-ah! There you go! Listen! The annoyance you

now feel for having gotten into this mess ought not make
you change your mind for still a third time!

Francesco.   Not at all! Not at all! Excuse me . . . you
said yourself that she went and confessed to Doro Palegari
that I was right in accusing her of treachery!

Diego.   You see? You see?

Francesco.   But what do I see, damn it all? If I discover that she is now accusing herself and saying that I
was right, why—of course—I change my mind and go
back to my first position! [*Turning to the others.*] Don't
you think I have a right to, you people?

Diego [*vehemently*].   But I tell you that she used him
treacherously . . . yes . . . if you insist on that word
. . . but only in order to free Giorgio Salvi from the
danger he was running in marrying her! Understand?
You have absolutely no right to claim that that was
treachery toward Salvi. On the contrary, I am ready to
defend her myself, even if she herself be her own accuser
. . . I'll defend her even against herself. . . .

Francesco [*giving ground with some irritation*]. . . .
In view of the reasons . . . yes . . . of the reasons advanced by Doro Palegari . . .

Diego.   . . . on account of which you . . .

Francesco.   . . . yes, . . . changed my mind . . .
changed my mind . . . exactly. . . . But the fact remains that as regards Rocca she was really treacherous
all the time.

Diego.   Treacherous? She was just a woman! Why not
stop at that? He approached her with the idea of having
his fun with her, giving her that impression also, so that
she in her turn made a fool of him. That really is what's
the matter with Michele Rocca! He is stung in his pride
as a man and as a male! He is not yet ready to admit that
he was just a helpless, stupid thing in the hands of a
woman, a doll which Delia Morello tossed aside and
broke to pieces after amusing herself in making it open

and close its arms in prayer—just by pressing the spring
of passion which that doll had in its insides somewhere!
Huh! The doll has been picked up again and set in place,
the wax nose of its wax face broken, the wax fingers on
its wax hands gone—cracks in its wax head and in its wax
body, and the spring—the spring of passion that it had in
its gizzard—has broken through the cloth covering and
is sticking out! But yet . . . no . . . the doll will not
have it that way! The doll keeps crying at the top of its
voice that it's not true; that that woman didn't make it
say its prayers; that that woman did not use it as a play-
thing, breaking it to pieces when the game was done! No
. . . no . . . it cries! Well, I ask you, did you ever see a
more absurd spectacle than that?

Prestino [*losing control of himself and almost shaking
his fist in* Diego's *face*].   Why are you trying to make us
laugh at such a serious matter, you clown?

Diego [*looking at* Prestino *in amazement, as the*
Others *do also*].   I?

Prestino.   You! Yes, you! Ever since you've been in
here, you've been playing the clown, trying to make a
fool of him, of me, of us, of everybody!

Diego.   But also of myself, don't you think?

Prestino.   Keep your compliments for yourself! It's
easy to laugh the way you do, making us all out so many
cocks on a weather vane which turns this way or that.
according as the wind blows! I'm tired of this nonsense!
How shall I describe it? When you talk that way you
seem to put poison in my soul!

Diego.   Not at all, my dear boy! I laugh because I
have reasoned my heart dry!

Prestino.   You said as much yourself . . . there is
nothing in your heart! It is empty, cold. dead . . . that
is why you laugh!

Diego.   That is why you *think* I laugh!

Prestino.   I think so because it's so! Even if it were

true that people are as you say we are, I should think
you would feel more like pitying us than laughing at us.

Diego [*offended in his turn, advancing toward* PRE-
STINO *aggressively, placing his two hands on the latter's
two shoulders, and bringing his face up close, looking the
man fixedly in the eye*]. Pity? Yes . . . if you let yourself be examined this way . . .

Prestino [*puzzled*]. What way?

Diego. This way . . . in the eye . . . just like this!
No . . . look at me! This way . . . naked as you are
. . . with all the filth and muck and smallness there is
in you! In you as in me . . . in me as in you—all the
fears—all the self-reproaches—all the hesitations and contradictions! Shake yourself free from the manikin you
create out of a false interpretation of what you do and
what you feel, and you'll at once see that the manikin
you make yourself is nothing at all like what you really
are or what you can really be! Nothing at all like what
is in you without your knowing that it is there—a terrible
avenger if you resist it; though it at once becomes chari-
table toward all your shortcomings if you just give in
and do not try to justify and delude yourself! Oh, I
know . . . to cast aside that manikin, that fiction, seems
in a certain way to be a denial of one's self, something
unworthy of a man; and it will always be that way so long
as we believe that humanness consists in what we call
conscience, in that courage, if you wish, which we have
shown on one single occasion rather than in the cowardice which on many occasions has counselled prudence.
You have agreed to act as Savio's second in this stupid
duel of Palegari's. [*Talking to* SAVIO.] And you thought
that Palegari kept calling you a clown yesterday? Huh!
He was calling names at that manikin which he could not
see in himself, but which he could see in you because you
showed it to him as in a mirror! I laugh . . . yes . . . I

laugh in my own way, and my ridicule falls upon myself sooner than on anyone else!

[*A pause.* THEY *all fall silent, each absorbed in his own thoughts. The following lines will be pronounced at intervals between pauses, as though each were talking to himself.*]

Francesco.   Of course, I have no real animosity against Doro Palegari. He kept leading me on from one thing to another. [*A pause.*]

Prestino [*after some seconds*].   So many times we have to pretend we are sure; and if such pretense only hurts us the more deeply, we are not more worthy of blame, but more worthy of pity.

First Friend [*after another pause, as though he were reading* FRANCESCO SAVIO'S *thoughts*].   Who knows? It must be splendid out in the country today!

Francesco [*answering quickly and without surprise, as though to justify himself*].   Why I had actually bought some playthings to carry out to my sister's little girl.

Second Friend.   A cute little tot she was that time I saw her.

Francesco.   Oh, a dear little thing! Prettiest child I ever set my eyes on! So wise, as she looks up at you out of her big eyes! An angel! A cherub!

Diego [*to* FRANCESCO].   Listen! If I were you, Francesco . . . [*The* BUTLER *appears in the doorway to the right.*]

Butler.   May I interrupt, sir?

Francesco.   What is it, Giovanni?

Butler.   A message for you, sir.

Francesco [*approaching the* BUTLER *and listening to what he has to say. Then with evident annoyance*]. Now? How can I? Impossible! [*He turns and stands looking at his friends, hesitant, in great perplexity.*]

Diego [*understanding*]. She is here?

Prestino. You cannot receive her! You must not!

First Friend. Of course not! You cannot while this point of honor is still pending!

Diego. Not at all! She has nothing to do with that!

Prestino. What do you mean? Why, she is the cause of the whole trouble? However, I won't argue the point. I am your second in this affair and I say no! I say you mustn't let her come in!

Second Friend. But you can't send a lady away like that, without even finding out what she's come for!

Diego. I really have no right to say anything.

First Friend [*to* FRANCESCO]. You might find out what she wants!

Second Friend. Yes, and if perchance . . .

Francesco. . . . she tries to put in a word about the duel . . .

Prestino. . . . end the interview at once! On that basis I consent!

Francesco. Very well! Very well! I'll tell her to go on about her business! That's what I'll do! Just leave it to me! [FRANCESCO *withdraws, followed by the* BUTLER.]

Diego. My only suggestion would be that he should advise her to . . . [*At this moment the veranda curtain is torn furiously aside and* MICHELE ROCCA *breaks in from the garden in the throes of a dangerous excitement which he has difficulty in restraining.* HE *is a person about thirty years old—black hair, dark complexion, traces of bitterness, of remorse, of passion, in the lines of his face. His whole expression, the nervous movements of his body, the twitching of his features, show that he is ready to go to any extreme.*]

Rocca. If I may! [*Then surprised at seeing so many people he had not expected to find.*] Is this the place? I have come to the right house?

Prestino [*voicing his own amazement and that of the others*]. Who are you?

Rocca. Michele Rocca.

Diego. Ah, so here he is!

Rocca [*to* DIEGO]. You are Signor Francesco Savio?

Diego. No, I am not. Savio is in the other room. [*He points to the door on the right.*]

Prestino. But if I may ask . . . how did you get in here in this way?

Rocca. I was shown to this entrance.

Diego. The porter thought he was one of Savio's friends!

Rocca. Am I mistaken? Did not a lady enter this house a few seconds before me?

Prestino. You mean that you were following her?

Rocca. Yes, I was following her. I knew that she was to come here.

Diego. So did I . . . and I knew that you would come here too.

Rocca. The most outrageous things are being said about me all over town! I know that Signor Savio, without ever having met me, has come to my defense. Now, he must not listen to that woman! He must not . . . without first hearing from me exactly how matters stand!

Prestino. But it's too late now, my dear sir!

Rocca. Too late? What do you mean?

Prestino. I said it was too late! Arbitration is now out of the question!

First Friend. A challenge has been made and accepted!

Second Friend. And the conditions signed!

Diego. And they both have changed their minds!

Prestino [*angrily to* DIEGO]. You will be so good as to refrain from any further interference! To put it plainly, please mind your own damn business!

First Friend. Why do you keep trying to mix things up?

Diego. I'm not mixing anything up. I'm making it clearer! This gentleman came here under the impression that Savio has been defending him. I am simply pointing out that Savio has changed his mind, and is defending him no longer!

Rocca. Ah, I see! So now *he* is blaming me, too!

Diego. He is not the only one, notice!

Rocca. You too, for instance?

Diego. Yes, yes! I—and everybody else here, as you may see!

Rocca. I can well believe it! So far, you've been talking only with her!

Diego. No! No! Not at all! None of us has seen her nor has Savio, until just now! He has this minute stepped into the other room to find out what she wants!

Rocca. Why do you blame me then? And why does Savio? At first he took my side! If he has changed his mind, why is he having his duel with Signor Palegari?

Diego. My dear sir, in your case—as I understand very well—in your case, madness assumes its most spectacular forms; but believe me, as I was saying just now, all of us are crazy in one way or another! This duel, as you must know, is being fought precisely because both the litigants have changed their minds!

First Friend [*along with the others, in some heat*]. Don't listen to this fellow! He is quite mistaken!

Second Friend. They're going on with the duel because, after the trouble night before last, Palegari got angry . . .

First Friend [*raising his voice*] . . . and called Signor Savio a clown!

Prestino [*raising his voice still higher*]. Signor Savio took offense at the insult and issued a challenge . . .

Diego [*raising his voice till it overrides the others*].

. . . though by that time they were both in perfect agreement!

Rocco [*vehemently*]. In agreement in condemning me without having heard my case? I should like to know— how is this worthless woman able to get everybody on her side like that?

Diego. Everybody except herself . . . except herself!

Rocca. Except herself?

Diego. Not quite that! Don't imagine that she is on one side or on the other! She doesn't know exactly where she stands! Examine your own state of mind, a little more carefully, Signor Rocca, and you will see that even you are not quite sure where you stand!

Rocca. I'm glad you enjoy your own jokes! However, will you kindly announce me, one of you gentlemen? Say that Signor Michele Rocca would like to be received by Signor Francesco Savio.

Prestino. But what do you want to see him about? I repeat, it's too late!

Rocca. What do you know about it? If he's against me now, all the better!

Prestino. But he's in the other room there with the lady!

Rocca. Better still! I followed her to this house on purpose! Perhaps it is just as well for her that I am meeting her with other people, in the presence, in fact, of a stranger whom chance has seen fit to involve in our troubles. So then, I have made up my mind—for anything! I was blind . . . blind . . . but now the simple fact that I find myself here unexpectedly with all you gentlemen . . . the simple fact that I must speak . . . answer your questions . . . well . . . I feel as though . . . I could—all of a sudden—breathe more easily . . . as though the atmosphere had been cleared! I had been keeping to myself for days and days! You gentlemen can't understand the agony I have been through! I tried

to save the man whose sister I was to marry, a man I had
come to love as my own brother . . . !

Prestino. You tried to save him? That's a good one!

First Friend. By running off with the girl he was in
love with!

Second Friend. The night before he was to marry her!

Rocca. No! No! Listen . . . listen, please! Not at
all! I wasn't trying to steal his girl . . . and you say he
was going to marry her! It wasn't much of a job to save
him! It was sufficient to demonstrate to him, to make him
see beyond any question of doubt that the woman he was
going to marry because he wanted her could be his—as
she could be anybody's—without any question of marriage!

Prestino. Anyhow, you spent the night with her . . . !

Rocca. But on a bet . . . on a bet!

First Friend. On what bet?

Second Friend. Bet with whom?

Rocca. Let me finish! Let me finish! A bet with him!
You see, it was by arrangement with his sister and his
mother! He had introduced her to the family, doing violence thereby to all his feelings of propriety; and I, by an
arrangement I made with his sister and his mother, followed the two of them to Naples with the excuse of
helping them get settled in their new house! He was to
marry the girl a few months later. However, there was a
quarrel . . . one of those quarrels that often arise between people about to get married. She lost her temper
and left him for some days! [*He covers his eyes with a
hand as though to hide a vision that tempts and horrifies
at the same time.*] Oh, she went away . . . and I can see
her . . . I can see her! . . . [*He lowers his hand, his face
showing greater and greater emotion.*] For I was present
at the quarrel! . . . [*Mastering his feelings.*] I seized that
occasion as a favorable opportunity for demonstrating to
Giorgio the absurdity of what he was about to do. It's in-

credible, isn't it? Incredible! And yet those women are
often that way, it seems! Do you know, she never gave
him the slightest concession?

First Friend [*intent, as all the others are, on the narrative*]. Of course!

Rocca. Not only that. At Capri there, she had shown
herself disdainful and contemptuous toward all the men,
keeping to herself . . . proud and reserved! "Well, I'll
bet you," said he to me, "I'll bet you!" And he challenged
me to do what I bet him that I could do, promising that
if I won the bet, he'd break with the girl and have nothing more to do with her! Well, instead, he shot himself!

First Friend. But I don't understand! You lent yourself to such a scheme!

Rocca. It was a bet! To save him!

Second Friend. But the treachery of it all!

Rocca. Yes, horrible . . . horrible!

Second Friend. But his treachery toward you, I mean!

Rocca. Yes, he did not play fair with me!

Second Friend. He shot himself!

Prestino. It's incredible . . . incredible!

Rocca. . . . that I lent myself to such a thing? . . .

Prestino. . . . No, that he allowed you to strike such
a bargain with him!

Rocca. But don't you see? He did it on purpose! Because he had noticed . . . noticed right away, you understand . . . that she had tried—from the very moment
when she saw me with his sister—she had tried spitefully,
with the most evil intent, to attract me . . . attract me
to herself, wheedling me with all her artfulness! Why, it
was Giorgio himself who called my attention to it! So it
was easy, you understand—it was easy to make the proposal I made at that moment, saying to him: "Why, you
know she would give herself even to me!"

Prestino. And in that case . . . well, I give up. He
dared you—but he was really daring himself!

Rocca. But he ought to have told me! He ought to have shouted it into my ears if necessary! He should have made me understand that he was lost, poisoned forever! That it was useless for me to try to cure him of a venom from that viper's fangs which had sunk so deep into his soul!

Diego. Viper? Viper? No, excuse me! I would hardly say viper!

Rocca. Viper! Viper! Viper!

Diego. I wonder . . . I wonder! A bit too ingenuous it seems to me, a bit too ingenuous, for a viper. If there was so much poison in her fangs, why should she have bitten you so soon, so immediately, I might even say?

Prestino. But she may have been bent on ruining Giorgio Salvi, breaking his heart, encompassing his death!

Rocca. She may.

Diego. And how is that possible? She had succeeded in forcing him to marry her, hadn't she? Why spoil everything before getting what she wanted?

Rocca. But she never suspected . . .

Diego. Why do you call her a viper then? A viper is always deliberate. A snake such as you say she is would have bitten afterwards, but not before! If now she did bite nevertheless, it means either that she is not so bad as you say she is, or else that she was not trying to harm Giorgio Salvi!

Rocca. So you think then . . .

Diego. It is you who make me think so, understand! You are trying to tell me that she is a treacherous woman. I am keeping to what you say yourself . . . and the case for perfidy doesn't hang together! You say she was trying to trick him into marrying her, but then just before the wedding she gives herself to you!

Rocca [*jumping to his feet*]. Gives herself to me? Who ever said she gave herself to me? I had nothing to do with the woman . . . nothing at all! And you imagine I ever could have thought of such a thing?

Diego [*in astonishment, like the rest*]. Ah, really?

The Others. What! Is it possible?

Rocca. You see, all I wanted was proof . . . proof that she . . . something in short to convince *him!* [*At this moment the door on the right opens and* FRANCESCO SAVIO *appears in great excitement and commotion. He has been in the other room with* DELIA MORELLO. *Fulfilling her promise to prevent the duel between him and* DORO PALEGARI, *she has used all her arts upon him, intoxicating him with herself. He at once assails* MICHELE ROCCA *vehemently.*]

Francesco. And what is this? What are you doing here? What do you want in my house? What mess are you trying to stir up here?

Rocca. I came to tell you . . .

Francesco. There is nothing you need to tell me!

Rocca. You are mistaken! I have something to say, and not only to you!

Francesco. I should advise you not to be quite so positive in your threats!

Rocca. I am making no threats. I was anxious to talk with you.

Francesco. You have been following a lady to my house!

Rocca. Ah, I have just been explaining to your friends here . . .

Francesco. What do I care about your explanations to my friends? You have been following a woman who was coming to see me! Do you deny it?

Rocca. Yes, because if you intend to fight a duel with Signor Palegari . . .

Francesco. What duel? Nonsense! I am not going to fight a duel with anybody!

Prestino [*in amazement*]. What is that you say? No duel?

Francesco. I am calling it off!

First Friend, Diego, Second Friend [*speaking at once*]. Are you crazy? Do you mean it? That's ridiculous!

Rocca [*also speaking at the same time, but in a louder voice, with a guffaw*]. Of course, you're calling it off! It's *her* work!

Francesco [*about to attack him physically*]. Shut your mouth or I . . .

Prestino [*running in front of him and holding him back*]. No! First you must answer me! You're calling this duel with Palegari off?

Francesco. Yes, I am calling it off! It's all nonsense, and I have no right to add to a woman's despair.

Prestino. But it will be worse, if you don't fight! The conditions of the duel have been drawn up and the papers signed!

Francesco. But it's sheer nonsense to have a duel with Palegari now! It's ridiculous!

Prestino. Why so ridiculous?

Francesco. Ridiculous! It's ridiculous because we are in entire agreement . . . Oh, you understand, Prestino, when you have a chance to figure in some affair like this, you are ready for a week's holiday!

Prestino. But Palegari insulted you, and you challenged him!

Francesco. But nonsense, nonsense, just as Doro said, nonsense! I am calling it off!

Prestino. This is incredible . . . incredible!

Rocca. He promised her he wouldn't fight with her champion?

Francesco. Yes, why shouldn't I, since I have you here?

Rocca. I see! That is why you promised not to?

Francesco. No, since you are here insulting me in my own house! What do you want of that lady, anyhow?

Prestino. You can't do that!

Francesco. He's been following her around for a day or more!

Prestino. But you can't fight with *him* now!

Francesco. No one can say I am challenging a less dangerous opponent!

Prestino. Not at all! Not at all! That won't make any difference! Because if I should go now and offer to fight Palegari in your place . . .

First Friend [*almost shouting at* FRANCESCO]. You will be disqualified!

Rocca. But I can ignore the disqualification!

First Friend. No, because we would prevent you!

Prestino [*to* FRANCESCO]. And you won't find a soul to act as your second! However, you have all day to think it over. I can't stay here any longer, so I'm going away!

Diego. He'll think it over, all right!

Prestino [*to the two friends*]. This is no place for us! Let's be going! [*The* THREE OF THEM *withdraw by way of the garden, rear.*]

Diego [*walking out on the veranda after them and calling*]. Not too fast, gentlemen, not too fast! [*Then turning to* FRANCESCO.] And you had better watch your step!

Francesco. You go to the devil! [*Again assailing* ROCCA.] And you!—you will find the door this way! Please make use of it! I am at your service when, where, and as, you wish! [*At this point* DELIA MORELLO *appears at the doorway to the right. The moment* SHE *sees* MICHELE ROCCA, *so changed from what he had been, another person in fact, she suddenly finds the mask lifted from her eyes—the mask, the fiction, which both she and he have hitherto been using to defend themselves against the secret passion by which from the very beginning they*

*have been madly attracted toward one another, a passion
which they have been translating before their own minds
into terms of pity and interest for* GIORGIO SALVI, *each
pretending to be trying to save him from one or the
other. With this fiction gone, destroyed by the sudden
shock they feel at being brought thus face to face,* THEY
stand looking at each other, pale and trembling.]

Rocca [*with a sob*]. Delia! Delia! [*He advances to
embrace her.*]

Delia [*sinking into his arms and accepting his kiss*].
No! No! My poor boy! My poor boy! [*To the horror and
disgust of* FRANCESCO *and* DIEGO, THEY *embrace fran-
tically.*]

Rocca. Delia! My Delia!

Diego. That is the way they hate each other! Ah, how
they hate each other! You see? You see?

Francesco. But it's absurd! It's monstrous! With the
corpse of a man between them!

Rocca [*gathering* DELIA *into his arms, like an animal
turning ravenously upon its prey*]. Monstrous? Yes! But
she must belong to me! She must suffer with me . . .
with me!

Delia [*suddenly horrified, and tearing herself loose
ferociously*]. No! No! Go away! Go away! Don't touch
me!

Rocca [*struggling to hold her*]. No! No! Mine! Mine!
Here, with me, in my despair! Here!

Delia [*still struggling*]. Let me go, I tell you! Let me
go! Murderer!

Francesco. Yes! Let her go! I say let her go!

Rocca. You keep your distance!

Delia [*freeing herself at last*]. Let me go! [FRANCESCO
and DIEGO *restrain* ROCCA *from throwing himself upon
her.*] I am not afraid of you! No! No! No harm can come
to me from you! Not even if you kill me!

Rocca [*speaking at the same time, struggling with the*

two men and shouting].   Delia! Delia! You must belong to me! You are mine! You must belong to me! I cannot live without you!

Delia.   I am free! I am free! I feel nothing, nothing whatever! It was an illusion! I thought it was compassion . . . fear . . . but no, it was nothing . . . nothing!

Rocca [*still struggling*].   Let me alone! Let me alone!

Francesco and Diego [*talking together*].   You are two wild beasts! Monstrous! Two monsters!

Delia.   Let him go! I am not afraid of him! I let him kiss me! But it was coldly, without passion! It was not fear! It was not pity!

Rocca.   Yes, you wretch! I know! I know your kisses are worthless, but I want you! I am going to have you!

Delia.   Any harm you might do me, even if you killed me, would not be so bad as that! Another crime! Poison! Death itself! I want to remain as I am! I want to suffer as I am!

Rocca [*still struggling to free himself from the two men*].   Her love is worth nothing, but all that I have suffered on her account gives it value to me! It is not love I feel for you! It's hatred! It's hatred!

Delia.   Hatred! Yes, it's hatred with me, too! Hatred!

Rocca.   The very blood that has been shed on her account! [*With a sudden burst of violence he succeeds in freeing his arms.*] Have pity on me . . . pity on me! [*He pursues her about the room.*]

Delia [*trying to keep away*].   No! No! Don't you touch me! It will be the worse for you!

Diego and Francesco [*getting hold of him again*].   But keep away, won't you? You must answer for this with me!

Delia.   It will be the worse for him if he tries to arouse my pity either for myself or for him! I have none! But if you have any regard for him, send him away from here! Send him away!

Rocca. How can I go away? You know that my life was drowned forever in Giorgio's blood!

Delia. The brother of the girl you were to marry! And you did not try to save him from dishonor!

Rocca. You lie! That is not true! You know that we have both been lying!

Delia. Yes, we have both been lying! Two falsehoods!

Rocca. You have wanted me as I have wanted you, from the moment when we first saw each other!

Delia. Yes! Yes! But it was to punish you!

Rocca. Yes, so with me! It was to punish you! But your life, too, has been drowned, drowned forever in Giorgio's blood!

Delia. Yes, you are right! You are right! [*She runs to him like a flame, pushing aside the two men who are restraining him.*] Yes, it is true! It is true!

Rocca [*embracing her again desperately*]. So we must both drown in that blood, but drown together . . . this way . . . in each other's arms . . . not I alone . . . not you alone . . . but both together! This way! This way!

Diego. If they don't change their minds!

Rocca [*carrying* DELIA *in his arms toward the door into the garden, leaving the two men standing there in utter astonishment and stupefaction*]. Yes . . . with me . . . with me! Come! Come! With me . . . away, with me . . . away, with me!

Francesco. Two lunatics!

Diego. You don't see yourself!

SECOND CHORAL INTERLUDE

Again the curtain rises as soon as possible after it has fallen on the second act; and again the theatre lobby appears with the entrances leading to the hall of the theatre. But this time no one comes out for some moments. The TICKET TAKER, *one or two* USHERS, MAIDS *from the*

*women's room are standing about in some apprehension;
because, along toward the end of the second act, they
have seen the* MORENO WOMAN, *despite the interference
of her* THREE MALE FRIENDS, *run through the corridor toward the stage entrance. Now the sound of shouting, clapping, hissing, comes out from the theatre, growing louder
and louder all the time, either because the actors have not
yet appeared before the curtain to make their bows to
the audience or because something strange and unusual
is going on inside.*

One of the Ticket Takers.   What the devil is the matter in there?

Another Ticket Taker.   Isn't it Pirandello tonight?
What else can you expect?

An Usher.   No, the audience is applauding, but the
actors refuse to come out.

A Maid.   But there's shouting and screaming on the
stage, don't you hear?

Another Usher.   And the house is in an uproar!

Second Maid.   Has that woman anything to do with
it?

Ticket Taker.   I imagine she has. The men with her
were having a devil of a time keeping her quiet!

First Maid.   She got in behind the scenes!

First Ticket Taker.   She was trying to get in at the end
of the first act!

Another Maid.   But hell is let loose in there! Don't
you hear? [*Two or three of the doors into the theatre are
thrown open and some* SPECTATORS *dash out into the
lobby, the uproar in the auditorium becoming louder for
the moment.*]

The Spectators.   But she got in there on the stage!
What's the matter? Are they fighting? [*Shouting. Scream-
ing.*] And the actors are not answering their curtain call!
[*More* SPECTATORS *appear, coming through the doors into*

the lobby and looking toward the stage entrance to the right. THEY *are followed by a great number of* SPECTA-TORS *who come on through the left. They are all shouting:*] What's the matter? What's going on? What's the trouble?

Confused Voices. There's a fight on behind the scenes! There . . . do you hear? On the stage! Why? Why? Who knows?

Gangway, please! What's happened? What's going on? Trouble tonight, all right! Let me get by! Is the play over? Isn't there a third act? There must be a third act! Make way there, please! Yes, at four o'clock sharp, so long! . . . Don't forget! But did you hear that? They're fighting! I am going in there myself! Do you hear that? It's scandalous! They've no right to! What's it all about? Why it seems that . . . God only knows! What the deuce! Why . . . why . . . there . . . there! The door is opening!

[*The stage entrance is thrown open, and for the moment the uproar on the stage—shrieks from the* ACTRESSES, *oaths from* ACTORS *and from the* STAGE MANAGER, *the voices of the* MORENO WOMAN *and her* THREE FRIENDS— *become louder. These noises will be drowned eventually by the confusion among the* SPECTATORS *crowding around the stage entrance, varied by the angry protests of a few people, some of whom are trying to get to the stage and others are trying to get away and out of the theatre.*]

Voices from the Stage [ACTORS *speaking*]. Get out of here! Get out of there! Back where you belong! Get that woman away! Have her arrested! She'll pay me for that! Back where you belong! Get out of here!

Voice of the Moreno Woman. It's a disgrace! It's a crime! I won't! I won't!

Voice of the Stage Manager. You just be moving along!

Voice of the Moreno Woman. You're insulting me publicly!

Voice of One of Her Friends. Remember she's a woman!

Voice of Another of Her Friends. Don't you dare strike a woman!

Voice of One of the Actors. Woman? Nonsense! She's making all the trouble! Get her out of here! Get her out of here!

Voices of Some Actresses. What a cat! For shame! For shame!

Voices of Some Actors. Lucky for her she's a woman! She deserves every bit of it! Get her out of here!

Stage Manager. Clear that doorway, there! Clear that doorway!

Voices from the Crowd of Spectators [*all talking at once, with occasional hoots, jeers, and applause*]. Signora Moreno! The Moreno woman! Who is she! She slapped the leading lady's face! Who? Who slapped her? Signora Moreno! The Moreno woman! Who is she? The leading lady! No! No! It was the author's face she slapped? Pirandello? She slapped his face! Who? Who slapped his face? Signora Moreno! No! The leading lady! The author slapped her face? No! No! The other way about! The leading lady slapped the author's face! Not at all! Not at all! Signora Moreno assaulted the leading lady and pulled her hair!

Voices from the Stage. Enough of this! Out of here! Put her out! Put her out! Cowards! Wretches! Call the police! What a woman! Put her out! Put her out!

Voices from the Spectators. Go on with the play! Put them out! Less noise! Shut up! Signora Moreno! Put her out! The third act! We want the third act! Pirandello!

Put him out! A speech! A speech from Pirandello! Put him out! A speech! He's to blame! Sh-sh-sh-sh! Make way there! The third act! Clear the way! Clear the way!

[*Some* ACTORS *and* ACTRESSES *from the play on the stage, more especially those appearing in the third act, elbow their way through the crowd gathered before the stage entrance. With them appear the* STAGE MANAGER *and the* TREASURER *of the theatre, the latter trying to persuade them to go on with the play. The lobby is thrown into the greatest agitation. At first the* SPECTATORS *are silent, eagerly listening to the dialogue of the stage people; though later on they will break occasionally into noisy comment of approval or disapproval.*]

Treasurer of the Theatre.   But for heaven's sake, use your brains. The crowd will want its money back! You want to stop the play?

Actors and Actresses [*talking all at the same time*]. Not on your life! I am going home! We won't put up with this! We are all going home! This is too much! It's a disgrace! We refuse to put up with it! We are going to strike in protest!

Stage Manager.   Protest? Who are you protesting against?

One of the Actresses.   Against the author, and rightly so!

One of the Actors.   And against the producer! Who ever thought of producing such a comedy as this!

Treasurer.   But you can't protest this way! If you go away and don't finish the play, we are ruined! This is pure Bolshevism!

Voices from Among the Spectators.   Fine! Fine! That's the way to talk! Not at all! The actors are right! They're right!

The Actors [*all speaking together*].   Yes! Yes! We protest! We protest!

An Actor.   You can't compel us to play a comedy with a key!

Voices from Some Ingenuous Spectators.   A key? Where's the key? What's a comedy with a key?

Actors.   We refuse! We refuse!

Voices of Other Spectators.   Of course! Everybody knows it! It's disgraceful! It's scandalous! You can't help seeing! The Moreno case! She's here! In the theatre! She got in behind the scenes! She slapped the leading lady's face!

Voices of Spectators and Friends of Pirandello [*all talking together and in great confusion*].   But nobody noticed! It's a good play! We want the third act! Give us our money back! We bought our tickets! The third act! The third act!

One of the Actors.   But we refuse to have our faces slapped!

An Actor.   Let's all go home! I, for my part, am going home!

An Actress.   The leading lady has already gone home!

Voices of Spectators.   Gone home? How did she go out? Through the stage entrance! Why?

Actress.   Because a woman came in on the stage and slapped her face!

Voices of Spectators in Argument.   Slapped her face? Yes! Yes! Signora Moreno! And she was right! Who was right? The Moreno woman? Why did she slap her face? The leading lady!

One of the Actors.   Because she saw an allusion to herself in the play!

Another Actor.   And she thought we had conspired with the author to make fun of her?

First Actress.   We refuse to be treated that way!

Baron Nuti [*accompanied by* Two Friends *as in the first interlude, more than ever excited and confused, pushes his way forward*]. It's true! It's unheard of! It's a disgrace! You're right in stopping the show!

One of His Friends. Hush! Don't make matters worse! Let's go home!

Baron Nuti. It's a disgrace, ladies and gentlemen! Two people pilloried in public! The private affairs of two people exposed to public ridicule!

Treasurer [*in despair*]. The play seems to have moved from the stage to the lobby!

Voices of Spectators Hostile to the Author. He's right! He's right! It's a disgrace! They ought to put a stop to it! They're right! They're right!

Voices of Spectators Favorable to Pirandello. Not at all! Not at all! It was a good show! The third act! Where is the third act. Give us the third act! Disgrace? Nonsense! It could be anybody! Where's the slander?

Treasurer [*to the actors*]. Shall we go on with the show or shall we not?

Baron Nuti [*seizing one of the* Spectators *by the front of his coat and addressing him so violently that everyone falls silent at the spectacle of his fury*]. You say it's all right? You approve? They have a right to take me and expose me there on the stage in public? Show me off, and all my sorrows, in the presence of a crowd? Make me say things that I never thought of saying and do things that I never thought of doing? [*In the silence that greets* Baron Nuti's *harangue, the* Stage Manager *will appear from the stage entrance, walking a few steps ahead of the* Moreno Woman *who, weeping, disheveled, half fainting, is being rather dragged than led out of the theatre by her* Three Male Companions. *The exchange of sentences between the* Stage Manager *and* Signora Moreno *will fall upon the silence as a reply to* Baron Nuti's *words. Everyone meantime will turn toward the stage entrance, mak-*

ing way for SIGNORA MORENO *and her* COMPANIONS. NUTI
will release his grasp on the SPECTATOR *he has been assailing, and turns to ask:*] What's the matter?

Stage Manager. But you know very well that neither
the author nor the leading lady have ever met you! They
don't know you at all!

Signora Moreno. She mimicked my voice! She used
my manner—all my gestures! She was imitating me! I
recognized myself!

Stage Manager. But why should you believe it was
you?

Signora Moreno. No! No! That isn't so! It was so
terrible to see myself there on the stage acting that way!
The idea! Why! I . . . I . . . kissing that man! [*She
suddenly becomes aware of* BARON NUTI'S *presence and
utters a shriek, covering her face with her hands.*] Oh!
Oh! There he is! There he is! There!

Baron Nuti. Amelia! Amelia!

[*General commotion among the* SPECTATORS, *who can
scarcely believe their eyes, as they see the very characters
and the very scene they have witnessed at the end of the
second act, present now before them. Their astonishment
should be manifested, however, only by facial expression,
by brief comments delivered in low tones, and a few
hushed exclamations.*]

Voices of Spectators. Oh! Look! Look! There they
are! Oh! In real life! Both of them! The same scene over
again! Look! Look!

Signora Moreno [*desperately, to the* THREE MEN *with
her*]. Take him away! Take him away!

Her Companions. Yes! Let's go away! Let's go away!

Baron Nuti [*dashing upon her*]. No! No! You must
come with me! You must come with me!

Signora Moreno [*tearing herself from his grasp*]. No!

Let me alone! Let me alone! Don't touch me! Murderer!
Murderer!

Baron Nuti. You heard that on the stage!

Signora Moreno. Let me alone! I am not afraid of
you!

Baron Nuti. But it was true! It's our punishment!
It's our punishment! And we must suffer it together!
Your place is with me! Come! Come!

Signora Moreno. Let me alone, I say! I hate you! I
hate you!

Baron Nuti. We are drowning . . . drowning in his
blood! It was true! Come with me! Come! [*He drags her
off to the left.*]

[*Most of the* SPECTATORS *follow with noisy comments
and exclamations.*]

Spectators. Oh! Really! It can't be! Incredible! How
horrible! There they are! Look! Delia Morello and
Michele Rocca! [*Other* SPECTATORS *continue standing in
the lobby, but looking after them and making more or
less the same remarks.*]

A Spectator [*who has not grasped the situation*]. And
they complain because the same thing was done on the
stage!

Stage Manager. Yes, and the leading lady had the
courage to come and slap my face . . . there, on the
stage!

Many Voices. Incredible! Incredible! Absurd!

A Spectator Who Understands. But no! It's all natural enough! They rebelled because they saw themselves
there, as in a mirror, forced into a situation that has the
eternity of art!

Stage Manager. They did it over again to the very
gesture!

A Spectator Who Understands. And that's natural,
too! They have done, here before our eyes and quite

involuntarily, something that the author had foreseen! [*Some of the* SPECTATORS *approve.* OTHERS *laugh.*]

Treasurer of the Theatre to the Stage Manager. But I should like to know whether you intend holding a debate right here?

Stage Manager. You want to close the theatre? What have I got to do with that? Tell them to get out!

Treasurer. Well, I can't have the third act! The actors have gone home!

Stage Manager. Post a placard calling the show off!

Treasurer. But some of the audience are still in their seats!

Stage Manager. Very well! I'll make the announcement from behind the footlights!

Treasurer. Yes, that's the way out of it! Go and do that! [*The* STAGE MANAGER *starts for the stage entrance, while the* TREASURER *begins shooing people out of the lobby.*] We are closing up, gentlemen! We are closing up! If you please, gentlemen, the play is over for tonight! The play is over for tonight!

[*The curtain falls, but immediately the* STAGE MANAGER *will make his way through the central opening of the curtain and come forward to the footlights.*]

Stage Manager. The management is grieved to announce that in view of unfortunate incidents which took place at the end of the second act, we shall be unable to continue the performance this evening.

APPENDIX I

PREFACE

to

Six Characters in Search of an Author

by

LUIGI PIRANDELLO

(1925)

IT SEEMS like yesterday but is actually many years ago that a nimble little maidservant entered the service of my art. However, she always comes fresh to the job.

She is called Fantasy.

A little puckish and malicious, if she likes to dress in black no one will wish to deny that she is often positively bizarre and no one will wish to believe that she always does everything in the same way and in earnest. She sticks her hand in her pocket, pulls out a cap and bells, sets it on her head, red as a cock's comb, and dashes away. Here today, there tomorrow. And she amuses herself by bringing to my house—since I derive stories and novels and plays from them—the most disgruntled tribe in the world, men, women, children, involved in strange adventures which they can find no way out of; thwarted in their plans; cheated in their hopes; with whom, in short, it is often torture to deal.

Well, this little maidservant of mine, Fantasy, several years ago, had the bad inspiration or ill-omened caprice to bring a family into my house. I wouldn't know where she fished them up or how, but, according to her, I could find in them the subject for a magnificent novel.

I found before me a man about fifty years old, in a dark

jacket and light trousers, with a frowning air and ill-natured, mortified eyes; a poor woman in widow's weeds leading by one hand a little girl of four and by the other a boy of rather more than ten; a cheeky and "sexy" girl, also clad in black but with an equivocal and brazen pomp, all atremble with a lively, biting contempt for the mortified old man and for a young fellow of twenty who stood on one side closed in on himself as if he despised them all. In short, the six characters who are seen coming on stage at the beginning of the play. Now one of them and now another—often beating down one another—embarked on the sad story of their adventures, each shouting his own reasons, and projecting in my face his disordered passions, more or less as they do in the play to the unhappy Manager.

What author will be able to say how and why a character was born in his fantasy? The mystery of artistic creation is the same as that of birth. A woman who loves may desire to become a mother; but the desire by itself, however intense, cannot suffice. One fine day she will find herself a mother without having any precise intimation when it began. In the same way an artist imbibes very many germs of life and can never say how and why, at a certain moment, one of these vital germs inserts itself into his fantasy, there to become a living creature on a plane of life superior to the changeable existence of every day.

I can only say that, without having made any effort to seek them out, I found before me, alive—you could touch them and even hear them breathe—the six characters now seen on the stage. And they stayed there in my presence, each with his secret torment and all bound together by the one common origin and mutual entanglement of their affairs, while I had them enter the world of art, constructing from their persons, their passions, and their adventures a novel, a drama, or at least a story.

Born alive, they wished to live.

To me it was never enough to present a man or a woman and what is special and characteristic about them simply for the pleasure of presenting them; to narrate a particular affair, lively or sad, simply for the pleasure of narrating it; to describe a landscape simply for the pleasure of describing it.

There are some writers (and not a few) who do feel this pleasure and, satisfied, ask no more. They are, to speak more precisely, historical writers.

But there are others who, beyond such pleasure, feel a more profound spiritual need on whose account they admit only figures, affairs, landscapes which have been soaked, so to speak, in a particular sense of life and acquire from it a universal value. These are, more precisely, philosophical writers.

I have the misfortune to belong to these last.

I hate symbolic art in which the presentation loses all spontaneous movement in order to become a machine, an allegory —a vain and misconceived effort because the very fact of giving an allegorical sense to a presentation clearly shows that we have to do with a fable which by itself has no truth either fantastic or direct; it was made for the demonstration of some moral truth. The spiritual need I speak of cannot be satisfied—or seldom, and that to the end of a superior irony, as for example in Ariosto—by such allegorical symbolism. This latter starts from a concept, and from a concept which creates or tries to create for itself an image. The former on the other hand seeks in the image—which must remain alive and free throughout— a meaning to give it value.

Now, however much I sought, I did not succeed in uncovering this meaning in the six characters. And I concluded therefore that it was no use making them live.

I thought to myself: "I have already afflicted my readers with hundreds and hundreds of stories. Why should I afflict them now by narrating the sad entanglements of these six unfortunates?"

And, thinking thus, I put them away from me. Or rather I did all I could to put them away.

But one doesn't give life to a character for nothing.

Creatures of my spirit, these six were already living a life which was their own and not mine any more, a life which it was not in my power any more to deny them.

Thus it is that while I persisted in desiring to drive them out of my spirit, they, as if completely detached from every narrative support, characters from a novel miraculously emerging from the pages of the book that contained them, went on living on their own, choosing certain moments of the day to reappear before me in the solitude of my study and coming— now one, now the other, now two together—to tempt me, to propose that I present or describe this scene or that, to explain the effects that could be secured with them, the new interest which a certain unusual situation could provide, and so forth.

For a moment I let myself be won over. And this condescension of mine, thus letting myself go for a while, was enough, because they drew from it a new increment of life, a greater degree of clarity and addition, consequently a greater degree of persuasive power over me. And thus as it became gradually harder and harder for me to go back and free myself from them, it became easier and easier for them to come back and tempt me. At a certain point I actually became obsessed with them. Until, all of a sudden, a way out of the difficulty flashed upon me.

"Why not," I said to myself, "present this highly strange fact of an author who refuses to let some of his characters live though they have been born in his fantasy, and the fact that these characters, having by now life in their veins, do not resign themselves to remaining excluded from the world of art? They are detached from me; live on their own; have acquired voice and movement; have by themselves—in this struggle for existence that they have had to wage with me—become dramatic characters, characters that can move and talk on their own initiative; already see themselves as such; have learned to defend themselves against me; will even know how to defend themselves against others. And so let them go where dramatic characters do go to have life: on a stage. And let us see what will happen."

That's what I did. And, naturally, the result was what it had to be: a mixture of tragic and comic, fantastic and realistic, in a humorous situation that was quite new and infinitely complex, a drama which is conveyed by means of the characters, who carry it within them and suffer it, a drama, breathing, speaking, self-propelled, which seeks at all costs to find the means of its own presentation; and the comedy of the vain attempt at an improvised realization of the drama on stage. First, the surprise of the poor actors in a theatrical company rehearsing a play by day on a bare stage (no scenery, no flats). Surprise and incredulity at the sight of the six characters announcing themselves as such in search of an author. Then, immediately afterwards, through that sudden fainting fit of the Mother veiled in black, their instinctive interest in the drama of which they catch a glimpse in her and in the other members of the strange family, an obscure, ambiguous drama, coming about so unexpectedly on a stage that is empty and unprepared to receive it. And gradually the growth of this interest to the bursting forth of the contrasting passions of Father, of Step-Daughter, of Son, of that poor Mother, passions seeking, as I said, to overwhelm each other with a tragic, lacerating fury.

And here is the universal meaning at first vainly sought in the six characters, now that, going on stage of their own accord, they succeed in finding it within themselves in the excitement of the desperate struggle which each wages against the other and all wage against the Manager and the actors, who do not understand them.

Without wanting to, without knowing it, in the strife of their bedevilled souls, each of them, defending himself against the accusations of the others, expresses as his own living passion and torment the passion and torment which for so many years have been the pangs of my spirit: the deceit of mutual understanding irremediably founded on the empty abstraction of the words, the multiple personality of everyone corresponding to the possibilities of being to be found in each of us, and finally the inherent tragic conflict between life (which is always moving and changing) and form (which fixes it, immutable).

Two above all among the six characters, the Father and the Step-Daughter, speak of that outrageous unalterable fixity of their form in which he and she see their essential nature expressed permanently and immutably, a nature that for one means punishment and for the other revenge; and they defend it against the factitious affectations and unaware volatility of the actors, and they try to impose it on the vulgar Manager who would like to change it and adapt it to the so-called exigencies of the theatre.

If the six characters don't all seem to exist on the same plane, it is not because some are figures of first rank and others of the second, that is, some are main characters and others minor ones—the elementary perspective necessary to all scenic or narrative art—nor is it that any are not completely created—for their purpose. They are all six at the same point of artistic realization and on the same level of reality, which is the fantastic level of the whole play. Except that the Father, the Step-Daughter, and also the Son are realized as mind; the Mother as nature; the Boy as a presence watching and performing a gesture and the Baby unaware of it all. This fact creates among them a perspective of a new sort. Unconsciously I had had the impression that some of them needed to be fully realized (artistically speaking), others less so, and others merely sketched in as elements in a narrative or presentational sequence: the most alive, the most completely created, are the Father and the Step-Daughter who naturally stand out more and lead the way, dragging themselves along beside the almost dead weight of the others—first, the Son, holding back; second, the Mother, like a victim resigned to her fate, between the two children who have hardly any substance beyond their appearance and who need to be led by the hand.

And actually! actually they had each to appear in that stage

of creation which they had attained in the author's fantasy at
the moment when he wished to drive them away.

If I now think about these things, about having intuited that
necessity, having unconsciously found the way to resolve it by
means of a new perspective, and about the way in which I actually obtained it, they seem like miracles. The fact is that the
play was really conceived in one of those spontaneous illumina-
tions of the fantasy when by a miracle all the elements of the
mind answer to each other's call and work in divine accord. No
human brain, working "in the cold," however stirred up it
might be, could ever have succeeded in penetrating far enough,
could ever have been in a position to satisfy all the exigencies
of the play's form. Therefore the reasons which I will give to
clarify the values of the play must not be thought of as intentions that I conceived beforehand when I prepared myself for
the job and which I now undertake to defend, but only as dis-
coveries which I have been able to make afterwards in tran-
quillity.

I wanted to present six characters seeking an author. Their
play does not manage to get presented—precisely because the
author whom they seek is missing. Instead is presented the comedy of their vain attempt with all that it contains of tragedy by
virtue of the fact that the six characters have been rejected.

But can one present a character while rejecting him? Obviously, to present him one needs, on the contrary, to receive him
into one's fantasy before one can express him. And I have actually accepted and realized the six characters: I have, however,
accepted and realized them as rejected: in search of *another*
author.

What have I rejected of them? Not themselves, obviously, but
their drama, which doubtless is what interests them above all
but which did not interest me—for the reasons already indicated.

And what is it, for a character—his drama?

Every creature of fantasy and art, in order to exist, must have
his drama, that is, a drama in which he may be a character and
for which he *is* a character. This drama is the character's *raison
d'être,* his vital function, necessary for his existence.

In these six, then, I have accepted the "being" without the
reason for being. I have taken the organism and entrusted to
it, not its own proper function, but another more complex
function into which its own function entered, if at all, only as
a datum. A terrible and desperate situation especially for the
two—Father and Step-Daughter—who more than the others

crave life and more than the others feel themselves to be characters, that is, absolutely need a drama and therefore their own drama—the only one which they can envisage for themselves yet which meantime they see rejected: an "impossible" situation from which they feel they must escape at whatever cost; it is a matter of life and death. True, I have given them another *raison d'être,* another function: precisely that "impossible" situation, the drama of being in search of an author and rejected. But that this should be a *raison d'être,* that it should have become their real function, that it should be necessary, that it should suffice, they can hardly suppose; for they have a life of their own. If someone were to tell them, they wouldn't believe him. It is not possible to believe that the sole reason for our living should lie in a torment that seems to us unjust and inexplicable.

I cannot imagine, therefore, why the charge was brought against me that the character of the Father was not what it should have been because it stepped out of its quality and position as a character and invaded at times the author's province and took it over. I who understand those who don't quite understand me see that the charge derives from the fact that the character expresses and makes his own a torment of spirit which is recognized as mine. Which is entirely natural and of absolutely no significance. Aside from the fact that this torment of spirit in the character of the Father derives from causes, and is suffered and lived for reasons, that have nothing to do with the drama of my personal experience, a fact which alone removes all substance from the criticism, I want to make it clear that the inherent torment of my spirit is one thing, a torment which I can legitimately—provided that it be organic—reflect in a character, and that the activity of my spirit as revealed in the realized work, the activity that succeeds in forming a drama out of the six characters in search of an author is another thing. If the Father participated in this latter activity, if he competed in forming the drama of the six characters without an author, then and only then would it by all means be justified to say that he was at times the author himself and therefore not the man he should be. But the Father suffers and does not create his existence as a character in search of an author. He suffers it as an inexplicable fatality and as a situation which he tries with all his powers to rebel against, which he tries to remedy: hence it is that he is a character in search of an author and nothing more, even if he expresses as his own the torment of my spirit. If he, so to speak, assumed some of the author's responsibilities, the fatality would be completely explained. He would, that is to say, see himself accepted, if only as a rejected character, accepted in the poet's heart of hearts, and he would no longer have any reason to suffer the despair of not finding someone to construct and affirm his life as a character. I mean that he would quite willingly accept the *raison d'être* which the author gives him and without regrets would forego his own, throwing over the Manager and the actors to whom in fact he runs as his only recourse.

There is one character, that of the Mother, who on the other hand does not care about being alive (considering being alive as an end in itself). She hasn't the least suspicion that she is *not* alive. It has never occurred to her to ask how and why and in what manner she lives. In short, she is not aware of being a character, inasmuch as she is never, even for a moment, detached from her role. She doesn't know she has a role.

This makes her perfectly organic. Indeed, her role of Mother does not of itself, in its natural essence, embrace mental activity. And she does not exist as a mind. She lives in an endless continuum of feeling, and therefore she cannot acquire awareness of her life—that is, of her existence as a character. But with all this, even she, in her own way and for her own ends, seeks an author, and at a certain stage seems happy to have been brought before the Manager. Because she hopes to take life from him, perhaps? No: because she hopes the Manager will have her present a scene with the Son in which she would put so much of her own life. But it is a scene which does not exist, which never has and never could take place. So unaware is she of being a character, that is, of the life that is possible to her, all fixed and determined, moment by moment, in every action, every phrase.

She appears on stage with the other characters but without understanding what the others make her do. Obviously, she imagines that the itch for life with which the husband and the daughter are afflicted and for which she herself is to be found on stage is no more than one of the usual incomprehensible extravagances of this man who is both tortured and torturer and—horrible, most horrible—a new equivocal rebellion on the part of that poor erring girl. The Mother is completely passive. The events of her own life and the values they assume in her eyes, her very character, are all things which are "said" by the others and which she only once contradicts, and that because the maternal instinct rises up and rebels within her to make it clear that she didn't at all wish to abandon either the son or the husband: the Son was taken from her and the husband forced her to abandon him. She is only correcting data; she explains and knows nothing.

In short, she is nature. Nature fixed in the figure of a mother.

This character gave me a satisfaction of a new sort, not to be ignored. Nearly all my critics, instead of defining her, after their habit, as "unhuman"—which seems to be the peculiar and incorrigible characteristic of all my creatures without exception —had the goodness to note "with real pleasure" that at last a *very human* figure had emerged from my fantasy. I explain this praise to myself in the following way: since my poor Mother is entirely limited to the natural attitude of a Mother with no possibility of free mental activity, being, that is, little more than a lump of flesh completely alive in all its functions—procreation, lactation, caring for and loving its young—without any need therefore of exercising her brain, she realizes in her person the true and complete "human type." That must be how it is, since in a human organism nothing seems more superfluous than the mind.

But the critics have tried to get rid of the Mother with this praise without bothering to penetrate the nucleus of poetic values which the character in the play represents. A very human figure, certainly, because mindless, that is, unaware of being what she is or not caring to explain it to herself. But not knowing that she is a character doesn't prevent her from being one. That is her drama in my play. And the most living expression of it comes spurting out in her cry to the Manager who wants her to think all these things have happened already and therefore cannot now be a reason for renewed lamentations: "No, it's happening now, it's happening always! My torture is not a pretence, signore! I am alive and present, always, in every moment of my torture: it is renewed, alive and present, always!" This she *feels*, without being conscious of it, and feels it therefore as something inexplicable: but she feels it so terribly that she doesn't think it *can* be something to explain either to herself or to others. She feels it and that is that. She feels it as pain, and this pain is immediate; she cries it out. Thus she reflects the growing fixity of life in a form—the same thing, which in another way, tortures the Father and the Step-Daughter. In them, mind. In her, nature. The mind rebels and, as best it may, seeks an advantage; nature, if not aroused by sensory stimuli, weeps.

Conflict between life-in-movement and form is the inexorable condition not only of the mental but also of the physical order.

The life which in order to exist has become fixed in our corporeal form little by little kills that form. The tears of a nature thus fixed lament the irreparable, continuous aging of our bodies. Hence the tears of the Mother are passive and perpetual. Revealed in three faces, made significant in three distinct and simultaneous dramas, this inherent conflict finds in the play its most complete expression. More: the Mother declares also the particular value of artistic form—a form which does not delimit or destroy its own life and which life does not consume —in her cry to the Manager. If the Father and Step-Daughter began their scene a hundred thousand times in succession, always, at the appointed moment, at the instant when the life of the work of art must be expressed with that cry, it would always be heard, unaltered and unalterable in its form, not as a mechanical repetition, not as a return determined by external necessities, but on the contrary, alive every time and as new, suddenly born *thus forever!* embalmed alive in its incorruptible form. Hence, always, as we open the book, we shall find Francesca alive and confessing to Dante her sweet sin, and if we turn to the passage a hundred thousand times in succession, a hundred thousand times in succession Francesca will speak her words, never repeating them mechanically, but saying them as though each time were the first time with such living and sudden passion that Dante every time will turn faint. All that lives, by the fact of living, has a form, and by the same token must die—except the work of art which lives forever in so far as it *is* form. —

The birth of a creature of human fantasy, a birth which is a step across the threshold between nothing and eternity, can also happen suddenly, occasioned by some necessity. An imagined drama needs a character who does or says a certain necessary thing; accordingly this character is born and is precisely what he had to be. In this way Madame Pace is born among the six characters and seems a miracle, even a trick, realistically portrayed on the stage. It is no trick. The birth is real. The new character is alive not because she was alive already but because she is now happily born as is required by the fact of her being a character—she is obliged to be as she is. There is a break here, a sudden change in the level of reality of the scene, because a character can be born in this way only in the poet's fancy and not on the boards of a stage. Without anyone's noticing it, I have all of a sudden changed the scene: I have gathered it up again into my own fantasy without removing it from the spectator's eyes. That is, I have shown them, instead of the stage, my own fantasy in the act of creating—my own fantasy in the form of this same stage. The sudden and uncontrollable changing of a visual phenomenon from one level of reality to another is a miracle comparable to those of the saint who sets his own statue in motion: it is neither wood nor stone at such a moment. But the miracle is not arbitrary. The stage—a stage which accepts the fantastic reality of the six characters—is no fixed, immutable datum. Nothing in this play exists as given and preconceived. Everything is in the making, is in motion, is a sudden experiment: even the place in which this unformed life, reaching after its own form, changes and changes again contrives to shift position organically. The level of reality changes. When I had the idea of bringing Madame Pace to birth right there on the stage, I felt I could do it and I did it. Had I noticed that this birth was unhinging and silently, unnoticed, in a second, giving another shape, another reality to my scene, I certainly wouldn't have brought it about. I would have been afraid of the apparent lack of logic. And I would have committed an ill-omened assault on the beauty of my work. The fervor of my mind saved me from doing so. For, despite appearances, with their specious logic, this fantastic birth is sustained by a real necessity in mysterious, organic relation with the whole life of the work.

That someone now tells me it hasn't all the value it could have because its expression is not constructed but chaotic, because it smacks of romanticism, makes me smile.

I understand why this observation was made to me: because in this work of mine the presentation of the drama in which the six characters are involved appears tumultuous and never proceeds in an orderly manner. There is no logical development, no concatenation of the events. Very true. Had I hunted it with a lamp I couldn't have found a more disordered, crazy, arbitrary, complicated, in short, romantic way of presenting "the drama in which the six characters are involved." Very true. But I have not presented that drama. I have presented another—and I won't undertake to say again what!—in which, among the many fine things that everyone, according to his tastes, can find, there is a discreet satire on romantic procedures: in the six characters thus excited to the point where they stifle themselves in the roles which each of them plays in a certain drama while I present them as characters in another play which they don't know and don't suspect the existence of, so that this inflammation of their passions—which belongs to the realm of romantic procedures—is humorously "placed,"

located in the void. And the drama of the six characters presented not as it would have been organized by my fantasy had
it been accepted but in this way, as a rejected drama, could not
exist in the work except as a "situation," with some little development, and could not come out except in indications,
stormily, disorderedly, in violent foreshortenings, in a chaotic
manner: continually interrupted, sidetracked, contradicted (by
one of its characters), denied, and (by two others) not even
seen.

There is a character indeed—he who denies the drama which
makes him a character, the Son—who draws all his importance
and value from being a character not of the comedy in the
making—which as such hardly appears—but from the presentation that I made of it. In short, he is the only one who lives
solely as "a character in search of an author"—inasmuch as the
author he seeks is not a dramatic author. Even this could not
be otherwise. The character's attitude is an organic product of
my conception, and it is logical that in the situation it should
produce greater confusion and disorder and another element
of romantic contrast.

But I had precisely to *present* this organic and natural chaos.
And to present a chaos is not at all to present chaotically, that
is, romantically. That my presentation is the reverse of confused, that it is quite simple, clear, and orderly, is proved by
the clarity which the intrigue, the characters, the fantastic and
realistic, dramatic and comic levels of the work have had for
every public in the world and by the way in which, for those
with more searching vision, the unusual values enclosed within
it come out.

Great is the confusion of tongues among men if criticisms
thus made find words for their expression. No less great than
this confusion is the intimate law of order which, obeyed in all
points, makes this work of mine classical and typical and at its
catastrophic close forbids the use of words. Though the audience eventually understands that one does not create life by
artifice and that the drama of the six characters cannot be presented without an author to give them value with his spirit,
the Manager remains vulgarly anxious to know how the thing
turned out, and the "ending" is remembered by the Son in its
sequence of actual moments, but without any sense and therefore not needing a human voice for its expression. It happens
stupidly, uselessly, with the going-off of a mechanical weapon
on stage. It breaks up and disperses the sterile experiment of

the characters and the actors, which has apparently been made without the assistance of the poet.

The poet, unknown to them, as if looking on at a distance during the whole period of the experiment, was at the same time busy creating—with it and of it—his own play.

(Translated E.B.   1950)

APPENDIX II

BIOGRAPHICAL AND HISTORICAL

IN THE Garibaldian era the Pirandello family were ardent partisans of the great rebel, but when Luigi Pirandello was born in 1867 the rebellion was over and Italians were eating the tasteless fruits of victory. Luigi's father was by now a fairly prosperous sulphur dealer in Agrigento, Sicily. Luigi was destined for a business career too. A studious bent, however, soon made itself felt, and he received a literary schooling at Palermo, Rome, and Bonn. His doctoral thesis at Bonn Universtiy (1891) was a study of his native Sicilian dialect. The young scholar also translated Goethe's Roman elegies.

Pirandello's first creative efforts were in the realm of verse. But when he settled down to taste the literary life of Rome, the influence he fell under was that of the Sicilian novelist, Capuana, who became his friend and adviser. Capuana turned his interest from what we would call "late-Victorian versifying" to naturalistic fiction. In 1893 *The Outcast* was written: the talent that is not so evident in the poems looks through all the cracks of this first novel.

Pirandello married, became the father of three and, because he thought it would be good to have a job for a time, accepted a post as teacher at a girls' school in Rome. When both his own family and his wife's lost their money in a mining disaster, the job became a necessity and a bugbear. The drudgery of it became one of the two great burdens he had to carry.

The other was his wife, who went insane. Nor, for many years, was she taken off Pirandello's hands and placed in a home. She persecuted him with an unprovoked and crazy jealousy.

As Dr. Johnson paid for his mother's funeral with his admirable story *Rasselas,* so Luigi Pirandello met the family's financial misfortune with his first widely recognized work: *The*

377

Late Mattia Pascal (1904). Before the First World War broke out ten years later, Pirandello had published two more novels and a good many short stories.

Although he had been induced to write a play or two at an earlier date, it was not till 1916 that further persuasion from actors precipitated a flood of dramatic works, beginning with *Pensaci, Giacomino!* (*Better Think Twice About It!*), and *Liolà,* and *Così è* (*se vi pare*) (*It Is So!, If You Think So*): they took, respectively, three days, a week, and six days to write. The first Pirandello play to enjoy a notable public success was *Come prima, meglio di prima* (*As Before, Better than Before*) in 1920. In a five-week writing bout Pirandello then created *Six Characters in Search of an Author* (three weeks) and *Henry IV* (two weeks). The first had a *succès de scandale* in Rome and a success without scandal in Milan. In the following year (1922) came the openings of *Henry IV* and *Vestire gli ignudi* (*Naked*), both successes. Komisarjevsky directed *Six Characters* in London. Brock Pemberton saw the production and proceeded to direct the play himself on Broadway. Reinhardt secured the German rights.

Between 1922 and 1924 Pirandello became a public figure, both at home and abroad. He and Mussolini announced their admiration for each other in the press. In Paris, Charles Dullin did *Il piacere dell'onestà* (*The Pleasure of Honesty*), and Georges Pitoëff did *Six Characters*. Pirandello himself went not only to Paris (where he received the Legion of Honor), but also to New York (where Pemberton planned to stage a whole cycle of his plays at the Forty-Fourth Street Theatre).

With the help of Mussolini, who graced the first performance with his presence, Pirandello opened his own Art Theatre in Rome in 1925. His company subsequently took his plays to London, Paris, Vienna, Prague, Budapest, the leading cities of Germany, and ultimately to the Argentine and Brazil. In 1931 Judith Anderson appeared in *Come tu mi vuoi* (As You Desire Me) on Broadway, and the Shuberts began buying even the maestro's untranslated plays. Miss Anderson was replaced in the film of *As You Desire Me* by a yet bigger name: Greta Garbo. In 1934 Pirandello was awarded the Nobel Prize. At his death in 1936 he was under contract to appear as the author in a Hollywood film of *Six Characters*.

Pirandello's whole life after 1918 was a success story. His wife was put in a home, and royalties enabled him to give up teaching. Pirandello's enthusiastic espousal of fascism, which appears to many non-Italians as a surprising blot upon his

career, was an integral part of it. Opposition to the fascist regime would have made serious difficulties for him; acceptance
of it meant subsidies and publicity. One should not imagine he
had anti-fascist scruples to overcome; he accepted money from
the fascist government in entire good faith. Nor can one believe reports that he later regretted the zeal of the early fascist
years. On his last appearance at the port of New York he
handed out a statement in favor of Italy's annexation of Abys-
sinia. He gave his Nobel medal to be melted down for the Abys-
sinian campaign.

Under fascism, Pirandello's playwriting entered a third and
more problematic phase. The first phase had been that of the
Sicilian folk-comedies like *Better Think Twice About It!*, *Liolà*,
and *Il berretto a sonagli* (*Cap and Bells*). The second was that
of the philosophical comedies in which Pirandello is less Sicilian than European: the phase of *Six Characters* and *Henry IV*.
In his third phase, Pirandello withdraws into a strange, sub-
jective world of his own—or, as he would probably prefer to
say, tries to create myths. Thus we have the social myth of
La nuova colonia (*The New Colony*), the religious myth of
Lazzaro (*Lazarus*), and the myth of art that is *I giganti della
montagna* (*Giants of the Mountain*). It would be either a stupid or an over-ingenious critic who would stamp any of these
works as fascist. They illustrate at most the plight of a playwright in a fascist state. They show that, in some degree, Pirandello lived in an "inner emigration" like many German writers
under Hitler. *The Giants of the Mountain* can be interpreted
as showing Pirandello's growing realization that the fascist-
giants were hostile to culture. A definitely fascist mentality is
present only in the anti-liberal animus of *The New Colony*
and the miracle-mongering of *Lazarus*.

The point is that Pirandello's success story of a career was
just as sad as most American ones. The strain and stress are
apparent in the whole last phase, and one play—*Quando si è
qualcuno* (*When You Are Somebody*)—presents the Pirandellian portrait of the literary bigshot: he is nameless and turns to
stone before our eyes. Pirandello was no happier as an international bigwig that he had been as a college professor. And,
if his marriage was a failure, it doesn't seem that the *grande
passion* which dominated his later life proved a satisfying alternative.

At Pirandello's death the fascists came to dress Pirandello in
a black shirt and give him a state funeral. But the maestro had
left instructions. "When I am dead, do not clothe me. Wrap

me naked in a sheet. No flowers on the bed and no lighted candle. A pauper's cart. Naked. And let no one accompany me, neither relatives nor friends. The cart, the horse, the coachman, *e basta*. Burn me . . ." This last "burn me" ended another flirtation of Pirandello's: one with the church, an almost necessary flirtation for a career man in Italy. The church does not believe in cremation and the party did not want a world-famous fascist to slip off naked—i.e., without his black shirt. These words of Pirandello's will sound a little melodramatic to non-Italian ears, yet if we ponder them we can begin to understand in what an agony of apartness this successful man lived. Apartness from church and state, the very sources and symbols of success. Small wonder that, in his creative life, he was not the celebrant of success, but the poet of apartness.

His influence has been considerable. The two principal Italian playwrights of today—Eduardo de Filippo and Ugo Betti—might almost be described as suffering under it. Outside Italy, Pirandello's influence has been most strongly felt in France. The French are most hospitable to a foreign writer whom they regard as a fascinating child of nature, whose barbarism will become significant when assimilated to their own civilization. So it is with Faulkner or Henry Miller today, and so it was with the Sicilian country boy, Luigi Pirandello. Crommelynk, who translated one of his plays *Come prima, meglio di prima,* is distinctly Pirandellian in his own work; and from Crommelynk to Anouilh is but a step. While Lenormand, in such a play as *Le Crépuscule du théâtre,*[1] takes over easily separable technical features of *Six Characters,* Crommelynk and Anouilh are Pirandellian in a deeper sense: they share his metaphysical anguish and, like him, they express it in a version of erotic relations *in extremis.*

In the American theatre I notice nothing so unequivocally Pirandellian.[2] At the first night of *Death of a Salesman* in Rome, everyone talked of *pirandellismo,* yet what has Miller

[1] English version: *In Theatre Street* by Ashley Dukes. Gollancz, London, 1937.

[2] In a note on Pirandello's influence (*Meridiano di Roma,* December 20, 1936), Silvio D'Amico mentions Eugene O'Neill, and specifically *The Great God Brown;* but how many American readers would feel convinced of Pirandellian influence here? The other writers mentioned by D'Amico are Marcel Achard, Denys Amiel (*L'Image*), Henri Bernstein (*Galerie des Spectres*), Jean Giraudoux (*Siegfried*), Kurt Goetz, László Krakatos, Henri Marx, Alfred Savoir; all of them European, all, except Goetz and Krakatos, French.

done to earn the description except write of illusion and reality and find the former more powerful? And surely Miller is criticizing Willie Loman's popular Pirandellism—his belief that what your customer thinks you are is more real than what you actually are? An American playwright much more likely to have been directly affected by Pirandello is that avid reader and linguist, Thornton Wilder. The use of commentators and plays within plays no longer indicates knowledge of Pirandello or any author of his time, but Thornton Wilder's interest in the perspectives that such devices provide in a world where reality itself is a maze in which we are lost (only a god can see a maze from above, and the gods are dead) suggests that he may have known his Pirandello before writing *Our Town* and *The Skin of Our Teeth*.

And there is much more in Pirandello for younger men to find.

APPENDIX III

THEATRICAL AND BIBLIOGRAPHICAL

A. The following is a list of Pirandello's plays with the date of the first Italian performance. When a play has been published in English, the English title is also given.

La morsa, 1910. (*The Vise*)
Lumìe di Sicilia, 1910. (*Sicilian Limes*)
Il dovere del medico, 1913. (*The Doctor's Duty*)
Se non così. 1915.
Pensaci, Giacomino!, 1916.
Liolà, 1916. (First published in the present volume, title unchanged)
Così è (se vi pare), 1917. (*It Is So!, If You Think So*)
Il berretto a sonagli, 1917.
La giara, 1917. (*The Jar*)
Il piacere dell'onestà, 1917. (*The Pleasure of Honesty*)
Ma non è una cosa seria, 1918.
Il giuoco delle parti, 1918.
L'innesto, 1919.
La patente, 1919.
L'uomo, la bestia, e la virtù, 1919.
Tutto per bene, 1920.
Come prima, meglio di prima, 1920.
Cecè, 1920. (*Chee-Chee*)
La Signora Morli, una e due, 1920.
Sei personaggi in cerca d'autore, 1921. (*Six Characters in Search of an Author*)
Enrico IV, 1922. (*Henry IV*)
All'uscita, 1922. (*At the Gate*)
L'imbecille, 1922. (*The Imbecile*)
Vestire gli ignudi, 1922. (*Naked*)
L'uomo dal fiore in bocca, 1923. (*The Man with the Flower in His Mouth*)

La vita che ti diedi, 1923.
L'altro figlio, 1923. (*The House with the Column*)
Ciascuno a suo modo, 1924. (*Each in His Own Way*)
Sagra del Signore della nave, 1925. (*Our Lord of the Ship*)
Diana e la Tuda, 1927.
L'amica delle mogli, 1927.
Bellavita, 1927. (*Bellavita*)
Scamandro, 1928.
La nuova colonia, 1928.
O di uno o di nessuno, 1929.
Lazzaro, 1929.
Come tu mi vuoi, 1930. (*As You Desire Me*)
Questa sera si recita a soggetto, 1930. (*Tonight We Improvise*)
Trovarsi, 1932.
Quando si è qualcuno, 1933.
La Favola del figlio cambiato, 1934.
Non si sa come, 1935.
Sogno (ma forse no), 1936. (*Dream, But Perhaps Not*)
I giganti della montagna, 1937.

B. The plays of Pirandello are today available collected in
four volumes under the title *Maschere Nude* (Mondadori, Milan, 1948-9). In English they are represented by five volumes,
excluding the present one, as follows:

Three Plays. (*Six Characters, Henry IV, It Is So!*). E. P.
Dutton & Co., Inc., New York, 1922; J. M. Dent & Sons,
Ltd., London, 1922.
Each in His Own Way and Two Other Plays. (*The Pleasure
of Honesty, Naked*). E. P. Dutton & Co., Inc., New York,
1923; J. M. Dent & Sons, Ltd., London, 1924.
The One-Act Plays. (*The Imbecile, By Judgment of Court,
Our Lord of the Ship, The Doctor's Duty, Chee-Chee, The
Man with the Flower in His Mouth, At the Gate, The Vise,
The House with the Column, Sicilian Limes, The Jar*).
E. P. Dutton & Co., Inc., New York, 1928.
As You Desire Me. E. P. Dutton & Co., Inc., New York, 1931.
Tonight We Improvise. E. P. Dutton & Co., Inc., New York,
1932.

One other play is known to have been published in English:
Dream, But Perhaps Not in *This Quarter,* Volume II, No. 4,
June 1930.

Some of the above plays have been performed in other than the published translations.

Some Pirandello plays have been performed in English but not published. Among these are known to be: *Come prima, meglio di prima (Floriani's Wife)*, *La vita che ti diedi (The Life I Gave You)*, *L'uomo, la bestia, e la virtù (Say It with Flowers)*, and *Lazzaro (Lazarus)*.

Some plays have been translated but neither published nor performed.

There are further details on these points (not always accurate, however) in the official Pirandello Bibliography (as listed below).

C. There are two books on Pirandello in English, and one in which he occupies a central place:

Luigi Pirandello: 1867-1936. By Walter Starkie. Second Edition, John Murray, London, 1937; E. P. Dutton & Co., Inc., New York, 1937.

The Drama of Luigi Pirandello. By Domenico Vittorini. University of Pennsylvania Press, Philadelphia, 1935.

The Age of Pirandello. By Lander McClintock. Indiana University Press, Bloomington, 1951.

In Italian there is a large number of books and booklets on Pirandello, among which the following are the most interesting either for information, critical insight, or the typicality of the point of view:

Bàccolo, Luigi: *Luigi Pirandello*. Second Edition, Bocca, Milan, 1949.

Di Pietro, Antonio: *Pirandello*. Second Edition, Vita e Pensiero, Milan, 1950.

Janner, Arminio: *Luigi Pirandello*. "La Nuova Italia," Florence, 1948.

Lo Vecchio Musti, Manlio: *L'opera di Luigi Pirandello*. Paravia, Turin, 1939.

Mignosi, Pietro: *Il segreto di Pirandello*. Second Edition, "La Tradizione," Milan, 1937.

Nardelli, F. V.: *L'uomo segreto, vita e croci di Luigi Pirandello*. Mondadori, Milan, 1932 and 1944.

Pasini, Ferdinando: *Luigi Pirandello (come mi pare)*. "La Vedetta Italiana," Trieste, 1927.

Petronio, Giuseppe: *Pirandello novelliere e la crisi del realismo*. "Lucentia," Lucca, 1950.

Puliatti, Pietro and Bottino, Egle: *Lineamenti sull'arte di Luigi Pirandello*. Intelisano, Catania, 1941.

Most of the really critical comment on Pirandello, as one would expect, is hidden away in periodicals and books on other subjects. The only systematic guide to this literature is the bibliography of Di Pietro (above), and even this is confessedly incomplete. The present editor has found the following especially suggestive:

Alvaro, Corrado: *Prefazione*. (Unpublished.)

Bontempelli, Massimo: "Luigi Pirandello," first published in *La Nuova Antologia*, February 1, 1937; reprinted in *Pirandello Leopardi D'Annunzio*, Bompiani, Milan, 1939; also in Lo Vecchio Musti's bibliography as listed below.

Brancati, Vitaliano: "Pirandello Diabolico?" in *Il Tempo*, March 8, 1948.

Debenedetti, Giacomo: " 'Una Giornata' di Pirandello," *Saggi Critici, Nuova Serie*, Edizioni del Secolo, Rome, 1945.

Gobetti, Piero: *Opera Critica*. Especially the Second Part, Section One, Chapters 7 and 14.

Gramsci, Antonio: "Il teatro di Pirandello," *Letteratura e Vita Nazionale*, Einaudi, Turin, 1950. (See also Second Part.)

Moravia, Alberto: "La lezione di Pirandello," in *Sipario*, November-December, 1946. (Reprinted in *La Fiera Letteraria*, December 12, 1946.)

Pandolfi, Vito: "Gramsci individua Luigi Pirandello," in *Il Dramma*, November 15, 1950.

Russo, Luigi: "Il noviziato letterario di Luigi Pirandello," in *Paesaggio*, April-May, June-July, August-November, 1946.

Tilgher, Adriano: "Il teatro di Luigi Pirandello," *Studi sul teatro contemporaneo*. Third edition. Libreria di Scienze e Lettere, Rome, 1928.

For further data, the reader must go to the official *Bibliografia di Pirandello*, of which a new and up-to-date edition is announced. The edition available to the present editor is in two volumes, dated 1937 and 1940 respectively, published by

Mondadori, Milan, and edited by Manlio Lo Vecchio Musti. The first volume lists all Italian editions of the major works of Pirandello up to 1937. It lists and gives particulars of first Italian performances of his plays. It provides facts as to translation into and out of dialect; movie scenarios; opera librettos. It includes thirty-three photographs of the maestro and essays by Bontempelli and Stefano Pirandello, not to mention a preface by His Excellency Dino Alfieri.[1] Volume Two is chiefly devoted to translations of Pirandello (thirty languages); scattered facts on foreign productions are also provided; and the listing of Pirandello's works in the original is completed with his contributions to newspapers and periodicals.

Postscript, 1957: Only a few changes would have to be made to bring this Appendix fully up to date. The reader's attention is called especially to the following items:

Lo Vecchio Musti, Manlio: *Bibliographia di Pirandello.* Second Edition. Mondadori, Milan, 1952.

Pandolfi, Vito: *Spettacolo del secolo.* Nistri-Lischi, Pisa, 1953.

Pirandello, Luigi: *Right You Are.* A stage version by Eric Bentley. Columbia University Press, New York, 1954.

Pirandello, Luigi: *Six Characters in Search of an Author.* Translated by Frederick May. William Heinemann Ltd., London, 1954.

[1] See the official bibliographer's *L'opera di Luigi Pirandello* (1939), page 23: "The Italian government ordered the compilation of his bibliography for the first anniversary of his death."